GREECE AND THE GREEK ISLANDS

Trip Planner & Guide

GREECE AND THE GREEK ISLANDS

Trip Planner & Guide
Paul Strathern

⬟ PASSPORT BOOKS

This first edition published 1994 by
Passport Books,
Trade Imprint of NTC Publishing Group,
4255 West Touhy Avenue,
Lincolnwood (Chicago), Illinois 60646-1975
U.S.A.

Conceived, edited, designed and produced by
Duncan Petersen Publishing Ltd, 54 Milson Road, London W14 0LB
from a concept by Emma Stanford

Typeset by Duncan Petersen Publishing Ltd;
film output by Reprocolor International, Milan

Originated by Reprocolor International, Milan

Printed by GraphyCems, Navarra

ISBN: 0-8442-9218-4

Library of Congress Catalog Card Number: 93-85443

Every reasonable care has been taken to ensure the information in this
guide is accurate, but the publishers and copyright holders can accept
no responsibility for the consequences of errors in the text or in the
maps, particularly those arising from changes taking place after the text
was finalized. The publishers are always pleased to hear from readers
who wish to suggest corrections and improvements.

Editorial director Andrew Duncan
Assistant editors Leonie Glass, Mary Devine and Laura Harper
Art director Mel Petersen
Design assistants Beverley Stewart, Chris Foley
Maps by Chris Foley and Beverley Stewart
Illustrations by Beverley Stewart

Photographic credits
Terry Harris: pp. 15, 26, 27, 30, 35, 40, 42, 46, 47, 54, 70, 77, 83, 86, 98,
102, 106, 107, 115, 122, 123, 124, 130, 150, 154, 190, 194, 214, 230, 231,
232, 233, 238, 239, 242, 243, 249, 250, 254, 255, 262. **Peter Ryan:** pp. 21,
22, 23, 24, 31, 36, 43, 73, 82, 85, 99, 101, 118, 131, 134, 138, 142, 146,
173, 177, 196, 198, 228. **Photographers Library:** pp. 45, 62, 74, 87, 90, 94,
95, 162, 163, 164, 166, 169, 170, 171, 175, 178, 182, 183, 186, 187, 202,
203, 206, 207, 218, 219, 222, 224, 226, 263, 266, 267, 274, 279.

Paul Strathern was born in 1940 and took a degree in philosophy at Trinity College, Dublin. He has written five novels and worked for more than 20 years as a travel writer, visiting four continents in the course of his work. He first saw Greece through the porthole of a tramp steamer on which he was working as a steward, and believed it was a mirage. He visited this mirage for the first time a year later and has been going back regularly ever since, living there on three separate occasions.

He has seen Greece at its best (spring in the Cretan mountains) and at its worst (during the grim and inept dictatorship of the Colonels). He has written several books on the Greek islands. His wide experience of Greek culture once led him to believe that he understood the Greek way of life: this illusion was shattered a few years ago when he watched Panathenaikos play Olympiakos in the Greek Cup Final. He has one daughter.

Master contents list

This contents list is for when you need to use the guide in the conventional way: to find out about where you are going, or where you happen to be. The index, pages 282-288, may be just as helpful.

HOWEVER...
There is much more to this guide than the region-by-region approach suggested by the contents list on this page. Turn to page 8; and see also pages 10-11.

Greece Overall
- *master map*

Greece Overall, pages 38-173, is a traveller's network for taking in the whole country, or large parts of it.

Each 'leg' of the network has a number (i.e., Greece Overall: 1); you will also find it described as a National Route, plus the number.

The term National Route does *not* simply mean a line on a map. Each 'route' leg features a whole region, and describes many places both on and off the marked route. Think of the National Routes not only as physical trails, but as imaginative ways of connecting all the main centres of Greece and of describing and making travel sense of the state as whole.

They are designed to be used in these different ways:

1 *Ignore the marked route entirely:* simply use the alphabetically arranged Gazetteer of Sights & Places of Interest, and the map at the start of each 'route', as a guide to what to see and do in the region, not forgetting the hotel and restaurant recommendations.

2 Follow the marked route by public transport (see the transport box), ferry, or by car. You can do sections of the route, or all of it; you can follow it in any direction. Link the routes to travel the length and breadth of Greece and the Greek Islands.

The routes are broken down into manageable legs. Each leg has a section to itself, beginning with an introduction and a simplified map. The page number for each such section is shown on this master map.

Always use the simplified maps in conjunction with detailed maps (suggestions are given on the introductory pages).

On the simplified maps:

RED *marks key sights and centres, not to be missed.*

BLUE *marks important places, certainly worth a visit.*

GREEN *places are for those who aren't in a hurry and want to experience the region in some depth.*

Some practical hints on how to travel red, blue and green are given in the introductory pages and the simplified maps, including key roads and their numbers. Generally, though, there are no absolute rules for going red, blue or green and you are meant to link the places, using a detailed road map, in whatever way suits you best.

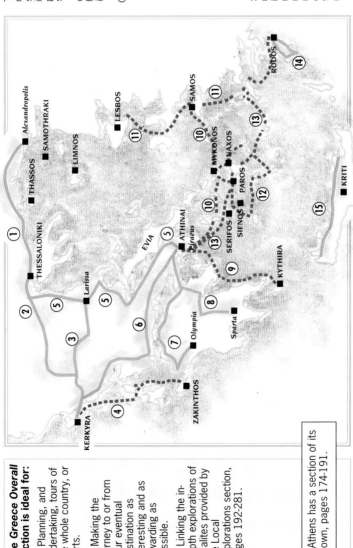

The *Greece Overall* section is ideal for:

■ Planning, and undertaking, tours of the whole country, or parts.

■ Making the journey to or from your eventual destination as interesting and as rewarding as possible.

■ Linking the in-depth explorations of localites provided by the Local Explorations section, pages 192-281.

Athens has a section of its own, pages 174-191.

The Local Explorations
- *master map*

The Local Explorations are strategies for exploring all the interesting localities of Greece and the islands. Also described as Local Tours, they complement the National Routes, pages 8-9. **They are designed to be used in these different ways**:

1 *Ignore the marked route entirely*: simply use the alphabetically arranged Gazetteer of Sights & Places of Interest, and the map at the start of each Local Exploration, as a guide to what to see and do in the area, not forgetting the hotel and restaurant recommendations.

2 Use the marked route to make a tour by public transport (see the transport box), ferry, or by car. You can do sections of the route, or all of it. (In the introduction it tells you how long you might take to cover everything the quickest way, by car.)

   If you are driving, you can generally follow the tour in any direction; usually, the route as marked is an attractive and convenient way to link the places of interest; you may well find other ways to drive it. Always use our map in conjunction with a detailed road map (suggestions are given on each introductory page).

The Local Explorations are ideal for:

■ **Planning single-centre holidays:** each Local Exploration encapsulates an area which would make a great holiday. The introductory page to each section is designed to tell you whether the area will suit you: what you can expect; and something of its history, geography, people, customs, food.

■ **Entertaining yourself while you are there:** each section is packed with ideas for things to see and do. The tour, followed in full, can fill several days, and will always make a memorable journey, but most of the the sights and places of interest make fascinating day or part-day trips in their own right, not to mention the detours.

■ **Planning multi-centre holidays.** The map on this page shows you at a glance all the interesting parts of Greece. Combine them at will to experience the different faces of the state; or link them, by means of the national route network.

The Local Explorations or Tours, pages 192-281, generally follow each other in a north-south/west-east sequence.

Athens has a section of its own, pages 174-191.

Conventions Used in this Guide

A single *drachma* sign – **D** – or several *drachma* signs, such as **DDD**, in a hotel or restaurant entry, denotes a price band. Its object is to give an indication of what you can expect to pay.
Bear in mind that accommodation offered at any one place may well span two or more price bands.

Hotels
For a double room (one night) at mid-season rate:

D   less than 3,000 drachmae
DD   3,000 – 7,000 drachmae
DDD   more than 7,000 drachmae

Restaurants
For a two-course meal with wine for one:

D   less than 1,500 drachmae
DD   1,500 – 4,000 drachmae
DDD   more than 4,000 drachmae

🛏 after a heading in **Sights and Places of Interest** means that there is an accommodation suggestion (or suggestions) for that place in **Recommended Hotels**.

✕ after a heading in **Sights & Places of Interest** means that there is a suggestion (or suggestions) for that place in **Recommended Restaurants**.

Hotels and restaurants in this guide are a selection of personal recommendations – not exhaustive lists. They have been chosen to represent interest and quality, or to satisfy specific needs, at every price level.

Opening times of restaurants
Restaurant opening and closing are intentionally not given in this guide. In Athens, Thessaloniki and the major resorts restaurant hours will tend to conform to general opening and closing hours, given on page 24. Outside these centres, and especially in remote country areas and on the islands, hours become flexible and informal, sometimes varying from day to day at the whim of the owner.

Opening times – museums and tourist attractions
The general rule is that museums and major sights in Greece open 8.30 am until 3 pm, and close on Mondays and on all public holidays. These are the *minimum* hours. Many places stay open until later (typically sunset). In practice, opening times are variable and subject to local whim. For that reason, specific opening times are not given in this guide. Before setting out on a long journey to see a sight, check the opening time with the local tourist office.

Mileages for routes and tours
Are approximate. In the case of National Routes, they represent the shortest distances you could expect to travel on the route, almost always the 'red' option.
In the case of Local Explorations, they also represent the shortest possible distance you could expect to cover, excluding detours.
Since the routes and tours are designed to be travelled in whole, in part, or indeed not at all, the mileages are given as much for passing interest as for their practical value.

Credit cards
The credit card revolution has not yet taken place in Greece, although expensive hotels and restaurants in the major cities and smarter resorts often accept the major cards – American Express, Visa, Diners Club and Access. For this reason, hotel and restaurant entries do not list credit cards accepted. As a rule, expect to pay in cash.

Spelling of place names
The spelling of Greek place names is

↗ After a place name on a map means that the sight or place of interest is covered in detail in another part of the book. To find out exactly where, look up the place in the **Sights & Places of Interest** gazetteer which follows the map: a cross-reference is given in every case.

still very unstandardized. Just as Shakespeare spelt his name in more than a dozen different ways, so modern Greeks enjoy varying their place name spellings. Moreover, the Greek alphabet does not exactly match the lettering in the German, Dutch or English alphabets.

In this guide, the place names are, as a rule, spelt in the way you will see them signposted in Greece, or at any rate the spelling in commonest use, or which best matches the way the name is pronounced.

Westernized versions are avoided where possible, except where they have become **very** current, for example, Crete for *Kriti,* Peleponnese for *Peleponnisos.* If you have difficulty matching a word in the text with what you see or hear, try playing around with some variations. Is and Ys are often interchangeable, so are H and I, as are CH and H.

Something for Everyone
Getting the most from your guide

Here is a *small* selection of ideas for enjoying Greece opened up by this guide, aimed at a range of needs and tastes. The list is just a start: the guide offers many, many more ideas for what really matters: suiting *yourself.* You'll find that it takes into account not only your tastes, but how much time you have.

Forget it all - faraway islands, Aegean sky
Local Explorations: 7, 8, 12.

Superb beaches, tourist facilities, yet a genuine island
Rhodes - Greece Overall: 14.

Picture-postcard Greek islands
The Cyclades - Greece Overall: 12 *and Local Explorations:* 10.

Day five: bored of your resort hotel on Crete's north coast?
Local Explorations: 13.

Combine Athens with some nearby island relief
Athens section, pages 174-191 *and Local Explorations:* 6.

Outstanding Classical sites
See especially Greece Overall: 7 *and* 9.

Sample a range of islands, with different characters
Greece Overall: 10 *and* 13.

Mix mainland and islands
Greece Overall: 9.

Discover the mainland outback
Greece Overall: 1.

The author's favourite island: beaches, celebrated ruins and a superb, unspoilt mountainous hinterland
Local Explorations: 12.

GREECE AND THE GREEK ISLANDS:
an introduction

The first wave of invaders came to Greece bringing with them a primitive form of culture. Four thousand years later, Greeks witnessing the latest arrivals often feel that little has changed. Visitors don't have much to offer the Greeks (apart from foreign exchange); they have plenty to offer us.

When I first arrived in Greece over thirty years ago, I thought I would never see a country so lovely. This still remains the case, despite the fact that much of the old unspoilt Greece has been transformed into holidayland. Even so, you seldom have to travel far off the beaten track before you find yourself in a landscape throbbing with cicadas, where the donkey paths wind through olive groves which have remained unchanged for centuries. Hidden coves beneath the cliffs, sheer-sided gorges winding through the mountains, the thin marble pillars of an ancient oracle overlooking the transparent sea, village festivals of wild music and dancing, crusader castles, a tiny whitewashed chapel perched high on a ridge, mountain peaks once inhabited by the gods – you'll find them all here.

Moreover, you will find that in Greece history is not confined to the history books: it is all over the place. You are never far from an ancient site: most of the mountains, plains and cities here have witnessed great events of one kind or another. This was where European civilization began – and what might appear as the minor skirmishes, imaginative fibs and simple thought processes of a distant millenium often had a crucial role in shaping what we are today. You can see the battlefields which stopped Europe from becoming a colony of Asia, visit the theatres where the first dramas ever written were performed, see the earliest truly naturalistic sculptures made by man. You can wander the streets where democracy came into being, where the early philosophers taught their pupils how to think coherently, and the foundations of mathematics and scientific thought were first discussed.

To this day the Greek language plays a major role in our own. Throughout this century of great discoveries, new developments and concepts, we have frequently turned to Ancient Greek to name these new ideas. Television, psychology, metropolis, and schizophrenia all come from Ancient Greek, as do many words which long ago took root in our language – such as philosophy, harmony, democracy, eroticism, sympathy and so forth.

• *Typical bright, hard Aegean light.*

Greece is less than half the size of Italy, yet it has almost 1,500 islands (170 of them inhabited). You will find its scattered inhabitants very different from one another. The nomadic shepherd amongst the snowy peaks of the Pindos Mountains near the Albanian border bears little resemblance to the tanned leather-skinned caique captain from Chios. And the moustachioed jack-booted Cretan is quite different from the flash bouzouki player in the Athenian nightclub. Yet they are all Greeks, and as such are likely to share those characteristics which make their nation the most open and welcoming in Europe.

Paul Strathern
Callow

Before You Go

When to go, and to which parts

If you have the choice, visit Greece in spring or autumn. In summer it can get very hot indeed. In winter it is seldom too cold, though snow has been known to fall in Athens. However, it can feel cold, as most of the buildings are designed for hot weather.

Hottest summer temperatures are more than 90°F (32°C). Spring is a pleasant 55-75°F (18-23°C).

Southern Crete tends to stay warmer than elsewhere in autumn, winter and spring. The north can get very chilly in winter, especially inland. In the mountains the temperature is of course always lower. Athens in summer always feels very hot: official temperatures often bear little relation to what is going on at sweltering street level.

The *Meltemi* wind keeps the Aegean islands from getting too hot in summer. The weather sometimes breaks here in September with a brief spell of storms.

During July and August the country is overrun with tourists, and the population of the country as a whole triples. However, away from the main resort areas it can still be relatively peaceful, even at the height of the season. Usually, the more difficult it is to get to a spot, or the longer it takes to get there, the fewer people there are around. But beware the exceptions: some islands, such as Zakinthos or Samos, are not particularly well known, and look remote on the map – but turn out to have airports that cater for holidaymakers in their thousands.

If you don't need to be by the sea, there are inland villages, especially in remote and mountainous areas, where you can still rent a room for practically nothing and hardly see a tourist – even in August. This is especially true of spots such as south-west Crete, Epirus and upper Macedonia.

Otherwise, if you are travelling during the season, be sure to book ahead, as accommodation is often limited. And don't expect to find a bed just because there are a number of large hotels at your destination: these are often completely taken over by block bookings for tourists on package holidays.

Greece now has a skiing season (Pindos mountains, Olympos) but it is only worth taking advantage of this if you already happen to be in the country. Don't expect the skiing to compare with that of alpine resorts.

Clothing

It's likely that during summer, you will get very hot, so pack your lightest clothes. Equally, pack a sweater or cardigan as well, for the evenings when you dine outside and it turns cool.

You will also need a hat to protect your head from the brain-frying heat of the midday sun. Likewise, be sure to cover up your arms and legs before walking in the sun. Sunburn is a major hazard.

If you want to walk any distance, don't forget some strong shoes or boots. Beach shoes are hopeless for walking the gorges and the mountains, as the rocks tear them to pieces.

Nobody dresses up for dinner in Greece: evening wear is strictly informal, except in Athens and a few exclusive spots.

Other essential items to pack include: sun glasses, sun-tan lotion, and treatment for 'holiday tummy'. Items best puchased when you arrive include: water container (plastic bottle); roll-up beach mat; and a plentiful supply of tissues which can be used as lavatory paper in places where such conveniences are not available.

Documentation

No visa is required for Greece if you are British, an EC member, Canadian or a U.S. national. If you want to stay in Greece for longer than three months, you will have to apply for a resident's permit when you arrive in the country. Drivers require a current driving licence from country of origin.

Travelling in your own car you need the registration document and insurance certificate. A policy extension (in the U.K., a 'green card') to make the cover comprehensive while motoring abroad is strongly recommended – without it your insurance is only the legal minimum. In Greece you cannot always be sure that the other person involved in the accident is insured, and it is not unknown for local witnesses to be somewhat biased.

Important: If you have recently visited the Turkish occupied section of Cyprus (the northern half) and have a stamp registering this in your passport, you won't be allowed into Greece. The best solution is to get a new temporary passport.

Medical and travel insurance

Not obligatory when visiting Greece, but a very advisable safeguard. Make sure that your cover includes accidents, especially motor accidents. When you hire a car or rent a motor bike in Greece, the insurance provided is often worthless in practice.

British and EC members qualify automatically for free medical treatment in Greece, provided they have the correct form. However, the cost of treatment and medication must be paid for at the time and reclaimed after a long-winded procedure. Also, as you quickly discover, the service in state hospitals is minimal. Private treatment is usually the simplest and safest option. Remember to keep all your medical receipts and bills, including those for medicines and drugs, in order to qualify for repayment.

If you lose anything, or have something stolen, the insurance policy will probably require you to report this at the local police station in order to validate the claim. This is not always as easy as it sounds, because the local police often consider all local theft as an affront to their reputation. This is no joke. If the local police prove uncooperative, go to the Tourist Police, who are not quite so touchy about these matters and will usually help out. Be sure to obtain an official piece of paper proving that you have registered your loss or theft.

Money

The Greek currency unit is the drachma (plural drachmae). The most frequently used notes are for 5,000, 1,000, 500 and 100 drachmae. Coins of lower denomination tend to be of so little value as to be a nuisance.

By far the best way to carry your money is in traveller's cheques. These are cashable in all banks and at many travel agents. (Check out the rate offered by some of the latter, as they are not always reasonable or consistent.) Everywhere but the most utterly remote spots, there is always someone who will change traveller's cheques.

Import duty

Customs regulations conform with the new EC norms introduced in January 1993.

Traveller's cheques are the trouble-free way to take money into Greece; it is best to carry only enough hard cash for your immediate needs.

On the way out through Greek customs, you can take almost as much as you want of anything, except Greek currency, on which the present limit is 20,000 drachmae. If this is important to you, check the latest regulations before leaving.

The consequences of being caught at Greek customs with drugs, even minor quantities of soft drugs, are a nightmare that can run for years.

Tourist information outside Greece

The Greek National Tourist Organization has offices in major capitals and distributes free literature including lists, regularly updated, of tour operators and special interest holidays.

Local customs: what to expect, how to behave

Greeks are tolerant prople, when you consider what tourism has done to their country.

Try to remember that you are, after all, only a visitor. A measure of decorum, and good manners, are always appreciated in Greece, where such things have yet to fall foul of political or psychological ideology. Attempts to speak Greek, no matter how hilariously inadequate, are often genuinely appreciated. But don't try this when you are standing at the head of a long queue at a kiosk.

Nude bathing and nude sunbathing are strictly forbidden by law. This means that you should engage in these pursuits with tact. They are OK on remote beaches, and most resorts have a discreet area, or nearby bays, where nudism is acceptable. But don't try it on the main family beaches as it gives offence, and often lets you in for some unpleasant attention.

When out walking on remote paths in the country, be sure to acknowledge any locals you come across: such commonplace politeness has not yet died out in Greece.

GETTING THERE

By air
The standard option. There is a wide variety of scheduled and charter flights, most visitors gaining notable bargains by booking package holidays, accommodation and flight included.

The independent traveller should note that there are direct flights from all major European air terminals to many Greek destinations. These include: Athens, Thessaloniki, Crete, Rhodes, Corfu, Xante, Skiathos, Kefalonia, Crete (Heraklion and Chania), Kos, Samos, Kalamata, Mikonos, Preveza (Aktion) and Santorini. Athens and Saloniki are served by scheduled and charter flights, the others mostly by charters. As a rule of thumb, there is one airport in every island group, served either by international or by domestic airlines.

Although some people choose to enter Greece via Athens, many prefer to save time by flying direct to a strategically located island and making any onward journey by ferry (see below).

It is a money-saving rule to book through a travel agent or discount flight specialist rather than directly with an airline. Doing so enables you to sift through the options on a route where competition between operators is intense.

By rail
This can be a more expensive option than taking a cheap air fare, and from northern Europe the journey time is two

• *Ferry routes.*

and a half days, via the Brindisi ferry. The leg from Milan to Brindisi (almost 20 hours) can be especially tiresome, with carriages often appallingly overcrowded.

The Eurail Pass, available only to non-European nationals, provides an economic and practical means of unlimited travel throughout Greece (and indeed continental Europe); but see below for comments on Greek railways. Certain age groups are eligible for valuable discounts. Enquire at a main railway station.

European nationals can buy similar unlimited travel passes (in the U.K., the Interail Pass) for railway journeys in Europe but outside their own country, again with discounts for certain age groups. Enquire at a main railway station.

By bus

Cheaper than the cheapest air fare, the journey takes two days from northern European cities, three from the U.K. An endurance test.

GETTING AROUND

By car

When you enter Greece in your car you are given a card, which is vaild for four months. This you must show on leaving. Don't try to sell your car in Greece, no matter how generous the offer, as this will involve you in a bureaucratic nightmare – and you will find it difficult to get out of the country without paying all kinds of duty, tax, local benevolent fund contributions and so on.

Car hire

You will find vehicles of some kind (including 'jeeps', motor bikes and mopeds) for hire in all main towns, all but the very smallest resorts, and at all but the smallest island airports.

The hire price usually includes insurance, which frequently turns out to be worthless if you have an accident. So if you are intending to hire a vehicle of any kind, make sure you are insured for any accident before you set out on holiday.

By the end of the season many vehicles for hire will have been driven by many different kinds of people who may not have the same respect for engines or bodywork as you. The harrassed Greek hirer may not have noticed the missing pedal, the dent, or the hole in the floor before you drove away. But you can be sure that he will when you bring the vehicle back. Indignant demands for recompense may well follow. Always check the state of a hired vehicle before you set out.

Car hire is comparatively expensive in Greece, though you will find some out-of-season reductions. For a car you can expect to pay around 6,000 to 10,000 drachmae per day, plus mileage.

Roads and driving regulations

There is a motorway from Athens to Thessaloniki, and a network of major roads links other main centres. These can become congested with slow-moving lorries. Minor roads, especially in the mountains, can be more exciting than you had bargained for, but the views can be second to none. Petrol in Greece is more expensive than in northern Europe and the price increases regularly. Lead-free petrol is widely available.

Distances are signposted in kilometres, and place names are given in Greek and Roman lettering.

All accidents must be reported to the local police, but try to contact the Tourist Police as well. Drinking and driving is not permitted but everyone does it. Drunken tourists on mopeds are a common hazard in resort centres at night.

Drive with caution in Greece. The country is second in the EC accident league table (after Portugal). A speed limit of 50 mph must be observed in towns and villages. Use of horns is not allowed in built-up areas.

Taxis

Contrary to universal myth, Greek taxi drivers are generally pleasant, friendly people, as long as they don't operate in Athens. In the big city, and sometimes in large provincial towns and tourist spots, keep your wits about you. Make sure the meter is on, and functioning (as is required by law), and that you are going in vaguely the right direction. Also, it is worth trying to establish what the approximate fare will be before you start. Curiously, however, tipping is not expected.

Out in the country and on the islands, your attitude to taxis and taxi drivers can be more relaxed. Usually you agree a price beforehand, and then set off. On longer journeys the driver will sometimes stop to see a friend *en route*, or inspect his melon patch in the mountains, or visit his favourite village café on the way. You are likely to be bought coffee, and will be expected to make a contribution to the conversation with your views on world affairs, the youth of today...and so on. In other words, the concept of a taxi as an express service between two places has yet to catch on.

Taxi rides are cheap in Greece, and this is often reflected in the age of the vehicles. The meters are usually in full working order, despite what is said.

Ferries

The Greek inter-island ferry service is generally excellent (despite the qualifications below), and even the remotest islands are linked most of the time by some kind of service.

The hub of the Greek ferry service is **Piraeus**, the port of Athens. Most of the main island services depart from here early in the morning. Be sure to get on board early, as final departure is usually accompanied by scenes reminiscent of Rome before the arrival of the Barbarians.

It is possible to hop from island to island all around the Aegean, and the Ionian sea. It is simplest to follow the 'spoke' routes out from Piraeus. You have to pay close attention to the complex schedules if you want to hop sideways and to make connections.

There are several different services linking the islands on the main routes from Piraeus, some fast and direct, others calling at a number of other islands on the way. A trip from Piraeus to Paros can take eight hours, and it can also take more than 12 hours, depending on which boat you take.

Out of season these services are reduced drastically, and in some cases daily services can even give way to weekly services.

You are always best off buying your ticket at one of the offices close to where the ferry departs. It is worth shopping around, as prices vary. Also, as the different offices have links with different operators, some tend to 'forget' to tell you about other services which better meet your requirements.

Tickets are very cheap, and become comparatively cheaper the longer your voyage. For example, you can pay around 2,000 drachmae for a short trip between two islands, but as little as 4,500 to cross the Aegean.

The cheapest tickets are deck class (ask for 'Touristiki' or 'gamma'). This gives you access to most of the deck areas, and theoretically entitles you to a reclining seat inside. But since the number of tickets sold invariably far exceeds the number of seats, the rule is very much first-come-first-served. In any case, it is much better out on deck – as any crew member will tell you when you protest. It is really only worth paying for a more expensive ticket if you are going through a misanthropic phase, or want a cabin for the night.

Most ferries also have a snack bar, a bar, and a restaurant. On all but the best ferries, these are usually a farce laid on for the entertainment of the crew, by the crew, at your expense. Toasted sandwiches inside toasted plastic wrappers, coffee consisting entirely of mud, and ouzo with a fly in it, are staple fare on some of the ferries. Standards tend to decrease with the increasing age of the ferry, which you may discover from a plaque in the saloon, plied the Channel or the North Sea some 20 years back.

It makes sense to take your own food if you are going on a longer trip on one of these old ferries. These atmospheric rustbuckets are alas rapidly being replaced by sea-going cafeterias staffed by friendly waiters.

Besides the ferries there are also hydrofoil services, known as Flying Dolphins. These connect Piraeus with the main islands of the Saronic Gulf, and go down the eastern coast of the Peleponnese to Kythira. They also do a circuit of the Cyclades, and ply between Rhodes and the other main Dodecanese. They are twice as fast, and twice as expensive as the conventional ferries, and usually have a snack bar where you can't even get a fly in your ouzo if you ask for one.

Domestic air travel

Olympic Airways runs an apparently adequate internal service that covers most large provincial cities and all the

main islands. The hub of this service is Athens, with flights departing from the West Terminal of Elleniko Airport, the one which caters exclusively for Olympic Airways.

The price of internal flights is reasonable. Athens to Corfu one way is around 14,000 drachmae (less than £45 or about $67 for 250 miles.) Services are frequent in the summer, and are considerably reduced in winter.

Unfortunately, at all times of year these services tend to be heavily booked up. Why, remains a mystery – for when you get on the plane you often discover that many of the seats are empty. However, if you're prepared to risk standby, you probably have a reasonable chance of travelling on the flight of your choice. Once you actually get to the airport, a seat is often guaranteed right away. However, this doesn't apply on Fridays and at the end of the weekend – when pale-faced, hollow-eyed businessmen from Athens tend to visit their families.

Buses

The Greek bus service is legendary. Most who travel on it remember the experience with great affection, and can bore you for hours with anecdotes about their adventures, the goat they sat next to (animal or human), or simply how they survived that dare-devil drive through the mountains.

Tickets are reasonably priced, and the service is far-reaching. Express services link the major cities and provincial centres, usually with several buses a day. Local services and cross-country links are usually adequate, too. But once you get to the villages, or start travelling the island routes, you

- *Ionian Islands-bound.*

enter another world. Here, where there is no need for precisely timed connections, a different order prevails. Your real journey begins with these local services.

Many of them use an aged school bus, driven by a local driver whose idea of time differs from that held by the rest of the world. Eccentricities are the norm. In Kefallonia, for instance, some of the drivers insist upon having the name of their village on the front of their bus, regardless of whether this has anything to do with the route they are travelling. For a while this even applied to the driver who took over the long-distance route to Athens.

So always check, and double-check, before relying on any service. That said, and allowing for peculiarities, local buses are magical conveyances which can take you through some of the most marvellous scenery in Greece – possibly with a chicken sitting in the seat beside you.

Trains

The rail network is not extensive. The Peleponnese is fairly well covered, there is a fast link between Athens and Thessaloniki, and there is a service from Thessaloniki to the Turkish border. But apart from the Athens-Thessaloniki express, and a superb little railway which runs from Diakofto on the Gulf of Corinth to the mountain village of Kalavrita (see page 104), there is little to recommend Greek trains except price. Fares are usually a little less than bus tickets. Most services are slow, or very slow.

ESSENTIAL PRACTICAL INFORMATION

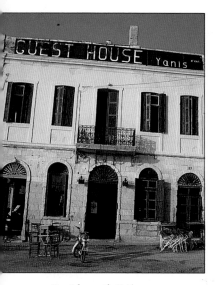

• *Guest house, the Dodecanese.*

Accommodation

Hotel prices at all levels in Greece tend to be inexpensive, and, at the bottom end of the market, very cheap indeed. However, hotel costs vary considerably throughout the year. Off-season rates are sometimes as much as 50 per cent lower than high season rates, especially in more remote spots which depend heavily upon tourism.

All prices, complete with seasonal variations, must by law be displayed in rooms on an officially stamped notice. These prices are the upper limit, and you will frequently find yourself being charged less if the hotel wants your custom. If this is the case, you may find that you can bargain.

(These seasonal variations don't officially apply in restaurants and cafés. Drinks prices at some of the more expensive 'holiday bars' can sometimes dip a bit at the end of the season.)

Banks and currency exchange

Banks are open from 8 am to 2 pm Monday to Friday. Some banks, especially in large centres, also open up again in the afternoon, at some seasons. But the first given times are the only ones you should *rely* upon.

All banks have display boards giving the exchange rates for major currencies. These are updated daily.

Breakdowns

The main automobile association of Greece is ELPA (Automobile and Touring Club of Greece). Its address is ELPA, Athens Tower, 2 Leoforos Messogion, Athens. Tel (01) 174.

This has more than forty offices throughout the country.

ELPA has a breakdown service, which is free to members of any other national motoring organization. To contact this, dial (01) 104. A warning triangle is required by law; however, you may find that some hire cars are not equipped with the triangle. If you consider this a Catch 22, this must be your first trip to Greece.

Electricity

Greece is mainly 220V 50 AC. Plugs are two-pronged. Take an adaptor for foreign electrical appliances. In some remote places the power is 110V DC.

Embassies and consulates

These tend to open between 9 am and 1 pm, sometimes longer. Foreign consulates are housed in the same buildings as embassies and include:

Australia 37, Soutsou St, Athens; tel (01) 644 7303.
Canada 4, Ioannou Genadiou, Athens; tel (01) 723 9511.
France 7, Vas. Sofias, Athens; tel. (01) 361 1663/5.
Germany 10, Vas. Sofias, Marousi, Athens; tel. 369 4111.
Ireland 7, Vas. Konstantinou, Athens; tel (01) 723 2771.
Netherlands 5, Vas. Konstantinou, Athens; tel (01) 723 9511.
U.K. 1, Ploutarhou, Kolonaki, Athens; tel (01) 723 6211.
U.S. 91, Leoforos Vas Sofias, Athens; tel 721 2951.

Emergencies

If you're in any difficulty anywhere in Greece, get hold of the Tourist Police by dialling 171. They usually speak English. It's also worth ringing them in case of motor accidents, breakdowns, lost property, or lost passport – *before* you ring other help lines (i.e., hospital, motoring organization, British Embassy, etc).

• *Opposite: Tinos.*

• 9 am, Leros.

Lost property
See Emergencies, page 22.

Measurements
Greece operates on the metric system: One litre = 1.7 pints (1 imperial gallon = 4.54 litres); 1 U.S. gallon = 3.73 litres.

One kilogramme (1,000 grams) = 2.2 lbs.

One kilometre (1,000 metres) = 0.62 miles. To convert kilometres to miles, multiply by five and divide by eight, and vice-versa.

Medical matters
You can get emergency medical attention at almost any hospital in Greece. The easiest one to get to in a hurry in Athens is Evangelismos, 45 Ipsilandou St; tel (01) 722 00 01. This is right by the Hilton, a destination any taxi driver will understand if he can't speak English.

If you're in need of medical treatment and can't travel, try telephoning 166. This line usually has someone who speaks English.

Another option is the Red Cross First Aid Centre, 21, 3rd Septemvriou Street, Athens; tel (01) 522 55 55. It is five minutes north of Omonia Square. English is spoken.

Outside Athens, dial 150. This line usually has someone who speaks English.

Chemists have a green cross motif outside. To find out which ones are open late in Athens, telephone 166. There is also a list of nearby late-opening chemists posted in the windows of most chemists. See also Emergencies, above, and Travel and medical insurance, page 17.

Opening hours
For banks, see above, under Banks and currency exchange.

Museums and tourist attractions: see *Versatile Guide* Conventions, page 12.

In cities you will find that shops tend to open from 8.30 am – 1.30 pm, and from 5.30 pm – 9 pm. However, these times may vary by as much as an hour. Away from the main holiday areas you'll find that the shops often don't bother to open for the afternoon session on certain days.

In Athens some shops and offices now no longer observe the long afternoon break, which means they tend to close earlier.

In Athens and the larger provincial centres most cafés open around 8 am and don't close until after midnight. A few might open earlier, especially near markets, ferry terminals and so on, and a few will stay open later, especially in 'late night' areas. Most night clubs and discos close at 3 am. Restaurants are open from noon until 3 pm, and from 7.30 pm or so until midnight.

In the country and the holiday resorts these hours are likely to be more flexible. For instance, many cafés will close during the afternoon, and ones by the harbour may open at 6 am.

Post and telephone
Allow at least four days for letters and postcards to reach a European address.

Most main post offices run a *post restante* service.

Post offices are open 9.30 am-1.30 pm, Mon-Sat. Main post offices in Athens generally open again in the afternoon, but with some variation according to district.

There are public telephones in kiosks and you can phone from a booth at the local OTE (Greek Telecom) office. Alternatively, you can phone from your hotel, usually at a much higher rate than the OTE meters.

You will probably need inexhaustable patience when dialling international numbers from Greece. Dial a few times, and if this doesn't work go and have a coffee. The Greek telephone system was installed to test your patience. A Greek friend of mine had to wait *eight years* after applying for a telephone before it was installed. Then within two months it broke down.

Public holidays
January 1 (New Year's Day); January 6 (Epiphany); Monday before start of Lent (Greek Orthodox); March 25 (Greek Revolution Remembrance Day); Good Friday to Easter Monday (Greek Orthodox); May 1 (May Day); June 15 (Pentecost); August 15 (Assumption); October 28 ('Ochi' Day); December 25 and 26 (Christmas).

Rush hours
The entire concept of 'rush' is foreign to the true Greek way of life. However, cities such as Athens and Thessaloniki have reluctantly imported these western notions. Here the morning rush-hour will tend to run from 7.30 am – 9.30. There is a midday rush-hour when everyone rushes from their office to the restaurants: at 1 pm it is usually at its height. And in the evenings there is a kind of rush-hour in reverse, when people come out to take their evening stroll (*volta*) in the main city centres. In one form or another this happens all over Greece, from the largest city to the smallest village, and usually takes place between 6.30 pm and 8.30 or around sunset.

Time
Greece is seven hours ahead of U.S. East Coast time, two hours ahead of British time, and one hour ahead of Continental European time.

Greek clocks are put foward by one hour on the first Sunday in April, and back one hour on the last Sunday in September.

Tipping
Tipping is not a widespread custom in Greece, and is not universally expected, but there exceptions.

If you visit a hairdresser (a shave at one of these is a supreme, and inexpensive, experience) you will be expected to tip around 25 per cent. Expensive restaurants expect 10 – 15 per cent. Cheap restaurants and tavernas used not to expect anything, but are beginning to pick up the habit – especially in the main tourist centres – Round up your bill to the nearest note and honour will usually be satisfied. The same can be done at cafés (or you can leave a few coins) – though again this is not universally expected.

The usual sad list of people who *do* expect tips includes the usual sad people who are underpaid and rely upon your generosity to make their work worthwhile. These include: cinema, concert and theatre ushers, night club check-in girls, hotel porters, lavatory attendants, car-park attendants and so on. You are unlikely to come across many of these outside Athens or Thessaloniki.

Tourist information
The Greek National Tourist Organization has offices in all main tourist centres throughout Greece. Their head office is:

2, Amerikis Street, Athens; tel. (01) 322 31 31. The Department of Information here, which deals with the public, is on the fifth floor.

GNTO also has a desk at the East Terminal of Athens Airport, and at 1, Odos Ermou, Athens; tel. (01) 325 22 67.

A BRIEF HISTORY OF GREECE

• N*axos*.

Earliest stirrings of civilization

Around 5,000 BC the first settlers began to arrive in significant numbers in Greece. They came from the Anatolian heartland of Asia Minor – modern Turkey. Ensuing waves of migrating tribes gradually occupied the Aegean islands.

By the middle of the 3rd millenium BC (i.e., around 2500 BC) Minoan civilization had begun to establish itself in Crete, with its royal palace at Knossos and its extensive trading links across the Aegean.

This civilization is named after its great king, Minos. Though perhaps Minos was not that great, because according to legend his wife Pasiphae took to coupling with the Cretan Bull. The result of this beastly habit was the birth of the Minotaur, who had the body of a man and the horned head of a bull. This early Cretan civilization appears to have been essentially peace-loving, and its art depicts a delightful, apparently care-free age – epitomized by the famous frescos of young girls leaping between the horns of bulls. Almost certainly, it was Minoan civilization which gave rise to the legend of the golden age of Atlantis, the lost continent which

is said to have sunk into the sea. This event is meant to have taken place beyond the Pillars of Hercules in the Atlantic (hence the name), but the description of what happened to Atlantis uncannily fits the end of Minoan civilization. Around 1500 BC a series of great earthquakes, the massive volcanic eruption of Thira, and tidal waves destroyed most of the Minoan coastal settlements throughout the Aegean.

This blow came at a time when a new, more war-like civilization was beginning to emerge on the mainland. This was centred on Mycenae, in the north-eastern Peloponnese.

The Mycenaeans were a Bronze Age civilization, in many ways less developed and less sophisticated than the Minoans. Their cities were surrounded by high, crude Cyclopean walls – so-called because they were said to have been built by one-eyed giants called the Cyclops. The Mycenaeans may not have been so cultured as the Minoans, but they created a series of myths and legends which appear to mark a distinct expansion of the human mind and its imagination. The myths of the Greek gods originate from this period.

According to one of these myths, Mycenae was founded by Perseus, the son of Zeus, who earlier had donned a helmet of invisibility to slay the hideous Medusa (the sight of whose face turned men to stone). These interwoven myths of semi-human gods and god-like heroes often painted a mythological picture of genuine historical events. The story of the siege of Troy and ensuing exploits, as recounted by Homer in the *Iliad* and the *Odyssey* about half a millenium later, are based on real events. Excavations have revealed that Troy was beseiged and fell in 1184 BC.

Much the same can probably be said of the blood-curdling events which befell the House of Atreus, the resident dynasty of Mycenae. This chronicle of rape, cannibalism, betrayal and vicious revenge, involving such figures as Clytemnestra and Agamemnon, was to be retold seven centuries later in the Greek tragedies.

The loose-knit Mycenaean empire came to an end with the migration into

• K*efalonia*.

Greece of the Hellenic tribes, starting with the first Dorian invasions around 1150 BC. For a while the destruction of Mycenaean civilization led to a dark age. This has yielded few archaeological remains to help us picture what exactly happened. But towards the end of this period the Greek alphabet appeared, and we can detect the beginnings of the city-state (*polis*).

The Classical era

What now took place in Greece has no precedent throughout world history. The 20th century may have witnessed a greater era of change, with great quantative advances, but they do not match the qualitative advances made in Ancient Greece.

The progress made during this brief period of a few centuries (and mainly during the course of one single century – the 5thC BC) changed the entire course of human development. This period marks the birth of philosophy, the inception of democracy, the start of true mathematical and scientific thought, the invention of drama (both tragedy and comedy), the perfection of sculpture and the transformation of architecture, to name but the major themes.

How this all came about still continues to puzzle historians. Many answers have been put forward as to why so much should have happened, and why it should have happened just here in this corner of the Mediterranean, but none of these answers is comprehensively satisfactory. Climate, the state of emergent human knowledge, evolutionary and racial factors, the advent of a period of comparative historical stability and prosperity giving the leisure to think, the stimulus of troubled times, diet even – these and many other contradictory explanations have been suggested.

But the truth is that neither the climate, nor the state of human knowledge, the immediate needs of humanity, the historical situation or social welfare were significantly more propitious than during a number of other eras. With all the benefit of hindsight, we still don't really know why this all happened in Ancient Greece, rather than say in Ancient Egypt, or much later during the Roman Empire.

So what exactly happened? Over much of Greece, city-states developed, each with its own distinctive character. The mountain remoteness of Sparta bred a philistine militaristic culture (which gave us the adjective spartan). Athens, on the other hand, developed into the centre whose culture was to change the world. Most of what we now refer to as Ancient Greek culture in fact derives from Athens.

But the rise of so many city-states inevitably bred great rivalries. The cities were constantly at war with each other. What we now call Ancient Greece consisted of many tiny squabbling centres of population who shared race, language, and certain elements of culture, but little else. (A recognizable Balkan situation to this day.) Celebrations of Greek togetherness were rare, though the cities did gradually become linked by treaties, and events such as the Olympic Games cemented a certain sense of shared racial tradition.

Partly because of the constant state of dissention, many Greek traders found it easier to emigrate. These emigrants founded colonies overseas, especially in Sicily, southern Italy and along the Black Sea coast.

The western coast of Asia Minor (now Turkey) had long been occupied by the Ionian Greeks. The very first philosopher, Thales of Miletus, came from here. But the Ionian cities soon found themselves blocking the path of aggressors from the east. The Persian Empire had already expanded to the borders of India, and as far south in Africa as Abyssinia. Now it began to expand westwards towards Europe.

By some miracle, most of the Greek city states managed to patch up their differences in the face of this common threat. (Though not all of them: Thebes even allied itself with the Persians in pursuit of its rivalry with Athens.) During the early decades of the 5thC BC, the Persians launched three successive full-scale invasions. Despite being heavily outnumbered by the vast Persian forces, the Greeks managed to repel each one of these attacks. The Greeks' defence of their homeland involved considerable bravery – Marathon and Thermopylae are remembered to this day – but the truth is that in the end they survived more by luck (and a measure of Persian incompetence) than by their own efforts.

So the Greeks survived, the Persian attempt to extend the borders of their Asian empire into Europe failed – and the city states of Greece continued to flourish. Athens now entered its golden age – when its citizens included the philosophers Socrates, Plato and Aristotle, the orators Demosthenes and Thucydides, the sculptor Praxiletes, the tragedian Sophocles and the comic playwright Aristophanes.

The city also now saw the rise of democracy – which literally means 'rule by the people', though in fact these 'people' did not include women or the large sub-class of slaves. The running of the city was decided by the Assembly, where all free citizens had their say. But as Athens became an increasingly busy trading centre, people found they had less and less time to waste on bickering in the Assembly, and power gradually began to polarize into factions as the citizens busied themselves making their fortunes.

But although this was a golden age of human development, all was not sweetness and light. The notion of individual freedom was not such as we would recognize today. The concept of democracy may have been born here, but the concept of liberalism was definitely not. Socrates was sentenced to death for teaching a philosophy that allegedly corrupted the young, and Aristotle would undoubtedly have met a similar fate if he had not left town in a hurry before his trial.

Meanwhile, the Spartans continued doing what they knew best: making war. At the height of the Athenian golden age, the city found itself involved in a series of wars with its Peloponnesian neighbour. These lasted for more than a quarter of a century, and were a great drain on resources – both economic and of manpower. And soon a new power began to emerge in the north, in Macedonia.

The kingdom of Macedon began expanding into Thrace, and Philip II then moved south and took over Athens. Philip was eventually succeeded by his son Alexander, whose 13-year rule witnessed the greatest expansion of empire yet seen by history. By the time Alexander the Great died in 323 BC he had conquered almost all the world that he knew existed. His empire extended east as far as Tashkent and the borders of India. (When Alexander reached the banks of the River Indus at the very limits of his advance, and realized that even he could go no further, he ordered tents, weapons and furniture to be constructed which were several times life-sized. These he left behind him, so that all who came across them would believe that they had been abandoned by a race of supermen.)

Alexander's empire did not last long. No sooner had he died than it split in three. But by then another great power was rising, this time in the west. The Romans soon conquered Alexander's divided empire, absorbing Greece and the nearer of its erstwhile colonies into its own.

The Romans recognized that the Greeks were in many ways more cultivated than themselves. The Roman Empire was the product of a civic and militaristic genius, and the spiritual vacuum this left was filled by Greek culture. Yet despite the Romans' partiality to Greek culture, their involvement in it was largely superficial. Rome produced several fine poets and orators, but made no significant advance in philosophy, mathematics or the sciences – apart from the strictly practical sciences of architecture, and civil and military engineering. Greek culture was largely decorative or decadent for the Romans, it was not a central driving part of their civilization. (Much the same has been said of European culture and late 20th century civilization. But this parallel breaks down in one essential aspect: we are progressive scientists, the Romans were not.)

During the era of Roman occupation, Greece was permitted a certain amount of autonomy. And where Roman and Greek civilization did not interfere with each other, they continued to accommodate each other. When the Emperor Nero attended the Olympic Games, competitions were duly arranged in singing and lyre-playing – so that he could take part and win these competitions. However, when he took part in the chariot race and fell out of his chariot, the judges were required to exercise their philosophical skills to the full in order to declare him the winner.

The Roman Empire, too, gradually began to sink into glorious decline.

Icon, St John's Monastery, Patmos.

Christianity filled the gap which Greek culture had never quite managed to occupy. Then the Empire split in two. In 330 AD the Emperor Constantine made Byzantium (soon to be known as Constantinople, after its founder, and today known as Istanbul) the capital of the Eastern Roman Empire. Just over a century later the Western Roman Empire was overrun by the barbarians from the north, and Constantinople became the last outpost of civilization as the Dark Ages descended over Europe.

The Byzantine Era, Independence and modern times

Despite being attacked by the Persians and the Arabs, Constantinople remained the capital of the Eastern Roman Empire. The Orthodox faith flourished and Byzantine culture took root throughout Greece – notably in such spots as Mount Athos and Ossios Loukas. But Greece was by now little more than a poorly administrated provincial backwater of the Empire. And before long, waves of foreign invaders from the north-west (mainly of Slav origin) began moving into the country.

These were followed by more organized occupations of patches of Greek territory. The Normans arrived at Corfu as early as 1085. Just over a century later came the armies of the Crusaders, who set up what virtually amounted to their own private kingdoms. Then for a while Byzantine influence showed signs of reasserting itself, until Constantinople was overrun by the Turks in 1453. After this the Turks began to take over Greece, absorbing it into the Ottoman Empire, and Greece once again became a forgotten backwater. The population in the countryside declined sharply.

But by the end of the 18thC resistance to Ottoman rule became increasingly organized. Byron's arrival at Missolongi to take control of the Greek army of independence, and his death there in 1824, captured the imagination of Europe – and the liberation of Greece became a popular cause. In fact, the European powers did not actually do much to assist the Greeks until 1827. The big three, Britain, France and Russia, sent their combined fleets in a show of strength to try and cow the Turks into granting autonomy to at least a few limited regions of Greece. But by accident the Turkish fleet engaged the combined European fleet, and a naval battle ensued off Navarino. By the time the smoke had died down, the entire Turkish and Egyptian fleet had been destroyed.

After this, Greek independence became virtually inevitable. The British, French and Russians forced the Turks to capitulate, and in 1830 Greece was proclaimed a republic. At this stage, its territory consisted only of the Peleponnese, Attica and the Cyclades. The ensuing history of Greece is largely a matter of Greek expansion at Turkish expense, as the Greeks took over their traditional lands.

There were several typically Balkan hiccups on the way. The first Greek president, Kapodistrias, was assassinated only a year after taking office; and the European powers saw fit to appoint the Bavarian Otho I as the first King of Greece. He lasted almost a couple of decades, before he had to be replaced by another European appointee for this difficult post: George I of Denmark. Within another 20 years, the Greeks had wrested Thessaly from the Turks. Then came the Balkan conflicts which erupted during the first decades of the 20thC – when everyone in the Balkans appeared to fight everyone else, and everyone fought against the Turks. Out of this massive confusion (which played an important part in

• *Mythological café sign.*

hastening the First World War, and has, worryingly, found new echoes today) Greece managed to take Macedonia and Epiros from the Turks.

During the First World War, the Greeks sided with the western Allies against the Turks. When the western allies were victorious, Greece was awarded Thrace and a region of the Asia Minor coastline around Smyrna (now Izmir), once ancient Ionia.

But the Greeks now had the bit between their teeth, and dreamt of even further expansion at the expense of the defeated Turks. Led by a general who was suffering from the delusion that his feet were made of glass, the Greeks launched into Asia Minor.

But by now the Turks had got rid of the decadent Ottomans and were being modernized by Attaturk. The Greek army in Asia Minor was put to flight, and in characteristic fashion the Turks moved into Smyrna and massacred every Greek they could find.

In common with a number of depressed nations of this period, Greece eventually began to recover its languishing national pride with a period of fascist-style dictatorship. This began when Metaxa took power in 1936. Despite this, Greece sided with the Allies at the outbreak of the Second World War. The country was now occupied by the Germans and the Italians, with a Nazi-controlled puppet government in Athens. The Greek resistance, with a little aid from British undercover agents, continued to harass the occupying foreigners. Unfortunately, the

31

Greek resistance was, for the most part, a communist organization. And when the division of Europe was agreed between the Allied Powers at Yalta, Greece ended up on the non-communist side of the divide. This meant that the communists were not allowed to take control of the country when the Nazis left in 1944.

Instead, the British insisted upon the Greeks accepting the royalist government which had sat out the war in exile. Churchill landed British troops in Athens to enforce this decision, and ensure that there was no communist take-over. There followed a period of bitter in-fighting and civil war. Atrocities and back-street executions were rife. Then famine once again spread throughout the land. More Greeks died during the four years of the Civil War than had died during the entire troubled period of the war itself.

The country which emerged from all this was heavily under American control. All orders signed by the Greek Prime Minister had to be counter-signed by the American ambassador before they could be implemented. The CIA continued to help suppress any hint of left-wing activity, and many Greeks were forced into exile.

There followed the problem over Cyprus, when the British refused to allow the island to decide its own destiny, and instead made it an independent country. Cyprus would almost certainly have voted for union with Greece, but the Turkish minority would almost equally certainly have suffered from widespread persecution.

Politics in Greece remained a volatile

KEY DATES

Ancient Greece

Earliest settlement of Crete by migrating tribes	5000 BC
Neolithic tribes occupy Cyclades	3000
Rise of Minoan civilization in Crete	2500
Achaian and Ionian invasions	2000
Decline and fall of Minoan civilization in Crete	1500
Rise of Mycenaean civilization on mainland and the Mycenean Empire (the period of Greek mythology, as later described by Homer)	12thC
Fall of Troy	1184
Dorian invasions	1150
Colonization of Asia Minor by Ionians	1100
Rise of the city state	900
First Olympic Games	776
Greek colonies founded throughout Mediterranean region, from Egypt to Spain and Black Sea; Odyssey and Iliad written by Homer	7thC

Rise of Sparta and Athens

First Persian invasion	500
Persians defeated at Battle of Marathon	490
Second Persian invasion, ending in defeat at Battle of Salamis	480
Final Persian defeat at Battle of Plataea	479
Periclean era heralds the Athenian Golden Age	5thC
Peleponnesian War between Athens and Sparta	431-404
Rise of Macedon under Philip II	350
Alexander the Great sets out to conquer Persians	336
Death of Alexander in Babylon	323
Romans conquer Greece	2ndC
The apostle St Paul preaches in Greece	AD 50
Roman Empire splits East-West; Barbarian invasions of Greece	3rdC

business, with the ruling government always dependent upon the support of the army, and the CIA lurking in the wings. Then in 1967 the army (almost certainly in collusion with the CIA) decided that they had had enough of this unstable situation. A junta of colonels seized power. This resulted in a vicious seven-year dictatorship, in which all liberal and leftist elements of Greek life were systematically eradicated.

The fascist colonels eventually brought about their own downfall in 1974, by trying to meddle in the politics of Cyprus with a view to annexing it to Greece. This dangerous game provoked a Turkish invasion of the island (the results of which have yet to be cleared up), and the army decided that enough was enough. The Colonels were granted early retirement and a small free room in a military barracks for an indefinite period.

In 1981 the Greek socialist party PASOK came to power, and a new era of political hope began. But by the end of the decade the goverment's position was a mockery – with the Prime Minister (attended by his air hostess girl friend) ruling the country from a hospital bed in England, and corruption rife throughout the country's institutions.

Since then the new government has begun the uphill struggle of trying to establish political credibility throughout the country, as well as abroad. It has been hampered in this task by a few own goals and Greece's deteriorating economic situation. But the country's main industry, tourism, continues to do well.

Middle Period

Greece falls under successive invasions of Franks, Normans, Venetians and Lombards	13th-15thC
Fall of Constantinople to the Turks; Christians defeat Turks at Battle of Lepanto, halting expansion of Turkish Empire	1453 1571
Turks complete conquest of Greece	1669
Venetians regain control of Peleponnese and Ionian islands	17th-18thC
Stagnation and desolation under Turkish rule	18thC
First independence struggles against the Turks	late18thC

The Modern Era

Start of War of Independence	1821
Byron dies at Missolongi	1824
Turkish fleet destroyed off Navarino	1827
Greece becomes an independent republic	1830
Otho I of Bavaria ascends Greek throne	1833
George I of Denmark replaces deposed Otho I; Britain cedes Ionian islands to Greece	1863
Greeks take Thessaly from Turks	1881
Balkan Wars	1912-13
Greece awarded Thrace and Smyrna (now Izmir, Turkey) after First World War	1919
War against the Turks, culminating in Smyrna massacre by Turks	1919-22
Germans occupy Greece	1941-44
Civil War and famine	1944-49
Dictatorship of the Colonels	1967-74
Greece joins European Community; Papandreou and PASOK (Greek Socialist Party) in power	1981
Fall of Papandreou amidst scandals	1991

SOME GREEK THEMES

The Gods

The Greek gods and the sexy, violent myths describing their exploits almost certainly date from the Mycenaean era, which started around the middle of the second millenium BC. This was a period when civilized restraint had yet to become an integral part of human nature. Memories persisted of more primeval human types who had been dispossessed and remained lurking in the undergrowth beyond the settlements – giving rise to stories about half human creatures such as satyrs (part human, part goat), centaurs (part human, part horse) and the like.

The Greek gods belonged to a religion utterly different from the Judaic heritage of Christianity. It had no moral code and no concept of sin. The gods represented the elemental forces of the universe, and thus were restrained by no human concepts such as justice (divine or otherwise). The gods were worshipped out of superstitious fear of the powers which they wielded, and were born in the human mind at a time when the world could be a very dangerous place. Experience had taught human beings that for much of the time they had no power to control their destiny. So in order to make sure the harvest was good, you gave a sacrifice to Demeter the god of agriculture; if you wanted to recover from an illness, you consulted Asklepios the god of healing; and if you were looking for someone to fall in love with, you appealed to Aphrodite, the goddess of love.

The oldest god was Gaia, the Earth Mother. She mated with her son Uranus, the sky god, and produced a number of offspring – including the serpent Python, the Titans and Chronos the god of time. Chronos had a fling with his sister Rea, and this produced Zeus, who became the leader of the gods and ruled from the top of Mount Olympos.

Zeus exercised his divine powers in much the way a human being would behave if placed in a similar position. He got up to as much mischief as he could, and slept with as many goddess and beautiful mortal women as he could lay his hands on.

As a result Mount Olympus soon became filled with gods and goddesses, who each had their own special powers – from wisdom (Athena) to eloquence (Hermes). Inevitably these gods and goddesses often crossed paths, giving rise to an endless soap opera of misdeeds, amorous pursuit, deceit, revenge and so forth.

A human being could contact a god by visiting the god's oracle. Here he would put his question to the god, and the attendant priests or priestesses would interpret the oracle's answer. There were oracles all over ancient Greece, the most famous of which was Apollo's oracle at Delphi.

The following list includes a few of the better known Ancient Greek gods and their powers:

Aphrodite: more frequently known as Venus. The goddess of love. She was the mother of Eros.

Apollo: the god of physical beauty and art, whose main oracle at Delphi was reckoned to be 'the truest of all'.

Ares: better known by his Roman name, Mars: the god of war.

Asklepios: the son of Apollo, patron of medicine and healing.

Athena: the goddess of wisdom, worshipped in Athens, at the Parthenon.

Dionysios: the god of wine, worshipped by an ecstatic cult; also known to us by his Roman name, Bacchus.

Hermes: the messenger of the gods, recognizable by his winged sandals.

Poseidon: the god of the sea and storms, usually seen flourishing a trident, often known by his Roman name, Neptune.

Zeus: called Jupiter by the Romans, ruler of the gods, and known as the Thunderer. Worshipped at Olympia and Dodoni.

Greek philosophy

Philosophy was started by the Ancient Greeks. The first philosopher is said to have been Thales of Miletus. He is known to have been alive and practising his trade in 585 BC, because he

• *Knossos, Crete.*

predicted an eclipse of the sun which took place in that year. Thales was the first to attempt to explain the world according to rational, universal concepts, and in terms of its observable nature, rather than in terms of mythology.

The main thesis of his philosophy was that everything is made up of water. Thales thus set the tone for all future philosophy by getting it wrong. On the other hand, if he had got it right, that would surely have been the end of philosophy, there and then.

Philosophy continued to flourish with a succession of errors (it wasn't water it was fire, then air, then pieces of light, and so on). But just over a century after its beginning, this new method of thinking was to enter a golden age, with the emergence of three of the greatest philosophers in history. The first was Socrates, who appears to have been something of a reprobate and never actually got around to writing anything down. This means that we only know of Socrates' teaching

through the writings of his famous pupil Plato, and it is sometimes difficult to separate their ideas.

Socrates developed a method of aggressive, negative questioning. This he used in dialogues to cut through the twaddle of his adversaries and arrive at the truth. Plato, meanwhile, persisted in the philosophical tradition of getting it wrong. He believed that the real world was that of ideas, and that the world we see and experience consists of no more than shadows of these pure ideas. Despite this unrealistic attitude, many are convinced that all of philosophy since has been no more than footnotes to Plato's writing. Though this is an exaggeration, it is certainly true that Plato was the first to formulate clearly many of the basic philosophical problems which still exercise us to this day. The third great Greek philosopher was Aristotle, a pupil of Plato's, who at least viewed the world realistically. The rules of logic and classification which Aristo-

• *Abbot Issidoros, Patmos.*

tle established laid the foundations for most philosophical and scientific thought during the next two millenia. Only now are we beginning to discover *how* he got it wrong. Aristotle himself appears to have understood that all comprehensive explanations were bound in the end to be wrong – but this did not stop him from having a go.

Without philosophy, which for centuries retained its distinctive Greek character, we would not be what we are today. We would have no science; and from the Greeks we have also inherited the view that unless a statement is objectively and logically proven, it cannot be regarded as 'truth'. (Incidentally, it has taken philosophers nearly 24 centuries of getting it wrong to conclude that getting it wrong isn't the point. They are now of the opinion that the mere practice of philosophy is what matters. Thus, according to the infallible categories of Aristotle, philosophy has now become an activity – like butterfly collecting or tax evasion. The last word remains with the Ancient Greeks, it seems.)

The Greek Orthodox Church

When the Roman Empire split into two in the 4thC, so did the church. The church of the Western Empire became the Roman Catholic church, and the church of the Eastern Empire became the Orthodox church. Like the other orthodox churches (such as the Russian Orthodox Church) the Greek Orthodox Church saw no Reformation. It retains the ancient Byzantine rites, and still looks to Constantinople (now Istanbul) as its religious capital. Its official head is still called the Patriarch of Constantinople.

Throughout the Turkish occupation of Greece (16th – 19thC) it was the largely suppressed Greek Orthodox

Church which kept Greek culture and Greece's sense of nationhood alive. And it was a Greek Orthodox priest, Patriarch Germanos, who first raised the Greek flag near Kalavritis in 1821 – the event which signalled the start of the War of Independence against the Turks.

Greek Orthodox priests and monks still wear the long black robes, black beards and tall black hats of their Byzantine predecessors. Village priests are allowed to marry, and often have to provide for their own living by working smallholdings. They are thus very much a part of country life, and share in the everyday fortunes of their parishioners.

The Greek Orthodox Church retains its Byzantine architectural and cultural heritage. The finest aesthetic product of this heritage is probably its icons, with their unique blend of stylization and individuality. Curiously, this is one of the few great art forms which has yet to be transformed at the hands of a 20th century master. The interiors of Greek Orthodox churches often appear somewhat cluttered and disorganized to western European sensibilities, though their formalized splendours and homely touches certainly seem more profoundly attuned to religious worship than the extravagances of the Baroque.

More than 95 per cent of the Greek population is at least nominally of the Greek Orthodox faith, and the national attachment to the church remains strong. Possibly this is because the church, like the Greek people, remains essentially relaxed and tolerant. Though the harsher traditions of monasteries and hermits have always been strong in the Greek Orthodox Church, these were accompanied by few of the neurotic excesses of self-fla-gellation, inquisitions, extreme asceti-cism, puritanism and fanatic sectarian-ism which became such a notable fea-ture of the western churches.

Greek popular music
You only have to tune in to any Greek radio station to discover that Greek popular music is different from that of the rest of Europe. Its purest form is what you will hear in the villages and country festivals; but the influence of the old folk music continues to perme-ate modern Greek pop and rock music. The main instrument is the *bouzouki*, a type of unwieldy steel-stringed lute which probably originates from the Lev-ant. Still popular in the Cretan villages is the *lyra*, a triple-stringed lyre which is played with a small bow. Another tra-ditional instrument is the zither-like *san-douri*, whose metal strings are played in the same way as a xylophone.

The music played by these instru-ments often accompanies traditional Greek dancing. There are several simi-lar but subtly different forms, the most popular perhaps being the *kalama-tianos*. This is the national dance, in which the dancers form a circle. The *zembetiko* (a Zorba-style solo) and other similar male dances are thought to have originated from the sacred dances of India.

Greece has also produced an indige-nous near-equivalent of the blues. This is *rembetika*, which started amongst the poor Greeks of Asia Minor, and flourished amongst the urban poor (especially those dispossessed by the Smyrna Massacre) during the 20s and 30s. The players of *rembetika* were celebrated for their notorious lifestyle – an evocative blend of sophistication and sleaze which permeated their songs: the rakish hat, the jacket slung over the shoulders, the hashish ciga-rettes, and the bitter-sweet romantic life of the gutter. (*Rembetika* is almost certainly derived from a Turkish word which means 'the gutter'.) True *rem-betika* is no more, except on a few ancient recordings. But its effect on the Greek popular tradition is indelible. A modern form of *rembetika* re-emerged in the left-wing clubs of Athens during the 1960s. This pro-duced vernacular political songs of the type which first brought Theodorakis to prominence. But all this was sup-pressed in 1967 by the Colonels, just as true *rembetika* had been sup-pressed by the dictator Metaxa in 1936.

The old political clubs have long since disappeared, but music with echoes of *rembetika* continues to be played. And to this day the *bouzouki* players working the club circuits of Athens like to imagine that their life-style has some of the panache of their heroic predecessors.

Between Thessaloniki and Alexandropolis
Macedonia and the North-East Coast

250 km; map Michelin 980, 1:700000

The territory covered by this route is not standard tourist fare, but it is nonetheless rewarding for that. It will particularly interest anyone who wants to see the ancient city of Thessaloniki, and wants to have a taste of the Orient while still within the borders of Greece.

Though Thessaloniki remains subordinate to Athens, it has a unique history of its own. This is the capital of Macedonia, the kingdom that produced Greece's best-known king, Alexander the Great (see page 29). The empire he subdued was in its time the largest the world had ever seen. Thessaloniki was founded by one of Alexander's sons-in-law, and named after Alexander's half-sister.

Assuming your starting point is Thessaloniki, you drive east along the main E90, reaching the coast at the resort of Asprovalta. From here you continue to the ancient ruined city of Amfipoli; then there is a superb drive along the E90, which keeps to the coast, until just before you reach the port of Kavala, with its picturesque old acropolis.

From Kavala you can take a detour to the ruins of Philippi, an ancient Roman town on the Via Egnatia, the ancient world's main trading route to the Levant. After Kavala you come to Xanthi, in the province of Thrace, a part of Greece that is often forgotten. In fact, it remained Turkish until just over 70 years ago, and it still has a sizeable Turkish population.

As you travel further east, you cannot escape noticing that you are approaching the Orient. There is a distinctly eastern feel to this part of the world, with mosques in the towns and oriental music playing from the radios in the Turkish quarters.

The E90 runs through the disappointing town of Alexandropolis, and then turns north beside the Turkish border towards Edirne, which is in Turkey. There are no great sights along this section of road, but it's worth the long drive if you are feeling curious: now a stretch of hinterland, this was one of the world's historic crossroads, where the Mediterranean world, Asia and Slavonic Europe all met.

The main part of the route between Thessaloniki and Alexandropolis can easily be travelled in a day. But if you wish to see all of it properly you should allow three days, and a day for returning to Thessaloniki.

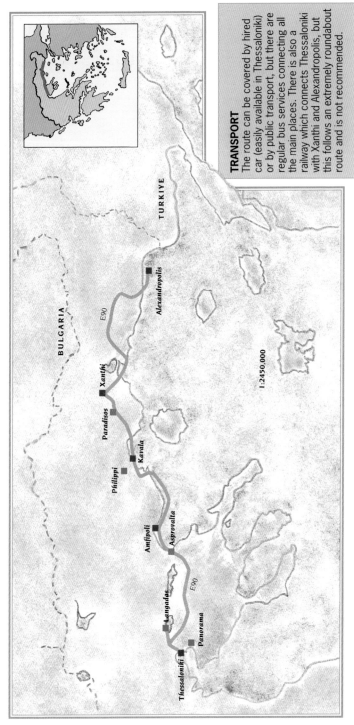

TRANSPORT
The route can be covered by hired car (easily available in Thessaloniki) or by public transport, but there are regular bus services connecting all the main places. There is also a railway which connects Thessaloniki with Xanthi and Alexandropolis, but this follows an extremely roundabout route and is not recommended.

• *Coast near Thessaloniki.*

SIGHTS & PLACES OF INTEREST

ALEXANDROPOLIS ⛴ ✕
NE coast of mainland, 20 km from the Turkish border. Easily the most depressing town in the whole of Greece. It isn't even named after Alexander the Great, but after Alexander I, the all-but-forgotten King of the Hellenes in 1919 when Thrace was handed back to Greece by the Turks. This almost says it all.

Nonethless, you'll find visitors here, but like yourself, they'll all be passing through: some to Turkey, some catching the ferry for Samothrace, some back from Turkey. If you're stuck, there's a beach. And if you're here in July or August, there's a rather spurious Wine Festival. The tedium comes into its own during the off season.

AMFIPOLI
107 km E of Thessaloniki, just inland off the E90. The site of ancient Amphipolis, the next important staging post east on the Via Egnatia (see Thessaloniki, page 43) after Thessaloniki.

The city was founded in the 5thC BC and rose to greatness a century later, when Macedon was ruled by Philip II and then his son Alexander the Great. Approaching Amfipoli from the west on the old road you'll see the superb **Lion of Amphipolis**, which stands by the

bridge across the River Strimonas. Stop and have a look. What you see is the solution to one of the great three-dimensional jig-saw puzzles of history. The original statue was erected at the end of the 4thC BC in honour of some timeless deed perpetrated by the illustrious Laomedon. During the ensuing centuries, some passing hooligans set about the lion, and for more than a thousand years its shattered fragments lay on the river shore. Then, in 1936, along came a team of restorers – and within a year, to the astonishment of the scoffers, they had the whole thing reassembled.

ASPROVALTA
87 km E of Thessaloniki. An attractive village on the Strimonic Gulf, the first stretch of sea you come to when you head east along the E90 out of Thessaloniki. There are miles of sand, and it's a great spot to stop for a swim, followed by something to eat at one of the pleasant cafés along the front.

KAVALA ⛴ ✕
182 km E of Thessaloniki on the NE coast. Kavala is the second city of Macedonia, though its population is less than 60,000. It is an attractive place, with a harbour, an acropolis, and a Turkish

aquaduct. It is also the centre of the Greek tobacco industry.

From here you can catch ferries to the islands of Thassos (see Local Explorations:7), Samothrace (see Local Explorations:7) and Limnos (See Local Explorations:7). It is not exactly a holiday spot, but if you want a swim there's a resort suburb to the west of town called Kalamitsa, which has a beach.

There has been a settlement on the site of Kavala since 3,000 BC. However, not much remains of Kavala's past, which was largely destroyed by the Turks, except a rather beautiful **old quarter** of the city surrounded by ancient walls. This is called **Panayia** (after the Virgin Mary), and is on the

> DETOUR – **PHILIPPI**
> If you've time while you're in Kavala, take a trip 16 km up the road north-west to the site at Philippi. There are some interesting Roman and Byzantine ruins, including a fine theatre and a section of the ancient Via Egnatia. The Battle of Philippi was fought west of here in 42 BC: it decided the fate of the Roman Empire after the assassination of Julius Caesar. Cassius and Brutus were defeated, and committed suicide in the time-honoured military fashion by falling on their swords.

RECOMMENDED HOTELS

ALEXANDROPOLIS
Motel Egnatia, D-DD; *on the main road into town; tel.* 051 28 661.

A pleasant modern motel, handy for a swim in the sea and with the distinct advantage of being out of town.

KAVALA
Oceanis, DD; *Erithrou Stavrou; tel.* 051 22 19 81.

A large modern hotel on the main street in the heart of town, and close to the port. It has good amenities, including that essential feature for all who find themselves wilting in the urban heat – a private pool.

Hotel Lucy, DD-DDD; *Kalamitsa; tel.* 051 83 26 00.

In the beach suburb of Kalamitsa, just to the west of town, this is a modern resort hotel with a picturesque setting above the sea.

PANORAMA
Nepheli, DDD; *tel.* 031 94 20 02.

Here you get a room with a view indeed, most mod cons, and willing if slightly dozy staff.

THESSALONIKI
As you'd expect, there is a wide choice of hotels in Thessaloniki. The nearer you are to the centre, the higher the decibel level, unless you're hermetically sealed in by air-conditioned luxury. The pleasantest hotels are mainly in the more residential areas.

Electra Palace, DDD; 5 *Platia Aristotelous; tel.* 031 23 22 21.

Right in the heart of town, opposite the sea-front, a large luxury hotel, whose prices approach the stratospheric. It compensates for being a little featureless with helpful, multi-lingual service.

Queen Olga, DD-DDD; 44 *Vasilissis Street; tel.* 031 82 46 21.

Some way south-east of the city centre, but near enough the sea to breathe. Some rooms have views of the bay, but you may have to employ a little skilful negotiation, and persistence if you want one.

Capsis, DD; 28 *Monasteriou; tel.* 031 52 14 21.

A large hotel close to the railway station on the western continuation of Egnatia Street. The bonus here is the pool, though it can become crowded when the package tourists arrive. In high season, when other hotels in town are booked solid, and there is not a room to be had anywhere, try making a personal approach to the desk here. It sometimes works.

Nea Orestias DD-DDD; 20 *Selefkidon Street; tel.* 031 51 94 11.

A hotel that combines value for money with peace and quiet. Popular with cheerful American students.

• *Harvesting tobacco, north of Thessaloniki.*

acropolis headland which juts out into the sea east of the port. This district is filled with narrow streets and tiny lanes which wind up towards the citadel.

In Panayia you will find the **home of Mehmet Ali**, a typical 18thC Turkish house, which is maintained in authentic style by the Egyptian government. Mehmet Ali's father was an Albanian muslim who had made his fortune out of the tobacco industry. Mehmet Ali served in the Turkish army, and in the late 18thC he went with the army to Egypt. By a series of implausible twists of fate, and some ambitious scheming of his own, he eventually found himself ruler of Egypt. He thus founded the dynasty which eventually tottered to a decrepit end under King Farouk. Also worth seeing is the nearby **Imaret**, a

superb grouping of domed Muslim buildings which looks over the harbour. This cries out to be restored to its former state (it was originally a charitable institution founded by Mehmet Ali), but owing to its despised Turkish origins it is now used as a warehouse.

There are fine views from the Kastro, the old Turkish quarter, which is above here, and also from the Belvedere at the tip of the acropolis.

LANGADAS

If you are in the vicinity of Thessaloniki on May 21, do all you can to get to the village of Langadas, which is just 22 km north-east of the city. Here they hold a mysterious fire-walking ritual called **Anastenaria**. Its origins almost certainly go back to prehistoric times, and as far as I know it is unique in Europe. The ritual involves a number of villagers walking barefoot on burning coals for anything up to 15 minutes. They emerge unscathed, which they put down to their belief in God, and to the fact that they are cleansed of sin. All sorts of explanations have been given – though the most obvious (hoax) was disproved several years ago when a young Dutch philosophy student tried to join in. He was taken off to hospital with severe burns, and then arrested by the police for disturbing the peace.

The ceremony tends to be commercialized nowadays (you have to pay to get in), but it makes a worthwhile day out. Be there soon after 5 pm if you want a decent seat for the grilling itself, which like all good barbecues begins around 7 pm.

(NB at time of going to press, this ceremony is temporarily suspended, allegedly owing to a dispute with the church authorities – so be sure to make enquiries at the tourist office before setting out.)

PANORAMA ⊨ ✕

About 8 km E of Thessaloniki's centre. If you are in or near Thessaloniki and feel the need to escape the pollution for a breath of fresh air, head for this aptly named village. Here you can look down on the entire city and the upper reaches of the Thermaic Gulf, while you sit at one of the cafés wondering whether you remembered to pay the gas bill before you left home.

PARADISOS

Heading east from Thessaloniki, 17 km before you reach Xanthi, this village is so delightful that it almost lives up to its name. An ideal spot to stop off for a coffee.

THESSALONIKI ⊨ ✕

N coast of mainland, at head of Thermaic Gulf. Thessaloniki has a population of more than 400,000, making it the second largest city in Greece.

It was officially founded in 315 BC by Cassander, who was married to Alexander the Great's half-sister. Cassander named the city after his wife (whose name translates into English as Sally).

• *Off Samos, eastern Aegean.*

Thessaloniki soon became an important staging post on the trading route to the east, and during the Roman Empire the city was to become rich from this trade. In those days, the trading route which led through Thessaloniki was known as the Via Egnatia, and to this day Egnatia Street is the city's main east-west thoroughfare.

The Via Egnatia linked the port of Dyracchium (modern Durazzo) in Albania to Asia Minor. This was a western section of the longest trading route the world has ever known, the Silk Road. As its name suggests, the route was used for bringing silk from China. At its height, the Silk Road linked the shores of the Yellow Sea with the Atlantic coast of the Iberian peninsula, a distance of almost 12,000 km. Although few Chinese travelled along its entire length, it is possible that the first Chinaman to see Europe came through Thessaloniki some time during the early centuries AD. What he saw here may well have been responsible for the Chinese deciding that it was best to remain in China.

St Paul arrived in the 1stC AD and began preaching Christian love – whereupon the local population pursued him through the streets and attacked the house in which he barricaded himself.

Three centuries later, the Emperor Galerius made Thessaloniki his headquarters, and at once set about vigorously persecuting the Christians. Later came the Emperor Theodosius, who fell ill in Thessaloniki. Believing himself on his death bed, he converted to Christianity. But when he recovered, he returned to his pagan ways. A special celebration was laid on in the local circus, and the entire pagan population was invited – to watch the massacre of 7,000 Christians. Theodosius later repented his deed and went to see St Ambrose, who told him to perform a penance, and to refrain from doing it again.

In 827 AD, the great St Cyril was born in Thessaloniki. In later years Cyril was to become a leading theologian, and also took Christianity to the heathen Slavs. He gave his name to the Cyrillic alphabet, which is still used by Russian and several of the Slavonic languages.

During the Byzantine era, Thessaloniki became the most important city in the Eastern Empire outside Constantinople (present day Istanbul). After the fall of Istanbul in 1453, the city was absorbed into the Turkish Empire.

In 1492 the Jews were banished from Spain, and more than 20,000 of them ended up in Thessaloniki. For years they lived here as an almost autonomous people, trading and speaking their own language, Ladino, a type of Castillian Spanish, but written in Hebrew characters. Once it had been uprooted from Spain, the language no longer developed. It thus preserved ancient Spanish Castillian as if in aspic, and this was the language which Cervantes used when he wrote *Don Quixote*. Four hundred years later, literary scholars would visit Thessaloniki to speak with the Jews here, in order to learn how the language which Cervantes had used actually sounded. To the British, this would be like going to a country where they still spoke perfect Shakespearean English.

During the final decades of the 19thC, Thessaloniki became a centre for dissent against the corrupt Ottoman rule of the Turkish Empire. In 1881, Kemal Attaturk, who was to become the first leader of modern Turkey, was born here.

In 1888 the railway from western Europe reached Thessaloniki (nearly 30 years before it was to reach

Athens), thus increasing the city's commercial importance. In 1912, nearly a hundred years after the main body of Greece had achieved independence, Thessaloniki was released by the Turks and became part of Greece. This resulted in a large exodus of the Turkish population, and at the same time there was an influx of Greeks from Turkey.

Through the centuries, Thessaloniki acquired a large mixed population, including Albanians, Slavs, Jews, Greeks and Turks (but no Chinese). Each racial group left its impact on the city, whose different quarters all preserved the different characteristics of their occupants. Unfortunately this unique heritage was almost entirely lost when a large fire swept the city in 1917. After this, the streets were laid out on a modern grid pattern which the city retains to this day. Only in the curving streets of the old Kastra quarter (see below), just over 1 km north of the sea-front towards the acropolis, do you get an idea of what old Thessaloniki must have been like. It appears very eastern here, more like Istanbul than Athens. In this part of the upper town you'll get some fine views out over the city, the harbour and the gulf.

Well into this century Thessaloniki remained one of the major Jewish cities in Europe – maintaining close trading links with similar Jewish cities as far afield as Antwerp and Prague. But after reaching a peak of nearly 70,000, the Jewish population started to dwindle. Some of the Salonika Jews, as they were known, began emigrating to Palestine. Then came the catastrophe of the Second World War and the Nazi occupation. It is believed that during this period more than 50,000 Jews were deported to the death camps of northern Europe. There is a **memorial** which commemorates this event at the end of Leoforos Langada.

Modern Thessaloniki is an attractive city – much more so than modern Athens. Though, like Athens, it suffers from pollution. On a steamy day in midsummer, with the traffic reduced to a horn-blaring standstill in the 30-degree heat, and effluents discolouring the upper reaches of the Thermaic Gulf, I can think of many places I'd rather be. Try exploring the city in the spring or autumn, though, and it's a different

• *The White Tower, emblem of Thessaloniki.*

story. A few years ago, in winter, I passed through Thessaloniki under snow, with the sea of the upper gulf frozen over, apart from the passages in the ice broken by the ships – a spellbinding experience. Apparently this happens more often than you'd expect, when the winter wind changes to the north bringing freezing air down from the Bulgarian mountains. Anyway, even if you don't bring your skates, there's plenty to do and see in Thessaloniki. Here are a few of the places you really ought to see if you have time:

The White Tower (Lefkos Pirgos)

This 15thC Turkish tower stands by the sea-front close to the Archaeological Museum. Despite its gruesome history, it has been adopted as the city's emblem.

This was where the sultan imprisoned any members of his personal guard whom he suspected of treason: the tower was in constant use. In 1826, the sultan's entire guard revolted against him, whereupon the sultan had them all imprisoned in the tower. Then he decided to have them all mas-

sacred instead. After this, the tower became known by the local people as the Bloody Tower. The Sultan's response was to have the tower whitewashed: from then on it was to be known as the White Tower.

Inside there is now a **Byzantine Museum**, and if you climb to the top, there is a fine view of the city and the harbour.

The Archaeology Museum

Close to the White Tower, this is more than a museum: it is a statement of nationhood. It contains the relics of the early Kingdom of Macedon, with a superb range of artefacts, gold masks, crowns and so forth, from the royal tombs of Philip II of Macedon, Alexander the Great's father. So why is this museum so significant politically?

The Greeks claim that early Macedon was essentially a Greek kingdom, run by Greek people, living a Greek way of life. According to them, the contents of this museum are irrefutable

45

evidence supporting this claim. The Slavs, on the other hand, claim that Macedon was a Slavonic kingdom, run by Slavonic people, and so on.

In fact, the ancient Kingdom of Macedon occupied a wide area of the Balkans, covering northern Greece, southern Bulgaria, and what used to be southeastern Yugoslavia. Until recently, the Bulgarians claimed the Greek part of Macedonia as theirs, and occupied it briefly during the Second World War until they were forced to give it back. Meanwhile, the part of Macedonia across the border in what used to be Yugoslavia has now declared itself independent and calls itself Macedonia. But the province in Greece, which is also called Macedonia, is not independent, and does not wish to become part of an independent Slavonic Macedonia...

The combustible possibilities are all too evident. This is indeed the Balkan politics of old – the complex and violent process which gave us the First World War.

St Demetrios Church (Aghios Demetrios)

North of the city centre on Aghiou Dimitriou, this is one of several interesting churches in Thessaloniki, (4thC St George's, and Aghia Sophia, in a garden with palm trees, are also well worth a visit). St Demetrios was originally built in the 7thC, but was devastated by the great 1917 fire. The surviving shell was then restored. You can see the remains of some Roman baths, and of the minaret which was added by the Turks when they converted the building into a mosque in the 15thC. It only reverted to being a Christian church in 1912. The present church is claimed as the largest in Greece, (along with two others which I mention in this guide). St Demetrios is the patron saint of Thessaloniki, and was martyred on the very spot where the church now stands. His relics were eventually returned here from Italy in 1980, where they had been for more than a thousand years.

• *Wayside shrine, Thessaloniki.*

• *Regional fare.*

Kastra

N of the city centre, this is the old Turkish quarter, the only part of the city which survived the great fire of 1917. Despite brutal modernization (Turkish buildings aren't worthy of preservation, in Greek eyes) the place still has a somewhat oriental feel to it. There are a number of ancient churches, several centuries-old mosques, and a fine 16thC Turkish bath house which is now used as a flower market.

Be sure to visit the **Byzantine ramparts**, which enclose the upper town and run down through the city in both directions, giving a clear indication of what used to be the old city limits.

Just east of Kastra, on Apostolou Pavlou, is the house where **Kemal Attaturk** (the founder of modern Turkey) was born in 1881. This is maintained as a museum, dedicated to its famous former inhabitant. However, owing to the way Greco-Turkish relations have developed during this century, the Greeks do not regard this as one of the great sights of Thessaloniki. Indeed, when the Turks wished to celebrate the centenary of Attaturk's birth here in 1981, a local Greek pilot had to be restrained from dive-bombing the place. (It is at present maintained by the Turkish government, and you'll need to bring along your passport if you want to get in.)

Swimming

Thessaloniki can get *very* hot in mid summer. Unfortunately, such is the local pollution that a dive into the sea is *not* recommended. If you must swim, head for the baths on Ayiou Dimitrou, which leads east out of the city centre. You'll find the swimming baths just 300 m before you get to the stadium.

For those who must have the sea, the nearest resorts where it's safe to swim are south across the gulf at Perea and Aghia Triada. You can get to these by boat – it's just 12 km. The road journey around the coast is 26 km. Yet even here the water is hardly pristine: it doesn't really start getting clear until you reach Nea Kallikratia, which is on the coast 30 km south of the city.

Festivals

Thessaloniki stages Europe's most boring trade fair in September, when hotels all over the city suddenly get booked solid. I have been here during this period, and had the pleasure of seeing the agreed price of my hotel room increase by 50 per cent.

Immediately after this, in late September, comes the Thessaloniki Film Festival, which can be one of the most interesting in Europe. As with some other film festivals, it is often the case that no-one knows it's happening. Be sure to ask.

At the end of October, Thessaloniki has its Dhimitria, when the city celebrates its patron saint, Aghios

---

RECOMMENDED RESTAURANTS

ALEXANDROPOLIS
Neraida, D-DD; *Platia Polytechnico*.

Tasty local specialities are served here, using imaginative ingredients. Check them before you order if you're not sure how bold you're feeling.

KAVALA
There are a number of good tavernas along the waterfront, many specializing in local and seafood dishes. None is particularly outstanding, and only one is so awful that the libel laws forbid me from mentioning it.

PANORAMA
Cyprus Corner, DDD; 16 *Komninon*; *tel.* 031 53 24 28.

A superb restaurant, with top-flight Greek cuisine. Live music (singer and accompaniment) can occasionally be a little intrusive if you're seated too close. An ideal spot for a romantic night out. (You can easily get a taxi from the centre of Thessaloniki and back, which is not prohibitive, as long as you make sure the meter is used.)

THESSALONIKI
Eating is only part of a night out in Thessaloniki. The evenings are long and easy-going. Try beginning with a pleasant stroll amongst the crowds wandering up and down the main thoroughfare of Dimitri Gounari. The best section is between the Arch of Galerius and the sea-front. Then you can enjoy a leisurely early evening ouzo and *meze* at one of the nearby

Demetrios. There is a good arts festival at the same time. But again, be sure to book ahead for a room. See also **Langadas**, page 42 and **Panorama**, page 43, for two pleasant excursions from Thessaloniki. For nightlife, see Recommended Restaurants.

XANTHI

Inland town 56 km E of Kavala. A pleasant small town just across the border into Thrace, where you really begin to feel that you're approaching the East. Turkey only surrendered Thrace to Greece in 1919, and the town itself still

has a considerable Turkish population. Relations between the Greeks and the Turks are still strained, but here at least they tolerate each other, or so it appears.

There is an old quarter, and a lively market. Just stroll through the streets, and you'll soon get the feeling of being on the edge of Asia. The old quarter has some pleasant cobbled streets and picturesque old houses.

---

cafés. There are plenty of places to choose from, but if you care to walk a few metres west, you can go to:

Aroopto, DD-DDD; 11 *Lori Margariti*.

This is one of the best ouzeri in town. Thessaloniki is famous for its traditional ouzeri, where ouzo is served with a range of little dishes called *meze*. These are appetizers in the manner of Spanish *tapas*, though with their own, distinct Hellenic flavour.

Above Aroopto there is a smart Italian restaurant, which is part of the same establishment.

Tottis, DD-DDD; 3 *Platia Aristotelous*; *tel. 031 27 59 60.*

Another highly recommended ouzeri, and one of the smartest in town, is just a few blocks west of Aroopto, above. Tottis has highly authentic and imaginative *meze*, and is a great favourite with my friend Nikos, who can be seen sitting pensively at a side table plotting yet another financial coup.

After this, you'll probably feel like something more substantial to eat. You'll find that restaurants in Thessaloniki are almost on a par with those of Athens. Here are a couple which I like:

Ta Nissia, DD-DDD; 13 *Proxenou Koromila*; *tel. 031 28 59 91.*

Just up the road from Aroopto (see above), this is also a good place for *meze*, but the main thing here is the superbly authentic regional cuisine, which covers a range of local and Macedonian dishes. It also has a friendly atmosphere, and is highly popular with the locals (always a good sign). It is only open in the evenings. If you want something of a similar standard for lunch, try:

Olympos Naoussa, DD-DDD; 5 *Leoforos Nikis, tel.* 031 27 57 15.

An excellent seafood restaurant, right on the sea-front, with a range of well-prepared local dishes and a fine local wine list. The waiters can be very knowledgeable and loquacious on this subject.

After this, you may feel like a night out on the town. Thessaloniki has a lively nightlife with establishments to suit all tastes – from the luxurious to the louche to the looney.

Mandragore, DD-DDD; 98 *Mitropoleos.*

A quiet, romantic spot, with a sophisticated, piano-bar atmosphere. They serve some fine wine, and an interesting range of *meze* – should you find that music alone is not the food of love.

The Milos, D-DDD; 25 *Andreadou Giorgiou; tel.* 031 51 69 45.

This place is huge, lively, and has just about everything. Bop, blues, jazz and straight disco are all played at different venues in the complex. A renovated flour mill, it is the in-place to go, and anyone who thinks that Greek rock is provincial and behind the times should pay a visit.

<u>Northern Mainland</u>

Between Thessaloniki and Corfu
Northern Greece and Epirus

300 km; map Michelin 980

Here is a region of Greece which remains largely untouched by the ravages of tourism. You are far from the crowded beach resorts, and can discover the isolation of the mountainous Greek hinterland.

If you start from Thessaloniki, drive west along the main E90 for Athens, turning off after 32 km for Veria. (This turn-off is in fact the continuation of the E90.) Just outside Veria you can visit the site of Vergina, once the capital of ancient Macedon and the burial place of Philip II, father of Alexander the Great. From here, you enter the mountains and travel on to Kozani, from where you can take a detour to the Aliakmona Barrage and its large artificial lake.

From this point on, the E90 climbs even higher into the mountains. Approximately 25 km to the west of Siatista you enter the Pindos range, where every kilometre of the road affords superb mountain views. Konitsa marks the beginning of gorge country. The region between here and Ioanina is known as the Zagoria. It has dozens of isolated unspoilt villages in splendid mountain valleys, and is ideal for hiking. The most spectacular hike takes you along the Vikos Gorge, which is even more awesome than the famous Samaria Gorge in southern Crete (see Local Explorations: 13), and attracts only a trickle of tourists each year.

A useful base for visiting this region is the city of Ioanina, where the tourist office will give you details of the many trails and facilities available along them. (It is essential to have this information before setting out, as you can often walk for several hours without coming to a village or even a source of water.) Ioanina is also worth a stop on its own account. It is the city of Ali Pasha, the so-called Lion of Ioanina, who once made the region virtually his own kingdom. From Ioanina you can also visit the Perama cave, the largest in Greece, and the ruins at Dodoni, the spectacular site of Greece's earliest oracle. If you travel west from Ioanina to Igoumenitsa, you can catch the ferry from here to end your journey at Corfu.

If you drive the direct route between Thessaloniki and Igoumenitsa and then make the short ferry trip to Corfu, it will take you a couple of days. If you want to stop and see a few places en route, and take some of the detours, you should allow at least five days.

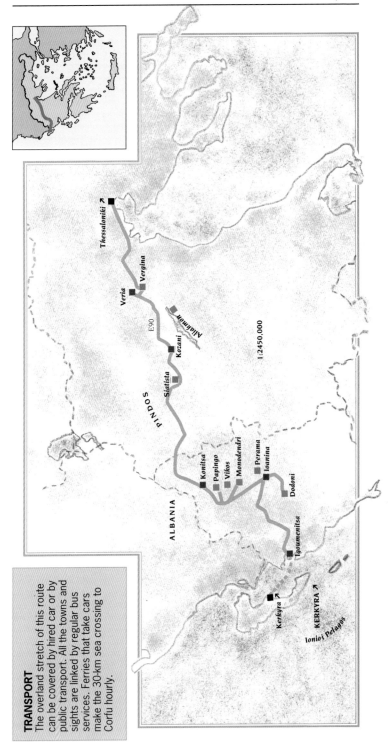

51

SIGHTS & PLACES OF INTEREST

CORFU

See Local Explorations: 5.

DODONI ✕

20 km S of Ioanina, west off E951 to Arta.
The road from Ioanina to this superb ancient site leads through the mountains. At one stage there is a great view of the city and lake lying far below at the foot of the mountains.

Dodoni is so far off the beaten track that it is almost tourist free, yet in its way the site is almost as important as Delphi. It was the location of the oldest oracle in Greece, and may well have been in operation 4,000 years ago. It is mentioned by Homer, and the early historian Herodotus perpetuates the myth of its origins. (Divine dove flies in from Egypt; perches on oak tree; oracle speaks through leaves.)

In ancient times people would come from far and wide with their problems. They would put their questions to the oracle: 'Theris asks Zeus if he should get married?' 'Am I her children's father?' 'About the woman N.' In reply the oracular oak tree would rustle its leaves. Many of the questions can be seen inscribed on ancient tablets in the Ioanina Archaeological Museum (see page 55).

The oak tree was tended by priests (or, according to some sources, priest-esses) who were required to sleep on the bare ground and never wash their feet. The priests would produce the oracle's answers by 'interpreting' the whispering of the leaves, whilst in a state of inspired frenzy, presumably induced by protracted insomnia. The site itself is in a picturesque setting, and has many fascinating things to see. Don't miss the **theatre**, which dates from the 3rdC BC and is one of the finest in the country. The ruined **Sanctuary of Zeus** now stands on the site of the ancient oracle, whose original oak was chopped down in 4thC AD by early Christian spoilsports.

Public transport to the site is infrequent and at highly inconvenient times, but you can get a taxi there and back for less than 3,000 D.

IGOUMENITSA ⛴ ✕

Northernmost port on W coast of mainland, opposite Corfu. This is the end of the line, and looks like it. Igoumenitsa is simply a busy ferry terminal port and has all the atmosphere of a transit camp. If you're arriving here by ferry from Italy, make sure you change your money at an exchange office on board or at a bank in town. If you're unlucky enough to find yourself stuck here for the day, catch a bus out to **Kalami**, which is 10 km south and has a beach.

The most interesting thing about Igoumenitsa is that most of its inhabitants are of Albanian origin. But even this won't be enough to keep you here.

DETOUR – **ALIAKMON BARRAGE**

To reach this sight, which is 30 km east of Kozani, take the road southwest from the town, then turn northeast along the lake shore. This road leads away to the left, but you have to turn right. Follow this road, and in 15 km you will reach the barrage, an impressive construction, which is over 300 m long and carries the road.

The lake here is an extraordinary archaeological site, with many important Macedonian relics lying beneath the waters. Just to the south of the barrage, you can see a tomb dating from the 3rdC BC, unearthed during the construction of the barrage.

IOANINA ⛴ ✕

Central Epirus, 101 km inland from northernmost part of W coast. Pronounced Yanina, the main town of the Epirus region stands on a promontory overlooking a lake – which is 10 km long, with an island in the middle.

Ioanina was founded recently compared with most other Greek cities. It probably dates from 540 AD, when the Roman Emperor Justinian established a camp here as part of his defensive network linking Albania to the Black Sea. The city almost certainly received its name from a 6thC Byzantine chapel dedicated to St John the Baptist, which was built by Justinian on the citadel promontory, though no remains of this chapel have been found. The octagonal defensive walls of the citadel fortress date from the 13thC, but were heavily restored by Ali Pasha.

Ali Pasha, the Lion of Ioanina, was born in Albania in 1744. After serving as a successful commander in the Turkish army, he was rewarded by the Sultan and appointed Pasha of Ioanina. From then on, Ali Pasha ran what was practically his own private kingdom. For the sake of form, he would pay the occasional tribute to the Sultan – sending him a few sacks filled with the heads of his enemies, and bribes to his ministers to put in a good word for him. Ali Pasha's rule was renowned for its spectacular cruelties. Enemies, slaves, tiresome courtiers, unwanted women, unfortunate visitors, all were regularly dispatched in various bloodcurdling ways – sewn into a sack with a wild cat and then thrown from the walls into the lake if they were lucky; having their limbs broken one by one with a sledgehammer in a protracted public ceremony, if they were less fortunate. He even sent a son-in-law to Constantinople bound in chains, and raped the wife of one of his sons (then had her drowned in the lake for infidelity).

Ali Pasha was obviously a difficult man to please, but when the occasion arose he could be as charming as any homicidal tyrant. He entertained a visiting British dignitary to a dinner which featured no less than 86 different dishes. (The dignitary survived this torture, and was most impressed.) But when Lord Byron visited Ali Pasha, he was less impressed. Later, Byron drew on this experience for a scene in his poem *Childe Harold's Pilgrimage*. Here the Pasha and his magnificent court are said to be implicitly disgraced by the darker 'deeds that lurk beneath' all the pomp and display.

When Ali Pasha omitted to send his tribute to the Sultan in Constantinople, the Sultan dispatched his army under the Grand Vizier to teach Ali Pasha some manners. The army laid siege to Ioanina from 1820 until 1822, and then

---

RECOMMENDED HOTELS

IGOUMENITSA
Astoria, DD; *tel.* (0665) 22 704.

A small hotel, which is fairly upmarket in atmosphere, furnishings and facilities, and handy for the ferry terminal.

Hotel Jolly, D-DD; *tel.* (0665) 23 970.

Small, but larger than the Astoria, and also handy for the ferry.

IOANINA
Hotel Bretannia, DD-DDD; *Platia Demokratia; tel.* (0651) [missing tel. no.]

A posh old pile, right in the centre of town. The best hotel in Ioanina, but not in the quietest district.

Hotel Tourist, D; 18 *Koletti; tel.* (0651) 26 443.

A friendly hotel with clean modern rooms, right in the heart of town, signposted off the main Averoff Street and close to the sights.

Vyzantion, D; *Leoforos Dodonis; tel.* (0651) 23 898.

A large hotel, which often has rooms when others are heavily booked. Conveniently situated on the main southbound road out of town (signposted for Arta), which, as the name indicates, leads to the Dodoni site.

KONITSA
Hotel Egnatia, D; *Platia; tel.* 22 083.

An agreeably decrepit old-style hotel on the main square.

PAPINGO VILLAGES
Nikos Saxonis, D; *Megalo Papingo; tel.* (0653) 41 615.

You're guaranteed a friendly welcome at this beautiful small hotel. Just the place to rest your feet – and all the other appalling aches – after hiking through the gorge.

VERIA
Aristidhis, D; *Platia Kendriki; tel.* (0331) 26 355.

More than 50 rooms, in a good location. Not exactly luxurious, but worth trying for a one-night stopover.

Veria, D-DD; *edge of town; tel.* (0331) 21 424.

A modern hotel with a range of amenities, including a pool and tennis courts. Something of a find in such a spot.

sacked the city. Ali Pasha was beheaded, and his head carried in triumph throughout his former 'kingdom'. At its height this kingdom had stretched from mid-Albania almost as far south as the mouth of the Gulf of Corinth, a territory larger than modern-day Albania. (It was in fact mistakenly called Albania by the European powers, who each in turn sought Ali's support in the regional balance of power.) During this period, Ali Pasha's capital Ioanina was the largest and most important city in Greece.

Nowadays the city is a modern, rather nondescript provincial capital, though it does retain certain intriguing aspects of its past. The citadel remains, as do several mosques, their derelict minarets now used for nesting by migrating storks. Many visitors simply pass through Ioanina, or only stop here to change buses, but this is a mistake. There are a number of sights, the like of which you won't see anywhere else in Greece.

The **fortress citadel**, overlooking the lake, was the ancient acropolis. It is protected by a ring of walls and once contained Ali Pasha's palace. It still has an early 17thC mosque (Aslan Aga), complete with minaret, which has been converted into a museum for popular art. There is also an old synagogue (during the last century almost one fifth of the population of Ioanina was Jewish), and in the narrow little streets that surround it there are some wonderful old houses.

• *Perama Cave.*

From the terrace by the mosque there is a fine view across the lake to the mountains, whose peaks remain snow-capped for much of the year. This citadel area with its little streets, houses and mosques retains a distinctly oriental atmosphere.

The lake, variously known as Lake Ioanina or Lake Pamvotis, provides a picturesque setting for the city. It is 10 km long and 4 km wide, and there are some pleasant walks along its shores, especially beneath the citadel ramparts. In places, the water is almost 12 m deep, but only those of iron nerve should contemplate a swim. The lake bed in the shallows is composed of squelchy mud, infested with eels (and, so I'm assured, vicious water snakes). In the middle of the lake there is an island, **Nisi Ioaninon**, which can be reached by a ferry that leaves from Dhionission, just beyond Platia Mavili, below the citadel ramparts. Wooded and bordered by reeds, the island has a number of monasteries and a village with several tavernas. The present inhabitants are said to be descended from 16thC refugees, who originally came from the remote Mani in the southern Peleponnese.

The most interesting of the monasteries on the island is the 16thC **Monastery of Pantelimon** (left of the street leading from the landing stage), where Ali Pasha finally met his end.

54

When the Sultan's army overran Ioanina, Ali Pasha managed to escape and hide upstairs in the monastery, where it appears he settled in for some time – you can still see his hubble-bubble pipe here. When the Sultan's men eventually caught up with him and summoned him down, Ali Pasha refused to listen to them, and presumably went on sitting up there, smoking his hubble-bubble. Obviously irritated, the Sultan's men fired some bullets up through the wooden ceiling. (The holes can still be seen in the monastery floor.) The tactic was doubtless intended to make Ali Pasha sit up and listen. But poor Ali Pasha appears to have received a number of bullets where he least expected them, and was mortally wounded. He was then ceremoniously beheaded.

Ali Pasha's headless body is now buried in the old Muslim graveyard on the citadel in Ioanina, beside the complete body of his favourite wife, the delightfully named Umm Gulshun. His head is said to have ended up stuck on a spike outside the walls of Constantinople.

Those with an interest in intriguing names will also want to visit the **Monastery of Aghios Nikolaos Spanos**, which stands on the rocks north of the village. It was founded in 13thC, is dedicated to St Nicholas the Hairless, and contains some interesting depictions of early Greek philosophers.

The **Archaeological Museum** is in the centre of the modern town, southwest of the Cathedral, just off Averoff. The museum contains a wide range of local finds, which fill in the historical background of this fascinating but largely neglected region. It also houses many of the best finds from Dodoni (see page 52), including a number of lead tablets inscribed with questions for the oracle. As is often the case, not so many of the great oracular replies have come down to us in such solid, verifiable form.

Less than five minutes' walk north of here is the **Old Bazaar** quarter, whose little lanes and tiny picturesque shops are well worth a visit.

KONITSA ⌑

65 km N of Ioanina on E90. This town is in the high mountain territory of the Pindos range, whose peaks rise to over 2,600 m near here. Albania is just 10 km away as the crow flies through the mountains to the north-west.

The town itself has a fine old bridge which dates from 1870, and some splendid views out over the mountain plain. The bridge has a bell beneath its arch, which would ring in high winds, warning travellers and their laden donkeys that if they tried to cross they were liable to be blown overboard.

In the winter of 1947-8 during the Greek Civil War, the Greek Army withstood a bitter three-week attack from the Communist Democratic Army, who wished to take the town and establish it as their mountain capital.

Just south of town there is a spectacular gorge where the Aoos River flows down from the high mountains. The road south leads to the Monastery of Stomiou. All around here there are fine walks over the mountains, with excellent views of the gorge, and occasional glimpses of rare wild life. (Some of the last lynxes in Europe are said to roam this region.)

KOZANI

137 km W of Thessaloniki on E90. The administrative capital of a small department, and a decidedly boring little place. Drive straight through, or arrive, change buses, and leave as soon as possible.

MONODENDRI

See Detour – Vikos Gorge, page 56.

PAPINGO VILLAGES ⌑ ✕

See Detour – Vikos Gorge, page 56.

PERAMA CAVE

6 km N of Ioanina. In a hill on the other side of the lake from Ioanina are the largest known caves in Greece. They were only discovered 50 years ago, when a ragged partisan, fleeing through the mountains from the occupying German army, was frantically searching for a place to hide.

Here you can see astonishing stalagmites and stalactites, together with limestone excrescences in many colours of the rainbow. You can even rap the stalagmites, which ring like distant church bells; then you can shout, and listen to your voice dissipating through the inner caverns. Unfortunately you can't see, or couldn't when I last visited, the fascinating collection of bears' teeth which are said to have been found here.

SIATISTA

5 km N of E90, just over 30 km W of Kozani. The mountains on either side of the road at Siatista rise to over 2,000 m. The town itself used to be a fur trading centre, and has seen better times. It was once on the main caravan route for Vienna, and the area was renowned for its fine wines, which were said to be as good as any in Austria. Unfortunately the phylloxera of the 1920s destroyed the vines, so this outrageous claim cannot be disproved.

Many of the fine old houses in town are decaying, giving the place a rather intriguing, dilapidated air. It is one of those places which either catches your imagination, or leaves you completely cold (and in winter it can be *very* cold here).

THESSALONIKI

See Greece Overall: 1.

VERGINA ✕

7 km S of Veria. Recent excavations here have uncovered the Royal Tombs of Macedon, and archaeologists have now conclusively proved that this was the site of ancient Aigai, the early capital of Macedon. It became the burial place of their kings, and modern discoveries have included the tomb of Philip II of Macedon, the father of Alexander the Great.

According to an ancient prophecy, if any king of Macedon was buried elsewhere, this would portend the end of the royal line. And when Alexander the Great died in Asia, and was buried in Alexandria, this is precisely what happened.

Just beyond Vergina you come to the ruins of **Palatitsa**, the small summer palace where King Antigonus Gonatus of Macedon came to get away from the summer heat, noise, traffic and endless string of foreign tourists in Aigai. The palace dates from the 3rdC BC, and was laid waste by the Turks several centuries later. Amongst the ruins you can see a mosaic, the central courtyard and several porticoes. From this site you can look out over the plains towards a number of pre-historic burial chambers which may be as much as 3,000 years old.

VERIA ⇄ ✕

73 km W of Thessaloniki on E90. A fruit marketing town whose modern appearance disguises a few hidden gems. During the centuries when Greece was ruled by the Turks, the local Christians

---

DETOUR - **VIKOS GORGE**

East of the E90, 30 km north of Ioanina, Vikos is the finest gorge in Greece, even more spectacular in places than the better-known Samaria Gorge in southern Crete. But unlike the Samaria Gorge, it isn't overrun with tourists.

You'll have to allow at least a day if you want to walk the gorge, then spend the night in one of the villages, and drive or catch the bus back the next day.

The best place to start is from the village of Monodendri, which is at the south end of the gorge. It is a perfect out-of-the-way spot, well worth a visit, even if you're not planning to rise at crack of dawn and set out on a gruelling eight-hour hike through the gorge. Walking the entire length of the gorge and on to one of the two Papingo villages, Megalo Papingo and Mikro Papingo (Big and Little

Papingo), where, exhausted, but exhilarated, you can have a meal and find a room for the night, will take you all of eight hours; though it only takes five hours if you stop at Vikos. It is a long hike, but there are some breathtaking views, with the walls of the canyon in some places rising many hundreds of metres above you.

Be warned: the buses from the Papingo villages only leave *most* days of the week. Before setting off on this jaunt, be sure to find out *all* the details of the gorge, places to stay, times of buses, and then decide what you will need to take with you: plenty of water, an emergency sleeping bag perhaps, food (dates and prunes are good), and so forth. The best place for information on the gorge is in Ioanina at the Greek National Tourist Office in Botsari Square in the town centre, or at the Hellenic Mountaineering Club, tel. (0651) 22 138.

were forbidden to build churches. The Greeks got around this edict by hiding their churches and disguising them as ordinary dwellings.

There are several in town, many concealed in delightful Byzantine courtyards and down little alleyways. You'll find **Aghios Christos** near the central crossroads. It contains some fine 600-year-old frescos. Ask also for Aghios Nikolaos and Aghia Fontini. You can walk along the ancient town ramparts, which give a fine view over the plain where much of the fruit is grown.

RECOMMENDED RESTAURANTS

DODONI
There is a café-restaurant just outside the gates of the site – an erratic but friendly hostelry whose staff are renowned for their long siestas.

IGOUMENITSA
There are a number of distinctly ordinary tavernas and restaurants in town, none of which is worth any special recommendation.

IOANINA
Ioanina is renowned for its regional cuisine, different from any other in Greece. Many of its best ingredients come from the lake. If you've never tried eel before, this is your chance (ask for *leli*). The lake also produces trout (*pestrofa*), and a form of fresh water crayfish, *karavidhes*.

However, the best local speciality has nothing to do with the lake. It is called *gastra* and is a form of stew, cooked in a similar manner to tandoori (though it tastes nothing like Indian food). A dish containing lamb stew is sealed, buried in the very heart of a glowing fire, and left to cook for hours. This results in extremely tender meat, which is full of flavour (none of the juices evaporates) and tastes superb.

The region is also renowned for its cheeses. *Tiri* is the general name for cheese (other than the ubiquitous *faeta*, which is usually imported from Denmark nowadays).

Owing to the long Turkish occupation, Ioanina also has excellent cakes and puddings. My favourite here is their version of custard tart (*bougatsa*), where the custard is flavoured with cinnamon.

There are a number of good restaurants in Ioanina. The restaurants on the island are the most interesting to visit – ferries run back to the mainland until quite late at night. There are also some worthwhile restaurants beneath the old city on Platia Mavili, which have fine views over the lake.

For a great meal on the island, try:

Pamvotis, DD; Nisi *Pamvotis.*
Here you can go to the tank and choose your dinner whilst it is still swimming. Do try the eels – though they're not cheap.

For sunset watchers, there's the café-restaurant **Litharitsia**, on the promontory overlooking the lake beside central Platia Akadhemias. On the opposite side of the main street is the best café in town, **Diethnes**, which is renowned for its fabulous chocolate-coated prunes, a delicacy for which true *aficionados* are willing to travel many miles.

PAPINGO VILLAGES
Both Megalo Papingo and Mikro Papingo have places where you can eat, after your gallant route march through the gorge. The best is:

Christodoulou's, D; Megalo *Papingo.*
This restaurant is in the square, and an ideal spot for meeting other intrepid souls, from whom you can learn the best international cures for blisters.

VERGINA
There is an unexciting bar-restaurant at the site. So, if you're planning to spend the day here, pick up a picnic in Veria, and just use the bar-restaurant for cold drinks.

VERIA
Phillipion, D-DD; Old Town.
One of several friendly restaurants in the old town. A good range of local and pan-Hellenic dishes. Go into the kitchen and point, as few of the waiters speak English.

Central Mainland

Between Larissa and Corfu
The Heart of Thessaly

200 km; map Michelin 980, 1:700000

This trail takes in the plains of Thessaly and the high Pindos Mountains, home of the mysterious Vlach nomads. Some of the sights are well off the beaten track, though this can't be said of the principal attraction: the Monasteries of Meteora. These are among the most spectacularly situated buildings you'll see anywhere in the world, perched high in the sky atop columns of rock, which rise sheer for hundreds of metres from the valley floor. They were once virtually inaccessible except by primitive ladders and even more primitive pulley systems, involving threadbare ropes and baskets. Nowadays there are steps carved into the rock face, and bridges span the chasms.

You might start your journey at the commercial town of Larissa, on the busy E75 highway, which connects Thessaloniki and Athens. From here you can take a number of side trips. The best of these is to the spectacular Vale of Tembi, once the narrow gateway through the mountains into Greece.

After this head west from Larissa on the E92 which leads across the plains of Thessaly to Trikala. From here you can take a detour to the village of Pili, with its nearby gorge and monasteries.

From Trikala you continue north on the E92 to Kalambaka. Just outside this town are the Monasteries of Meteora, and if you stop for nothing else on this route, be sure to allow a day to visit them. They are an unforgettable experience.

From Kalambaka you continue west along the E92, which now climbs high into the Pindos Mountains and eventually leads across the Katara Pass, the highest permanently open pass in Greece. Just beyond here is Metsovo, a historic Vlach village. The surrounding peaks rise to well over 2,000 m, and are snow-capped for much of the year. Not surprisingly there is a ski resort nearby, which flourishes during the winter season.

From here you take the E92 down to the historic city of Ioanina, and then continue down to Igoumenitsa, where you can catch the ferry for Corfu.

To do justice to this route, and stopping off to see a few of the sights, you should allow at least three days.

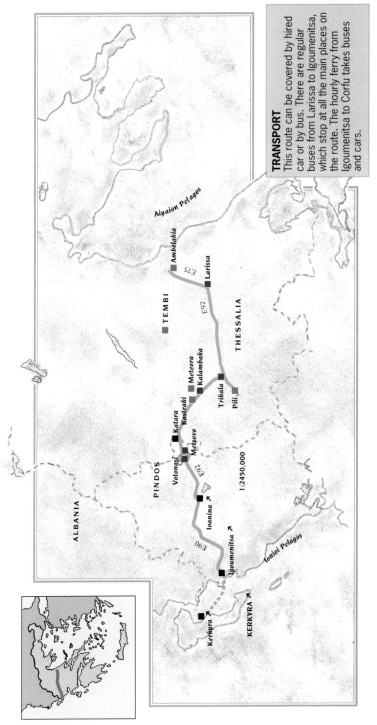

SIGHTS & PLACES OF INTEREST

CORFU
See Local Explorations: 5.

IGOUMENITSA
See Greece Overall: 2.

IOANINA
See Greece Overall: 2.

KALAMBAKA ⇌ ✕
85 km W of Larissa on E92. In the old days this was quite a picturesque spot. Then the Nazis moved in and the whole town was flattened, apart from the **cathedral**. This dates from the 14thC, and its walls contain bits and pieces from earlier ruins; its fine old bell tower is permanently occupied by a large stork's nest.

The only good reason to come to Kalambaka is because it makes a good base for visiting the Monasteries of Meteora (see page 62), which are just to the north of town.

KASTRAKI ⇌ ✕
See Meteora, page 62.

LARISSA ⇌ ✕
151 km S of Thessaloniki on E75. There is nothing wrong with Larissa: it is just a

---

DETOUR – AMBELAKIA

About 27 km north of Larissa: turn east off the E75, the main Athens-Thessaloniki highway. Ambelakia is a small town, nestling amongst oak trees on the slopes of Mount Ossa, with views down over the valley of the River Peneios towards the peaks of Mount Olympos.

During the 18thC the town became the world's first industrial co-operative. The townspeople ran factories producing and dyeing cotton, silk and other textiles. At its height there were more than 700 members of the co-operative, which had agents and offices operating as far afield as London, Lyons and Vienna. Although the town was theoretically under Turkish rule, it operated as a virtually autonomous unit, with its own democratically elected assembly, free medical services and education, and weekly performances of the ancient Greek tragedies and comedies.

This was embryo socialism at its most optimistic and efficient stage, and it would be interesting to know what might have become of it, if it had been allowed to continue. Unfortunately it was way ahead of its time, and more regressive forces were soon to intervene. In 1811 the army of Ali Pasha, the Lion of Ioanina (see Greece Overall: 2), took over the town, and a heavy tax was then imposed on all the town's produce. At the same time, European trade was being disrupted by the Napoleonic Wars. The final blow came when the bank in Vienna where the co-operative kept its cash went bust.

There used to be more than 500 mansions in Ambelakia; now only a few dozen remain. One has been restored, and from it you get a good idea of the town's prosperity during its co-operative period. The house of George Schwartz, the last elected president of the town co-operative, has some beautiful carved partitions, painted landscapes, and many other curiously Greco-Turkish features. You can also see the president's office on the ground floor.

Incidentally, George Schwartz was not German, as his name might suggest. His real surname was Mavros (which means black in Greek). Schwartz was the Viennese bank's translation of his name, which they used for financial dealings with him while he was president.

A modern echo of the town's socialist past is to be found in the Women's Tourist Co-operative, which is similar to the one at Petra in Lesbos (see Greece Overall: 11). Women's co-operatives, of which there are now more than half a dozen in Greece, rent out rooms and run restaurants, craft workshops and information centres. If you arrange to stay with them you can take part in local farming activities and get to know how the real Greece functions. (For further details of the Women's Rural Co-operatives and their locations, contact the Greek National Tourist Office.)

RECOMMENDED HOTELS

KALAMBAKA

Aeolikos Astir (Aeolian Star), D-DD; *Central Square.*

An adequate, central hotel with rooms at a fairly moderate price in a town where everything is somewhat over-priced.

Hotel Meteora, DD; 14 *Ploutarchou* St; *tel.* (0432) 22 367.

Just west of town, with superb views of the cliffs and distant valley, is the one exceptional hotel in Kalambaka. It is worth trying to get a room, particularly if you 'phone well ahead, though it is nearly always booked solid.

Motel Divani, DDD; *on* E92 *to Trikala;* *tel.* (0432) 23 330.

The most expensive hotel in town, with most of the amenities you'd expect. They believe in making their money during the season, and close down during the winter. This said, it is a reasonable hotel – and does have a swimming-pool.

KASTRAKI

Kastraki Hotel, D-DD; *Kastraki; tel.* (0342) 22 286.

Of the several good places to stay in Kastraki, this is my favourite – a pleasantly eccentric spot in a great setting.

One of the three camping sites here, **Camping Vrachos** (the first you come to), is exceptional, with a small swimming-pool and spotless facilities (very inexpensive).

LARISSA

Metropole, DD-DDD; *in town centre; tel.* (041) 22 99 11.

A hotel in town with the bonus of a private swimming-pool.

Motel Xenia, DD; *on* E75 *Athens to Thessaloniki highway; tel.* (041) 23 81 83.

A couple of kilometres outside town, and handy if you're simply passing through this rather dull part of the country. It has its own restaurant.

Pantheon, D; S *of town centre; tel.* (041) 23 67 26.

Spartan accommodation by the railway station at budget prices.

METSOVO

Hotel Egnatia, DD; *on main* E92; *tel.* (0656) 41 263.

By far the best place to stay in Metsovo, this hotel is in the centre of the village, with rows of geraniums in pots along the balconies. Step through the door and you enter old Metsovo. The furnishings and fittings are delightfully authentic, with old stone flags, chintzy woodwork and ethnic drapes. It is always booked solid during the ski season.

Victoria, DD-DDD; *just* E *of town, off main road; tel.* (0656) 41 898.

An alternative to the Egnatia and with the attraction of a superb view and exceptionally helpful and friendly staff.

PILI

Babanara, D; *town centre; tel.* (0431) 22 325.

The hotel to stay in here (because there isn't another). It has pleasant staff, and is a useful base for exploring this largely undiscovered region.

TRIKALA

Achillion, DD-DDD; *near town centre; tel.* (0431) 28 291.

Boring but reliable, with no surprises. Just the place for some reassuring comfort.

Palladion, D; 4 *Odos Vironos; tel.* (0431) 28 091.

Handy for the city centre, but popular with Greek travelling salesmen.

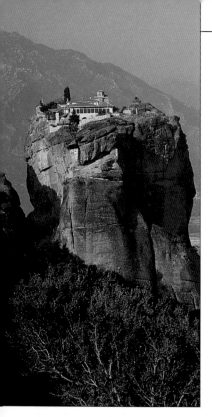

• *Aghios Stefanos, Meteora.*

METEORA

6 km N of Kalambaka, off E92. The monasteries of Meteora are equal to any you're likely to see from Tibet to Timbuktoo.

The best place to start a walking tour of the monasteries is the village of **Kastraki**, just below the rocks. (Kastraki is 20 minutes' walk or a short bus ride from Kalambaka.) Otherwise you can drive to the monasteries, or join an excursion which will take you around the best of them.

Important note: the monastic dress code is strictly enforced here. This means that men must wear long trousers, and women must wear skirts that cover their knees; both men and women must have their arms covered, preferably to the wrist. If you are not dressed correctly, you will not be allowed in.

The monasteries are in a large valley where erosion has left 60 or so tall, isolated columns of sandstone which rise a sheer 300 m from the valley floor. Around 900 years ago one of these columns took the fancy of a passing hermit. Here at last was a place where he could achieve true isolation from the world and its wicked ways.

Word quickly spread on the hermit grapevine, and soon more than a dozen of the columns each had its own hermit-in-residence high in the sky. (The name Meteora comes from a corruption of the Greek for 'middle of the air'.) In the 14thC, brigands from Serbia began to terrorize the region. Not surprisingly (and presumably not for the first time) the hermits found themselves somewhat exposed. Those who hadn't planned on martyrdom were thus forced to abandon their happy state of hermitude. For reasons of safety the ex-hermits reluctantly put up with each other, and teamed up to form monasteries.

The first of the monasteries (Megala Meteora) was founded in 1336 by St Athanasius, who had originally come from Mount Athos. According to legend, he reached the top of the high rock on which the monastery now stands by riding there on an eagle's back. The legend doesn't explain either how he got down again (even ascetics surely have to eat sometimes), or how he managed to get the materials up

rather ordinary city, in the middle of the rich farming region of Thessaly, on the main highway. There are good bus and rail connections, so you might well find yourself spending some time here.

In classical times Larissa was the leader of the Thessalian alliance of cities which at one stage ganged up against Athens (unsuccessfully, owing to internal quarrels). Later Larissa fell under the influence of the Macedonians, then the Romans, then the Byzantines, and finally the Turks, who ruled the city in their usual desultory fashion for almost 500 years (1389-1881). You can still see remnants of their rule in the Turkish houses along main Venizelou Street. The **Archaeological Museum** in the square at the end of this street is a former mosque, and contains a large collection of fascinating ancient relics.

If you're feeling energetic, there are a couple of interesting side trips you can make from Larissa, to Ambelakia (see page 60) and the Vale of Tembi (see page 65).

there in order to build his monastery. On the other hand, none of the more down-to-earth explanations is flawless. Or much more plausible. Yet there the monastery stands, in all its glory – a miraculous and permanent monument to human perversity.

St Athanasius was to be succeeded as abbot of Megala Meteora by St Ioasaph, who had turned down the throne of Serbia in favour of life 300 m up on this bare rock. (And when you consider the history of Serbia, who can blame him?) When you visit this monastery you can see a fresco depicting St Athanasius and St Ioasaph, and you will find St Ioasaph's tomb in the narthex, the vestibule at the west end of the church, behind a screen, which is where the women traditionally worshipped in early Christian churches.

By the 16thC there were no fewer than 24 monasteries on the high rocks of Meteora. Access could only be gained by climbing the sheer rock face, the last stretches sometimes being covered by rickety 40-m ladders, and sometimes by a pulley and a basket on the end of a rope. The ropes on these pulleys became something of an article of faith, as they were never replaced until they snapped.

Life at the top was of necessity fairly ascetic. Every morsel had to be hauled up from ground level, and, with the inevitable scarcity of water, one doubts whether much of it was used for washing. High on their pinnacles in the sky, the monks remained far from the sins of the world. Yet even here it seems, misdemeanours were not unheard of, and a form of punishment was found necessary. Some of the monasteries constructed rickety plank punishment platforms: the miscreant monk was forced to sit out on the very edge and contemplate his sins – making sure at the same time that he didn't fall off, or tremble too much and cause the entire platform to collapse. (Some did, and you'll understand why when you see the ones that remain.)

During the 19thC, Meteora became a less attractive prospect to young men starting out in life. A decline set in, and this has continued to the point where there are now only six monasteries in operation. These are, in approximate order of attractiveness and popularity: **Megala Meteora**, with its fine narthex, and **Varlaam**, which was founded in 1518 on the site formerly occupied by the virtuous hermit Barlaam, after whom it is named. It also has a fine narthex, with 16thC frescos. Nearby **Aghios Nikolaos** has a marvellous 'restored' fresco by the great 16thC Cretan icon artist Theophanes. Across the valley, **Roussanou** is reached by a death-defying footbridge, as is **Aghios Stefanos**, which has a working population of 20 nuns, and a museum with some excellent illuminated manuscripts. **Aghia Triada** is up a flight of hundreds of steps, but has a wonderful little garden at the top.

The entire circuit of these monasteries is about 20 km, and takes almost six hours by foot. The excursion buses of course complete the tour in far less time, in a comfort which, in the eyes of the monks, would have rendered one fit only for the punishment platforms.

If you intend to walk, be sure to enquire about the opening times of the monasteries before you set out. Each monastery has its own entirely different system of opening hours, which are likely to defeat all but the most expert scholars of theological observance, viz. 'closed on the vigil of the martyrdom of St Charalambos' (whose head, incidentally, is kept as a venerated relic by the nuns of Aghios Nikolaos).

METSOVO ⚓ ✕

56 km E of Ioanina off E92. This delightful village stands high in the Pindos Mountains just west of the Katara Pass, which is almost 1,700 m above sea level. The village has 200-year-old stone houses with slate roofs and wooden balconies, and is Greece's answer to the Alps, in more senses than one. In season it can all be rather predictably twee, with lines of traditionally-clad tourists looking at the lines of traditionally tatty souvenirs. Even so, it's well worth a stopover. The sheer setting dwarfs any superficial touristic tawdriness. Dividing the village there is a ravine, and high above the rooftops the nearby peaks rise to over 2,000 m.

Metsovo has an odd history. In the 17thC a Turkish vizier who had fallen foul of the sultan's wrath sought refuge in the village, where a shepherd hid him and looked after him. When the vizier returned to power, he repaid the shepherd's kindness by granting Metsovo a special status: it became virtually autonomous within the Turkish Empire, occupying a position similar to that of Andorra in the Pyrenees. Several well-off Christian families from Turkish-occupied Greece came to live in Metsovo, and the village prospered, its quasi-independent status enabling trade to flourish.

DETOUR - PILI 🖼️

If you like exploring off the beaten track, this is the place for you. Pili lies 20 km south-west of Trikala on the banks of the small Portaikos River, below a picturesque gorge, and there are several sights worth seeing near here. Follow the river upstream and you come to the church of Porta Panayia (Sanctuary of the Virgin of the Gateway), parts of which are more than 700 years old. Its two buildings are in distinct eastern and western styles. It has been suggested that this was an eastern outpost of the Cistercian order, which is quite possible, as the Franks ruled this part of Thessaly during the 13thC. No one lives here, but you can get the key from the small house on the nearby hill.

Inside the church there are some lovely frescos and mosaics, and outside the setting is enchanting. Further upstream there is a fine old stone bridge, which crosses the valley in a single span. It is said to have been built single-handed in the early 16thC by a monk called the Blessed Bessarion.

A few kilometres' walk in the other direction from Pili leads you to the Monastery of Dousiko, which stands on a leafy slope, and was founded by the Blessed Bessarion in 1515, three years before his great solo bridge-building feat. It is a large monastery, which was apparently intended to contain 365 cells, one for each day of the year. Perhaps they hoped to choose the monks so that it was always somebody's birthday. Unfortunately they only got to 336 cells, so the monks had to endure a whole month without birthday cake. Unfortunately, even after the long walk in the heat of the day, women are not allowed into the monastery.

The majority of Mestsovo's inhabitants are Vlachs, the nomadic shepherds of the Pindos Mountains, who used to trade wool and leather with the caravanners who passed through Metsovo, bound for the markets of Vienna and Constantinople. Trading came to an abrupt end when Ali Pasha took over the region (see Ioanina, Greece Overall: 2).

Today Metsovo is once again a privileged village, due to a philanthropic banker in Switzerland whose family originated here. When the banker died, he left his fortune to the village, and the money has been used to finance a saw mill, a factory, dairy farming and various cottage industries. It has also been used to restore the old home of the banker's family, and you can now visit the **Tossitas mansion**, which is furnished in typical 18thC local style. Here you can buy some of the excellent locally woven rugs, which aren't cheap, but are as good as any you'll find in Greece.

There is also a surprisingly good small **art museum**, founded by another locally born plutocrat and philanthropist, Averoff. It features works by artists from all over Greece.

If you want an idea of what Metsovo was like in the days before the influx of tourists, cross the ravine to its twin village, known to the locals as **Anilio**, meaning 'out of the sun' (the main village is known as Prosilio: 'facing the sun'). Anilio is much more of a genuine Vlach community, though both halves of the village still retain the Vlach language and many of their customs.

The **Vlachs** are one of the mystery tribes of Europe. They are a nomadic people who live as shepherds in the high Pindos Mountains and, across the border, in Albania. Nowadays, to a certain extent, they have abandoned the more rigorous elements of their nomadic way of life, and maintain a relatively settled existence, and homes, in high villages such as Metsovo.

The Vlachs have their own language, which is recognizable as a Romance language with affinities to both Italian and Romanian. Its Latin-based vocabulary meant that the Vlachs readily understood the Italians when they invaded the region during the Second World War.

Numerous theories have been put

forward about the origins of these people. Some say they are Slavs, who drifted south with their grazing sheep at the break-up of the Roman Empire (hence their Latin tongue). Others say they are descended from groups of Roman legionnaires who settled here, and another theory is that they've always been here (and thus are true Greeks) and only learned their language from the Romans who travelled along the trading routes which passed through their territory.

TRIKALA 🛏

63 km W of Larissa, on E92. Trikala is another town, which, though pleasant, has little out of the ordinary to recommend it to the passing visitor. It has a population of more than 40,000, is the third largest town in Thessaly (after Larissa and Volos), and is the seat of an archbishop.

Trikala, along with nearly half a dozen other places, is said to be the birthplace of Asclepios, who was the son of Apollo and said to possess great healing powers. To back up its claim, the town contains the (very fragmentary) ruins of the earliest known Asclepion (Sanctuary of Asclepios). This served as a form of early hospital-cum-faith healing centre (with the emphasis on 'faith', when you consider the methods used). In ancient times the plains around here were famous for their horses, which are featured on the Parthenon's frieze.

The River Letheios runs through the town, and there are some pleasant cafés and restaurants along the river shore. If you find yourself here for the day, take a trip out to Pili (see above).

VALE OF TEMBI

20km N of Larissa on main E75. This unexpectedly beautiful valley follows the course of the River Pinios, and was once the gateway to Ancient Greece. It has two ruined castles and is good for hiking. Unfortunately its atmosphere is somewhat reduced by the main road and railway which run through it.

VOTONOSI

10 km W of Mesovo, on descent towards Ioanina. There is some mountain scenery near here, but the village itself is of interest only in terms of history. It was here that Greece's first collaborationist prime minister, Tsolakoglou, signed the Greek armistice with the Germans in 1941. Perhaps it is appropriate that in summer this village is dotted with blazing Judas trees.

RECOMMENDED RESTAURANTS

KALAMBAKA
Restaurant International, D-DD; *Platia Riga Fereou.*

As its name suggests, this restaurant caters largely for the tourist trade, but it is the pick of a rather ordinary bunch and has a fair selection of local dishes. As you'd expect in this region, the lamb ones are the best.

KASTRAKI
Boufidis, D-DD; *outside village on the road to the monasteries.*

A recommended local taverna, which serves much more authentic cuisine than you have a right to expect in such a tourist-dominated spot.

LARISSA
The best restaurants and cafés in Larissa are by the central square, Platia Stratou, on the banks of the Pinios River. If you don't fancy any of these, there are some OK places in the nearby Alcazar Park, which is also by the river.

METSOVO
For once, almost all the restaurants here are good of their type. The local cuisine isn't fancy, but it is appetizing. The best dishes feature lamb or, for the more adventurous, goat (the Greek word for this hardy mountain beast is *katsika*).

Kryphopholia, D-DD; *main square.*
A mouthful of a name, whose menu and portions live up to its promise, and are excellent value.

Metsovitiko Saloni, DD-DDD; *main road.*
The best restaurant in town and as elegant as you'll get in such a spot.

Between Corfu and Zakinthos
The Ionian Islands

280 km; map Michelin 980, 1:700000

This route takes you to all the Ionian islands, with the exception of Kythira, which only became an Ionian island by virtue of politics politics (see Greece Overall: 9) and Corfu (see Local Explorations: 5.)

The Ionian islands are quite different from most of the other Greek islands. For a start, they tend to be larger and greener. Instead of the parched barren rocks of the Aegean islands, here you come across mountains covered with pine trees, olive groves pierced by slender cypress trees, and vineyards which produce some of the finest wines in Greece. There are also many superb beaches. Some, such as those of Corfu and Zakinthos, have developed into major resorts. Others, less accessible and on less visited islands, are as unspoilt as you'll find anywhere in Greece.

You might choose to start this route at the holiday island of Corfu, where there is a huge variety of sights to see before you even start on your main island-hopping route. From Corfu, you voyage south to the little island of Paxos, from where you can cross to the mainland resort of Parga for a visit to Nekromandio, the site of the ancient Oracle of the Dead.

The next island south after Paxos is Levkas. Here you can visit the famous white cliffs, from which the poet Sappho is said to have leapt to her death, see the tiny island which was once owned by Aristotle Onassis, and take a detour to Preveza on the mainland to visit the site of ancient Nikopoli, the Roman 'victory city'.

South of Levkas is the Homeric island of Ithaka; then it is a short hop to the largest Ionian island, Kefalonia. From here you continue across the water to end your journey at the popular resort island of Zakinthos.

The route can easily be covered in two or three days, but will take at least a week if you want to stop off and take in some of the islands at leisure.

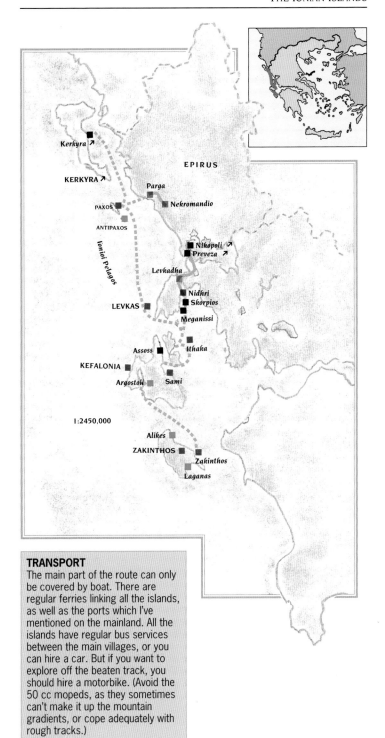

TRANSPORT
The main part of the route can only be covered by boat. There are regular ferries linking all the islands, as well as the ports which I've mentioned on the mainland. All the islands have regular bus services between the main villages, or you can hire a car. But if you want to explore off the beaten track, you should hire a motorbike. (Avoid the 50 cc mopeds, as they sometimes can't make it up the mountain gradients, or cope adequately with rough tracks.)

67

SIGHTS & PLACES OF INTEREST

ANTIPAXOS
See Paxos, page 75.

ARGOSTOLI
See Kefalonia, page 69.

ALIKES
See Zakinthos, page 76.

ITHAKA ⌦ ✕
5 km E of Kefalonia, 120 km S of Corfu.
Homer has made Ithaka one of the most famous of all the Greek islands. It was the home of Odysseus, to which he eventually returned after all his wanderings. It also features in a famous poem by Cavafy, the greatest modern poet in the Greek language. Loosely translated and paraphrased, this begins:

> When you start out for Ithaka
> pray that your journey be long,
> full of incident and wisdom.
> Be not afraid of the mythic
> monsters or the angry gods.
> These you will never meet
> as long as your spirit remains
> true and pure,
> as long as they are not there
> within you...

For the full poem, properly translated, see The Complete Poems of Cavafy (translated by Keeley and Sherrard). Despite its literary fame, Ithaka remains largely undeveloped. It has some remarkable scenery, and there are many excellent walks. Although the island is 25 km long, it is seldom more than 5 km wide, so you're never far from the sea. You'll find some woods, a number of fine beaches (mostly pebble), and a few sandy coves. There are also some superb views, especially on the road along the west coast to Stavros.

The island is virtually divided in two by the long curving inlet which ends at the port of **Vathy**. Both parts are largely barren and mountainous – the northern half rising to over 800 m.

In the middle of the inlet opposite Vathy there is a tiny island known as **Lazaretto** – so named because it once served as the island's quarantine station. It is said that when the poet Byron visited Ithaka he swam out to this island. (In my Byronic youth, I too once swam out to this island, but I'd advise against any attempt to swim to Lazaretto nowadays – you're liable to get run down by a ferry or cruise liner.) Ithaka attracts a number of cruise liners (presumably because the name adds a touch of class to the advertised itineraries), but they're only here for the day, and as soon as these floating gin palaces depart in the afternoon, Vathy once more returns to its sleepy state. Night falls, the tavernas and cafés along the waterfront open, and the real show begins.

As is often the case with important mythological sites, there are several places on Ithaka which claim to be site of Odysseus' palace. The great German archaeologist Schliemann thought he'd located the site on the slopes of

Mount Aetos, but this has since been discounted because it was not old enough. Another possibility is near Stavros. The island abounds in places which match lines in Homer's poem, and if you feel like doing some detective work of your own, it is well worth bringing a copy of *The Odyssey* to read while you're here. There are also occasional lectures on Homer, given at the small cultural centre in Vathy.

KEFALONIA ⌖ ✕

120 km S of Corfu. Kefalonia is the largest of the Ionian islands, and is reputed to be the least interesting. But as all the Ionian islands have more than a few things of interest, you shouldn't let Kefalonia's reputation put you off.

The island is 50 km long, yet owing to its deep bays and inlets it has nearly 200 km of coastline. Much of this is particularly beautiful, which means that all the north-western, western and eastern coastal roads have excellent views. Be warned: the bus service on the island can be very erratic, and the twisting roads dangerous for motorbikes and scooters. By far the best way to see the views is on foot, or by car (with one person intently driving, whilst the other marvels at the panorama). Inland, Mount Enos rises to more than 1,600 m and the island's main roads skirt its fir-covered lower slopes. The island is said to be named after the fir trees, which are of the species *abies cephaloniensis*. Although, according to a knowledgeable local I once encountered, it is the other way round, which does seem more logical.

During its long history, Kefalonia's ownership appears to have been passed on from one part of Italy to

---

A real find, though unfortunately it has already been found by enough people to keep it pretty heavily booked during the season. The views from the windows are of the kind you dream about on cold February nights, and the rooms are wonderfully furnished in 'ethnic' style.

LEVKAS – Levkadha
Levkadha Hotel, DD-DDD; *tel.* (0645) 32 916.

The best hotel here. Modern, slightly characterless, but utterly reliable. You can usually be sure that one of its 90 rooms will be free.

Hotel Vyzantion, D; *Dorpfeld Strasse* (Odos Dorpfeld); *tel.* (0645) 22 692.

Close to the harbour, on the street named after the great German who tried so hard but erroneously to put Levkas on the Homeric map. Spick and span, but no frills.

PARGA
Lichnos Beach, DD-DDD; *beyond edge of town on way to beach; tel.* (0684) 31 257.

As well as the main building, this hotel also has some fine chalets in a citrus grove which slopes down to the sea. Tucked away from the crowds.

PAXOS
In Paxos you're best off taking a room. People offering accommodation will meet you as you step off the boat. Be sure to get the price, location of the room and the length of your stay firmly established right at the start. But be warned: in July and August rooms can rocket in price (to as much as a medium/expensive hotel room), and there are often so few that you'll be lucky to get one at all. If you've tried everywhere, and still can't find a room, try contacting: Paxos Holidays (off the main square; tel. [0662] 31 381), where they're usually as helpful as it is possible to be.

Paxos Beach, DD-DDD; *outside Gaios; tel.* (0662) 31 211.

The best (and only real) hotel on the island, which, as its name suggests, is handy for the beach.

ZAKINTHOS – Alikes
It is still just possible to get a pleasant room here away from the lowing of the main herd. Ask around.

ZAKINTHOS – Zakinthos Town
Libro D'oro, DD; *on the way to the sea; tel.* (0695) 23 785.

Useful as a base for exploring the island, and near enough the sea to swim before you set out and when you get back.

• *Assos, Kefalonia.*

another. Amongst others, it has been ruled by the Romans, the Sicilians, the Pisans, the ruler of Brindisi, the Orsini family, the Tocchi family, then by the Venetians – and eventually, during the Second World War, by the whole of Italy.

In 1943 the Italian garrison in Kefalonia, which consisted of 9,000 men from the Alpine 'Acqui' Division, refused to capitulate to the Germans. After the ensuing hard-fought battle, which lasted over a week, the 3,000 Italian survivors finally surrendered – and were promptly shot, on Hitler's orders. Apparently 34 managed to survive by pretending they were dead. (There is no graveyard as evidence of this atrocity, as the bodies of the victims were removed and reburied across the Ionian Sea in Bari ten years later.)

Lord Byron lived here for a while, in the village of **Metaxata**, before setting off on his fateful journey to take command of the Greek Army of Indepen-

dence in Missolongi, where he died. According to my knowledgeable local friend who may or may not have put me right about the fir trees, Byron's behaviour was a source of great interest to the locals. Apparently his lordship had a special extension built on to his house, in which he kept a pet peacock that had been given to him by one of his Italian mistresses. But the cries of the peacock early in the morning so exasperated the late-rising Byron that eventually he shot the bird and ate it. Unfortunately the house where Byron lived (along with its peacock wing) has long since vanished, so it is impossible to tell whether there is even a grain of truth in this story.

Metaxata presumably has some link with the Greek dictator Metaxa, who was born in Kefalonia in 1871. Metaxa ruled Greece with an iron hand during the 1930s, and became a kind of Balkan Mussolini. But when Mussolini demanded that Metaxa should hand over Greece to him, Metaxa sent his celebrated reply on 28th October 1940: *Ochi* (No). To this day, *Ochi* Day is celebrated as a public holiday in Greece on October 28.

The main ferry port of Kefalonia is **Sami**, a rather nondescript place since its old Venetian buildings were completely flattened by the 1953 earthquake. But nearby you can visit the famous **Drogarati Caves**. They have an inner lake, filled with sea-water that was said to flow along a hidden fault through miles of undiscovered caverns deep beneath the 1,000-m mountains, from some swallow-holes on the far side of the island. This unlikely story for the entertainment of the tourists was astonishingly proved to be true, when two die-hard Dutch realists, determined to win a late-night bet made over a few glasses of *ouzo*, poured some potassium permanganate into the swallow-holes and met their come-uppance when the purple dye appeared in the lake of the cavern.

One of the best places to stay on the island is the small resort of **Poros**, which lies beneath the slopes of Mount Enos in the south. Another pleasant spot is **Argostoli**, 15 km west of Sami, at the end of a small inlet, off a much larger inlet. From here you can take a ferry across the larger inlet to an unspoilt peninsula with cliffs and long beaches.

Towards the northern end of the island, on the west coast, **Assos** stands on a hillside, beneath a large 16thC castle, overlooking its small harbour. The central square is called Paris Square, because it was rebuilt after the 1953 earthquake with money sent by the city of Paris. From here it is just a short walk to **Myrtos Beach**, one of the finest in Greece.

Some 13 km north of Assoss is **Fiskardo**, which also has a French connection. It is named after Robert Guiscard, the Norman king of Sicily who died here in 1085, and is thought to be buried somewhere by the ruined Norman church across the bay. Picturesque Fiskardo managed to escape the ravages of the 1953 earthquake, and has instead suffered the worst ravages of tourism.

LAGANAS

See Zakinthos, page 76.

LEVKADHA

See Levkas, below.

LEVKAS ⊯ ✕

About 80 km S of Corfu. Levkas (often known locally as Levkadha, which is the accusative) is named after the Greek word for white. This almost certainly refers to its white cliffs.

The island is 30 km long and 10 km or so wide, and its mountains rise to over 1,100 m. In fact, Levkas isn't really an island at all; it is joined to the mainland by a sand bar, though this is bisected by a ship canal. It is said that the first canal was cut through the sand bar as early as the 7thC BC by Corinthian colonizers. This would make it a candidate for the title of earliest ship canal in Europe, though the ancient historian Thucydides mentions that it had silted up by 427 BC. The Roman Emperor Augustus built a bridge across the re-dredged canal, the remains of which can still be seen on its banks. Now there is a pontoon bridge.

The approach to the island is guarded by the ruined fort of **Santa Maura**, which dates from the 14thC, though the present ruin contains much later Ottoman and Venetian additions. The castle was originally encircled by water from the nearby lagoon, and had to be approached by a bridge. Despite being on the mainland, Santa Maura was the island's capital until 1684. (The island is still occasionally referred to by its older inhabitants as Santa Maura, its former name.)

In common with many other Ionian islands, Levkas has been ruled by the Franks, the Turks, The Venetians, the British, and even for a brief period by the Russians (1798-80). It didn't become part of Greece until 1864.

Although Levkas is now a popular holiday destination, it has by no means been completely ruined. There are many fine beaches, particularly along the north and west coasts, and the inland mountain villages are a delight. Many are composed of little medieval houses along narrow lanes with blazing Judas trees, picturesquely situated above fertile green valleys where you can sometimes still see the older women working in traditional costume. The vineyards here produce some good wine – Levkas retsina is justly renowned, and be sure to try a bottle of red Santa Maura. The largest mountain village **Karya** is famous for its embroidery.

The main town on the island is **Levkadha**, which suffered badly in the earthquakes of 1948 and 1953. Some of the upper storeys of the buildings are still made out of ugly painted sheet metal, which gives the place a slightly ramshackle air, though there are still a number of the original old houses, as well as some Italianate churches, a few of which date from the late 17thC. The town is a popular yachting haven, and there are pleasant beaches beyond the windmills on the sand bar, which is the other side of the Yira lagoon. The lagoon itself is not good for swimming: it is only 1 or 2 m deep and is full of eels. The picturesque lagoon and nearby fish ponds have their drawbacks – in the form of mosquitoes and occasional fishy odours. If you're in Levkadha during August there is a lively theatre and arts festival, which is well worth a visit.

The best way to explore the island is by hired car or moped, both of which can be easily obtained in Levkadha. Just west of the town the road climbs to the **Faneromani Monastery**, which has great views out over the coast. Further down this coast you come to some fine beaches (mainly pebble, but some suitably remote for nude bathing). Unfortunately when the wind gets up (as it often does in the afternoons), these beaches become almost uninhabitable.

The afternoon is the best time of day to explore the protected east coast. Just over 10 km south of Levkadha, there is a delightful, almost landlocked bay. **Nidri**, on the north-west shore of the bay, is a popular resort which attracts a large number of yachts. Beside the harbour is a statue to Wilhelm Dorpfeld (1853-1940), the German archaeologist and follower of the great Schliemann. Dorpfeld was convinced that Levkas was the real Ithaka described by Homer in The Odyssey. He was wrong – but the Levkadians have never forgotten his attempt to put Levkas on the map (albeit under a different name). Dorpfeld's grave is across the bay at Aghia Kiriakai, near the house where he died, and one of the main streets in Levkadha is named after him.

Nearby **Vlikos**, which stands at the head of the bay, is renowned for its bouzouki festival. Further south is the village of **Piros**, below which there is a less crowded beach; and just over 16 km west of here you come to the seaside village of **Vassiliki**, a popular windsurfing centre.

For something really out of the ordinary, head on for **Cape Levkas**, which is west of here, but can only be reached by driving up to join the road from the north (off which there are a couple of superb beaches beneath the cliffs). Cape Levkas has spectacular 70-m-high white cliffs, and is the southernmost tip of the island. It is also known as Kavos tis Kiras, which derives from the Greek for 'Lady's Leap'. The lady in question is the poet Sappho, who was born on the island of Lesbos in the 7thC BC. She is said to have leapt from this cliff to her death in the blue waters far below, after she had been spurned by a good-looking young lad called Phaeon. At least part of the legend is untrue. Sappho was sapphic, a lesbian through more than the island of her birth. (The sexual meaning of both 'sapphic' and 'lesbian' derives from her.) However, Sappho also fell in love with a number of men. It is the other part of the story that is untrue: there is no historical evidence whatsoever that Sappho leapt to her death from here.

Later there was a temple of Apollo on this site, and a curious form of sacrifice took place here for more than 500 years. A local criminal or lunatic would be selected by the priests of the temple. A ceremony would then take place, in which he would have birds tied to his arms and feet, and then be cast off the cliff. The birds were optimistically intended to break his fall, by acting as a kind of fluttering feathered parachute. Miraculously, according to Cicero, some of these reluctant early aeronauts lived to tell the tale (what happened to the birds, one wonders). A modern lighthouse now stands near the site of the ancient temple of Apollo and its early experimental launch pad. Nowadays the criminals and lunatics have been replaced by hang-gliders, who hold a tournament here each summer (though you don't see many birds around here these days).

Levkas also has strong literary associations: the great turn-of-the-century poet Sikelianos was born here, as was the intriguing short story writer Lefcadio Hearn. The latter was born in 1850, the son of an Irish army surgeon, who became an American missionary, and a Greek woman from Kythira. They decided to name their offspring after the island of his birth (Lefcadio is an Italianate version). But Lefcadio evidently harboured a secret longing to rid himself of his eponymous Christian name. Despite achieving renown under the name of Lefcadio Hearn, he ended his days in 1905 as a naturalized Japanese called Yakumo Koizumi.

Just off the east coast of Levkas there are a number of small islands, the most interesting of which you're not allowed to visit. From Nidhri you can take an excursion boat all around **Skorpios**, but you can't set foot on it. It is the private island once owned by the billionaire shipowner Aristotle Onassis, lover of the great opera singer Maria Callas, and then husband of Jackie Kennedy. Their marriage took place on this island in 1968, in private, with a dozen helicopters containing the world's press circling halo-like above. Onassis himself was buried here in 1976. Nearby Madhouri island (also private) was the home of 19thC Greek poet Valaoritis.

The one island that you *can* visit off the east coast of Levkas, **Meganissi**, is something of a hidden gem – with superb views, a whitewashed village, and some marvellous swimming.

NEKROMANDIO

22 km S of Parga, E off main E55, by Mesopotamo. Nekromandio is the site of the notorious Oracle of the Dead, where people would come to question the spirits of the departed. The oracle was particularly well sited for this purpose, being on an island in a lake, from which the River Acheron flowed down into Hades (the Underworld). Homer describes the instructions given to Odysseus about how to enter Hades at this place (*Odysseus Book 10*, lines 510 onwards). The site has changed drastically since Homer's day. The lake

• *Ouzo and* meze.

has now dried up, and the 'thunderous waters of Acheron' are very much more placid. Even so, there are some interesting ruins, and this is indisputably the site which was described by both Homer and the historian Herodotus.

In ancient times people came here and made votive offerings to question the dead. This necromantic spot remained in business for almost 1,500 years (which is more than can be said for many more straightforward businesses). So what was the secret of its success?

Unfortunately modern excavations of the oracle site have shown the whole thing to be an elaborate hoax. As soon as the pilgrims arrived on the island, they were shown into a pitch dark windowless room, where they spent the night, enduring various spooky special effects laid on by the priests. After this long softening-up process, they were made to sniff some hallucinogenic fumes and led along a dark corridor, which brought them to the centre of the sanctuary. Drugged and terrified, they were then lowered down a shaft into the smoking antechamber of

• *Shipwreck Bay, Zakinthos.*

Hades itself. Here amidst the billowing fumes the priests laid on a show of gibbering spectres and squeaking disembodied souls. (The spirits of the dead only gibbered and squeaked in those days: the moaning and the howling of the damned came later with the Christian concept of hell.) The pilgrim then put his (or her) question to the departed spirits. Some form of gibbering answer was presumably provided, and the pilgrim was then assisted speedily back into the blinding sunshine minus his expensive votive offering.

Apprentice illusionists will be pleased to know that it is still possible to visit the antechamber where the terrified pilgrims had their audience with the dead. Iron-nerved rationalists will be disappointed to learn that it is no longer possible to spend the night here at the gateway to hell.

NIDRI
See Levkas, page 72.

NIKOPOLI
See Greece Overall: 6.

PARGA ⇥
Mainland resort on W coast, opposite Paxos.
Parga has quite a history. It was where Octavius harboured his fleet before the battle of Actium in 31 BC (when Cleopatra deserted Antony). In the 14thC, when Venice ruled all the offshore Ionian islands, Parga was the only piece of the mainland to become

part of the Venetian Republic. This it remained for over 400 years – with one brief interruption when the notorious pirate Barbarossa sacked it in 1537. The Venetian castle on the promontory was rebuilt after this, in 1624, and you can still read the inscription beneath the Lion of Venice on the walls, commemorating this fact. Later, the French took Parga. Then, briefly during the 19thC, it became an independent state, supporting itself by trade in olive oil and citrus fruits (in particular, the locally grown citron, a lemon-flavoured fruit the size of an orange, which was popular with Jewish communities throughout Europe and the Near East as a traditional decoration for the tabernacle during the feast of Sukkoth).

Finally the British took over Parga and, despite all assurances to the contrary, immediately sold it to the notorious Ali Pasha. Rather than live under this bloodthirsty tyrant, the citizens moved out lock stock and barrel for the islands. They even exhumed the bones of their dead, and burnt them, so that Ali Pasha couldn't defile them. Ali Pasha then moved in a Muslim population, which remained here after this part of Greece became independent in 1913. But the Muslims were forced to move out in 1924 (when Greco-Turkish relations reached an all-time low after the Smyrna Massacre), and they were replaced by Greeks from Istanbul.

Until recently, this was one of the most beautiful bays on the coast, with two fine beaches divided by the high castle-crowned promontory. Unfortunately, nowadays during the season you can hardly see these beaches for the bodies roasting voluptuously in the carcinogenic rays of the sun. Parga is overrun by package tourists and continues to become increasingly built-up. If you find yourself here, be sure to visit Nekromandio (see above), which is just 22 km to the south.

PAXOS ⌘ ✕

15 *km S of Corfu*. Paxos is just 9 km long and 3 km wide. The main port of **Gaios** is guarded by a small island with a ruined Venetian castle. Gaios has a pleasant harbour front, with coloured Venetian houses, and a row of yachts from which Italians emerge at night in full glitter. The port and its surroundings can get a little crowded during the daytime by trippers from Corfu and the mainland port of Parga (just 13 km to the east). However, when the boats return and evening falls, things quieten down considerably.

Inland, the whole island is covered with olive groves, and rises to just over 200 m. A lovely gentle walk takes you from Gaios up the main road, which leads through the centre of the island, to **Lakka** in the north. This is situated on an almost totally enclosed lagoon, where you can have a pleasant swim at the end of your two-hour walk. (There are regular buses, if you decide to take the easy way home.)

A few years ago the actor Peter Bull used to live here. (He played the bull-faced Russian ambassador in *Dr Strangelove*.) I once briefly encountered his puce, ferocious features in mid lagoon as we swam past each other in opposite directions. ('Kali mera, Mr Bull.' 'Afternoon, dear boy.') Lakka also boasts one of the world's most user-friendly aquariums – a small but ecologically sound institution, whose amiable proprietor is one of its main attractions. The aquarium contains small octopi, eels, squid, crabs, and a smattering of fairly unspectacular local fish. Like us, the exhibits are only here for the season and, at the end of summer, the proprietor releases them back into the sea.

There are fine walks all over the island, which is renowned for its flowers and the variety of its bird life. The great thing about these walks is that they're never very hard, and never very long, and there is almost always some shade. The west coast of the island is particularly beautiful, though it is best seen by boat. Regular caique tours leave from the harbour in Gaios for the cliffs and the seven famous caves. Homer describes how the one called **Ipapando** was the home of the sea god Poseidon, and was decked out in gold, though no evidence of this fabulous grotto remains.

Another pleasant boat trip is to the smaller nearby island of **Antipaxos**, which is only inhabited in summer by a few locals who tend the vines that produce its delicious red wine. The island also has a stunning beach, though it is often filled by day trippers. In the early autumn Antipaxos plays host to flocks

75

of migrating birds, which make easy prey for the local hunters and not particularly nourishing stews.

PREVEZA

See Greece Overall: 6.

SAMI

See Kefalonia, page 69.

ZAKINTHOS ✍ ✕

160 kms S of Corfu. In the days when this island was ruled by the Venetians, they referred to it as:

Zante, Zante,
fior di Levante.

which translated into English becomes:

Zakinthos, Zakinthos,
flower of the Levant.

In those days the island was renowned for the beauty of its Venetian architecture, which was all destroyed in the terrible 1953 earthquake. A few of the old landmarks and churches have been rebuilt – but only a few, and rather sporadically.

Nowadays Zakinthos has succumbed to a severe dose of mega tourism. Unfortunately this has transformed the island's charms as drastically as English transformed the island's delightful Italian jingle. The locals unwittingly did their best to forestall this later disaster. Several years ago, at great expense, a new airport was built, in the hope of attracting more tourists. That summer, squadrons of charter flights began arriving from all over Europe to fill the new hotels. Unfortunately, the labour force had been too busy building the airport to start work on the hotels, which were still in the blueprint stage. Just as they had been promised, thousands experienced a holiday they would never forget.

For a few years after this, Zakinthos reluctantly became the least-known gem of the Ionian islands, until finally such convincing photographic evidence of the new hotels began reaching the travel agents of Dortmund, Birmingham and Rotterdam that they decided to try again.

Despite the influx of tourists, the island is large enough to have plenty of unspoilt countryside. The cliffs of the north-west coast are truly spectacular, and the fine sandy beach at **Alikes** on the north-east coast is long enough not to get crowded. Down in the south it is pure holidayland, where you can't savour the wonderful scenery, sea and beaches, which the inevitable cocktail bars and discos. The main beach here at **Laganas** used to be home to thousands of rare loggerhead sea turtles (species *caretta caretta*); now the population is down to a few hundred. At night volunteers attempt to rescue the eggs, which the turtles come ashore to lay whimsically amongst the abandoned sandcastles, beach umbrellas and forgotten buckets and spades. Measures have been taken by the local authorities to protect the species. But none has really worked.

Out of season is a different matter. In spring and autumn Zakinthos lives up to its name 'flower of the Levant', with the hillsides ablaze with different coloured blooms. Hire a sturdy motorbike and explore the inland trails to the villages, and you'll be pleasantly surprised. The local people are very hospitable and their villages are largely unspoilt.

You can also see a few interesting natural phenomena on the island. Near **Keri** in the south-west you'll find pools of natural tar, which the locals have used for caulking boats since ancient times. At the other end of the island are the **Kianou Caves**, whose blue waters are great for snorkelling. The spectacular cliffs in the north-west are also worth a visit. You can have a drink at the taverna here 100 m above the ultramarine sea far below. The sunsets at this spot are fabulous – alas, serenaded in season by a symphony of clicking camera shutters.

Zakinthos was the birthplace in 1798 of the poet Solomos, who wrote the Greek national anthem and survived this feat to become a fine poet. The island is also the birthplace of the even finer poet Foscolo (1778-1827), whose Ionian origins are frequently overlooked because he wrote in Italian. Foscolo became one of the great Italian romantic poets and, after a life of suitably romantic, political and emotional turmoil, took refuge in England, where he died in poverty.

RECOMMENDED RESTAURANTS

ITHAKA – Vathy
Kantouri, D; *sea front.*

Right in the middle of the action by the harbour, Kantouri attracts a jolly crowd. The menu is filled with reliable old favourites.

If you want to dine in a secluded, romantic spot, try the village of **Frikes** on the north-eastern coast. There are several old-style tavernas by the jetty overlooking the beach. Just as one always imagined it would be.

KEFALONIA – Fiskardo
The best and most romantic dining spots tend to be around the harbour. Unfortunately they aren't very large, and not surprisingly are the most expensive. But it is worth trying one of these for a special occasion. My favourite is:

Dendrinos, D-DD; *waterfront.*
Out of season, this is a delight. Otherwise, get here early.

LEVKAS – Levkadha
Agrambeli, DDD.

For smart dining amongst the smart yachting set. The seafood here is superb, but you pay for it. They also stock a range of local Ionian wines.

If you just want a pleasant meal, and not such a stiff bill, you're better off heading out to one of the beach-side tavernas on the coast. Here they serve the usual fare in a jolly atmosphere, with a view that's worth more than any lobster.

PAXOS
This is a small island with a short season, which sees itself as catering for a cut above the package tourists, so don't expect much in the way of bargains.

PAXOS – Gaios
Spiro's, D-DD; *off main square.*

The best informal restaurant to eat at in Gaios, where busy waiters run

• *Zakinthos Town.*

about in jovial mayhem, shouting 'A messos' ('I'm coming straight away'), although this often takes some time. You do eventually get served some good authentic dishes, and the leisurely service tends to breed camaraderie amongst the customers – who usually manage to find bottles of wine regardless. A really friendly spot.

ZAKINTHOS – Alikes
This resort has a few pleasant tavernas overlooking the sea, and an excellent small café with a friendly, intimate atmosphere, run by Anita from Germany, at a house in the middle of a vineyard just inland.

ZAKINTHOS – Zakinthos Town
To Tavernaki, D-DD; Ignatiou Street.

The name (which means 'the little Tavern') may not be imaginative, but the food here is. An unpretentious spot, popular with a lively young clientele.

Otherwise, head up to the old Bohali quarter of town, by the castle. The main square here has a number of good tavernas.

<u>Central Mainland</u>

The Road to the North
Between Athens and Thessaloniki

350 km; map Michelin 980, 1:700000

Greece's two major cities are connecetd by the highway on which this route is based. It is a toll route, and a few of its busier sections are dual carriageways: a demanding drive, due to the number of lorries on the road. But this does provide a speedy link to the north – and off it you'll find some of the most varied sights on the Greek mainland.

Assuming you start from Athens, immediately you leave the capital on the main E75 for Thessaloniki you'll see the Parnitha Mountains rising to your left. Take a detour into these mountains and you'll find some pleasant woodland hikes. Just beyond there is a plethora of sights. Curiously, those of greatest historical importance (such as Marathon and Thermopylae) tend to be the most disappointing in reality. It is the more remote sights, such as Ramnous and Amfiaraio, that you'll probably find most pleasant to visit.

When you get to Volos there is a wonderful circuit you can make around the Mount Pelio Peninsula This is a wooded, mountainous region, filled with picturesque little villages, which has a character quite distinct from the rest of Greece.

North of Volos you pass through Larissa and then come to Mount Olympos, which rises inland to the west. If you have a couple of days to spare, and you're feeling energetic, you can climb the mountain and visit the home of the ancient gods in the clouds. On the northern slopes you'll find the ruins of Dion, the sacred city of ancient Macedon. Then you continue up the coast of the Thermaic Gulf to Thessaloniki.

The main part of this route can be covered easily in a day. If you want to turn off and see some of the sights, and follow the detours, you should allow four to five days.

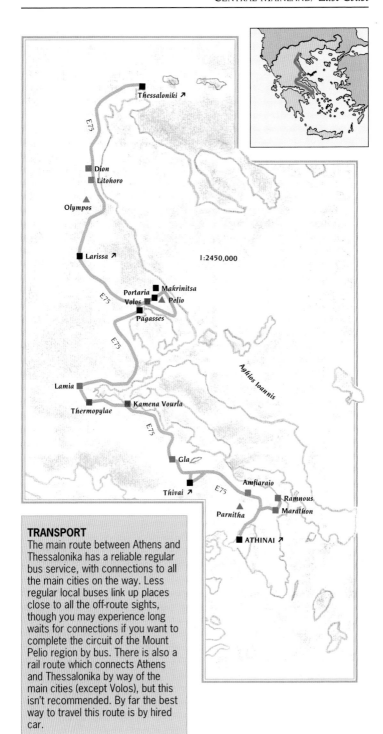

TRANSPORT

The main route between Athens and Thessalonika has a reliable regular bus service, with connections to all the main cities on the way. Less regular local buses link up places close to all the off-route sights, though you may experience long waits for connections if you want to complete the circuit of the Mount Pelio region by bus. There is also a rail route which connects Athens and Thessalonika by way of the main cities (except Volos), but this isn't recommended. By far the best way to travel this route is by hired car.

SIGHTS & PLACES OF INTEREST

AMFIARAIO
10 km N of main E75 Athens to Thessaloniki highway; going N, turn off right for Kalamos, 8 km beyond turn for Marathon. This ruined 4thC BC sanctuary was dedicated to Amphiaraos, who was King of Argos and a renowned interpreter of dreams. According to legend Amphiaraos never died but was swallowed up by the earth and became a god. His sanctuary here was a dream oracle for the treatment of the sick.

The patient would lie down to sleep on the portico (still visible), wrapped in the skin of a sacrificial lamb, whereupon Amphiaraos would speak to him in a dream. The priests would interpret this dream, discovering in it how the patient should be treated. Grateful patients who had been cured threw coins into the fountain. The site contains the ruins of a Doric temple and a theatre which seated 3,000 people.

ATHENS
See pages 174-191.

DION
87 km S of Thessaloniki, 4 km W of E75. This site is on the northern flank of Mount Olympos, and was once a seaport. (The sea has now receded by 6 km, to the modern village of Dhion by the E75 highway.)

Ancient Dion was the sacred city of the Macedonians. It had sanctuaries to many of the main Greek gods, as well as a few Egyptian ones, such as Isis and Anubis, for good measure. This hedging of bets obviously worked: Alexander the Great came here to seek divine assistance for his forthcoming ambitious expedition to conquer the world (there are times when megalomania alone is not enough).

At its height, the city of Dion had a population of over 15,000, and even ran its own Dion Olympic games, which attracted competitors from all over Greece. You can see the ruins of the sanctuaries, and some fine mosaics (especially one of Dionysius riding in his chariot). The ancient **theatre** here stages regular performances of ancient Greek drama (both comedy and tragedy) during July and August.

During the Roman conquest Dion became a Christian centre, and in the 5thC it even had a bishop. But this switch of allegiance obviously didn't appeal to the gods on nearby Olympos. After an earthquake it was covered by a torrent of mud from Olympos, which caused a hasty exodus.

Modern excavations here have continued to throw new light on the history of ancient Macedon. Some of the latest finds can be seen in the **museum**. Many have been excellently preserved through the centuries by the mud.

GLA
E off E75, 107 km S of Lamia. This ancient Mycenaean fortress once stood on an island in the middle of Lake Copais, which was drained just a century ago. The perimeter walls extend over 3 km, making them larger even than those at Mycenae; yet this site remains a mystery. No one really knows precisely who lived here, nor what happened to this once powerful and thriving community.

Amongst the ruins you can make out the market place and a palace. This is an ideal spot for Ozymandias-type thoughts about the passing of history into oblivion.

Nearby on the slopes of the 700-m-high Mount Ptoo is the **Sanctuary of the Ptoan Apollo**, which contains the remains of a temple and the cave of the oracle. Doubtless threatened by its more famous competitors, this oracle claimed (like all optimistic and ambitious tipsters) to be absolutely infallible; though there is no historical evidence to substantiate this claim.

KAMENA VOURLA 🛏
40 km E of Lami, on E75. A pleasant spa resort, which is largely a Greek holiday centre and has a decent beach.

LAMIA 🛏
143 km S of Larissa. A provincial town, by-passed by the main E75, which is a convenient place to stay the night, as it is almost halfway between Athens and Thessaloniki.

The town has a population of just over 40,000, and its own archbishop. The storks' nests perched on the tiled rooftops give the place a slightly raffish air. The inhabitants don't disturb these nests as they're said to be a sign of good luck.

There is nothing of real interest to see in Lamia, and not much of importance has happened here since it was first settled in the Bronze Age.

If you spend the night in this congenial, utterly Greek town, you will glimpse how the Greeks live out of sight of the tourists' cameras. The locals are very friendly.

LARISSA
See Greece Overall: 3

LITOHORO ⇔ ✕
See Mount Olympos, page 82.

RECOMMENDED HOTELS

KAMMENA VOURLA
Delfini, D; *on seafront; tel. Kammena Vourla 22 321.*

A small beach-side hotel with clean rooms and sound plumbing, which includes showers that work in most rooms. Deservedly popular, but if they're full, they usually know of somewhere that isn't.

LAMIA
Only stay here if you're caught by nightfall on the E75 main Athens to Thessaloniki highway. There are several inexpensive hotels in the city centre, none of which is very special. Try:

Samaras, D; *tel. Lamia 28 971.*

or:

Vyzantion, D-DD; *tel. Lamia 25 025.*

LITOHORO
Myrto, D-DD; *main street; tel. (0352) 81 398.*

Not so spartan as most of the other hotels, and when the temperature drops (as it does quickly out of season), the place is kept beautifully warm.

If you prefer to stay down by the sea, there are a number of inexpensive hotels and rooms to rent at the nearby beach-side villages of **Plaka**, **Limenas Litohorou** and further south at **Platamonas** (where there is a fine Crusader castle).

MARATHON ⇔
27 km beyond northern suburbs of Athens, off E75. In the immortal words of Byron:

> *The mountains look on Marathon*
> *And Marathon looks on the sea;*
> *And musing here an hour alone,*
> *I dreamt that Greece might still be free:*
> *For standing on the Persians' grave,*
> *I could not deem myself a slave.*

The plains here were the scene of the famous Battle of Marathon in 490 BC, when the Athenians defeated the might of the Persian army.

MARATHON
Gold Coast, D-DD; *tel.* (0294) 92 102.

A large hotel with a range of amenities, including tennis courts and a swimming-pool. Despite the name, it is quite a way from any swimmable sea.

MOUNT OLYMPOS
Spilios Agapitos (Refuge A); *altitude 2,100 m; tel.* (0352) 81 800.

This is the refuge where you can spend the night between Priona and the final climb to the peaks. In summer it is essential to 'phone ahead and book a place for the night. Turning up on spec can prove to be a very chilly disappointment.

VOLOS
Aegli, DD; *24 Odos Argonauton (Road of the Argonauts); tel.* (0421) 23 500.

Your best bet if you have to stay in town. It is handy for the ferry and such attractions as there are in the centre of Volos. An old-style provincial pile, it is right on the front. Those who really enjoy watching the movement of shipping will love the ever-changing nautical view.

Hotel Kypseli, DD; *1 Ayiou Nikolaou; tel.* (0421) 24 420.

You'll find this hotel on the corner close to the cathedral (Ayiou Nikolaou), in a relatively quiet part of town.

• *Volos.*

Darius, the leader of the Medes and Persians, ruled an empire which stretched as far east as India, and as far south as Abyssinia. His 490 BC expedition, backed by a large fleet, intended to take Greece and press on to the west. Had he defeated the Greeks, it is more than likely that he would eventually have overrun Europe. It was the Battle of Marathon that stopped him.

The sides weren't quite as uneven as some exaggerated early historical records suggest, but even so the Athenian force was probably only 10,000 men, whilst the Persian army almost certainly numbered more than 25,000. About 6,000 Persian soldiers lost their lives, whilst the rest fled in disarray – according to legend, as a result of divine intervention by the god Pan.

Disbelievers in such tales may scoff, but the word used to describe the effect of Pan's intervention at Marathon remains with us to this day. The Persians fled in the first ever 'panic'.

During the slaughter of the Medes and Persians, the Athenians lost fewer than 200 men, who were all buried on the spot with full military honours. Meanwhile, a messenger set out to run from Marathon to Athens, where he finally arrived to announce the famous victory before he collapsed from exhaustion and died. Since then, a 'marathon' has always been raced over the precise distance between Marathon and Athens: 42.1946666 recurring km.

Had the Athenians lost the Battle of Marathon, we would not have seen the glories of Ancient Greece, from philosophy and tragedy to mathematics and unlikely legends.

Nowadays, Marathon is a rather ordinary spot, though, according to a story that has persisted through the centuries, on the anniversary of the battle (September 12) the huge emptiness of the plain of Marathon is filled at night with the ghostly clamour of battle. Those who have heard it speak of the ringing of metal swords, the cries of the combatants and the distinct whinnying of horses. Unfortunately, modern research has conclusively proved that no cavalry took part in this battle.

Just 10 km to the east is the superb ancient site of Ramnous (see below), which easily makes up for the disappointment of modern-day Marathon.

MOUNT OLYMPOS 🛏

E off main E75, 92 km S of Thessaloniki. Mount Olympos is the venue of the world's earliest and longest running soap opera: this is the home of the Greek gods.

The massive mountain skirts the eastern shore of the Thermaic Gulf, and the main Athens to Thessaloniki

• *Sunset near Olympos.*

highway runs along the coast in its shadow.

Olympos is the highest mountain in Greece and has no fewer than six peaks over 2,780 m. The highest is **Mytikas** (sometimes known by its more evocative name Pantheon), which rises to 2,917 m. The easiest to climb is nearby **Profitis Ilias**, which rises to 2,787 m and has a small chapel on top.

The peaks are snow-capped from late September until April, and during the summer are often shrouded in cloud. Owing to their geographical location they are the scene of frequent thunderstorms, which, to the ancient Greeks, represented anything from Zeus' indigestion to outbursts of Titanic rage (the Titans lived here too).

While Zeus and his riotous crew of fellow gods lived up here no mere mortal would have dreamt of trying to make an ascent of the mountain. No one attempted it until 1669 when Sultan Mehmet IV mounted an expedition for the peak, which failed. The heady combination of the Romantic Movement and the revival of interest in Ancient Greece soon inspired further attempts. In 1862 the intrepid Heinrich

DETOUR – **MOUNT PELIO**

The tour of Mount Pelio, which is 25 km east of Volos, is a tour within a tour; the full circuit of the main villages covering around 80 km. The route is largely on twisting mountain roads, with many steep gradients. There are several places you'll want to visit, so it is worth allowing at least a day for the whole route if you're driving yourself. There are buses from village to village, but you can spend a long time waiting for connections.

• *View of Mount Pelio.*

The scenery here is subtly different from other parts of Greece. As well as the distinctive beauty of each little village, you'll see a succession of superb views out over the mountains and coast, woodlands, olive groves and fruit orchards; the entire region feels steeped in legend, which indeed it is. The woods here were once the haunt of the centaurs (top half man, bottom half horse), who were notorious for their carousing and sexual profligacy. The equine proportions of these creatures appear to have held a great fascination for the women of Ancient Greece, whom the centaurs preferred to their own kind. Some of the centaurs were sensitive, intelligent creatures, such as the wise and benevolent teacher Cheiron, who gave private lessons to the young Achilles, instructed Asklepios in the art of herbal medicine, and taught Jason how to build his ship, the *Argo*, which was constructed out of trees from Mount Pelio.

Driving north-west from Volos, going clockwise, you pass through Ano Volos and Episkopi (see Volos, page 88). At Portaria you turn left for Makrinitsa, which was founded over 700 years ago by refugees from the first sack of Constantinople. Here you'll find a street named after Charles Ogle, a reporter for *The Times* of London, who was killed at Makrinitsa when caught up in a skirmish between the Turks and some Greek resistance fighters. At a café just beyond the main square you can see a mural by the eccentric primitive painter Theophilos (see Volos).

From Makrinitsa, return to Portaria and continue along the road through Hania (a popular ski resort in winter, like several other towns in these mountains). The road now twists and turns with a vengeance until you reach the charming village of Tsagora, the largest in the region. From here, head back to the main route, and then continue south-east through the mountain villages above the sea. At Anilio you can follow a winding detour down to Aghios Ioannis, which is on the sea. There is a lovely walk from here, south along the coast to Damoukori, with its houses around a little bay. From a little further on you can ascend some breathtaking (in all senses) steps inland to the main road, and then continue back to Anilio and down again to Aghios Ioannis, where, if you wish, you can stay in one of the pleasant little hotels or rented rooms along the front. (Allow a full half day for this walk – though you can easily hitch the last sections if you get tired.)

From here the main road continues around the mountain peaks, which rise to 1,400 m. Then you drive down to the west coast of the peninsula, eventually arriving at the fine sandy beach of Kala Nera, where there are inexpensive holiday hotels and rooms to rent. I'm told there used to be a wonderful railway which followed the coast back to Volos, but sadly it no longer exists.

Barth finally made it to the lesser peak of Profitis Ilias, only to discover, to his astonishment, that there was already a small chapel here. Some Greek monks had beaten him to it by 500 or so years.

Yet still the main peak remained unscaled. After two daring but unsuccessful attempts, Edward Richter was well on his way to the top in 1910 when he was captured by bandits and, much to his indignation, held to ransom. Then in 1913 Mytikas (which means 'the needle') was finally conquered by the Swiss pair Baud-Bovy and Boissonas who weren't even professional mountaineers – just a couple of artists, but, according to the records, were led by a Greek guide, Christos Kakalos.

Nowadays it is very different, and the peak even has a little metal Greek flag and a visitors' book, which is filled by visitors with the usual witticisms at the expense of their hosts. ('The gods are dead, said Nietzsche. Nietzsche is dead, say the gods.')

A word of warning here: it is still a difficult climb to the top, and can take you a couple of days. The best place to start from is the mountain village of **Litohoro**, which is 6 km inland from the E75. If you want to reach the peak by foot you'll have to start from Litohoro at 7 am. A four-hour walk through the woods brings you to **Priona** (though there is a road as far as here). At Priona there is an eccentric little mountain restaurant, where you can stock up for the forthcoming ascent with a well-simmered bowl of bean soup.

Then it's onwards and upwards through the woods (once the haunt of wolves, mountain lions and bandits) for another three hours to the **Spilios Agapitos** hut at 2,100 m, frequently known by its more purposeful name of Refuge A. You can stay the night here (on the way up or on the way back) in the company of the rather gruff warden and your fatigue-dulled fellow climbers. But it is a night you won't forget, with a sunset view to the Throne of Zeus above.

The final stretch to Mytikas takes a couple of hours, and if you're not an experienced climber you should try and attach yourself to a group with a guide at this point. The guides are fairly expensive (6,000 D or more per day),

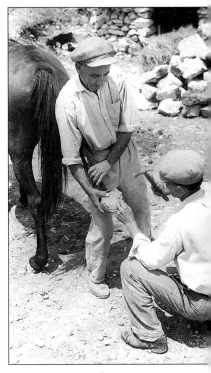

• In *the Parnitha Mountains.*

but groups will often let you join them if you offer to make a contribution. It is only a strenuous hike up the meadows and over the steep vertiginous trails, rather than genuine mountaineering, but mountains are not to be fooled with at this altitude.

For details before you set out, contact the EOS Mountaineering Club office at Litohoro, which runs Refuge A. Another club, the SEO Mountaineering Club of Greece, also has an office in Litohoro, and runs another refuge (Refuge B) on a different part of the mountain. This refuge is closer to the summit, has even more superb views, and is less likely to be filled with singing students – but it is generally reckoned that this route is more difficult for beginners.

As well as the routes to the summit, there are a number of excellent hiking trails all over the slopes of Olympos, especially Lower Olympos to the south. (See also Dion above.)

Mount Olympos was the home chosen by Zeus, chief of the Ancient Greek

85

gods. His father was the Titan Chronos, who castrated his father with a flint sickle and married his sister Rea. Domestic life must have been fairly fraught in the Chronos home as Chronos had been warned that one day he also would be deposed by one of his sons, just as he had deposed his own father. Chronos decided to take the rather drastic precaution of devouring his offspring one by one as they arrived, but Rea managed to give birth to baby Zeus and hide him before dinner.

Zeus grew up and duly deposed his father. He made Chronos regurgitate his two brothers, Hades and Poseidon, and then consigned Chronos to the Underworld. Zeus then threw lots with his brothers to see who should rule the different regions of the world. Poseidon won the sea, Hades won the Underworld (where presumably their father still languished), and Zeus won the sky. The earth was ruled by nobody, and was looked upon as a place where any of the gods could impose their will.

Zeus now settled down to the serious business of ruling the gods from Olympos, his home in the sky. He took up with Dione, but soon tired of her and fell for his sister Hera. In order to attract Hera's amorous attentions, Zeus is said to have turned himself into a cuckoo, which was astute as Hera turned out to be a bird lover and the two of them were soon living together as god and goddess.

Originally Hera had power over all living things and even had vegetable life in her sway. Her powers appear to have dwindled though, and in the end she was reduced to being just the goddess of marriage and childbirth. Despite being the mother of a number of baby gods and goddesses, she was able to renew her virginity annually by immersing herself in the waters of the magic spring at Argos. (Sadly this spring does not appear to exist any longer.)

Zeus obviously didn't like being married to a virgin, for his attentions soon began to wander, and Hera became extremely jealous. Eventually Zeus married Hetis (by whom he had a baby

• *Lamia.*

• *Volos, with Mount Pelio in the background.*

goddess), and after that he married Themis (two small gods followed). In between he also had a fling with his sister Demeter (result, one goddess), a couple of unrelated goddesses and a Titaness called Mnemosyne (who consequently gave birth to all nine Muses). As if this wasn't enough, he also managed to have his godly way with several mortal women (who gave birth to a whole tribe of little gods and goddesses). In order to have his way with Leda, he went back to his old bird trick and forced his attentions on her in the form of a swan (she consequently gave birth to two eggs). And so it went on, the success of this long-running early soap opera by now guaranteed, with a nationwide audience of mortals hanging on each new episode.

PARNITHA MOUNTAINS ×

Just beyond the northern suburbs of Athens. The highest peak in this range, Mount Parnis, is over 1,400 m, and the slopes of the mountains are covered with pine trees. In the days of ancient Greece these woods were hunting grounds filled with wild boar and wolves. It is said that they even contained some of the last lions in Europe. There are several drives up into the mountains. The best takes you through Aharnes and up a torturous road towards the peak. If you don't fancy driving, you can take the funicular, which goes higher than 900 m, and provides a spectacular view out over the farmlands of Attica. Incongruously, there is a casino here.

The other route, further to the east, takes you up to Varimbombi. Outside the village is the graveyard of the former Greek royal family, which contains the tombs of the Duke of Edinburgh's father and mother.

RAMNOUS

10 km E of Marathon, by the coast. A beautiful isolated spot on a headland above a cove – the kind of romantic Greek site you always expected to find, but never did. Here there is a fine **Temple of Nemesis**, which is Doric in style, as well as the ruins of a 5thC BC **Temple of Themis**. Nemesis was the much-feared goddess of retribution, who always caught up with you, just

87

when you thought you'd got away with it. Nemesis allegedly laid an egg, which gave birth to Helen. Themis, on the other hand, was a mere Titaness, who used her titanic powers to decide what was permitted under divine law (almost anything, to judge from the behaviour of the Greek gods).

THEBES

See Greece Overall: 6.

THERMOPYLAE

14 km S of Lamia, on E75. This pass gave its name to one of the most famous battles in ancient history. Around 2,500 years ago, Thermopylae was a narrow pass, with the mountains rising almost sheer from the sea, which has now receded several kilometres away to the north-west.

Here in 480 BC Leonidas led 300 Spartans in a heroic stand against 30,000 Persians under the command of Xerxes. The Persian commander called on Leonidas to surrender, warning him that he had so many archers that their hail of arrows could blot out the light of the sun. Leonidas retorted with his famous remark: 'So much the better, we will fight in the shade.' And so they did, fighting to the bitter end. (It is said that only two survived out of the original 300.) In the customary chivalrous manner of the time, Xerxes then had Leonidas' body decapitated and nailed to a cross.

The battle is described in heroic terms in Herodotus (*Book 10*), which makes superb reading as a companion guide to the site. Several of the features in his description are still recognizable; and you can see the burial mound, which allegedly contains the bodies of the heroic Spartans. Opposite is a modern statue to Leonidas, with the inscription: *Stranger, tell the Lacedaemonians [Spartans] that we lie here, obedient to their command.* A truly memorable place, whose name stirs the hearts of all Greeks.

Just beyond the site are the hot springs from which Thermopylae takes its name. In winter they sometimes steam in a dramatic fashion, but during the summer they often appear almost cool.

THESSALONIKI

See Greece Overall: 1.

VOLOS ⇌ ✕

60 km SE of Larissa, off E75. Volos holds little appeal for the traveller. It is a booming commercial port, with expanding factories and clouds of dust raised by the constant stream of noisy juggernauts. Look at the number plates of some of these lorries and you'll be surprised. Volos has a direct ferry link 1,500 km across the Mediterranean with Tartus, and is a staging post on Syria's main commercial route to western Europe.

The recent facelift given to Volos by the civic authorities has only marginally improved its situation. The fact is, there are several sights of great historic interest around Volos, each with a fascinating story to tell. Unfortunately, when you arrive at them there isn't really much to see.

Take **Pagasses**, for instance, which has a perfectly reasonable beach and a rather boring looking archaeological site, most of which is fenced off. Yet this seemingly ordinary spot was where Jason launched the famous Argo. According to legend, Jason crewed his Argo with a motley bunch of gods, heroes and other largely mythological characters, known as the Argonauts.

Jason then set off for the Black Sea in search of the Golden Fleece, which he eventually managed to steal, with the aid of Medea, who fell in love with him. She came back with Jason, but turned out to be quite a handful – chopping up her brother and persuading Pelias' daughters to pop him in the pot and boil him alive. Jason soon decided that he'd had enough, and went off with Glauca. Whereupon Medea murdered all her sons by Jason, instigated Glauca's murder, and swept away in a chariot born aloft by winged serpents – before finally achieving the rare feat of becoming an immortal. (Judging from her mortal history, she certainly had the right qualifications.)

Another site with a fascinating tale and little to show for it is **Iolkos**, on the outskirts of town, on a slope overlooking Volos. Here there is admittedly a fine view out over the blue waters of the gulf, and you can visit the (slightly irrelevant) Byzantine church of Episkopi. Much more interesting however is the fact that this is the spot where the first beauty contest was held.

This event wasn't organized, but came about almost by accident. One of the argonauts, Peleus, was getting married to a young sea nymph he'd met called Thetis, and all the gods were present for the big occasion. Unfortunately they'd forgotten to invite Eris, the goddess of discord, who was so miffed that she flung down a golden apple inscribed 'to the fairest'. This certainly succeeded in introducing discord into the harmonious proceedings. A slanging match developed between Hera, Athena and Aphrodite, each of whom claimed the apple as rightfully hers. So they decided to hold the earliest known beauty contest, with Paris of Troy as judge. Paris chose to give the apple to Aphrodite, and from then on was a marked man in the eyes of Hera and Athena (but that's another story).

Other nearby sites of little visual interest include: **Dimini** (3 km west of town), a neolithic site dating from 4,000 BC, which has six rings of walls; **Sesklo** (7 km west of town), which claims to be the oldest fortified settlement in Europe; the 18thC tower houses at **Ano Volos**; and in a house in the same suburb the 'fascinating' early 20thC frescos by the famous primitive painter Theophilos, who died in 1934. Theophilos lived the life of an itinerant eccentric, wandering the countryside dressed up as a soldier from the time of the War of Independence. He painted pictures for anyone who would give him food and shelter – frescos in the winter because it was colder, you worked inside, and they took longer.

RECOMMENDED RESTAURANTS

LITOHORO
Olympus, D; *main street; tel.* (0352) 82 178.

Among several inexpensive small restaurants along the main street, this one offers good standard fare at excellent prices; ideal if you want to stoke up for your ascent of Mount Olympos. The friendly young clientele includes many determined characters with rucksacks.

MOUNT PELIO REGION
This region is renowned for its distinctive cuisine, which features rich, hearty game stews. If you don't fancy rabbit, pigeon or goat, then you should stick to the dishes you recognize. Contrary to wine buff lore, in the hot season these casserole dishes are best eaten with a local cold white wine, which has enough bite to stand up to the herbs and spices.

MOUNT PELIO REGION – Aghios Ioannis Ostria, DD; *tel.* (0426) 31 331.

An exceptional spot, which boasts the most authentic cooking in Aghios Ioannis (their speciality is a superb local spinach dish), and outdoor dining in the garden, with views down to the sea.

MOUNT PELIO REGION – Portaria
Pakoulorizos, D-DD; *off* Platia.

The best food in town, with a menu specializing in a range of regional dishes.

PARNITHA MOUNTAINS
A popular destination for Athenians who want to get out of town and away from the dreaded Nephos for the weekend. Consequently you'll find plenty of roadside restaurants, particularly near the start of the most popular trails through the woods. A few have elaborate, wildly over-priced menus, but most are good inexpensive tavernas.

VOLOS
The best place for eating in Volos is along the waterfront, but when you get here you'll find that everyone else seems to have heard of this too.

Nautilia, D-DD; 1 Odos Argonauton.

Right by the harbour and just the place for watching all the action of the port over a drink and a plate of imaginative *meze*.

If you head east along the promenade until you come to **Anavros** district, you'll find the town beach, which has a number of quieter, more picturesque tavernas.

Central Mainland
Between Athens and Corfu
West from Athens: Delphi, Thebes and the Oedipus Crossroads
400 km; map Michelin 980, 1:700000

The longest tour in the book, this route takes you from Athens along the northern shores of the Gulf of Corinth, and then all the way up the mainland's west coast as far as Corfu.

Besides the direct route, there are a number of detour options, such as the one suggested from Preveza to the southern Ionian islands. The direct route can be driven in a couple of days, but it can also quite easily be extended into a fascinating two-week holiday, ending with a boat trip back to Athens. There is plenty of variety: sights of major importance; spectacular mountains; sleepy provincial towns and picturesque, remote ruins.

The ancient road from Athens to Thebes started at the Acropolis and led along the Sacred Way to Eleusis. Today, the modern E962 out of Athens still follows this historic route, though to begin with you will sense little historic about the urban sprawl of modern Athens beside the westward road along the upper reaches of the Saronic Gulf.

Assuming you are travelling from Athens westwards, you continue along the road that Oedipus trod, passing the haunting Oedipus Crossroads on your way to Delphi. Despite the large crowds which Delphi attracts, it would be a crime to miss out on this major attraction.

From here you continue west to Missolongi, where Byron died more than 150 years ago as he was about to lead the Greek Army of Independence against the Turks. After this you strike north, passing Arta, towards the port of Igoumenitsa, where you catch the ferry for the resort island of Corfu.

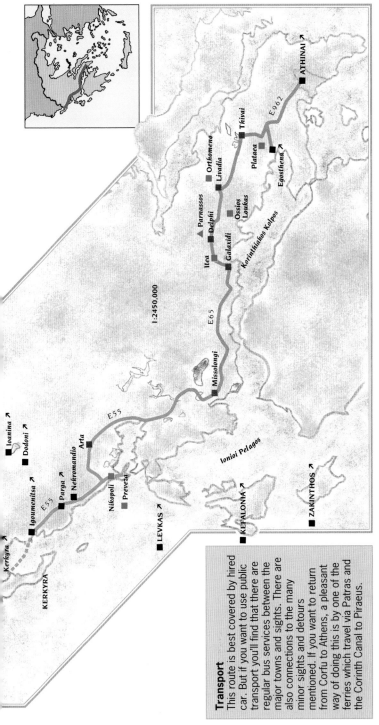

Transport

This route is best covered by hired car. But if you want to use public transport you'll find that there are regular bus services between the major towns and sights. There are also connections to the many minor sights and detours mentioned. If you want to return from Corfu to Athens, a pleasant way of doing this is by one of the ferries which travel via Patras and the Corinth Canal to Piraeus.

SIGHTS & PLACES OF INTEREST

ARTA 🏠

30 km inland from NW *coast, on the* E951 *100 km* N *of Patras.* This was the capital city of King Pyrrhus of Epirus, who ruled during the 3rdC BC and won the first Pyrrhic victory. ('Another victory like that, and I'm finished', he's reported to have said.)

Arta attracts few tourists, but you'll find it's a provincial town with a distinctive character, as well as a few things worth stopping off to see.

The ancient arched stone bridge here is said to be the oldest in Greece. It certainly has foundations which date back well over two thousand years. It also has a myth attached to it, which crops up about a number of old bridges all over Mediterranean Europe – a curious story, which has yet to find a wholly convincing explanation. According to the myth, the original builder of the bridge found that every morning when he woke up, all his previous day's building had been washed away by the current. He was at his wits' end, until one day he happened to listen to the advice of a passing bird, which told him that the only way he would be able to support the bridge properly would be to brick up his beautiful young wife in the supporting arch. This the builder duly did – and the bridge remained standing. But for ever afterwards, those who crossed the bridge at night would sometimes hear the ghostly voice of a woman crying out from below.

The town also has a fine 13thC church with no fewer than half a dozen domes. These domes are said to have been inspired by those of Santa Sophia in Constantinople. There are also the rather picturesque remains of a Byzantine castle.

ATHENS

See pages 174-191.

CORFU

See Local Explorations: 5.

DELPHI 🏠 ✕

13 km inland from N *coast of Gulf of Corinth, on* E962 *162 km* W *of Athens.* Delphi is one of the major sights of Greece – both in importance, and in revenue derived from the tourist trade. You have to see it, but if possible, try to see it out of season.

As usual, there is a legend about the origin of this historic spot. Zeus, wishing to discover the centre of the world, ingeniously dispatched two eagles from the opposite ends of the earth (which, being a god, he knew was flat). The two eagles duly flew towards each other, and collided over the centre of the world. They fell to earth at Delphi. A stone called the Omphalos still marks this spot, which was considered by the ancients to be the navel of the world.

The oracle here was dedicated to the cult of Apollo, who is said to have arrived in Greece from Crete on the back of a dolphin. The Greek word for dolphin is 'delphoi', and this is claimed as the origin of the name Delphi. Its setting is spectacular, beneath the crags of Mount Parnassos, looking down over a gorge covered with olive trees which leads down to the sea.

For more than a thousand years, this was the greatest oracle of Ancient Greece, consulted by poor peasants as well as major leaders from all over the ancient world. Such was the oracle's importance that in 6thC BC it became an autonomous state. Pilgrims would come from far and wide, making their way over the mountain tracks. They would bring an offering for sacrifice (often a sheep or a goat) and submit their question to the Pythian priestess. This wise old woman, elected by the priests, sat above the Omphalos wreathed in the steaming vapours which rose from the chasm of the oracle itself. The vapour would literally give the priestess an 'attack of the vapours' (the phrase is thought to originate from here) and in an ecstatic frenzy she would deliver the oracle's reply. As this reply was usually incoherent, it would be 'interpreted' by the priests, who would pass it on in verse form to the eager pilgrim.

The priests here were no fools, and gathered information from all over the ancient world to help them with their prophetic replies. This enabled them to give astute answers to the tricky political questions put to them by worried leaders. The answers tended to be enigmatic, often more like a riddle than a reply. Very seldom was the advice given by the oracle demonstrably wrong, and the oracle thus retained its reputation as the truest of all for many centuries.

There is a great deal to see at Delphi, and if you want to see it all you should allow at least a day. If you take the trouble to do this, it's also worth reading in detail about the history, function and remaining ruins of the oracle in a specialized guidebook devoted entirely to this subject. You'll find these on sale in both Delphi and Athens.

On a brief visit, be sure at least to see the **Sanctuary of Apollo**, the superb **Museum** (which contains the justly famous Charioteer of Delphi), the **Theatre** (which dates from 4thC BC and could seat 5,000 spectators), and the delightful **shrine of Tholos**.

The first time I came here I spent the

RECOMMENDED HOTELS

ARTA
Xenia Hotel, DD; Kastra; tel. (0655) 27 413.

Small hotel in superb setting inside the walls of the old castle. They only have a couple of dozen rooms here, so it's advisable to book. An ideal base for touring the region.

Besides the sights mentioned on the preceding pages, (see particularly Preveza entry), you're also within reach of Dodoni and Ioanina (see Greece Overall: 2). If the Xenia is full, try:

Anessis, DD-DDD; 7 Mitropolitou Xeno poulou; tel. (0655) 25 991.

Off the main tourist trail, this is travelling salesman's territory: pleasant, but nothing out of the ordinary.

DELPHI
Can be extremely crowded during the high season, so be sure to book.

Vouzas, DDD; I Pavlou and Frederikis Street; tel. (0265) 82 232.

Right by the site, with all the advantages and disadvantages that this implies. The bonus is the spectacular view over Pleistos Gorge. Just over 50 rooms, so essential to book.

Hotel Pan D-DD; 51 Pavlou and Frederikis Street; tel. (0265) 82 239.

On the same street as the Vouzas, above, by the bus station. A friendly welcome and big reductions out of season.

If both of these are full, your next stop should be the Tourist Office, 45 Apollonou Street, tel. (0265) 82 220. They are helpful. If this fails, as it may during July or August, try at neighbouring Itea or Galixidi – see below.

GALIXIDI
Pension Ganimede, DD; off Platia; tel. (0265) 41 328.

A real find, with a lovely courtyard garden and 'ethnic' decoration. Run by a Greek-Italian family.

ITEA
Hotel Galini, DD; Poseidon Street; tel. (0267) 32 278.

In the centre of town, not too far from the sea. Most rooms have bath or private shower.

LIVADIA
Livadia Hotel, DD; town centre; tel. (0261) 23 611.

Probably the most salubrious accommodation in town, though don't expect anything out of the ordinary.

MISSOLONGI
Theoximia, DD-DDD; pleasantly situated by the sea; tel. (0631) 28 098.

Large hotel with a range of amenities including tennis courts.

PREVEZA
Aktaeon, DD-DDD; I Kolovou; tel. (0682) 22 258. OK for a night.

If you prefer to stay outside town, try:

Margarona Royal, DD-DDD; 4 km from the town by the coast road; tel. (0682) 24 361.

Large resort hotel with 100 rooms; range of amenities includes pool and lively disco; good for families.

THEBES
Meletiou, D-DDD; Epaminon Street; tel. (0262) 27 333.

Small provincial hotel on one of the two main north-south streets. Most rooms have a shower or private bath.

night under the stars beneath the thin marble columns of Tholos, a night I shall never forget. Unfortunately, this is no longer possible – it's forbidden, and if it wasn't you'd probably find yourself lying in the midst of a night of a thousand guitars. The crowds at Delphi can be a real problem – but the sight itself more than makes up for this.

DODONI
See Greece Overall: 2.

EGOSTHENA
See Greece Overall: 7.

ELEUTHERA
East of the E962 from Athens, just over 20 km before Thebes. The ruined fortress here was originally built by the Athenians in 4thC BC. The remains are well preserved, particularly the northern walls and eight of the protecting towers.

GALAXIDI ⇌ ✕
31 km S of Delphi on th E65. In the 19thC this was one of the main shipping towns in Greece. Its population of 60,000 boasted no fewer than 60 shipping magnates (i.e., one in every hun-

• Mount Parnassos.

dred, though this figure reduces drastically in the tax returns of the period.) The present town has a harbour, a few nearby stony beaches, and a number of fine mansions dating from its time of prosperity.

The main thing to see here is the superb **Maritime Museum**, which may be tiny but contains a fascinating collection of nautical relics. Also, there's usually a line of laid-up shipping anchored out in the gulf. An absolute must for all nautical buffs, the place remains largely unspoilt by tourism.

IGOUMENITSA
See Greece Overall: 2.

IOANINA
See Greece Overall: 2.

ITEA
On the coast S of Delphi. A small resort, useful as a back-up if accommodation at Delphi is full. Don't expect much of the beach. See Recommended Hotels, page 93.

• Sanctuary of Athena, Delphi.

LIVADIA ⌂

113 km W of Athens on the E962, 46 km from Delphi. A small provincial town whose main business is the milling of cotton. It is located at the edge of the Erkinas Gorge, once thought to be the entrance to the Underworld. A walk up this gorge brings you to the **Springs of Remembrance and Forgetfulness**. The Spring of Mnemosyne (Remembrance) has some niches carved into the cliff where votive offerings used to be placed in classical times, and one larger one where the local pasha used to smoke his hookah during the Turkish occupation.

Nearby is the Spring of Lethe (Forgetfulness): people who bathed in the waters of this spring were granted release from past memories. These two curiously touching functions reveal how little the contradictory needs of the human psyche have changed in the past 3,000 years.

MISSOLONGI ⌂

At the northern entrance to the Gulf of Corinth on the E951 42 km NW of Patras. Missolongi is just as dire a place today as it was when Byron died here in 1824. It is usually hot and muggy, due to the nearby lagoon and marshes, the happy breeding ground of a particularly virulent species of local mosquito. Even so, anyone interested in the history of modern Greece should stop a while here.

Byron's involvement in the Greek struggle for independence is typical of the blend of high farce and genuine nobility which characterized so much of the Romantic Movement. Lord Byron, the club-footed British aristocrat whose libertine behaviour and romantic poetry had stirred the female hearts (and male jealousies) of European society, arrived in Missolongi in January 1824. Here, despite his total lack of military experince, he took charge of the Greek army fighting for independence from the Turks.

Byron arrived with a complete wardrobe of six expertly tailored 'Classical Greek' uniforms (and assorted 'Hellenic' helmets) designed by himself for his dashing role in the coming campaign, and was welcomed ashore with a 21-gun salute. But the 5,000 soldiers who greeted him turned out to consist of a largely brigand army which was riven with factions and internecine rivalries.

Byron brought with him to Missolongi several trunks filled with cash raised by well-wishers for the cause of Greek liberty. These were largely European philhellenes, whose classical education led them to believe that they were helping an army of clean-living Spartans and noble Athenians, rather than the bunch of whiskered desperadoes whom Byron encountered.

Byron did his best to unite the Greek forces, allocating cash as prudently as he could amongst the warring Greek factions. Sometimes he almost despaired, yet he couldn't help but deeply admire the simple bravery of these men who had rallied to the cause of their nation's freedom. They may not

BYRON'S RETURN FROM MISSOLONGI

Byron caught a fever and died in Missolongi on 19th April 1824. His heart was removed from his body and is now buried in Missolongi beneath his statue. Much as Byron would probably have wished it, his body was then embalmed in a barrel containing 180 gallons of alcohol.

Barrel and contents were then loaded on to a sloop, which was given a 31-gun salute as it left the harbour bound for the nearby island of Zakinthos. Eventually, Byron's body (heartless in death as it had been in life, according to one commentator) was transported to London on board the British brigantine *Florida*.

But it was still only just over a decade since Byron had been ostracized from London society and forced into exile on account of his scandalous behaviour. Despite his acclaim all over Europe, Byron still wasn't forgiven for his social misdemeanours at home, and any suggestion that he should be buried at Poet's Corner in Westminster Abbey was rejected. Not until 1969 was a plaque finally erected to his memory in this hallowed spot commemorating Britain's finest poets.

have looked like the heroes of Thermopylae and Marathon (though they probably looked a lot more like them than the philhellenes and classics professors of Europe imagined), but there was no doubting their commitment and courage.

Unfortunately, Byron was to catch a fever while out hunting one day, and it soon became obvious that he would not survive. As he lay on his deathbed, even Byron recognized that perhaps his greatest contribution to the cause of Greek liberty would be his death. And so it was to be. Byron's death made headlines all over Europe, rallying both governments and Romantic artists to the cause of Greek liberty. When Missolongi fell to Turkish beseigers in 1826, the press throughout Europe raised a storm – which eventually resulted in the French and British navies destroying the Turkish fleet off Navarino, the event which turned the tide in the struggle for Greek independence.

Nowadays, O Lordos Vironos (The Lord Byron) is part of the pantheon of Greek heroes, and you can see an Odos Vironos (Byron Street) in towns throughout the land.

In Missolongi you can visit the Garden of Heroes, which contains the bodies of the Greeks who died defending the city against the final Turkish assault. Here there is also a statue of Byron, placed on the very spot where his heart is buried. The house where Byron lived (and died) was destroyed during the Second World War, and its site is now occupied by a rather tired-looking memorial garden.

MOUNT PARNASSOS
Inland from N coast of Gulf of Corinth, N of Delphi. This large mountain has two peaks, the highest of which rises to 2,457 m. This is called Lykeri (Wolf Peak) and may account for the persistent rumour that there are still wolves on the mountain (while others claim that these beasts became extinct in Europe more than 40 years ago).

Parts of the mountain remain very remote and inaccessible. A party of Greek communist resistance fighters from the civil war is said to have held out here into the 1950s.

In ancient times, this was the home of Apollo and the Muses. It thus became sacred to the poets of ancient Rome, and to this day remains a poetic cliché.

The peak is snow-covered for much of the year, and during winter becomes a popular skiing area. It's possible to climb to the top of the mountain during the height of summer. If you drive up beyond the ski resort, you can get within an hour's walk of the summit, which has one of the most fabulous views in Greece. On a clear day you can see as far as Mount Athos in the north, south to the Peleponnese, and east to the islands of the Aegean. People who have seen this at dawn often never recover from the urge to describe the scene over and over again. Unfortunately, or perhaps fortunately, the peak is more often than not shrouded in cloud.

NEKROMANDIO
See Greece Overall: 4.

NIKOPOLI
5 km N of Preveza on the NW coast.
This was intended to be a great city, but it never really caught on. It was founded in the 1stC BC as a 'victory city' by Octavius, to mark his victory at the Battle of Actium. At this great sea battle, fought off the nearby coast in 31 BC, Octavius defeated Antony and Cleopatra, and thus secured himself as sole ruler of the Roman Empire in succession to Julius Caesar.

Nikopoli was built out of bits and pieces from a number of nearby ruins. Water had to be brought in from the nearby Louros River by aquaduct, and the population was conscripted from neighbouring regions.

But when the Romans left, so did almost everyone else. Consequently, the ruins are still quite impressive.

OEDIPUS CROSSROADS
24 km W of Livadia. This is the crossroads where the ancient road from Thebes to Delphi meets the road from Daulis (modern Davlis) to Ambrossos (modern Distomo). The ancient road used to run further down in the gorge than the present road. At the ancient crossroads, Oedipus had a fateful meeting with a stranger. They quarrelled, and Oedipus killed the stranger – not realizing that this was his father King Laius of Thebes, and that he was

97

thus fulfilling the first part of the prophecy that he would kill his father and marry his mother. See Thebes, page 100.

The crossroads itself is at a particularly desolate spot. Years ago, when I first arrived here alone on foot as the afternoon light was fading, I found myself experiencing an eerie feeling of horror and menace which I imagined was induced by my little classical learning and an over-active imagination. (The fact that Sophocles sets the murder here in his drama is hardly a historical confirmation of what is largely myth anyway.) Later I was given a lift by the driver of a lorry full of water melons, who was not in the least surprised

• *Off the coast of Missolongi.*

by my weird experience. He said that it was quite common, and had nothing to do with Oedipus. According to him, this chilling spot was haunted by the villagers of Distomo just over the hill, who had all been massacred in a Nazi reprisal during The Second World War.

ORTHOMENO

14 *km* NE *of Livadia.* These ruins are all that remains of what was once the wealthiest city in Greece. In pre-historic times it was the capital of the Minyans, a people whose origins are uncertain. They inhabited Thessaly and Boetia in the early second millenium BC, and

may possibly have come from Ancient Egypt. Indeed, the city was so wealthy that it was specifically compared by Homer to Thebes in Egypt.

Orthomenos remained a power throughout the Mycenaean era, and probably thrived until the time of Alexander the Great.

The main sites include a fine ancient **theatre** and the so-called **Treasury of Minyas**, which is in fact a large Mycenaean tomb. Nearby is the Byzantine **Church of the Dormition**, which dates from the 9thC. Interestingly, this is completely constructed out of column drums and pieces of stone salvaged (or pillaged, depending upon your point of view) from the surrounding ruins.

OSSIOS LOUKAS

Inland from N coast of Gulf of Corinth, off the E962 36 km SE of Delphi. This is one of the finest Byzantine monasteries in the country, and its splendour is only increased by the austere remoteness of its setting 500 m above sea level in the mountains. The slopes nearby are covered with olive groves, and in the distance you can see the peaks of the Elikonas Mountains, which rise to nearly 1,750 m.

The monastery is still a going concern, complete with a small community of Orthodox monks, so suitable clothing is required for a visit. (Calf-length skirts, long trousers, covered arms.)

The monastery was founded by the hermit Luke the Styriot, who was probably born in Delphi of a Lesbian family (from the island of Lesbos). Luke died here in 953, whereupon a sacred tree sprung up through the floor of his monastic cell. As a result of Luke's great healing powers and his ability to foretell the future, the hermit's tomb became an object of pilgrimage and the monastery is named after him.

Ossios Loukas (Holy Luke's Church) dates from the 11thC and contains some superb mosaics depicting various biblical scenes. Four hundred years ago, the monastery was badly damaged by a succession of earthquakes, but was later restored.

This is a particularly striking and evocative spot, and well worth the 12-km detour. Signposted south from the main road 20 km W from Livadia.

• *Livadia.*

PARGA

See Greece Overall: 4.

PLATAEA

Four km W of Erithes, off the main E962 road from Athens to Thebes. There are extensive ruins here of the ancient city which in 490 BC sided with Athens in an attempt to break free from the domination of nearby Thebes. Heroically, the city despatched its whole army of just 1,000 men to fight alongside the Athenians at Marathon. Owing to Plataea's unfortunate geographical position between Athens and Thebes, it was razed to the ground on several occasions during classical times.

Nearby is the site of the Battle of Plataea, which took place in 479 BC, when the combined Greek force finally managed to defeat the Persian invaders, despite being outnumbered three to one. (For the best description of this battle see Herodotus Book 9.) The battle marked the end of Persian attempts to conquer Greece and turn it into an Asiatic colony.

PREVEZA 🏨

On the NW coast, 96 km S of Igoumenitsa. This is really rather an ordinary spot, just a small town at the entrance to the

99

Amvrakic Gulf. However, it makes a useful base for visiting a number of nearby attractions. Nikopoli (see page 97) is just a few kilometres north of here, Nekromandio (see page 73) is only 35 km further on, and Arta (page 92) is just across the gulf. You're also within easy distance of Levkas (page 71).

From here you can also begin a pleasant mini-tour of the southern Ionian islands of Ithaka, Kefalonia and Zakinthos, all described on pages 68, 69, 76.

THEBES ⌁
On the E962, 69 km NW of Athens. Thebes has a rich mythological past, but not all that much to show for it nowadays.

The city was founded by Cadmos, the son of the King of Phoenicia and a grandson of Poseidon the sea god. Zeus happened to abduct Cadmos' sister, and Cadmos went looking for her.

RECOMMENDED RESTAURANTS

DELPHI
Delphi is very much a tourist spot, and this reflects in the restaurants. Don't expect charmingly relaxed service and a menu with a long list of authentic local delicacies. This said, the best restaurants are those overlooking the gorge, with views down towards the distant sea. The most dependable of these tend to be the ones attached to hotels.

Try the restaurant belonging to Vouzas (see Recommended Hotels, page 93), which serves standard fare at moderate prices; a memorable view.

Otherwise a safe bet is Grigori's, which has a fine simple menu, served by affable express waiters in the open air.

GALAXIDI
Restaurant Alekos, D-DD; *on the sea front, at the junction with the main street.*

Popular local spot with range of standard pan-Hellenic fare and a friendly atmosphere. Just by where the main street reaches the sea.

But when he consulted the Delphic oracle on the matter, he was told to forget about his sister and instead follow a magical cow. On the spot where the cow sat down, he was to found a city. Astonishingly, this is just what Cadmos did. When the cow sat down, he founded Thebes. (Which was all for the best, as Cadmos's sister Europa was quite happy with Zeus and in the end they had three children together.)

During the legendary era, Thebes was for a time the home of such celebrated figures as Dionysios, Heracles (Hercules) and Tiresias. Dionysios was born out of Zeus' thigh, raised by nymphs, and started a cult for drunken orgies. Heracles stalked a huge lion for 50 days, slew it with his massive club, and was rewarded by the grateful King Thespius with all his 50 daughters (hence the term Herculean strength.) Tiresias was a blind prophet who is said to have possessed both male and female physical attributes.

But these characters pale into insignificance compared with Thebes' most famous son Oedipus, whose story is said to cause such deep psychological stirrings in us all.

One day Oedipus' father Laius, the King of Thebes, visited the Delphic oracle where he received some unsettling news. He was told that he would be killed by his son, who would then marry his mother, Laius's widow. In order to put a stop to this, Laius abandoned baby Oedipus on a mountainside, with his feet firmly nailed together just in case he should try and crawl away over the mountain tops.

However, a wandering shepherd came across Oedipus and took pity on him. The shepherd ended up by giving Oedipus to the King and Queen of Corinth, who brought him up as their own son.

When Oedipus grew up, he learned about the prophecy that he would kill his father and marry his mother. Believing that the King and Queen of Corinth were his true parents, he left town at once.

By one of those coincidences which make myths what they are, Oedipus happened to encounter Laius at a crossroads on the way to Thebes (see Oedipus Crossroads, page 97). After an argument, he killed Laius, and unaware of the identity of his victim,

• *Thebes.*

Oedipus then continued to Thebes. As a reward for solving a riddle posed to travellers by the monstrous Sphinx (it killed those who failed to give the correct answer), he won the hand in marriage of the Queen, Jocasta, his mother. When Oedipus discovered what he had done, he blinded himself. Jocasta hanged herself. Though Greek tragedies begin in the legendary 'once upon a time', they always end up realistically enough with nobody living 'happily ever after'. This myth, and later disasters to the House of Thebes which flowed from the original debacle, formed the basis for the plots of several of the great Greek tragedies written several centuries later.

Thebes was to become one of the leading city-states during classical times. Briefly during the 4thC BC, the famous 'seven-gated city' was the most powerful in the land, but for much of its history it suffered from its rivalry with neighbouring Athens. Though Thebes never matched Athens in cultural standing, it made a number of essential contributions to Greek civilization. It was here that the Greek alphabet was invented; the great poet Pindar was born in Thebes; and it was the Theban army which first introduced the phalanx into military tactics. (At the time, Philip of Macedon was a hostage here, and pinched the technique, passing it on to his son Alexander the Great, who used it to conquer practically all of the known world – more than can be said of modern military aids, including nuclear weapons.)

During the centuries since the classical era, Thebes was ruled by the usual succession of Franks from Champagne, Normans from Sicily, Lombards from Italy, Turks and so forth. It has now ended up as a rather sleepy provincial town of just under 20,000 inhabitants. Practically nothing of the early Mycenaean settlement and the later classical city remains, apart from the **Kadmeion excavations** and the exhibits in the **Museum**. The Kadmeion excavations are on the site of the palace of the city's founder Cadmos (and quite possibly the site where the original magical cow sat down). The excavations have revealed some spectacular finds, but most of the palace remains inaccessibly buried beneath the modern city. The Museum contains exhibits ranging through most periods of the city's history, including parts of a mural from Cadmos' palace, some fascinating examples of the early Greek alphabet, and a number of marble torsos.

The other sites around the city are really only of interest to historians with a detailed knowledge of early Theban history.

Peleponnese

Between Athens and Olympia
The Northern Peleponnese

260 km; map Michelin 980, 1:700000

This route explores the northern Peleponnese, along the shores of the Gulf of Corinth. At one end is Athens, and at the other the site of the original Olympic Games. It offers some spectacularly situated ancient ruins and castles. You can travel on a unique narrow-gauge railway up a gorge into the mountains, visit a remote monastery with an icon said to have been painted by St Luke, and stop to swim and laze at some inviting beaches on the way. The entire trip is 260 km, but it is best to allow four or five days if you want to do justice to the many sights.

Assuming you start from Athens, head for Corinth on the E94. From here drive west along the road to Patras. If you have time, be sure to take the minor coast road – rather than the main E65. It has the best views out over the Gulf of Corinth and passes through some appealing towns. At Patras take the E55 for Pirgos. This leads you around the north-western shoulder of the Peleponnese. At Pirgos you take the road inland for Arhea Olympia.

At Olympia you can link up with Local Explorations: 3. Alternatively, if you want to get back to Athens by a different route from the one you came by, try the road east from Arhea Olympia, through the mountains of Arcadia to Tripoli. This is a particularly beautiful route. At Tripoli you can either take the motorway back to Athens, or cover the early stages of Greece Overall: 8.

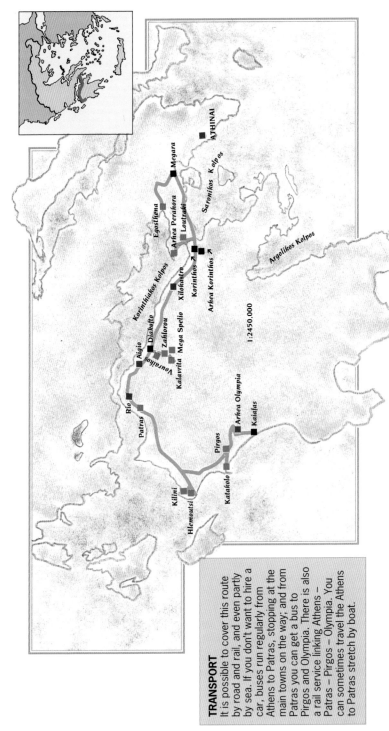

TRANSPORT

It is possible to cover this route by road and rail, and even partly by sea. If you don't want to hire a car, buses run regularly from Athens to Patras, stopping at the main towns on the way; and from Patras you can get a bus to Pirgos and Olympia. There is also a rail service linking Athens – Patras – Pirgos – Olympia. You can sometimes travel the Athens to Patras stretch by boat.

SIGHTS & PLACES OF INTEREST

AIGIO ⚓

34 km E of Patras. This small port on the southern shore of the Gulf of Corinth. is where the cross-gulf ferry from Aghios Nikolaos puts in. Aigio earns its name from that of a local goat, which is said to have suckled Zeus in his infancy: this early diet may well account for some of this god's rather dyspeptic and goatish episodes later in life. Although there has almost certainly been a settlement here since early Neolithic times, not much of interest appears to have taken place over the past 4,000 years. And it shows. However, this is a useful accommodation base and there is an attractive sandy beach at Rhodhodhafni, less than 1 km further west.

ARHEA (ANCIENT) PERAHORA

To get here take the coast road N from Loutraki, along the hillside towards the Cape, passing through the modern village of Perahora on the way. For the energetic and daring, this can be reached by a three-hour walk along the cliff path from Loutraki. At the end, keep to the south side of Lake Vouliagmeni. This delightful lake is almost a lagoon – you have to swim across the narrow channel connecting it to the sea, so be prepared.

At the end of the lake you will find some tavernas and a place to swim. Incidentally, the old cistern here is said to date from the 4thC BC, and to have been in continuous use ever since.

The main attraction of Ancient Perahora is its setting. It overlooks the final neck of the Gulf of Corinth (150 km to the west is the open sea) and the view of the coast, mountains and sea is superb, especially at sunset. The promontory has several ruins, including two sanctuaries, and for snorkellers, there is also submerged masonry from the ancient port. The locals will warn you not to swim out beyond the cove, where the currents are dangerous. If you show signs of disbelief, they may tell you the local shark story, which will probably put you off swimming altogether.

ARHEA (ANCIENT) OLYMPIA ⚓ ✕

Seventeen km E of Pirgos. This was where the original Olympic Games were held, for more than a thousand years. The experts believe the games probably started around 11thC BC and according to one legend they were initiated by Hercules, who perhaps regarded his earlier Labours as mere training exercises. These local games soon evolved into a massive event held every four years, attracting competitors from all over the Hellenic world, which at the time included Asia Minor and southern Italy. When the games were in progress a 'sacred truce' was declared throughout the entire region, to enable the competitors to travel in safety.

Athletics and wrestling events were held in the **Stadium**, whose start and finish lines are still visible amongst the ruins. Early events were often fairly violent. Wrestlers were sometimes killed in combat, or returned home dismembered. (However, no biting was allowed.) Yet the only prizes for winning

---

DETOUR – KALAVRITA ⚓

This is the beautiful small town at the head of the **Vouraikos Gorge** (see the separate entry, page 105), and the terminus of the narrow-gauge railway, which runs up the gorge.

Kalavrita is something of a historic centre for the Greeks. The Monastery of Ayia Lavra, 6 km from here, is where the Archbishop of Patras raised the Greek flag on March 21, 1821, signalling the start of the successful War of Independence against the Turks.

More recent local history is less heroic. On December 13, 1943, the occupying Germans executed all 1,436 male inhabitants of the town in reprisal for partisan activities. The church clock still stands at 2.34, the exact time of the killings. As a result, the town has dedicated itself 'to fight for world peace'. Since 1962 the schools here have been endowed with a grant from the German government.

Kalavrita can also be reached by the picturesque road which winds up from the coast just east of Trapeza.

were a palm and an olive wreath. Inevitably the games produced their heroes. The greatest of all was Milo of Croton, who won the wrestling event six times, which means he must have defeated all comers over a period of 20 years. In his prime, Milo was said to be able to outrun a racing horse.

By the fourth century the original Olympic spirit had declined. Professionals were now entered, with the aim of bringing prestige to their city. They were accompanied to the games by packs of rowdy partisan supporters – such classic behaviour dies hard, it seems.

In late Roman times the games degenerated into a farce. When Emperor Nero attended, he insisted there should be competitions for singing and lyre playing, so that he could enter. Predictably, Nero was judged winner of no less than seven events – including the chariot race, despite the fact that he fell off his chariot and was unable to make it to the finish.

When visiting this site, be sure to see the **Temple of Zeus**. It was once as large as the Parthenon in Athens, and contained the celebrated Olympian statue of Zeus. This was over 12 m high and one of the 'Seven Wonders of the World'. Like all the others except the Pyramids, no trace of this remains, except for a few tantalizing pieces of the pedestal.

(Guide books are on sale at the site for those wishing for more Olympic lore.)

CORINTH AND ARHEA KORINTHOS (ANCIENT CORINTH)

See Greece Overall:8.

EGOSTHENA

13 km W of the E962, Athens-Delphi road, at E end of the Gulf of Corinth. This out-of-the-way site was never of any great

---

DETOUR – **VOURAIKOS GORGE** ⊨ ✕

This spectacular gorge plunges from Kalavrita in the northern central Peleponnese, down to the coast of the Gulf of Corinth at Diakofto (see Recommended Hotels, page 108). It is almost as breathtaking as the famous Samaria Gorge in Crete, but nowhere near as crowded. The big bonus here is that you don't have to hike anywhere to see it. There is an excellent small railway which runs the entire length.

The 20-km **narrow-gauge railway** was built by the Italians in 1895 as part of a mineral mining venture, and is an impressive feat of engineering. En route there are tunnels, sheer drops, high cliffs and narrow canyons. After an hour's journey you come to the railway station for the hamlet of **Zahlorou**, where you can eat at one of the local tavernas, or even stay at the hotel, see page 109.

From here you can go by mule on a 45-minute climb to the **Mega Speleo Monastery**. It sits in a breathtaking setting by a cave beneath a sheer cliff. Mega Speleo means large cave.

The original monastery on this site was said to be the oldest in Greece. Unfortunately the last trace of it was destroyed in 1934 when a long forgotten, 100-year-old powder keg exploded.

The modern monastery has a hostel where men only can stay overnight. There is a great view of the gorge, which is said to be spell-binding at dawn. If you are interested in ancient icons, the monastery has some of the finest you will see outside the major museums. They include the usual 'miracle-working' icon – a murky blackened image of the Virgin Mary, allegedly painted by Saint Luke. Its style is said to be unlike that of any other icon, thus apparently confirming its authenticity. It seems rather churlish to dismiss this as an obvious fabrication: however, the alternative is sensational. If it is genuine, this is a portrait of the Virgin Mary by someone who actually saw her.

Suitable dress is required for visits to the monastery. For those who have forgotten what this is: long sleeves, and long trousers or skirts, are essential if you wish to avoid disappointment at the end of the long, hot hike.

From Zahlorou, the railway continues up the gorge for another half an hour to **Kalavrita** (see page 104).

historical importance. Perhaps for this reason, it is one of the best preserved ancient forts in the land. Experts rate it a perfect example of late 4thC BC military architecture. Even if you are no expert, it is still an evocative sight, with its remnant walls built of huge blocks of stone, and its towering turrets. As you stroll around you get a real sense of what it must have been like in its time.

HLEMOUTSI

At the end of the westernmost peninsula of the Peleponnese. This hexagonal Frankish castle was built in 1220 by William de Villehardouin, the man from Champagne who put Mystra on the map (see page 115). Try a walk along the ramparts for a view out over the sea. You can usually see two, and sometimes three, of the Ionian islands in the distance.

KATAKOLO 🛏

Several choices of places to stay here. See Recommended Hotels, page 108.

KILINI 🛏 ✕

A useful ferry port for the southernmost Ionian Islands, Zakinthos and Kefalonia.

LOUTRAKI 🛏

10 km N of Corinth. The springs here produce the most famous water in Greece. Until recently the place was a typical sleepy spa town, with faded architectural grandeur to match. Then in 1981 came the Corinth earthquake. Loutraki was at the epicentre, and the place collapsed like a pack of cards. Since then it has been rebuilt in more 'modern' style. Even so, the place retains a distinct charm of its own – with its palm tree-lined promenade, the views of the Gulf of Corinth, the luxury hotels, the public gardens smelling of oleander blossom, the little harbour, and behind it all the rising mountains. One disappointment: the beach is rather stony.

As for the famous water, it bubbles out warm, is said to be highly curative, and is officially described as radioactive.

• *Taverna, Patras.*

• *Loutraki.*

PATRAS 🛏 ✕

NW Peleponnese, at entrance to Gulf of Corinth. Patras is the only real city in the Peleponnese, and the second most important port in Greece (after Piraeus). And that's about it. If you arrive here off the ferry from Italy, keep going – there's plenty to see, and it's all out there beyond the city limits.

If you have to stay in Patras – which is uncharacteristically rather ordinary and an unfair introduction to Greece – there are two things worth seeing. The local **Cathedral of St Andrew** is the largest of its kind in the land. It is said to have been built on the site of St Andrew's crucifixion, which took place on an X-shaped cross (hence the diagonal white cross on his flag, adopted by Scotland). After St Andrew's death, his devotees would place an X at the end of their letters in memory of his death, and kiss it. This is said to be the origin of putting an X at the end of a letter as a kiss.

The other site worth visiting is the **Achaia Clauss winery**, 7 km southeast of town. Their wine label is the one seen in every Greek restaurant from Birmingham to Berlin. After the obligatory tour you get a free drink of their famous Mavrodhafni, a sticky dark wine, said to be named after the girl

107

with whom the original Clauss fell in love.

If you want a swim, the best beaches near Patras are at **Rio**, 6 km northeast along the coast. They are pleasantly sandy.

PIRGOS 🛏

Eastern central Peleponnese, 13 km inland from the coast, 96 km S of Patras. This nondescript market town is a centre for the currant trade. It even has an institution where you can study this wizened

fruit. If you are stuck for the night, head 12 km west to the attractive little port of Katakolo, which has nearby beaches and a fascinating harbour – if, like me, you are are interested in rusting old hulks.

XILOKASTRO

42 km W of Corinth. This popular seaside resort on the southern shores of the Gulf of Corinth has beaches, and an impressive mountain backdrop. Mt Ziria, at 7,860 m, is the second high-

---

RECOMMENDED HOTELS

AIGIO
Hotel Galini, DD-DDD; *town centre*; *tel. 0691 26 150*.

At the town centre, you'll see its large sign. A medium-sized hotel with 30 rooms (most with private shower or bath). Friendly staff, some of whom speak English and German.

DIAKOFTO
Helmos, D; *main road*; *tel. 0691 41 236*.

Rather spartan, undistinguished rooms. But you get a friendly welcome, and they will give you information about the railway.

KALAVRITA
Hotel Paradissos, D-DD; *Kalimani Street*; *tel. 0692 22 210*.

Friendly spot, which attracts an interesting clientele. A former, occasional, long-term resident Canadian claimed to have been the world checkers (draughts) champion. He said he came here 'to study his game and perfect his moves in preparation for the big season.'

KATAKOLO
There are several hotels here, but ask for a room in one of the chalets at the top of the steps. In spring some of these are surrounded by a blaze of blossom. If you want a hotel, try:

Delfini, D; *tel. 0621 41 214*.

Sunset addicts and helio-romantics should try a late-afternoon stroll from here along the headland to the lighthouse.

Glaretzas, DD; *Glaretzas Street*; *tel. 0623 92 397*.

Modern decoration, with private shower or bath in most rooms. Not too far from the beach and the main night-time action (such as there is).

LOUTRAKI
Pappas, DD; *Pefkaki Beach*; *tel. 0741 43 936*.

Large spa-style hotel, frequented mainly by Greek families who appear to be uninterested in the famous waters. For all this, it is a friendly, fairly lively spot. If this is full try:

Brettania, DD; *28 Yiorgos Lekka Street*; *tel. 0741 42 349*.

OLYMPIA
There are many hotels, of all classes, at Olympia. During the tourist season they tend to be block booked by package tours and coach groups. Sometimes, at the height of the season, there is, literally, not a room to be had. This leaves the local campsites as your only choice. The best is Camping Diana, which is well signposted from the main Kondhili road. So if you plan staying the night at Olympia be sure to ring in advance. Also, be warned that the place closes out of season – from the end of October to just before Easter. An exception to this winter closing is:

Europa Hotel, DDD; *by the site*; *tel. 0624 22 650*.

Generally considered the best hotel in town. All kinds of sporting facilities, including a private pool. If you need the sea, head for nearby Katakolo, see page 107 and Pirgos, above.

est peak in the Peleponnese. (They say you can climb it from here in three to four hours.) The beach can get crowded at weekends with families from Corinthos.

Those interested in Greek poetry may want to ask for the Sikelianos Villa, now a museum devoted to the memory of the great Greek poet Sikelianos who died in 1951.

Hotel Alexandros, D; 5 S*piliopoulou* Street; *tel.* 0624 22 549.

This is at the bronze medal end of the Olympic market.

The Olympic Village, DD-DDD; *tel.* 0624 22 211.

Ideal for who wish to impress their athletic friends or would like a story to embellish upon for the grandchildren.

PATRAS
Astis, DDD; 16 A*giou Andreou; in the street that runs parallel to the harbour and the seafront, one block inland; tel.* 061 27 5021.

The most outstanding hotel in town, with its own roof garden and private pool – a real bonus in hot, sticky Patras.

Hellas, D-DD; 14 A*giou Nikolaou; central situation near the start of the street that leads from the waterfront to the Acropolis; tel.* 061 273 352.

An easy-going hotel based in an historic building. Inside this shell, the rooms are pleasant enough.

PIRGOS
Pantheon, DD-DDD; 7 T*hemistokleous* Street; *tel.* 0621 29 747.

Reasonable for the price. Better choices in Katakolo, 12 km down the road.

ZAHLOROU
Romantzo, D; *by the station.*

A wonderful small hotel in one of the most 'romantzo' spots you are likely to find.

RECOMMENDED RESTAURANTS

KILINI
Sou-Sou, D; *at the beach.*

Unpretentious seaside spot with lively young clientele. Renowned for its moderately priced seafood.

OLYMPIA
Olympia has a large range of restaurants and souvlaki joints. Owing to the nature of the place these are exclusively for tourists, so don't expect special or authentic cuisine. For a reasonable meal, try:

Pritanio, D-DD; K*aramani* Street.

Pleasant tourist taverna, with typical examples of the species on migration from almost all European countries.

PATRAS
Eating out in Patras is a disappointment. Mediocrity (at all price ranges) and fast food are the hall marks of the place. If you don't mind mediocre food, so long as there's a view, try one of the tavernas along the waterfront. Just beyond the hazy shore across the water lies Missolongi, where Byron died waiting to lead the Greek army against the Turks in the War of Independence.

Evangelatos, DD; 7 A*ghiou Nikolaou.*

The fish here can be the best in town, if the chef is in the mood. Ask your waiter – one of them, at least, is quite frank about best dishes of the day.

If you have to wait here for a boat, or a bus, you could do worse than have a snack at the Europa Centre, the ticket and information centre on the waterfront just south of Karolou St. The bar-restaurant here is reasonably priced and quite serviceable.

ZAHLOROU
Messinia, D-DD; *in the village street.*

Pleasant, friendly restaurant in this idyllic spot, within sight of the most enchanting railway station in Greece.

Peleponnese

Between Athens and Sparta
Central Peleponnese

Up to 250 km; map Michelin 980, 1:700000

This route explores the north-eastern and central Peleponnese, taking in Sparta, the city which was the main rival of Athens in Classical times, and its bitter opponent in the Peleponnese War of the 5thC BC.

On your way you'll see some superb sites, dating from each of Greece's historic eras – Mycenean, Classical (both Greek and Roman), and Byzantine. At the Athens end of the route there are some fine coastal views; at the other you are in the heart of the mountains. Allow at least four days if you want to explore all the blue and green detours, and the ancient sites, properly.

If you start from Athens, the straggling suburbs west along the coast road are hardly encouraging. But from Megara onwards you are treated to extensive views of the shoreline, stretching right out into the Saronic Gulf. On a clear day you can see easily as far as the island of Aegina. You then cross the Corinth Canal, one of the engineering wonders of the 19thC, and enter the Peleponnese.

At this point you can take a detour to the great theatre at Epidavros. Here they still put on performances of Ancient Greek tragedy, just as it was staged over 2,000 years ago.

Back on the main (red) route, your first stop is Arhea Corinthos. These are the ruins of the only Ancient Greek city state to rival Athens in history and civilization. About 30 km on down the road you come to the site of an earlier civilization – Mycenae – once the home of Agamemnon and other Homeric heroes (see page 34). Continuing south you pass other Mycenaean cities at Argos and Tirintha, until you arrive at the charming town of Nafplio, the capital of Greece just over a century ago.

From here you head west to Tripoli, the capital of the evocatively named province of Arcadia. Then begins the 50-km stretch south to Sparta on the E961. The second half of this stretch has some dramatic views of the wild and mountainous Peleponnesian hinterland. Finally, once at Sparta, you can take a side trip to the fabled Byzantine city of Mystra. It is worth making an effort to see this one – it's the most spectacular site of its kind in Greece.

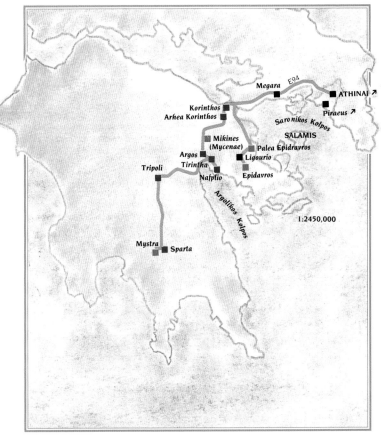

TRANSPORT
This route can easily be covered
by public transport or hired car.
Buses run regularly from Athens to
Corinth, and then on into the
Peleponnese, with connections for
Nafplio, Tripoli and Sparta. A
railway also runs from Athens to
Corinth, with connections for
Argos and Tripoli.

SIGHTS & PLACES OF INTEREST

ARGOS

54 km S of Corinth on the road to Nafplio.
Once a major Mycenaean city, though the present ruins date mainly from Classical times. Be sure to visit the **Theatre**: it is larger than the more celebrated one at Epidavros.

Argos is said to have been founded by an Ancient Egyptian called Danaos, and to be the oldest continuously inhabited town in Europe. However, this claim is duplicated by at least three other places I know of in Greece.

ARHEA CORINTHOS 🚩 ✕

7 kms SW of Corinth. Nowadays, Arhea (ancient) Corinth is a vast mass of ruins. From earliest times, Corinth's position – guarding the isthmus to the Peleponnese – gave it great strategic power. In Ancient Greece, for many years it was second only in importance to Athens. In Roman times the city became a religious centre and a popular home for retired soldiers from the Roman legions. This seems a curious combination, until you discover that the religion concerned was the worship of Venus (the goddess of love). Her temple on the Acropolis (now occupied by the ruins of Acrocorinth) employed over a thousand sacred prostitutes whose original role was to 'cleanse' soldiers after battle.

When St Paul arrived at the city in AD 54 he was horrified, and immediately set about trying to convert the avidly religious old soldiers to the more restrained ways of Christianity. Riots ensued, and St Paul had to make do with merely writing an angry letter, which achieved Biblical immortality as the *Epistle to the Corinthians.*

Allow at least a day for this site. Highlights include **The Roman Town**, whose layout is clear when viewed from the modern road above. It has a

RECOMMENDED HOTELS

ACROCORINTH

If you're feeling adventurous, and don't mind the long climb up to Acrocorinth, ask at the café there for an overnight room. They only have three rooms, so be sure to ask early in the day. The accommodation isn't exactly palatial, but the setting is what counts here – a night to remember amongst the ruins.

Hotel Belle-vue, DD; *Dimaskinou Street; tel.* 0741 22 088.

Pleasantly situated, right on the waterfront. Tends to be popular in late summer, so be sure to book ahead.

CORINTHOS

Xenia, DD; *at Arhea Corinthos; tel.* 0741 31 203.

Spotlessly clean. Well-kept pension-style rooms in the modern village at the entrance to the ruins.

EPIDAVROS

Xenia, DD-DDD; *right by the ruins; tel.* 0753 22 003.

Two dozen pleasant, chalet-style rooms, all with own private shower.

MIKINES

As you'd expect, many of the establishments here are named after figures from ancient Mycenae. Since many of these characters behaved in gruesome fashion and met hideous ends, this doesn't make such establishments sound so promising. An exception is:

Hotel Belle Helene, DD; *up the hill on the main road; tel.* 0751 66 255.

Named after the lady whose face launched a thousand ships. This hotel is the very same town where Schliemann stayed during his historic excavations. Other celebrated names in the visitor's book include Virginia Woolf, Debussy and mine.

Klytemnestra, DD; *on main road beside ruins; tel.* 0751 66 451.

Klytemnestra, the ogress of the Oresteia tragedies, murdered her husband in the bath, with the help of her lover Aegisthus – so if you're feeling superstitious you may well prefer a room with only a shower here. The lady of the house is most hospitable and bears no resemblance whatsoever to Aeschylus' immortal heroine.

theatre for 3,000 spectators. The **museum**, in the main site, houses a pottery collection, some produced to not very high standards – see if you can spot the wobbly lines and animals grotesquely elongated to fill the required space. The **agora** (market place) has remnants of shops, rather hard to visualize, and on one corner the **Peirene fountain**, a natural spring whose water was stored behind an arcade before channelling into the pool in front.

Do make the effort to climb (two hours, in easy stages, with plenty of water) to Acrocorinth. It contains the remains of the Turkish city – Corinth's third great flowering, which lasted from the Byzantine era until the early 19thC.

CORINTH CANAL
Links the Saronic Gulf with the Gulf of Corinth. The famous waterway cuts through the 6.5-km isthmus which joins the Peleponnese to the Greek main-land, slicing almost 480 km off the sea route between Athens and Patras.

Stop by the bank of the canal and walk on to the bridge. You get a spectacular view of the narrow canal (only 24 m wide) passing between the high vertical cliffs of the cutting. If you're lucky you may see one of the cruise liners being towed through by a tug – otherwise the canal is used mainly by small coastal craft.

The idea for a canal at this spot is said to date from the early Classical era. The Roman Emperor Nero did start a scheme in AD 67 – with his own hands, and the aid of a silver trowel – before handing the work over to 6,000 convicts shipped in from Judea. If Christ had been spared by Pontius Pilate, he might well have ended up working, and even dying, on this scheme.

In 1882 a French company started to dig a canal, but the venture failed in 1889. It was eventually completed by

MYSTRA
The main accommodation here is at the village of Nea Mistra, close to the site.

Hotel Byzantion, D-DD; *Nea Mistra; tel.* 0731 93 309.

Just by the site, with 20 rooms. Be sure to arrive early in the day, or book well ahead.

NAFPLIO
Prices are tend to be high, reflecting the place's popularity.

Xenia Palace, DDD; *Akronafplio; tel.* 0752 28 981.

Luxury hotel between the Kale fortress and the Palamede Fort, overlooking the beach, with views out over the Argolic Gulf.

King Otto Hotel, D-DD; *3 Farmakopoulou; at the end of the street running from the port towards the Kale Fortress; tel.* 0752 27 585.

Slightly austere accommodation.

PALEA EPIDAVROS
There are a number of cheap rooms available a couple of kilometres down the road from Epidavros at Ligourio. But if you're going to travel, it's best to head that little way further on to Palea Epidavros.

Paola Beach, D; *Palea Epidavros; tel.* 0753 41 397.

Two dozen rooms, some with private shower. Friendly welcome, and helpful service.

SPARTA
If you're spending the night in this area, your best option is to head for Mystra. For those who insist upon staying in Sparta, or have no alternative, there is:

Hotel Kypros, D; *66 Leonidou Street; tel.* 0731 26 590.

A suitably Spartan spot, though the friendly young international clientele easily makes up for this. Rooms are small, so ask for one with a balcony (which will also be small).

TRIPOLI
If you find yourself stranded, or insist upon staying in Tripoli overnight, try:

Alex, DD; *26 Vassileos Yioryiou; tel.* 071 22 3465.

This is very much a Tripolitan C class hotel, but pleasant enough.

the Greeks in 1893, but was never a great commercial success as it was not wide enough.

At Diolkos, at the Gulf of Corinth end of the canal, you can see the remains of the methods used by the Romans to drag ships on logs across the isthmus. It conjures up images of a Cecil B. de Mille cast of bawling taskmasters brandishing whips over lines of sweating slaves, with Kirk Douglas heaving manfully in the ranks.

EPIDAVROS ⊨ ✕

68 km S of Corinth on the Argolida peninsula. Epidavros began as a quasi-religious medicinal centre around 5,000 BC. According to legend, Asklepios, son of Apollo, and god of healing, was born here. In ancient times people came from far and wide to be healed by the sacred serpent that was kept in the Sanctuary. Snakes were involved in several of the centre's treatments (see below) and indeed the serpent of Epidavros remains the traditional emblem of the medical profession.

The psychosomatics, hypochondriacs and geriatrics (all words readily comprehensible to Ancient Greeks) who regularly visited Epidavros for the cure would often need distraction during their prolonged treatments, so entertainment was laid on. Thus Epidavros also became established as a centre for the arts. Today it is best known for its magnificent **theatre**, which dates from the 4thC BC, and was restored in 1954. It seats 14,000, and its acoustics remain as perfect today as they were almost two-and-a-half millenia ago. During the summer season, Greek tragedies are staged. Those lucky enough to have seen Maria Callas on stage here say she gave a performance fit to have inspired Aeschylus, the founder of Greek tragedy, who once sat in the audience. The great Greek leader Kolkotronis proclaimed Greece independent from the Turks at Epidavros in 1822.

Other major features of Epidavros are the **museum**, with its stone plaques listing cures achieved by Asklepios (one woman, suffering from infertility, became pregnant with twins after sleeping with a snake); the huge **gymnasium**; the **stadium** for athletics and wrestling competitions, with starting and finishing lines still dis-

cernible; the **Abaton**, a dormitory where patients rested after initiation (snakes would be released during the night to aid healing); and the **Tholos**, a temple giving access to a labyrinth (walls still evident) through which patients are said to have groped in the dark towards a central chamber swarming with snakes. A theory suggests that this was an early form of shock treatment.

MIKINES

42 km S of Corinth, off the road to Nafplio. Mikines is the site of ancient Mycenae, the main city of the civilization which preceded Classical Greece.

The Mycenaeans arrived here before 2,000 BC and set up a Bronze Age civilization. The previous, more primitive, inhabitants of the region were driven into the wilds – and these little-known, unshapely people may well be the origins of ancient myths about satyrs, centaurs and other creatures which were half animal, half human.

The Mycenaeans were the heroes who featured in Homer's *Illiad*. For centuries, this work was believed to be merely a legend. However, in the 19thC the brilliant German amateur archaeologist, Heinrich Schliemann, began to suspect otherwise. After following the geographical clues in Homer's poem, he astonished the world by discovering the ruins of ancient Troy. He followed up this success by discovering Mycenae. Here he unearthed a fabulous golden mask, which he believed to represent the face of Agamemnon. This mask is at present in the Archaeological Museum in Athens, and is now known not to be the face of Agamemnon, since it dates from several centuries before the Trojan Wars. However, it seems likely that Agamemnon and many of the heroic characters did indeed exist.

When Minoan civilization collapsed in Crete, the Mycenaeans took over and became the main power in Greece. Their inscriptions, in what is known as Linear B, are the earliest known form of Greek writing. Around 1200 BC Mycenaean civilization collapsed. To this day, the reason for this remains unclear – though it may well have been caused by Dorian invaders from the north.

There is much to see at Mycenae:

• *The harbour, Nafplio.*

the site brings to life several ancient myths, especially those that featured the House of Atreus, subject of several of the great Greek tragedies. Be sure not to miss the **Acropolis**, the famous **Lion Gate**, and beside it the **First Circle of Royal Tombs.** Buy the site guide and explore these; also the **Royal Palace**; the **Secret Cistern** and the finely constructed **Treasury of Atreus**, actually a beehive-shaped tomb, which conceivably might have been Agamemnon's burial place. Stamp your foot and listen to the echo.

MYSTRA ⊨

5 *km E of Sparta*. This is one of the most striking sights in the Peleponnese: a complete, deserted Byzantine city situated on a hillside dramatically overlooking the Lakonian plain. This city, which once housed a population of more than 40,000, was known as the Florence of the Orient – on account of its beauty and artistic achievement.

Its history is equally astonishing. The spot came to prominence when a fortress was built here in 1293 by William de Villehardouin, who came from Champagne in northern France. Later the city was held by the Byzantines, the Turks, the Venetians, the Russians, and even for a brief period by the Albanians. By the time the great French romantic writer Chateaubriand arrived in 1806 there were only 8,000 people living in the city, and it was finally abandoned altogether in 1834.

NAFPLIO ⊨ ✕

66 *km S of Corinth, at the head of the Argolic Gulf.* This is a gem. Its setting on a peninsula jutting out into the blue waters of the bay is one of the most picturesque urban sights in Greece.

Nafplio was occupied over the years by the Turks and the Venetians, who have both left their legacies in the city's architecture. One of its three ancient mosques is now a cinema, and many of its houses, as well as its famous forts, show their graceful Venetian origins.

The best view of the city is from the walls of Palamedes Fort, which is on the hillside 200 m above the sea. From the ramparts here you can look down over the bay and the romantic island castle of Bourdzi, which once held the key to the city.

On the walls of the Palamedes Fort you can still see images of the Lion of

RECOMMENDED RESTAURANTS

CORINTHOS
Corinthos itself has a justifiably bad name for restaurants. There's just a run of souvlaki joints and rather tacky tavernas along the waterfront, whose only saving grace is their cheapness and the view. An exception to this depressing rule is:

Theodorakis, D-DD; G *Seferis Street.*
You'll find it at the north-eastern end of the waterfront. The fish here is excellent, and they serve some acceptable, moderately priced white wine to go with it. Greek poetry *aficionados* will be pleased to see that the street is named after the great modern Greek poet, George Seferis, friend of Lawrence Durrell and sometime Greek ambassador to London, who won the Nobel Prize for Literature in 1963. As far as I know, Seferis had no particular connection with Corinth, though he probably visited it. As you finish your bottle of wine, you might care to gaze over the water and reflect on some of his lines:

Angelic and black light,
Laughter of waves on highways of the sea,
Laughter between the tears...

EPIDAVROS
The nearest restaurant is at Ligouri, a couple of kilometres down the road from the site. Here you'll find:

Oasis, D-DD; *road to Nafplio; tel. 0753 22 062.*
A pleasant lively spot, justly renowned for its excellently cooked local specialities.

MIKINES
Aristides O Dikeos, DDD; *main road; tel. 0751 66 252.*
Sound local cuisine, whose intricacies are helpfully explained by your genial host.

NAFPLIO
Ellas, DD; *Syntagma Square.*
Pleasant popular local taverna on the main square. Open-air dining with a range of local dishes on the menu and pan-Hellenic standards.

Kolios, DDD; *Bouboulina; tel. 0752 27 675.*
They do squid here in a way I've never found anywhere else – and it's absolutely superb. Pleasant dining on the waterfront, with a romantic view out over the bay (which can occasionally become obscured by street vendors).

SPARTA
Spartan restaurants tend to live up to their name, whereas the bills sometimes show no such restraint. If you must eat in town, select one of the more ordinary restaurants filled with locals. Otherwise, head out a couple of kilometres to Parolis, a village less than a kilometre from the site at Mystra. Here you'll find:

Taverna, D; *Parolis.*
A delightful rural spot where you dine by waterfalls.

TRIPOLI
For those who need a meal whilst waiting for a bus, try:

To Konaki, D-DDD; *Petropoulou Street.*
A range of well-prepared standard dishes, and a few esoterica. Waiters are pleased to explain in three languages, though not always ones you'll understand. If you've got to while away some time waiting for a bus, try playing a game of chess here after your meal (you'll need to bring your own set). There used to be a local expert, called Giorgo, who would join you, courteously appoint himself adviser to your opponent, especially if female, and proceed to take you apart in the most ruthless possible manner while keeping up a charmingly polite conversation.

Venice, the symbol of the Venetian Republic. The original stone lion, which now stands in St Mark's Square, Venice, was captured from Constantinople. According to a Nafplion legend, the ship carrying it from Constantinople to Venice put in here, and a crafty local sculptor made a copy of it. He sold it back to Constantinople for his own weight in gold. Another version of this story has the sculptor substituting his copy for the original. These are intriguing tales, unsubstantiated by historical record, but not untypical of local enterprise through the dark ages of foreign rule.

In 1829 Nafplio became the capital of the newly independent Greece. Two years later the Greek leader Kapodistrias was assassinated here (his assassins suspected him of being a Russian spy). In 1833 the new King of Greece, Otho of Bavaria, arrived to take up his throne. But a year later the capital was moved to Athens, and Nafplio slipped gracefully into the backwaters of provincial life.

PALEA EPIDAVROS ✎

On the coast, E of Epidavros. Fine broad views, but the beach is only good for a quick refreshing dip. A useful accommodation base for Epidravros: see Recommended Hotels, page 112.

SPARTA, MODERN AND ANCIENT ✎ ×

Southern Peleponnese, 43 km N of the Lakonic Gulf. Spartan history is full of tales of valour: so the sight of overweight modern Spartans allowing their wives to shoulder the luggage while they stroll on ahead down the street may come as something of a disappointment. Are these the descendants of the warriors of Thermopylae? Fortunately, yes. The inhabitants of modern-day Sparta are amiable, easy-going, and have little in common with the élitist prigs who fought the Peleponnese Wars over 2,000 years ago.

The ancient Spartans, hell-bent on their philistine Spartan life, didn't have time for monuments, so there's not much to be seen of the city that once took on Athens. Beyond the football stadium to the north of town, you can see the remains of the **Acropolis** in the middle of an olive grove. Near here there is also the remains of the large

theatre, whose masonry was vandalized by the ancient Spartans themselves. From several accounts, these Spartans could have looked like football hooligans, too.

If you came here to see something interesting, best head straight on for Mystra.

Ancient Sparta: The ancient Spartan way of life has become a byword that has entered the language. At the age of seven, young Spartans started on the tough regime which was designed to turn them into the most fanatic soldiers in Greece. The training involved sleeping on the ground, training for hours each day at combat and athletics, and shunning all softening luxuries. Spartan soldiers were expected to die rather than surrender. They lived up to all expectation at Thermopylae, where 300 of them held up the entire might of the Persian Army and fought to the last man.

However, contrary to popular belief, this tough regime was far from being as upright and puritan as is often supposed. Spartan girls, who were put through an almost equally tough training programme, were notorious throughout Ancient Greece for their dresses, which exposed their breasts. And Spartan women were not required to remain faithful to their husbands – they were allowed to choose suitable lovers in the 'interests of procreation'. Also, Spartan youths were encouraged to steal, but were severely flogged if caught. This gave rise to the legend of the youth who stole a fox cub. Someone saw him, so he hid it in his tunic and let the fox cub eat out his heart rather than give himself away by calling out. A likely story.

TRIPOLI ✎ ×

Central Peleponnese, 56 km E of Nafplio. In bygone times when Latin was widely taught, a Classics teacher would use the cliché 'in Arcadia ego' whenever he found himself amidst some particularly pleasant surroundings. Arrive in Tripoli, and you are literally in Arcadia, for this is the capital of that ancient province. Alas, modern Tripoli has little to recommend it – except that from here you can catch buses for places all over the Peleponnese.

Peleponnese

Between Athens and Kythira
The Eastern Peleponnese

200 km; map Michelin 980, 1:700000

This is an expedition for those who can't choose between the islands and the mainland. It includes visits to two very contrasting islands and a long stretch of largely unspoilt Peleponnese coastline. On the way you can see the haunting pinewoods which featured in a famous novel, a Byzantine stronghold, a remote monastery high in the mountains, and a ruined town which has been deserted since it was sacked by the notorious pirate Barbarossa nearly five hundred years ago.

It is possible to cover this route by hired car, but it is far easier by boat. This way, the entire trip is just over 200 km. If you stay on board you can travel the main red route in a day. But there is plenty to see if you disembark, so you would do well to spend at least a day at some of the ports of call, and allow no fewer than three days for the island of Kythira. This way, the entire trip will take around a week.

Assuming you start from Athens, the voyage begins at Piraeus. You sail first to Ermioni, on the Argolida, the eastern arm of the Peleponnese. At Ermioni you catch the boat for the island of Spetses, the setting of John Fowles' novel *The Magus*. From Spetses you catch the boat across the Argolic Gulf to the little port of Plaka, and then coast-hop down to the Byzantine stronghold of Monemvassia. After Monemvassia the boat takes you to the pleasant resort of Neapoli in the southern Peleponnese. Then there's just a short trip across the strait to the island of Kythira. This is one of my favourite Greek islands, and to this day remains largely unspoilt, despite its size. Here there are many interesting haunts – from an ancient Minoan site to a cave with Byzantine frescos, as well as one of the prettiest beach resorts in Greece.

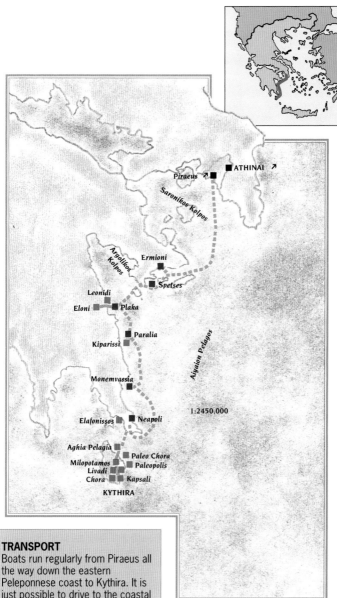

TRANSPORT
Boats run regularly from Piraeus all the way down the eastern Peleponnese coast to Kythira. It is just possible to drive to the coastal spots on the route, and there are ferries which take cars to both Spetses and Kythira. You could combine land and sea by taking the coach from Athens to Ermioni, or even as far as Leonidio, just above Plaka, and then catching the boat. However, I strongly recommend taking the boat all the way.

SIGHTS & PLACES OF INTEREST

ELAFONISSOS
See Neapoli, page 123.

ERMIONI ⌇
Resort at the end of the Argolida Peninsula opposite the fashionable island of Hydra. This pleasant fishing village has a beautiful bay and swimming at the end of the headland.

Recently some early Christian mosaics were uncovered near the school. There is a local ravine, which in ancient times was believed to be a short cut to Hades (the land of the dead). Normally, to enter Hades, one had to cross the River Styx in Charon's boat. On account of this, the canny locals gave up the ancient custom of putting a coin in the mouth of the dead – Charon's fee for the crossing. Their modern descendants are, however, far from mean with their money.

KYTHIRA ⌇ ×
Island off the SE Peleponnese. This is one of the last remaining unspoilt islands in Greece, although even Kythira shows signs of change. You might expect a small island to be forgotten, but this one is surprisingly large: 40 km from tip to toe, and nearly 24 km wide in places.

Kythira has remained off the tourist trail for a combination of reasons. For a start it *is* off the trail – at the end of one of the more remote ferry runs, and on the way to nowhere (although it does have the occasional ferry service to Kastelli, on the western end of Crete). Another factor is that the Kythirans are not particularly interested in

RECOMMENDED HOTELS

ERMIONI
Costa Perla, DD; *Ermioni; tel. 0754 31 112.*

Large hotel with a wide range of entertainment and sporting activities. Facilities include chalets and private pool.

KYTHIRA – Aghia Pelagia
This little north-western port is where many of the boats put in. It has a beach, but it is not a very attractive spot. It's wise to move on south (to Kapsali or Chora) as soon as you arrive, taking the bus which meets the ferry. If you have to stay overnight, your best bet is one of the rooms for rent near the jetty.

KYTHIRA – Chora
This, too, can be very booked up in high season, so be sure to ring ahead if you can. In summer many places want you to stay more than one night, and some even insist on a minimum of three nights. If you plan to stay for only one night, you may have to ruffle a few feathers when you ask for your bill next morning.

Hotel Margarita, DDD; *Chora; tel. 0735 31 711.*

Sophisticated old-style hotel with superb views out over the valley. There is a wide range of facilities and very helpful staff who are capable of communicating in a wide range of languages.

Pension Kaite, DD; *28 Livanou Street; tel. 0735 31 318.*

Small, highly recommended spot in the centre of the old town, just off the main square.

If you are really stuck, try the travel agents in the main square: *tel* 0735 31 390.

KYTHIRA – Kapsali
The big speciality here is self-catering rooms – there's a good, well-stocked supermarket just up the road at Chora. The rooms are close to the beach and the cafés, which can be quite lively at night. If you want something quiet, try Chora – if you can face the trek down to the beach in the morning.

At the height of the season all the rooms are likely to be full. If you want to book in advance, try ringing: 0735 31 340 or 31 232.

MONEMVASSIA
Hotel Malvasia, DD-DDD; *Kastro; tel. 0732 61 323.*

This is easily the most atmospheric spot in town, in the heart of the old

tourists, nor, it appears, in the money tourism brings.

Kythira is in the rare situation of being the only Greek island (and probably the only island in the world), to be supported by the Australian social security system. I've heard many explanations of how this came to pass, including the suggestion that Kythiran doctors working in Australia sign fake medical certificates for returning emigrés, who then receive their benefit for life, and even pass on these certificates from generation to generation. In fact, this alleged ruse disguises a rather more poignant truth. Since the Second World War, a staggering 75 per cent of the island's population has been forced to emigrate. Most go to Australia, which is now referred to rather touchingly by the locals as 'Megala Kythira' (Greater Kythira).

These emigrés regularly send money to those left behind, and also come to Kythira on holiday. You will hear 'Strine' spoken all over the place by the younger visitors, who otherwise look Greek through and through.

Since earliest times, Kythira has been looked upon as the island of lovers. According to legend Aphrodite, the goddess of love, who was born out of the foam, was assisted to her first landfall at Kythira by the breath of the Zephyrs. Later Paris is said to have built the first temple of Aphrodite here. By a strange coincidence, in 1900, a sponge diver working the sea bed by the offshore island of Antikythira discovered a statue which is thought to be a likeness of Paris. This was found to date from 4thC BC, and is now in the Athens Museum, where it is known as the Ephebe of Antikythira.

city. It consists of a couple of old houses which have been renovated. Impossible to recommend this one too highly, if you want a night to remember.

If that is full, you might try the **Byzantio** in the main square. If there are no rooms to be had anywhere on the Kastro, try:

Actaion, D-DD; 23rd Iouliou (23rd July) Street; tel. 0732 61 324.
Handily close to the causeway across to the Kastro, or old city. Modern, pleasant, bright rooms, most with private balcony, some with private bath or shower, but nowhere near as full of character as those on the Kastro.

NEAPOLI
Aivali, D-DD; Neapoli; tel. 0732 41 287.
Small hotel, handy for the ferry, and a pleasant beach.

PARALIA
There is an unusually large number of rather ordinary hotels here, without much to choose between them. If only for the name, try:

Muse's Beach, D; tel. Paralia 61 212.
A friendly welcome; they also have a pleasant restaurant of their own.

PLAKA
Olympios Zeto, DD; Plaka; tel. 0757 22 115.
Large, rather out-of-place hotel, complete with chalets and sports facilities.

SPETSES
Accommodation can be very difficult here during the height of summer, as many of the establishments in the main town become booked out *en bloc* by package tours. If you have difficulty, contact:

Takis Travel: tel. 0754 72 888
You can't miss it – on the left as you come off the boat.

If you can get in, do try:

Hotel Possidion, DD-DDD; waterfront; tel. 0754 72 208.
The island's most famous hotel, which features in John Fowles's *The Magus*. A grand old pile, which in its heyday was one of the most sophisticated spots in the region.

If this is full, try:

Saronika, DD; waterfront; tel. 0754 73 741.
Lively views out over the busy seafront. Not for those who plan to go to bed early.

• *Kythira.*

Although Kythira is one of the Ionian islands, the nearest other island in the group, Zakinthos, is nearly 250 km away on the other side of the Peleponnese. When the Ionian islands came under British rule in 1809, Kythira too became part of the British Empire. Despite Greek Independence in 1822, the Ionian islands remained under British control, and it was not until 1864 that Kythira became part of independent Greece. There are several things well worth seeing in Kythira:

Chora
This is the main town, also known as Kythira. *See Recommended Hotels.*

Kapsali
Two beautiful, sand-sculpted bays and a small harbour set below the main town of Chora. One of the least spoilt spots in all the islands.

Livadi
See Recommended Restaurants.

Milopotamos
Considered to be the island's star attraction, this is a small, peaceful village in the centre of the island with a stream running through it – now almost deserted. If it is Sunday, don't miss the excellent local market. The best buy is a pot of fragrant Kythira honey, but don't expect a bargain – they know it's famous. Also, production is often severely limited, owing to the frequent bush fires which sometimes set the entire island ablaze for days on end. These conflagrations are spectacular, and although the locals claim they are harmless, there may be an element of Kythiran insouciance here.

Thirty km west are the **Aghia Sophia** caves, which have some Byzantine frescos in the part once used as a church.

Paleo Chora
The hidden city which was once the island's capital, set in a stunning secret site inland from the north-west coast, 6 km south of Aghia Pelagia. Deserted and in ruins since it was raided by the pirate Barbarossa in 1537.

Paleopolis
This ancient Minoan site on the west coast south of Avlemonas was excavated by the British around 20 years ago. The crates of finds, unopened, used to be stored in Chora. In fact, this is a deserted site on a rather undistinguished remote stretch of coast, but it is worth searching about in the refuse – I once came across a Roman coin with Emperor Vespasian's head clearly visible, although how it arrived at a Minoan site is a mystery.

MONEMVASSIA ⊨ ✕
SE *Peleponnese, on E coast 30 km N of Cape Maleas.* The name Monemvassia derives from the Greek words *Moni emvasis*, which mean 'one entrance'. This refers to the causeway you see as you sail in, linking the ancient city to the modern settlement on the mainland. This causeway is less than a hundred years old, but in the old days a long wooden platform joined Monemvassia to the mainland.

Monemvassia was a Byzantine stronghold of considerable importance, controlling the vital seaway between Venice and Constantinople (now Istanbul, formerly Byzantium). In the 13thC, William of Villehardouin managed to capture the place for the Franks after a seige lasting three years. Later it became a strategic revictualling port for the fleets setting off for the Crusades.

The 'lords of Monemvassia' were renowned for their cultivated ways, and this is said to be the first spot where forks were used as cutlery in Greece. According to a local historian I met, this made the lords of Monemvassia a laughing stock throughout Laconia, as the peasants imagined the lords were eating with pitchforks – the only forks they had ever heard of.

Another local cultural first was the introduction to western Europe of Malmsey wine. This was originally a sweet wine grown on the nearby hills, and Malmsey is a corruption of the name Monemvassia, allegedly via the French name for the wine: *vin de Malvoisie*.

After the Franks, the place was occupied in turn by the Turks, a mixed bag of international ruffians under the Papal flag, the Venetians and others, until eventually it was occupied by 4,000 New Zealand soldiers fleeing from the German invaders during the Second World War.

The **old town** is still a remarkable spot, all winding alleyways, steps, little courtyards, and dozens of churches. Be sure to see the frescos in **Aghia Sophia** ('restored' in 1950s); the **Venetian campanile**; and the **ramparts**, which have superb views out over the sea. But the main thing here is the maze of alleyways – ideal for walking and getting lost.

There are beaches up and down the coast, which often remain deserted, even in high season – probably because they are pebbly.

NEAPOLI

On the Vioatic Gulf at the SE tip of the Peleponnese. The name comes from *Nea Polis*, which means New City (just as Naples does). There is little historic in appearance about this rather ordinary small resort, although it is not a new city – there has probably been a settlement of some kind here even longer than at Naples.

Despite its remoteness, the place is

• *Monemvassia.*

surprisingly popular with Greek tourists, who spread out in family groups along the sandy beaches which stretch east and west.

Across the gulf is the island of **Elafonissos,** separated from the mainland by a channel 0.5 km wide. You can get to the island by boat from Vinglafia, opposite, on the mainland. It is worth the trip just to explore the island (3 km wide and 3 km long), swim from the beach, and have a plate of squid and a glass of retzina at one of the tavernas – a day well spent.

PARALIA ⊠

On the SE Peleponnese coast 30 km N of Monemvassia. An extremely remote little harbour with houses rising on the slope behind and a long beach to the south. Curiously, despite its remoteness, this spot can get crowded at the height of the season. It is most easily reached by the boat which plies along the coast, although there are rumours of a track which winds up through the mountains from Leonidi (see Plaka, below). This road route is marked on the maps, but with such lack of confidence that I wouldn't trust it. (I have followed many a road marked on maps with much firmer intent that quickly petered out into tracks negotiable only by goats.)

A short drive inland from Paralia is the lovely isolated village of **Kiparissi**

• *Spetses.*

amongst the olive groves. This is strictly for 'get away from it all' types' – a sheer joy for those who believe in following tracks simply because they are there and don't mind a night gnawing at crusts under the stars wondering when they will ever meet another human being.

PLAKA ⊠

On the E Peleponnese coast across the Argolic Gulf from Spetses. If you like the look of the place, do try going ashore (you can always catch the next boat out again). Here, what you see is what you get – just a couple of tavernas on the waterfront and a beach to the south. Nothing to do? Take the bus to the nearby market town of Leonidi, then head up the road into the mountains to the **Eloni Monastery** (16 km). This is a superb mountain road through a gorge, which climbs towards the peaks. These rise to nearly 2,000 m, and are said still to be prowled by wolves.

When you arrive at last, panting at the monastery gate, pull hard on the wire, which rings a distant bell. You will be welcomed by a charming ageing nun, who will show you around the chapel with the icons, and offer you a glass of the freshest water.

SPETSES ⌘ ✕

Island off the Argolida Peninsula, at the head of the Argolic Gulf. Fans of the British author John Fowles will regard Spetses' main claim to fame as the setting for his remarkable novel *The Magus*, which has been translated into umpteen languages. (In the novel, he calls it Phraxos.) Away from the main tourist spots, the hilly pine woods and some of the remote little coves still have that same eerie, haunted quality which Fowles evoked so brilliantly. This is great walking terrain. The town of Spetses has two smallish harbours, some attractive streets and a number of pretty cobbled courtyards. At the height of the season, however, they can become intolerably overcrowded.

The school where Fowles taught, Anaryiros College, is just to the west of the main town. It used to be a Greek version of a minor English public school – but this attempt at cross-cultural symbiosis has now lapsed, and the place is an occasional conference centre. Only 10 km long, Spetses has over 50 km of coast.

RECOMMENDED RESTAURANTS

KYTHIRA – Chora
Zorba's Taverna, D-DD; *main street.*
Just before you reach the main square. Friendly, relaxed international clientele of regulars.

KYTHIRA – Livadi
O Toxotis, DD; *Livadi.*
This is the best restaurant I know of on the island – in the small town just 5 km north of Chora. The chicken dishes served here are justly renowned. *Toxotis* means 'The Archer' – apparently a good old Greek name for a restaurant. It implied that the owner was a hunter, who went out with his bow to find fresh game for the pot.

Kythira – Kapsali
Antonis O Magos, DD; *on the front.*
This is a different sort of place entirely to the last-mentioned. Antonis O Magos – 'Tony the Magician' – does, indeed, work magic with his fish, although the wine can sometimes leave a little to be desired. Good for seafood; lively clientele; affable service.

MONEMVASSIA
Matoula, D; *Kastro.*
Although the restaurant is on the main tourist route in the old city, this is only a disadvantage in crowded mid-season, when you have to arrive early for a table. The big bonus here is the superb view from the leafy terrace, which looks out to sea. Try their fresh fish with a glass of delicate white wine, for the perfect accompaniment to a romantic evening.

Those who fancy a more lively evening, or have not yet found the romantic partner of their choice, could head over to:

Angelo's Bar, DD; *Kastro, 50 m up the main street on the right.*
Serves superb fruit juices and a range of standard exotic cocktails (with rather exotic prices). Friendly clientele.

SPETSES
Trehandiri, DD-DDD; *waterfront.*
This is where the smart Athenians on holiday come for their seafood. Generally considered one of the finest fish restaurants in the region, with views of the harbour. Choose carefully, or the bill may get out of hand.

For slightly less sophisticated dining, try:

Lirakis, D-DD; *waterfront; tel.* 0754 72 288
Wide range of standard pan-Hellenic dishes and local specialities. Fine view out over the waterfront.

Spetses is renowned for its cuisine and has several local specialities. If you like seafood, be sure to try their Spetsiotika, a powerful concoction of white fish, garlic and tomato, but which tastes delicious if you have no preconceptions. Also worth a try is the famous island sweet, Amigdolato. Don't be put off by one notice which advertises it as 'famous old Spetses sweat'.

Aegean Islands

Between Piraeus and Samos
The Heart of the Aegean

300 km; map Michelin 980, 1:700000

This route links the Port of Piraeus with the island of Samos, just off the Turkish coast. On the way you call in at a string of quintessentially Aegean islands of widely different character. Assuming you start from Piraeus, your first stop is Kithnos, in the Cyclades group. It is renowned for its bubbling thermal springs, and is one of the less spectacular (and thus less visited) of the archipelago. Its neighbour Siros was once the busiest harbour in the Aegean, but beyond its port you'll find some pleasant beaches and lively resorts. However, if you want live it up, Mykonos is the place: its legendary beauty is matched only by its legendary nightlife.

Ikaria, last stop after Mykonos, has an altogether different beauty from the stark splendour of the Cyclades. Here you'll find mountains and woodlands, steep cliffs and isolated coves. Samos has some similarly spellbinding inland scenery, but this island has now become one of the main tourist destinations of the eastern Aegean – so again, the nightlife is there if you want it after your days exploring the mountains.

You can catch the boat direct from Piraeus to Samos, and just call in at the main islands on your way. This way you can do the entire trip in a day. But if you want to do justice to the islands, you should go ashore and explore a few of the ones that take your fancy. If you do this, the trip can easily take you a week or more.

As the map shows, you can make a detour from Kithnos to Kea. After Kithnos you island-hop to Siros and Mykonos. From here I strongly recommend the brief detour to Delos. You then continue to Ikaria, where you can take another detour to tiny Fourni. From Ikaria you continue to journey's end at Samos, where you can spend several days exploring the inland mountains and villages and, of course, link up with other routes in this guides, such as Greece Overall: 11, exploring the Dodecanese north to Lesbos and south to Rhodes.

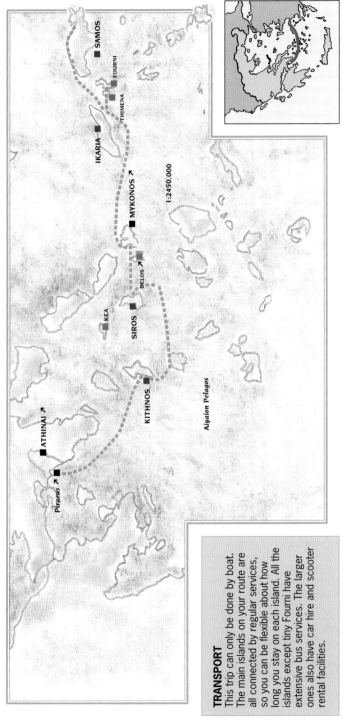

SAMOS

FOURNI

THIMENA

IKARIA

MYKONOS ↗

1:2450,000

DELOS ↗

KEA

SIROS

KITHNOS

Aiyaion Pelagos

ATHINAI ↗

Piraeus ↗

TRANSPORT

This trip can only be done by boat. The main islands on your route are all connected by regular services, so you can be flexible about how long you stay on each island. All the islands except tiny Fourni have extensive bus services. The larger ones also have car hire and scooter rental facilities.

SIGHTS & PLACES OF INTEREST

DELOS
See Greece Overall: 12.

IKARIA ⌨ ✕
30 km W of Samos. As usual there are several explanations for the name of this island. The one best supported by the facts is that the name comes from the Phoenecian word 'ikor', which indicated that it was surrounded by rich fishing grounds.

But by far the best story is that it is named after Icarus, son of Daedalus. The well-known myth of Icarus tells us that in order to escape from Crete, Daedalus created two pairs of wings out of feathers and wax. In defiance of the laws of both gravity and credulity, father and son took off and flew some 250 km out over the Aegean. At this point, Icarus flew too close to the sun, which started to melt the wax holding together the feathers. He plunged into the sea and his distraught father then glided down to bury him on the nearest island. To perpetuate the myth, there is now a rather ungainly metal statue of the falling Icarus on the pier at Aghios Kirikos, the island's main port.

Ikaria is a stunningly beautiful island, which attracts fewer tourists than you would expect. Its rocky shores rise in steep high cliffs, giving way to a number of idyllic little coves and some fine beaches. The mountainous hinterland has a number of remote villages, and there are some lovely walks over the terraced hillsides and through the woods.

Take the bus up from Aghios Kyrikos to **Evdhilos** on the other side of the island, and you'll get a fair picture of the beauty of the place. You wind through some spectacular scenery up towards the high ridge, with its covering of cloud. (The highest peak here is over 1,010 m.) Then you plunge down towards the blue unbroken horizon of the Aegean. If you're lucky, on a very clear day you can just make out the southern mountains of the island of Chios, 70 km to the north.

Evdhilos itself is set on a slope amongst the woods, within easy reach of some lovely beaches.

Five kilometres further west along the coast you come to **Armenistis.** Contrary to modern myth, this spot is not so-named because of grateful passengers uttering the first two syllables when emerging shakily from the bus

RECOMMENDED HOTELS

FOURNI
There are rooms for rent here: usually you'll be met at the boat by people offering accommodation. If not, start making enquiries *as soon as* you get off the boat. Accommodation is limited, and in season there is sometimes not enough to go around.

IKARIA - Aghios Kirikos
Toula, DD-DDD; *just outside town; tel.* 0275 22 298.

A large development with more than 200 rooms, many in chalets. The range of facilities includes a private pool and tennis. Excellent access to the beach. Often has a room to spare when other places are booked solid.

IKARIA - Armenistis
Armenistis Inn, DD; *tel.* 0275 41 415.

Delightful spot up on the hill; rooms with balconies looking out to sea.

Armenistis is likely to be heavily booked during July and August. Even so, you can sometimes find a room if you persist in asking around. If you are in difficulty, try:

Rooms Eligas; D; *tel.* 0275 41 445.

They speak English here, and are very helpful. Rooms right by the sea.

KEA - Korissa
Pension Korissa; DD-DDD; *tel.* 0288 31 384.

Just around the corner from the beach.

KEA - Koundouros
Kea Beach; DD; *on the shore; tel.* 0288 31 230.

Attractive modern development complete with chalet accommodation. A range of amenities includes private pool and private beach.

after the heart-stopping approach through hairpin bends. It is a wonderful place – a pleasant seaside village with a long sandy beach, which out of season is often all but deserted. When in this part of the island, try to visit the ruins of the Byzantine palace, the Roman relics, and the tiny museum at **Kambos**, which is a couple of kilometres down the road from Evdhilos. I say 'try to visit' because it's often difficult to get in. Ask around in Evdhilos for the whereabouts of the curator, Vassilis Kambouris.

The museum itself has just one room, but contains some fascinating pieces found off the coast, as well as a fragment of a marble statue and little carvings. It is that sort of place: worth the effort of trying to get into, if you feel like doing something just to see what happens.

Walk even further west along the coast from Armenistis and you come to a couple of remote hamlets, a little chapel on a tiny island and an idyllic beach. If having reached here you have surplus energy, head inland where there are some larger villages amongst the hills. Follow this inland track to its end and you will reach the southern tip of the island. Here you'll find the truly enchanting village of **Karkinagri** looking down over the sea – a real end-of-the-world spot.

KEA ⌘ ✕

20 km E of Cape Sounion. Kea is the closest of the Cyclades to the mainland. Herein lies its main advantage and its main disadvantage. It is a popular resort with weekenders from Athens, who flock here on the ferry during the season. For this reason, and because it is so unadventurously close to the mainland, it is often overlooked by foreign tourists. Yet during the middle of the week, even at the height of summer, it can remain surprisingly uncrowded – especially in the fertile and mountainous hinterland.

Kea is 20 km long and 10 km wide, so there is room to explore. The boat puts in at the somewhat nondescript port of **Korissia**. Just north of here is the yachting resort of **Vouraki**, a popular port with the Athenian nautical set. Just a couple of kilometres further north you come to the island's main archaeological site, **Aghia Irini**. Here you can see the remains of some buildings and a temple, all dating from around 2000 BC.

The best sight on the island is the

KEA - Loulida (Chora)
Hotel Ioulis Keas; D-DD; *tel.* 0288 22 177.

Each room has its own balcony, where you can sit looking out at the spectacular view over the island.

KITHNOS - MERIHAS
Kithnos Bay; DD

Here you can be sure of a warm welcome. Clean, pleasant rooms.

If this is full, there are rooms available for rent around the port.

KITHNOS - Loutra
Xenia Anagenissis; DD; *tel.* 31 217.

You can take the spring waters at this hotel, located in the old spa centre, by the sea. Beach nearby.

SIROS - Ermoupoli
Hotel Omeros; DDD; *by the harbour.*

Exceptional old-style provincial hotel with views of the harbour. Staying here is something of a historic experience.

Athina Hotel; D-DD; 4 *Antiparon Street; tel.* 0281 26 165.

A short walk from the harbour, and handy for the ferry. A cool base in hot Ermoupoli.

KITHNOS - Kimi and Galissas
Both these resorts have plenty of rooms for rent. Simply enquire as soon as you get off the bus.

KITHNOS - Agathopes
Delagrazia, D-DD; *Agathopes; tel.* 0281 42 225.

A real find in a delightful beach-side setting; only worth trying out of high season, as it is usually booked out.

THYMINA
The small island close to Fourni. There are some rooms for rent in the little port, also known as Thymina. Enquire at the quayside.

• *Kithnos.*

famous **Lion of Kea**, which is just outside the picturesque capital of **Ioulidha**, up in the hills above the port. Set off on the path towards the Kastriani Monastery, and you come to the lion in 20 minutes. It dates from pre-historic times and is remarkable for its odd face.

Other celebrated figures from Kea's past include the 5thC poet Bacchylides who wrote verses in praise of a horse which won the Olympic Games, and Ariston the Peripatetic philosopher. In ancient times the islanders were also famous throughout the Greek world for their rather Draconian solution to the problem of care for the aged. Anyone who reached the age of seventy was required to mark his (or her) birthday with a glass of celebratory hemlock.

KITHNOS ⚓ ✕

30 km SE of Cape Sounion. Kithnos is also known as Thermia, because of its thermal springs. In fact, it's really a rather boring little island – without much to see, and no great isolated beaches. Athenians come here in the

summer, and a number of the less adventurous roving tourists arrive here because it's on the map and fairly close to Athens. Still, if you're suffering from your round of some of the more hectic Cyclades, this might be just the spot for you. Here you can soothe your liver by taking the waters, which are also highly recommended for gout and hysterical disorders. The islanders are friendly, and the place has been renowned for its cheese since Roman times.

Apart from the numerous springs, there is a cave at **Dhriopidha**, the former island capital, and a resort at **Loutra** (complete with abandoned spa).

Kithnos briefly entered history nearly 2,000 years ago. After Nero died, an ingenious hoaxer decided to set up as an impostor of the famous Emperor who had fiddled while Rome burned.

• *Opposite: Off Ikaria.*

The hoaxer's days of living it up at the expense of others came to an end when his boat was blown ashore at Kithnos during a storm. Clapped in irons, he was dragged before the local proconsul, who gave his act the 'thumbs down' – the death sentence.

MYKONOS

See Greece Overall: 12.

SAMOS

See Local Explorations: 12.

SIROS 🚢 ✕

80 km SE of Cape Sounion. If you enjoy rusting old mercantile harbours, your spirits will rise as you enter **Ermoupoli**, the port where the boats put in at Siros. A hundred years ago, this was the major sea port of the Aegean, far outstripping Piraeus, the port of Athens, which is now the third largest in the entire Mediterranean.

Ermoupoli was a bunkering port, and coal-fired ships plying the Aegean would put in here for fuel, which was delivered by grimy coalers from northern European ports. Then came oil-fired ships, and the trade dwindled. Even the famous Neorion shipyard now has a derelict look.

Incidentally, this port is named after Hermes (Ermoupoli = Hermes-polis =

DETOUR - FOURNI 🚢 ✕

20 km E of Ikaria. This is the largest of the archipelago of small islands that you can see from the port of Aghios Kirikos on the east coast of Ikaria. There is a regular caique which runs from Aghios Kirikos to the island's small port, also called Fourni, which spills down the sheer hillside to the harbour. Fourni has a pleasant sandy beach, but not much else. Down the path leading south, beyond the windmills, there are some better, more remote beaches.

If you're feeling adventurous you can step off the boat when it calls in at the small island of **Thimena,** which lies a couple of kilometres to the west of Fourni. There is a tiny landing place, the Monastery of St John (Aghios Ioannis), and some accommodation (see Recommended Hotels).

In past centuries this island used to be a stronghold of Corsair pirates from the Barbary Coast of North Africa. Some scholars think, contrary to the popular conception of pirates, that these were seldom independent operators. Much of the time they were probably a loosely linked force under such fearsome commanders as the notorious Barbarossa.

Barbarossa – 'Red Beard' – is the name that has come down to us of a notorious pirate who was feared throughout the Mediterranean during 16thC.

In fact, there were two Barbarossas – brothers. They were both originally Greeks, but became Muslim pirates operating out of North Africa. This is why Barbarossa is often refered to as a Corsair pirate.

One of the Barbarossas, born in 1473, allied himself with the Court of the Tunisian Sultan. He specialized in raiding Spanish coastal towns, but the Spaniards eventually caught up with him. The alleged details of his long and extremely gruesome end are probably untrue.

The second Barbarossa brother then took over the family business and did so well that he was eventually appointed as the Turkish sultan's deputy in North Africa, then part of the Turkish Empire. He later served as pasha to Suleiman the Magnificent.

The Greek islands were an ideal environment for piracy. Raids were commonplace on the richly laden merchant shipping that plied the archipelagoes. The Turkish sultan gave Barbarossa the task of clearing the seas for his shipping. Barbarossa not only eliminated competitors from the field, but terrorised the Greek islands for his personal profit, inflicting bloodthirsty raids on their inhabitants.

However, he did make one contribution to humanity: on orders form his Turkish masters, he ferried thousands of Moors to safety as they fled the Spanish Inquisition. He lived to a safe old age, dying at 80 in Constantinople.

City of Hermes). Hermes was god of commerce and travellers, but he also patronised thieves. Either way, Hermoupoli flourished.

Nowadays, Hermoupoli is the largest town in the Cyclades and also the administrative capital for the islands. The town is unique in Greece as a centre of Roman Catholicism, the comunity here being descendants of 16thC Venetians and Genoese. Nowadays, however, the community contains as many Greek Orthodox as it does Catholics, and there is both a Roman Catholic and a Greek Orthodox bishop in residence.

Most people call in at Siros simply to change boats. This is one of the main ferry terminals in the islands. If you are on an island and are told it's impossible to get to where you want to go, the answer is often to get there via Siros.

Explore the island and you will be pleasantly surprised. Across the mountains, on the south and west coasts, there are a number of agreeable resorts. **Kimi**, directly across from Ermoupoli, has a fine beach – as has **Galissas**, which is some 20 km to the south-west.

Ermoupoli is renowned for its bouzouki music. One of the all-time great players, **Markos Vamvarkaris**, was born just north of here in the village of Ano Siros, where he has a square named after him. No visit to Siros is complete without a pilgrimage to Ano Siros. As you would expect, it is where you can hear some of the finest and most authentic bouzouki music in Greece. For a great evening of *real* Greek music, try **Lilli's**.

In the upper town of Ermoupoli, by the Catholic cathedral (Aghios Georgios), there is a British cemetery containing the graves of more than a hundred British soldiers drowned when the troop ship **Arcadian** was torpedoed off the island in 1917.

RECOMMENDED RESTAURANTS

FOURNI
This is an out-of-the-way spot, so don't expect a great range. One thing you can expect is fresh fish, which is well cooked and attractively served at the local tavernas by the port. I once had some exceptional charcoal-grilled *barbouni* (red mullet) here. But it wasn't any cheaper than anywhere else: the season is short, and they have to make a living.

IKARIA - Aghios Kirikos
Adelfia Taverna, DD.
The best restaurant in town, though don't expect too much. The menu has a range of pan-Hellenic and local specialities, and a fair selection of admittedly rather fair wines.

IKARIA - Armenistis
Delfini, D-DD.
Delightfully situated; fresh seafood and friendly service.

There is also a handful of adequate inexpensive tavernas along the harbour, where the international backpackers make for pleasant, informal company.

KEA - Korisssa
I Tzi Mas, D-DD; *by the beach;* tel. 0288 31 222.
Pleasant restaurant attached to small hotel, where they serve the usual range of Greek and international specialities in an attractive setting.

KITHNOS - Chora
To Kentron, D-DD.
Don't expect novelties – but the standard fare here is excellent value. The company is young and lively.

KITHNOS - Loutra
Xenia Anagenissis, DD; *close to the beach;* tel. 31 217.
Well-run restaurant serving a range of Greek and local specialities.

SIROS - Ermoupoli
Tempelis, DD; 17 *Anastaseos.*
Well worth the hot uphill walk. Nothing special to look at, but this one serves a *very* good range of *real* Greek island dishes, and a few local to Siros. Try to be adventurous – though don't expect much help from the waiters if you don't speak Greek. An opportunity to try out your phrasebook.

Aegean Islands

Between Rhodes and Lesbos
The Dodecanese

380 km; map Michelin 980, 1:700000

This route takes you through the Greek islands that lie in the lee of the Turkish mainland. Each island here is unique. Rhodes and Lesbos are amongst the largest in the Aegean, yet their history and appearance are utterly different. Rhodes was the ancient stronghold of the Knights of St John, and is now a major tourist destination. Lesbos, on the other hand, is the island of poets, whose inland mountain villages remain largely unspoilt. Kos is also a major tourist destination, with a distinct history of its own. At Patmos you will find a curious blend of the sacred and the secular. It is the Aegean's holy island, where St John the Divine wrote the *Book of Revelations* – yet it is also a smart resort, with some beautiful beaches. Also on your route is Samos, whose famous sweet wine was commended by Byron. You may not care for the wine, but don't let that put you off the island, which has many secrets to be explored. The same is true of Chios, which may well have been the birthplace of Homer – an idyllic spot with medieval villages, ancient monasteries and miles of unspoilt countryside.

If you begin at Rhodes, you take the boat for Kos. From there you head north to Leros, and then on to Patmos. At Patmos you can take the green detour to one of the more remote islands, Agathonissi, which lies just off the Turkish coast. The next ports of call are Samos, Chios and Lesbos – it is worth allowing several days to explore each of them. Although you can cover this route in a couple of days, it is best to allow at least a week.

At the end of the route you can choose between catching the boat directly back to Athens, or hopping across to Limnos, where you can continue with Local Explorations: 7.

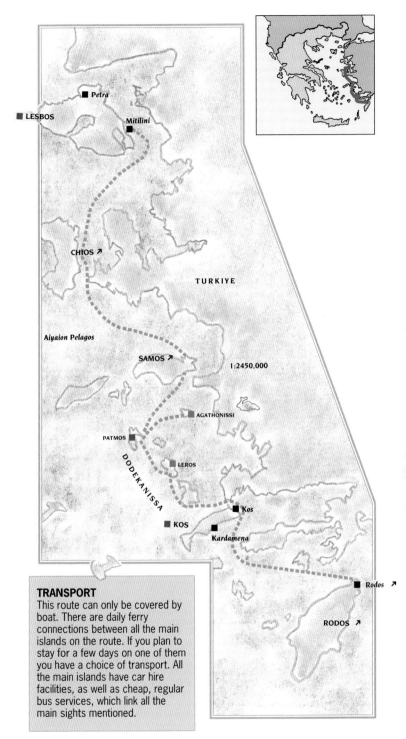

Petra

LESBOS

Mitilini

CHIOS ↗

TURKIYE

Aiyaion Pelagos

SAMOS ↗

1:2450,000

AGATHONISSI

PATMOS

LEROS

DODEKANISSA

Kos

KOS

Kardamena

Rodos ↗

RODOS ↗

TRANSPORT
This route can only be covered by boat. There are daily ferry connections between all the main islands on the route. If you plan to stay for a few days on one of them you have a choice of transport. All the main islands have car hire facilities, as well as cheap, regular bus services, which link all the main sights mentioned.

SIGHTS & PLACES OF INTEREST

AGATHONISSI ⌂ ✕

Around 20 km from the barren Turkish coastline, 25 km S of Samos, and 40 km NE of Patmos. This tiny remote island is just 7 km long, and named after the island's main vegetation – thorn bushes.

Agathonissi has a permanent population of just a hundred people, who live in a small village. History and tourism have largely passed by this haven – as does the ferry service. It is a difficult island to get to, and even more difficult to get away from. There used to be a ferry only once a week or so, but the locals say this will change soon.

If you read the *Book of Revelations* in Patmos, this is the ideal place to catch up on reading the rest of the Bible. There isn't much else to do here except savour the solitude – a rare enough experience. The island attracts a few intrepid souls in the high season. Out of season, however, it's the per-fect setting to test out life as a hermit.

CHIOS
See Local Explorations: 11.

KOS ⌂ ✕

80 km NW of Rhodes. Kos is the second largest of the Dodecanese, after Rhodes. Like Rhodes, it flourished in Classical times, and was occupied by the Knights of St John of Jerusalem during the 14th and 15th centuries. Today, like Rhodes, it has become a major tourist destination, mainly for holidaymakers from Britain and Scandinavia.

The most famous inhabitant of Kos was Hippocrates, the so-called Father of Medicine. He was born here in 460 BC, and according to the records died in 357 BC. This would make him 103 when he died – so despite the primitive state of medicine in his time, it appears that he knew how to treat his most important patient. His medical advice has survived even longer. To this day, before doctors can practise they have to take the Hippocratic Oath,

RECOMMENDED HOTELS

AGATHONISSI
There is a pension at the little port where the boat puts in, or if you ask around, someone will soon fix you up with a room. Don't expect choices, or quality: this place is at the back of beyond.

KOS - Kos Town
Be warned: at the height of the season Kos Town is often completely booked with package tours. But try:

Hotel Koala, DD-DDD; *Harmilou Street; tel. 0242 22 897.*
Small hotel, which, as its name suggests, has Antipodean connections. Foreign visitors are assured a friendly reception. Handy for all the main sights, and close to the harbour.

Continental Palace, DDD; *Kos Town; tel. 0242 22 737.*
A massive resort development down by the sea. Here you have the use of a wide range of facilities, including a luxurious private pool. Ideal for families.

If in trouble consult the EOT (Tourist Office) at Akti Koundouriotou – the waterfront where the ferry puts in.

KOS - Kardamena
The main resort area close to the airport.

Norida Beach Hotel, DD-DDD; *Kardamena; tel. 0242 91 220.*
Massive hotel with more than 400 rooms and a wide range of amenities, including its own pool and tennis courts. Usually block-booked with package tours – but with skilful negotiation, an empty room can sometimes miraculously be found when no such thing exists anywhere else on the island.

LEROS - Laki
Hotel Leros, D; *Laki; tel. 0247 22 940.*
Small hotel, handy for the ferry, on the front. Large, old-style rooms with balconies and views out over the bay. Most rooms have private showers, and many of them even work.

which binds them to the ethics of the profession. This oath largely derives from a treatise Hippocrates wrote, that commits a doctor to treat anyone in need of medical attention.

The present name of this island derives from the rather unfortunate Turkish name it was given in the Middle Ages – Stin Ko. The islanders eventually got rid of the Turks and their name. Today they are known as Koans, though I once heard a Belgian student arguing that they should be known as Les Costives.

The island's long history and frequent occupation by foreign powers has left it with a mixed heritage. The island boasts ancient Greek ruins, a Roman site and a number of Knights' castles. Its architecture shows Turkish, Crusader and Italian influences. Inland, the lower ground is unexpectedly fertile. Unlike many Greek islands it attracts a fair amount of seasonal rain, giving rise to many springs. This accounts for the island's most famous produce: Kos Lettuce. There are also carefully cultivated fields of melons, orange groves and vineyards full of grapes.

But the main feature of Kos today is its beaches, most of which now have their carefully cultivated crop of hotels.

Kos Town

At NE *of the island, on the coast*. This is the island's major town and the centre for much of the resort accommodation. It also contains most of the interesting sights.

In the square just up from the harbour *(Platia tou Platanou)* stands the famous **Plane Tree of Hippocrates**. This venerable old tree has a massive girth of around 14 m and is propped up by ancient pieces of marble and some more modern pieces of scaffolding. According to legend, Hippocrates gave medical lessons in the shade of this tree. Unfortunately, even Hippocrates' celebrated longevity was unequal to this claim, as the tree is only just over 500 years old. Even so, this 'only' makes it one of the oldest

---

LEROS - Platanos
Eleftheria, DD; *by main square; tel.* 0247 23 550.

Comfortable accommodation in the island capital. Close to the action down the slope in Pandeli, but away from the noise.

LESBOS - Molivos
Elaiotriveo, DDD; *Molyvos; tel.* 0253 71 205.

Fairly expensive, but one of the most exceptional hotels in the country. Housed in what was an old olive mill, down by the beach.

LESBOS - Skala Eressou
Thassos House, DD; *Skala.*

Fine large rooms, many with private shower or bath.

Petra Women's Agricultural Tourism Collective, DD; *main square; tel.* 0253 41 238.

The collective acts as an information agency and room-letting service. Started up by the women of the village in 1984, when, as far as I know, it was the first of its kind in Greece. Besides somewhere to stay, it offers a unique opportunity to learn about the day to day life of a Greek village.

PATMOS - Skala
Once again, be sure to book in advance here during July and August.

Astoria Hotel, D; *on the waterfront; tel* 0247 31 205.

Pleasant small hotel with old-style charm, close to where the boats put in.

If this is full, you could try:

Rex Hotel, D; *on the waterfront; tel.* 0247 31 242.

At the end of the front. Large rooms, some with private shower or bath. Friendly service; usually someone available to speak English.

PATMOS - Hora
It is almost impossible to stay in Hora. You are better off trying for accommodation in Skala or by one of the beaches, such as:

PATMOS - Lambi
Dolphin Hotel, DD; *Lambi; tel.* 0247 32 060.

Delightful small hotel – an idyllic spot towards the end of the season.

• St John's Monastery, Patmos.

standing (or leaning) trees in western Europe. When the first green shoots of this tree sprouted from the earth, Columbus was still contemplating an epoch-making voyage to China – and perhaps more relevantly, medicine was still in a largely hit or miss state. Beside the tree is a **Turkish Fountain,** partly made out of pieces from ancient ruins. The basin of the fountain was once a stone tomb.

A bridge from Platia tou Planatou (or Plane Tree Square), leads to the **Knights' Castle**. This has two protective walls, one dating from the 15thC and the other from the early 16thC. Like the Turkish Fountain, parts of this building were constructed out of fragments from earlier ruins. Above the entrance you'll see an Ancient Greek frieze. From the ramparts fine views extend out over the harbour towards the Bay of Bodrum on the Turkish mainland, and you can walk along the former moat, now lined with palm trees.

Below the castle you can see the foundations of the **Agora** and the harbour quarter of what was once the Ancient Roman town. This was destroyed in the great earthquake of 554 AD, and by a quirk of fate the ruins were revealed by another earthquake in 1933.

The town also has a fine **Archaeological Museum**, housing a number of interesting exhibits found at sites all over the island. Inevitably, these include a statue of the island's most famous son, and leading contender for the title 'Patron Saint of Kos Tourism', Hippocrates. There are also statues of Aphrodite, the goddess of love, and Eros, who gave us the word erotic – both of whom are also strong contenders in the Patron Saint of Kos Tourism stakes. In the courtyard you can see a fine mosaic showing Hippocrates greeting Asklepios, son of Apollo, another celebrated early medical luminary.

Sanctuary of Asklepios

Four kilometres south of Kos Town, these remains date from the 4thC BC. There are a number of interesting ruins in a pleasant setting with cypress trees and a backdrop of Mount Dhikeos (which rises to nearly 850 m). The Sanctuary site itself was wrecked by an earthquake, possibly the one that destroyed the Ancient Roman Agora and harbour quarter. Centuries later the Knights of St John pillaged stones from the ruins here to build their castle.

Kardamena

30 km from Kos Town in the middle of the SE coast. This is the second resort centre of the island. It has excellent beaches on either side – but for how long? If the local architects and planners have their way, this will soon be Kos's answer to Miami Beach. Give it another ten years, and they could well have succeeded.

If you want to lie in the sun and listen to ghetto blasters, this is the place for you. You can water-ski, windsurf, paraglide, or just sit on the terrace and watch the world go by through rose-tinted cocktails.

About 15 km south of Kardamena is **Paradise Beach**, which lives up to its name in appearance, although your idea of paradise may not include quite so many Club Mediterranée inhabitants.

Just 5 km off the north coast lies the pretty little island of **Pserimos**, which unfortunately suffers during the season from being pretty little when the day trippers invade in their hordes.

LEROS ⛴ ✕

Island 40 km NW of Kos. Leros has few tourists, but it also has a bad name. During the notorious Colonels' Regime (1867-74) this island was used as a concentration camp, with hundreds of political prisoners confined under hideous conditions. But this is not the only blot on Leros's name.

For a long time, Leros has been a psychiatric dumping ground, a shame on the Greek medical service. Incurable psychiatric patients and mentally handicapped children were, and still are, sent here from all over Greece and kept in 'centres'. A few years ago, a British newspaper exposed the appalling conditions which prevail in these centres – more reminiscent of Eastern Europe than a government which allegedly subscribes to the principles of the EC. Since then, apparently, some improvements have been made. But be warned: if you come here, it is wise to avoid any mention of these places – many of the locals are employed in them, and see them as their livelihood. Under these circumstances, suppressed moral qualms have been known to lead to aggression.

That said, Leros is largely unspoilt. Its five main bays have some lovely beaches and provide some of the most spectacular anchorages in the Aegean. The boat puts in at **Laki**, whose Italian buildings date from the occupation of the Dodecanese during the first half of this century. They now look slightly down at heel.

The best place to head for is **Platanos** on the other (eastern) side of the island. This spills down on either side of a hill towards two bays. The Venetian **Castel** is reached by a long flight of steps, said, as is so often the case, to number one for each day of the year.

The fishing village of **Pandeli**, down the hill from Platanos, is where you will find the action: several lively discos and bars are situated on or near the waterfront. Historians who wish to check on the Colonels' former concentration camp will find it at the army base by the little village of Partheni, in the north of the island, although the chances of being allowed in are remote.

LESBOS ⛴

NE Aegean, off Turkish coast, 240 km NE of Athens. Lesbos, sometimes known as Mitilini, is the third largest of the Greek islands, after Crete, Euboea and Rhodes. To drive from one end of the island to the other you have to cover 70 km.

Lesbos is perhaps best known as the birthplace Sappho, the great woman poet who lived here during the 6thC BC:

Love seized my heart
like a mountain wind
that shook the oak trees.

According to the story, Sappho fell in love with Phaeon, and when he betrayed her she threw herself from a cliff to her death. This is probably a fib, cultivated by Victorian classicists to mask the true nature of Sappho's sexuality. Sappho was a lesbian – and not just because she was born in Lesbos. She wrote some superb love lyrics, and is generally recognized as the first woman poet. Together with her contemporary Alcaeus, also a lesbian, Sappho virtually created subjective lyric poetry. The long tradition of poetry expressing intense personal feelings owes its origins to these two. Just imagine what we would have missed, and how little would be left of world literature, if this side of human nature had never been articulated through poetry.

Lesbos seems to be conducive to literature. Aesop is said to have been born here, as was Arion (the creator of the ancient Greek choral lyric form known as the dithyramb). Lesbos was also the birthplace of the philosopher Theophrastus, who ran the Lyceum – the school in Athens founded by Aristotle. More recently, the last Greek poet to win the Nobel Prize for Literature, Odysseus Elytis, was born here in 1912:

I've dragged my heart this far:
a line sliced into the sand
which the sea will soon erase.

Lesbos is curiously shaped, with two almost landlocked gulfs. Inland it is hilly, and comparatively fertile, with an abun-

139

dance of trees – something of a rarity on an Aegean island. There are several pine woods, and some olive groves reputed to be more than 500 years old. This is great walking country.

The locals are known as avid supporters of the Greek Communist party, which has done much good on the island, setting up collectives and helping poor farmers. Appropriately, one of the first womens' collectives in Greece was founded here in Petra – where it runs the tourist office and the taverna and rents rooms.

There is plenty to see on Lesbos, and not simply because it occupies almost as much space as Luxemburg. Yet there are no truly spectacular sights.

Mitilini

The capital, it has a **Genoese castle** and an excellent small museum, **The House of Lesbos**, with local examples of popular art.

The **Teriade Museum**, 4 km S down the road south at Varia, celebrates the life and work of Teriade, the Parisian art publisher, born here in Lesbos. Colourful lithographs by many of the great 20thC names are here, including Picasso, Matisse and Chagal.

Regular buses run to Varia from Mitilini waterfront. Sadly, you have to pay to get on to the beach at Mitilini, and when you do, it is unexciting. Instead try:

Petra

The home of the womens' collective, a 40-km bus ride from Mitilini. This has a beach, and forms an ideal base for walks and explorations. Try a visit to the petrified forest at **Sigri**, at the western end of this coast. Although it is not a wildly exciting sight – petrified forests don't tend to be lively – the nearby village has a pleasant beach and a castle.

Around 15 km south of here you come to **Skala Eressou**. The beach is excellent, although you will find that others have discovered this too. Sappho was born here in 612 BC, and, not unnaturally, attracts a number of her followers to the site of her home up on the hill overlooking the bay.

On the way back to Mitilini through the southern part of the island you can call at **Ayiassos**, a beautiful mountain village on the side of Mount Olympos.

From here you can go for walks through the pine woods and unspoilt valleys to a number of remote hillside villages.

PATMOS ⇔ ✕

40 km S of Samos. After Orestes had killed his mother, he was pursued by the Furies and forced to seek refuge in Patmos. The most famous figure to be exiled in Patmos, however, was St John the Divine (who may have been the Apostle St John). In 95 AD, St John was banished to Patmos by the Roman Emperor Domitian for outraging the locals at Ephesus by preaching Christianity. While St John was on Patmos he had a revelation as he was sitting in a cave. When he had finished dictating it to his disciple Prochoros, it came to over 22 chapters. This now forms the last book of The Bible and is known as *The Revelations of St John*. Regardless of your religious inclinations, it is hard not to find this book a rich source of subconscious and archetypal images. Essential reading if you are staying any length of time in Patmos, St John's apocalyptic descriptions conjure up an eschatological nightmare which adds a strange dimension of shade to this sun-drenched isle.

Patmos is a blend of the sacred and the profane. It has long been a religious centre of particular importance to the Greek Orthodox Church, and indeed was once known as 'the second Athens'. It has also recently become a centre for the more discriminating, but often profane, tourist. The Agha Khan and Axel Springer – a suitably contrasting pair – both had holiday homes here; and many of the characteristic white-washed houses of the ancient inland capital Hora have been refurbished by artists, who are not generally known for their sacred behaviour. Yet towering above the rooftops of these whited buildings is the dark, brooding fortress-like structure of **St John's Monastery**, which was 900 years old in 1988. It was founded by the blessed Christodoulos, a prominent religious of his time. For me, this spot has an atmosphere like no other in Greece. Be sure to see the **frescos** illustrating scenes from St John's life – including a scene where he turns the magician Kynops into a stone as he leaps into the sea.

The **museum** here has one of Greece's finest collections of orthodox manuscripts, including 33 pages of the *Gospel According to St Mark* in silver on parchment. It also has some impressive icons – one of them a 17thC depiction of St John dictating his revelation to Prochoros. This event is said to have taken place at the nearby **Monastery of the Apocalypse**, constructed around the cave itself.

More secular pursuits are best carried out at **Skala**, where the boats put in. This has a run of smart cafés and restaurants lining the waterfront. The most exciting local beach, though also the most popular, is in the next bay to the north: **Meloi** – pronounced appropriately 'mellowy'.

A more secluded resort is **Lambi** on the north coast (see Recommended Hotels, page 136), with an attractive pebbly beach. See also the restaurant recommended at **Grikou Bay**.

RHODES
See Local Explorations: 12.

SAMOS
See Greece Overall: 10.

RECOMMENDED RESTAURANTS

AGATHONOSSI
There are a couple of tavernas (and a third which is sometimes closed) down by the jetty where the boat puts in. You may well be stuck here for a week, so be sure to reserve your visit to the second one until you have completely exhausted the range of choices at the first. Basic, but none the worse for that.

HORA
Vangelis, D-DD; *the main square.*
Best of the range of tavernas in the centre of Hora.

However, if you are looking for top-of-the-range food at top prices, try the excellent:

Patmian House, DDD; *off the main square.*
First-class cuisine in a beautiful old restored house.

KOS - Kos Town
Romantika, DD; *Akti Koundouriotu; on the harbour front, towards the castle.*
The best of a mediocre collection. You pay for the location, rather than the food. But they do serve some respectable local dishes and the service is friendly. An authentic tourist spot.

For peace, try:

Kivolos Tea House, D-DD; *Ipirou Street.*
Tempting cakes and some superb fresh fruit juices. Just over 0.5 km inland from the harbour beyond the Roman amphitheatre.

LEROS - Laki
Laki is rather disappointing for restaurants. The food is of better quality, and cheaper, a couple of kilometres up the road at Platanos. If you are stuck in Laki, there is a pleasant taverna down on the beach at Koulouki. Here you can lunch off a plate of moussaka and a carafe of retzina, and then spend the afternoon gazing through your binoculars at the line of rusting old tramp steamers anchored out in the bay. This is a popular haven for Greece's enormous mothball mercantile fleet – many of whom will one day miraculously put to sea again when the world-wide recession ends.

LESBOS - Mitilini
Restaurants are not Mitilini's strength. Just choose one where you see a preponderance of locals eating.

PATMOS - Skala
Arion, DDD; *the waterfront.*
Old-style bar-restaurant, the place to see and be seen in on Patmos. Ideal for a drink and to watch the world go by – or to have a meal, and do serious damage to your wallet rather than to your liver.

PATMOS - Grikou Bay
Flisvos Taverna, DD; *Grikou; tel.* 0247 31 380.
Friendly spot in a lovely location on the spur looking down over the beach. It sometimes has a few rooms to rent.

A *Circuit from Paros*
The Cyclades

360 km; map Michelin 980, 1:700000

Here is the archipelago which represents the classic, travel brochure notion of Greek islands. You can wander down tiny twisting lanes of whitewashed cubist houses; happen upon little blue-domed chapels; and muse over views of a pristine blue Aegean beneath a swooning blue sky. Surprisingly, despite the inroads of mass tourism, it remains like this in much of the Cyclades (so-named because the islands form a circle). Even in high season, at the most popular tourist spots such as Paros and Mykonos, it is possible to stroll through the heat of the day down deserted alleyways, with the cats snoozing in the shade; though at other times of day you are unlikely to be so lucky.

The Cyclades are full of history, and this tour takes you to all the main places of interest. You call at Santorini, whose spectacular cliffs were formed by an ancient volcanic explosion; and at the sacred island of Delos where you can see the famous stone lions which still gaze out to sea, just as they did two and a half thousand years ago.

But there is more to the Cyclades than history. These are the fun spots of the Aegean, where young and old, rich and not so rich, come for that all-over suntan, and to live it up at night beneath the stars. For those who prefer a quieter way of life, there are a number of spectacu-larly remote and almost completely unspoilt little islands.

I have suggested a clockwise circuit of the main islands. The others are covered in other tours – look for the cross-references. It does not much matter where you start, but Paros is conveniently central. There is a blue detour to Delos from Mykonos, and from Ios a green detour to the remote islands of Sikinos and Folegandros.

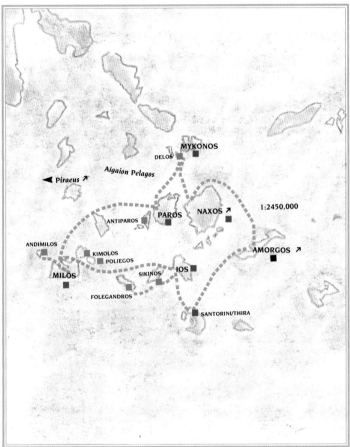

1:2450,000

TRANSPORT
The only way to cover this route is by boat. There are regular ferries between all the main Cycladic islands. The larger islands have car hire facilities, and even the most out-of-the- way islands have bus services connecting the main villages.

143

SIGHTS & PLACES OF INTEREST

AMORGOS
See Greece Overall: 13.

ANDIMILOS
See Milos, page 146.

ANTIPAROS
See Paros, page 147.

DELOS
SW of Mykonos. Ferries for Delos leave from the pier in Mykonos port at 9 am, returning for lunch.

This was once the richest and most powerful of all the Aegean islands. But how could this have come about – on a barren island less than 5 km long and 2 km wide, stuck in the middle of nowhere? The legendary answer is that this was the birthplace of Apollo and Artemis. By the time Ionian civilization arrived here around 1000 BC it was already the centre of a flourishing reli-

gious cult. A more prosaic explanation is the fact that its anchorage is the safest, and probably the handiest, between Europe and Asia – right in the middle of the main sea lanes that connected the two continents in ancient times.

Either way, Delos had risen to become a great power by the 2ndC BC. Yet a century later it was destroyed, its civilization laid waste. The ruins we see today are all that remain after the centuries of abandonment and casual plundering.

No trip to Delos would be complete without a visit to the famous **Terrace of the Lions.** The wind and sand have blurred their features, and only five of the original nine remain. (A missing one can be seen outside the Arsenal in Venice.) Also well worth seeing is the **Theatre District**. Its dilapidated theatre was once capable of seating an audience of five thousand, and the House of Masks has some intriguing mosaics.

RECOMMENDED HOTELS

FOLEGANDROS
Pension Fani-Vevis, D-DD; Kastro-Chora; tel. 0286 41 437.

A real find in such an out-of-the-way spot. A small establishment, but clean and friendly. Island living as you hoped to find it.

IOS
Mare-Monte, DD; Ios Town; tel. 0286 91 564.

Small, well-run establishment. About as good as you will get in town.

If you want to be by the beach, try:

Petradi's, DD; Ios Town; tel. 0286 91 510.

Located out of town, on the road to the beach. Rooms with balconies looking out over the sea. You are spared the nightly decibel epicentre down the road, but it is not always as quiet as an equivalent spot might be on another island. People don't come to Ios to go to sleep.

MILOS
Venus Village, DDD; Adamas; tel.

0287 22 030.

Large resort development just above the sea to the west of town with nearly a hundred rooms, including some attractive chalets. A range of amenities includes private pool and tennis courts. Ideal for children.

Semiramis, DD; 25th Martinou Street; tel. 0287 22 117.

In contrast to the Venus Village, this is a peaceful small hotel with no spectacular amenities and a friendly personal welcome.

MYKONOS
Some of the hotels here can be very expensive indeed. The places recommended below fall within our usual price guidllelines (page 12), so DDD does not mean ruinous.

MYKONOS - Mykonos Town
Apollon, Odos Mavroyenis. DDD; tel. 0289 23 271.

If you want to be right at the centre of the action, this is the place to stay. It is the oldest hotel on the island, and has bedrooms overlooking the main harbour, with superb, but not very peaceful views.

FOLEGANDROS 🛏

W *of Ios and Sikinos.* This is one of those small islands that people tend to forget, yet it is well worth a visit, if only to see its spectacular capital, **Hora**. This is perched on the plateau above 300-m cliffs, and is filled with little medieval dwellings.

It used to be the island where Greece's more authoritarian governments sent internal political exiles. Apart from Hora, the only attractions are the spectacular cliffscapes, and a cave with stalactites at **Hrissospilia**, which is only accessible by boat.

The ferry puts in at Karavostassi, and there is a stony beach just down the coast at **Livadi**. The best beach is at **Livadaki** (Little Livadi), 10 km away at the other end of the island.

IOS 🛏 ✕

S *of Naxos.* I find it difficult to know what to say about Ios. It is either 'the greatest' or 'the grossest', depending upon your point of view, your age, and your tolerance level.

Over a decade ago, Ios became famous as the 'Rock Island'. Word quickly got around, and the young from Dublin to Dusseldorf flocked to Ios for the music. To the horror of less hedonistic generations, they set about enjoying themselves wholeheartedly – in a fashion seldom witnessed since the days of the original Bacchanalian and Dionysian revels. (Greece has a long and glorious tradition of such behaviour, even if it has lapsed a little during the centuries since modern 'civilization' arrived.) Sex, drink and rock-and-roll filled most of the night, and lazing naked on the beach accounted for the hangover. This barren little island, with but one village and a few heavily overcrowded beaches, soon began to witness all that the parents of its holiday inhabitants confined to their worst nightmares.

The locals did not like it either – but they have decided to accept it (often grudgingly) for the sake of the money.

Hotel Phillippi, DD; *Kaloyera; tel.* 0289 22 294.

This one is a short walk in from the harbour, and much quieter than the Apollon, above. It has a beautiful garden and large clean rooms. An ideal base for a few days' stay on Mykonos, with very helpful staff, some of whom speak English.

MYKONOS - Aghios Stephanos
The beach a couple of kilometres north of Mykonos Town.

Alkistis, DD; *by the beach; tel.* 0289 22 332.

Large establishment with nearly 100 chalet-style rooms overlooking the sea. Can be hectic during the height of the season, but it is usually quieter here than in Mykonos Town. Easy walk into town for the evening's revels.

PAROS - Parikia
Dina, D; *by the market; tel.* 0284 21 325.

Delightful, romantic spot with pleasant rooms offering balconies and showers. Very helpful English-speaking staff.

SANTORINI - Thira Town
Atlantis Hotel, DDD; *Thira; tel.* 0286 22 232.

The best hotel in town, on the edge of the cliff with panoramic views out over the sea far below. Worth splashing out on this one for a romantic night.

Towards the other end of the market is:

Villa Maria, D-DD; *25th Martinou Street; tel.* 0286 22 168.

A pleasant, airy spot, just off the main square.

MYKONOS - Perissa Beach
Christina's, D-DD; *Perissa; tel.* 0286 22 586.

Small, with just seven rooms – so be sure to book ahead. Right by the beach, with its own friendly restaurant. A useful base for visiting the Ancient Thira site.

SIKINOS
You will find a few rooms down by the port where the boat puts in. For romantic peace and views, try for a room up at Kastro-Hora.

• *Mykonos.*

Money is a problem here – thieving is not unknown and Ios has never developed, as Mykonos has, into a respectable hedonistic resort. However, this is where you come to serve your apprenticeship, and it can be a gruelling initiation.

Like it or not, nightlife is the thing on Ios. It can be loud and hectic, although most of the bedlam is harmless fun. For a night out you'll never remember, try **The Slammer Bar**, in Ios Town.

The name says it all. You could also try **Dido's**, also in Ios Town, which has a reputation for perpetual party atmosphere.

Those who want something other than 'youth culture' will want to visit the island's sights. To the north, is a place alleged to be **Homer's tomb**. Historians discount this, but according to legend Homer was washed ashore here and buried by the beach. Those who contend that Homer was in fact several different people living at the same time, one of whom was probably blind, will notice plenty of Homeric look-alikes on the island.

The island also has several hundred charming little chapels scattered about its 120 square kilometres and some typical Cycladic windmills.

KIMOLOS
See Milos, below.

MILOS ⌷ ✕
W *of Folegandros.* Even if you have never heard of this island, you are likely to know of the Statue, Venus de Milo (Greek name, Milos Aphrodite).

In 1820, a visiting French admiral noticed this 2,000-year-old statue standing in the garden of a local farmer. After a year of bargaining, skulduggery and even physical violence, the statue was eventually bought, given to Louis XVIII of France, and ended up in the Louvre in Paris. Sources disagree as to whether the arms disappeared during or before the disputes accompanying its purchase.

Milos has another claim to fame. At the end of the 17thC, a group of islanders led by Archbishop Georgirenes emigrated to London. Here the Duke of York gave them a site on which to build a Greek Orthodox church, the first of its kind in London. The church has long since disappeared, but the street in Soho where it stood is still known as Greek Street.

Despite all this, Milos is one of the least known islands of the Cyclades. This is largely because for many years it was a mining centre. Once a volcano, its rocks are rich in minerals, and parts of the mountains have been gouged out to provide obsidian, perlite (an acid volcanic glass), baryta (used in cylindrical moving-point recording apparatuses) and other such useful substances.

This meant that tourism came late to Milos, and out of season it remains relatively quiet. The boat puts in at Adamas, which has a fine natural harbour. The best places to stay are around **Plaka**, 4 km north, at the entrance to the bay.

If you can, take a boat out to any of the three small offshore islands, which have some spectacular basalt cliffscapes. To the north is the largest, **Kimilos** (meaning chalk, which was mined here). This is an inhabited island, and there is some accommodation. Nearby **Poliegos** is used for herding goats; and **Andimilos** to the west is the home of a rare type of antelope, said to be similar to the elusive Kri-kri of Crete.

MYKONOS ⌷ ✕
N *of* Naxos. Mykonos is the Aegean's answer to the South of France. The Riviera used to be astonishingly beautiful, Mykonos still is. This is the island of blindingly whitewashed cubist houses, little chapels sillhouetted against the blue, blue sea, and paradise beaches.

Mykonos has a typical recent colonial history. The earliest western European colonizers were primitive, though fairly well-heeled, bohemians and artists, who began arriving in the late 1950s and early 1960s. The second wave of invaders appeared to be of more barbarian stock, with a rudimentary lifestyle to match. Yet, for the most part, the Hippies were no marauders, and were content to set up their primitive culture on the beaches. Then came a rather more sophisticated invasion, marked by exotic cultural displays and even more flamboyant tribal dress – or none at all. For many years Mykonos thrived as a gay centre, although in time the ascendancy of these invaders also began to wane. Now Mykonos civilization is an easy-going blend of pleasure-seeking cultures.

This is the place to have fun, but be prepared – it can get expensive. Everything you may have heard about Mykonos nightlife is likely to be true. (For specific recommendations, see page 149.) The gourmet restaurants, smart bars, and wildly sophisticated (or camp) discos provide ample opportunity for mayhem, broken hearts and broken glasses. A regular part of the morning, easing into early afternoon, is set aside for nursing the collective hangover. Sizzling afternoons are for wanton sunbathing and gossip. Then cocktail time arrives and the whole process begins again.

The best, and most famous, beaches are on the south of the island. They can be reached by caique, by foot or by taxi. On this stretch, the white sands of **Psarou** are the closest to Mykonos Town. Next one along is **Piranga**, which has some exciting snorkelling among the rocks. Beyond this is **Paradise Beach**, where any kind of clothing used to be frowned upon. Further on is **Super Paradise Beach**, where nothing is frowned upon, and even further on, the last resort, is **Elia Beach**. Nowadays these beaches no longer observe a strict undress code, and tolerance has long since been extended towards heterosexuality.

The best view on the island – and arguably in the whole Aegean – is from the 400-year-old **Boni Windmill**, which stands on the hill above the town. The harbour front is also a delight, and no visit to Mykonos would be complete without a stroll through the narrow winding alleyways of the **old town**. These were purposely constructed to defeat the intentions of invading pirates. Fleeing into the maze of alleyways, the women could avoid rape, and the men could prey on any foreign invader who became separated from his companions. Centuries later, these alleyways can serve a similar purpose late at night.

Those who take an interest in old bones and old stones should visit the **museum**, which contains a number of finds from nearby Delos.

NAXOS
See Local Explorations: 10.

PAROS ⚑ ✕
W *of Naxos*. Deep in the winter night of Europe, freezing impoverished students in their garrets discuss dreams of idyllic summer in the Greek Cyclades. Months later, these dreams materialize – Scandinavians, Dutch, Germans, French, Irish, rainbow-haired punks and Luxemburgers emerge from the Piraeus ferry on to the quayside at Paros: first stop on their tour of the Cyclades. They give the island a pleasantly innocent party atmosphere, a contrast to the more sophisticated hedonism of Mykonos, or the hard-core pandemonium of Ios.

Parikia Town, where the boats put in, is at first glance a little tasteless – cocktail lists, garish postcard scarecrows and scooter hire notices jostle amongst the tourist tavernas. Yet behind this is a maze of beautiful narrow back streets, with whitewashed buildings and little domed chapels.

The church here, **Panagia Ekatondapiliani**, is regarded as the finest in the Aegean. Its name means 'one hundred doors', and according to one expert, 99 of these have been found. The last one was allegedly stolen by the Turks and taken to Istanbul – a popular Greek excuse for any relic that can't be found.

Then there is **Petaloudhes**, 'the Valley of the Butterflies', and, as usual, some superb monasteries in impossible locations. If you have come here for the beaches, they are scattered all around the coast, in varying degrees of respectability and remoteness. For surfing try **Santa Maria**, at the northeastern end of the island.

For a wild time with a difference, try heading across the strait to the small island of **Antiparos** – where the over-thirties are so rare as to be something of a protected species.

POLIEGOS
See Milos, page 146.

SANTORINI/THIRA 🛥 ✕
S of Ios. Named after Saint Irene of Salonika, the island has recently taken to using its ancient name Thira. Santorini is formed from the remains of an ancient volcano which blew up with a force only matched by that of Krakatoa. This explosion diverted the course of European civilization. When the volcano erupted in 1450 BC there were earthquakes all around the Aegean, huge tidal waves destroyed coastal settlements througout the region, and the entire south coast of Crete was thrust 5 m higher by the tectonic plate shifting beneath it.

This catastrophe virtually destroyed Minoan civilization throughout the Aegean, dealing it a blow from which it never fully recovered. Had this apparently easy-going culture been able to continue, the development of Ancient Greek history might have taken a dif-ferent course. Ensuing civilization might have evolved without the need for philosophers, badly behaved gods, mathematics or tedious Greek tragedies – and instead we could have lived happy mindless lives watching topless girls athletically hurling them-selves between the horns of bulls (i.e., not that different from the philosopher-less beach culture of today.)

The destruction of Santorini, or per-haps Minoan culture as a whole, entered Ancient Greek history as the legend of lost Atlantis, a golden civilization which is said to have sunk into the sea.

Nowadays, Santorini is one of the most spectacular holiday spots in the Aegean. Its high cliffs (the walls of the ancient volcano) enclose a bay (the col-lapsed flooded crater). The volcano has not finished, however. One of those charred islands in the middle of the bay is in fact a dormant volcano. It only appeared in 1772, and expanded with a series of eruptions in 1866, 1925 and 1956.

The approach by boat is spectacu-lar. High above the water, perched on the tip of the cliff, you can see the tiny white houses and churches of the town

---

RECOMMENDED RESTAURANTS

IOS
Pavlos, D-DD; *Ios Town.*
A real find – except that many other people seem to have found it, too. Imaginative menu, with local spe-cialities and some local inventions. Friendly clientele.

MILOS
Trapetselli's, DD-DDD; *Adamas.*
Down the road to the beach. This is the best restaurant in town, and it also boasts a romantic setting by the sea.
There are also some pleasant tav-ernas on the waterfront in town.

MYKONOS
Antonini's, DD-DDD; *on the waterfront.*
A venerable old Mykonos institu-tion, renowned for its fine Greek cuisine.

El Greco, DD; *Mykomnos Town.*
Excellent Greek menu, with some international dishes. Delightful garden atmosphere.

PAROS - Parikia
For the best food in town at a reason-able price, try:

To Tamarisko, DD; *near the market.*
Real Greek food in a delightful gar-den setting.

For further choices, and possibly for a wild time, head for the bar com-plex at the top end of the harbour. Here you will find such all-time favourites as The Hard Rock Café, The Downunder and so on.

SANTORINI
Camile Stephani's, DD-DDD; *Kamari.*
This used to be the best restaurant in Thira Town, now it has moved to where the action is. Pleasant spot with up-market trimmings, right by the beach. Delicious seafood, and they even have their own special wine.

of Thira. To reach Thira from the landing jetty, you have to climb 582 steps, hire a mule, or take the cable car.

When you get to the top, the view is breathtaking. With its little cobbled streets and whitewashed houses, it is still very beautiful, in spite of tourism.

From here you can catch buses to the other side of the island. Santorini is only 20 km long, and just over 4 km wide at its widest. Inland the volcanic soil is highly fertile, and vineyards proliferate. The wine has a sweet, strong muscatel taste. According to some vigorous oneological researchers I once met here, the way to avoid a hangover is to drink it with ice cubes.

The beautiful sandy beaches are made of black volcanic sand – disappointing only to bucket and spade enthusiasts. Non-purist seven-year-olds can enjoy themselves on fine beaches at **Perissa** and **Monolithos**, but avoid Kamari, which has died the death of a thousand tourists.

Despite its reduced size, Santorini has remains from all the main periods of early Greek history: Minoan, Mycenaean, Classical, Byzantine.

The Minoan site just below **Akrotiri** in the south was heroically excavated by Professor Marinatos, who was reburied here after his excavations collapsed on top of him in 1974. This is an interesting site, but unfortunately the best frescos were stolen by Athens, where they remain in the Archaeological Museum.

Ancient Thira is in the south-east, by Perissa Beach, and has ruins dating from the 9thC BC to the Byzantine era. Inland, and nearly 600 m up, at the island's highest point, stands the small early 18thC monastery of **Profitis Ilias**. Inside, this has an interesting little museum of icons, and outside a garden full of spectacular radio masts and radar discs – seemingly engaged in a high-tech search of the heavens.

SIKINOS 🏝

SW *of* Ios. This is just the place if you want peace and quiet after the chaos of Ios. It is only 14 km across the water, but it feels like a world away. Tourism has made few inroads – there are no very obvious attractions, and as yet few amenities.

Sikinos used to be known as 'Wine Island', but its once-fertile vineyards

have now vanished. There is a harbour at Alopronia, and the sleepy capital Kastro-Hora is on the ridge. Between them they contain less than three hundred permanent inhabitants. On the hill stands a derelict monastery. The best beach is at Aghios Nikolaos, up the east coast from the port.

The northern tip of the island has the curious name of Kavos tis Maltas (Cape Malta). Various theories have sought to explain this odd name. My own is that it was named after a band of Maltese pirates who are known to have plied their trade in this part of the Aegean several hundred years ago. One of their bases was on the Dodecanese island of Astipalea: the village where they lived is still known as Maltesania.

MYKONOS - BARS & NIGHTLIFE

Montparnasse, DD; *Aghios Ayarginos* Street.

Down by the beach to the west of the main harbour, in the direction of Little Venice. One of Mykonos' most famous 'sunset' bars, complete with classical music. Just the place to start the ball rolling for the evening.

Scandinavian Bar, DD; *close to south-western end of waterfront.*

Vast bar and menagerie. Perennial party- atmosphere-cum-hysteria. A typical holiday bar that can become addictive.

Yacht Club, DD; *by the port.*

An island institution, whose clientele is likely to cover the entire social range from top to bottom. *The* place to go on to, at the end of the night. Usually quite lively until it closes around breakfast time.

Other spots to be spotted in:

Oasis, *on Mitropoleos Street.*

La Mer, *near Oasis and slightly smarter.*

Pierro's, *Matayianni Street, near the waterfront.*

Once almost exclusively gay (despite appearances to the contrary). Now appearances are no longer so deceptive.

Between Athens and Rhodes
Aegean Crossing

440 km; map Michelin 980, 1:700000

This route has something for almost all tastes, and makes an ideal introduction to the different aspects of the Greek islands – whether you favour splendid isolation, or living it up in the resorts. It takes you across the breadth of the Aegean, from the Greek mainland to Rhodes, off the Turkish mainland.

Paros and Naxos are two of the largest and most popular of the Cyclades, the islands best known for their lovely whitewashed villages, quaint chapels, and wild taverna nights. Further east, you come to the Dodecanese, the group of islands scattered alongside the Turkish coast. Some of these are the most remote of all the islands. Here you can visit deserted villages high in the mountains, isolated monasteries where you can stay the night, and the grumbling crater of a dormant volcano.

The natural starting point is the Athens port of Piraeus, but as with all the routes and tours in this guide, you can start (and finish) where you like. You take the ferry to Paros, which lies at the hub of the Cyclades. From Paros it is just a short hop to Naxos, another popular resort island with some beautiful inland scenery. After Naxos you come to Amorgos, one of the lesser-known Cyclades.

Next stop, Astipalea, is the first of the Dodecanese, although you only really begin to appreciate the difference between these two island groups when you arrive at your next stop, Kalimnos. A further hop takes you to Kos, renowned for its beaches, nightlife, and rare inland pastures. From here you go to the even more popular resort island of Rhodes, travelling by way of the green route via the tiny, almost unspoilt islands of Nissiros, Tilos, and Simi.

You can sail directly from Athens to Rhodes in less than a day. However, if you spend a day or so on the islands that take your fancy, you could easily spend a week on the crossing.

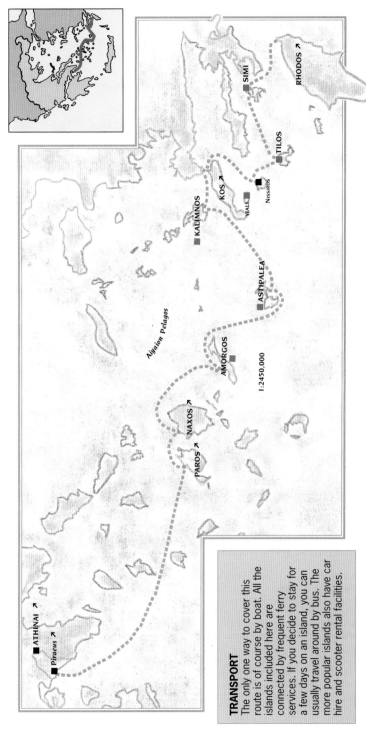

TRANSPORT

The only one way to cover this route is of course by boat. All the islands included here are connected by frequent ferry services. If you decide to stay for a few days on an island, you can usually travel around by bus. The more popular islands also have car hire and scooter rental facilities.

SIGHTS & PLACES OF INTEREST

AMORGOS ⌔ ✕

The outermost of the Cyclades group, 30 km SE of Naxos. This is a barren, out-of-the-way spot with a hidden charm of its own, which soon becomes apparent if you stay for a few days.

The island is just over 30 km long and only 6 km wide. A high, ridged spine runs along the centre, rising to three peaks. The highest, Krikelas, is in the north-east, and rises to 780 m. Seeing its barren slopes nowadays, it's difficult to believe that this mountain was once covered in woods.These were all burnt down in the 19thC by a spectacular fire which lasted three weeks. According to a contemporary report by an understandably anonymous witness, the islanders are said to have 'gaped in stupid idleness and wonder as the great fires lit up the night sky and burned their island home to barren rock.' What else do you do, when there are no roads, and no fire brigade?

According to tradition, Amorgos women are renowned for their beauty. It is possible that this tradition has now lapsed – I have never noticed any exceptional beauties here. This island was also the home of the ancient poet Simonides, who came from Samos but emigrated to Amorgos, apparently to found a colony. Simonides also appears to have been disappointed with the beauty of Amorgos women, for he wrote a number of poems comparing them to various animals. Visitors who wish to take a more positive approach than Simonides should seek out the island's indisputable geographical and cultural beauties. There are several places well worth a visit:

Katapola

This is the port where the boats put in, on the middle of the west coast of the island. Take the steps up the hillside and you come to the ruins of ancient **Minoa**. The most interesting finds from here, including some fine Cycladic idols, were stolen by the French at the end of the 19thC and are now in the Louvre. If you're feeling adventurous, continue on the path south from the ruins. This leads through some beautiful little unspoilt villages to a tower at **Aghia Triada** which is more than 2,000 years old.

Hora

Four km from Katapola, this is the island's ancient capital, sometimes known as Kastro, or simply Amorgos. It has a 13thC Venetian castle, which looks down over the coastline. Hora is around a thousand feet above sea level, and the walk up from Katapola takes just under an hour; or you can take the bus, which has an unsettling tendency to return a little earlier than you have been led to believe.

South of Chora there are some fabulous sandy beaches, and the cliffs along the south coast are exceptionally beautiful. But the main thing to see at Chora is the famous Chozoviotissa or **Convent of the Presentation of the Virgin**. It is in a shimmering setting beneath huge cliffs and just half an hour's walk north east of Chora. Inside, one of the monks will take you to see the famous 11thC icon of the Virgin which originally came from Cyprus. Then he'll give you a coffee and a sweet. Be sure to dress properly (no bare legs or arms, male or female), and don't come after 2 pm, as the siesta hour here is inviolate and appears to continue until next morning at sunrise.

Egiali

This is the port at the north of the island, 17 km from Katapola. From Katapola you can either take the ferry, or travel by caique. Alternatively, it *can* be reached by a five-hour inland walk, which is said to lead through some superb unspoilt countryside. Egiali may seem a remote spot, but people still find their way here in the summer. The beach is pleasant, and in the hinterland there are some wonderful walks through unspoilt countryside to some truly idyllic villages – notably south to the whitewashed churches of Potamos, north up the hillside to enchant-ing Langada, and along the beach and up the valley path to Tholaria, which has some Roman tombs.

ASTIPALEA ⌔ ✕

70 km SE of Naxos, 40 km SW of Kos. Astipalea is the first of the Dodecanese islands you encounter as you travel eastwards across the Aegean. In fact, its barren geography is much more like

RECOMMENDED HOTELS

AMORGOS - Katapola
The ferry tends to put in here rather late at night, so if you are coming in high season you may have to take your chance with any rooms available for the first night of your stay.

Minoa Hotel, D-DD; *Katapola.*
One of the very few hotels on the island, handy for the ferry.

Otherwise the main accommodation here is in rooms. The best of these are at:

Pension Amorgos, D; *Katapola; tel.* 0285 71 013.
Just by the quay where the ferry puts in.

AMORGOS - Egiali
Mike, D; *seafront; tel.* 0285 71 252.
Small hotel right by the beach, at this pleasant northern resort. Be sure to ring ahead in July or August.

AMORGOS - Chora
A number of places let out rooms here. Naturally these tend to be rather spartan, though inexpensive.

ASTIPALEA - Astipalea Town
Both the hotels I have recommended are in the lower town, close to the action. Those wanting a more peaceful atmosphere might prefer to try the upper town, where there are a number of inexpensive rooms for rent.

Hotel Paradissos, D-DD; *on the waterfront; tel.* 0243 61 224.
Right by the sea, for a night in paradise. If cleanliness is next to godliness, this place can be said to live up to its name; but don't expect heavenly accommodation at this price.

Hotel Astynea, D; *on the waterfront; tel.* 0243 61 209.
Another cheap and cheerful small hotel down by the port.

KALIMNOS - Pothia
Themelina Hotel, DD-DDD; *close to the Museum.*

Old-style courtesies are observed here, and there is a distinct atmosphere of gracious living. The new chalets and private pool should be ready by the time this book is published, but don't count on it – you are in the islands.

KALIMNOS - Mirties
Zephyros, D; *Mirties; tel.* 0243 47 500.
Pleasant, unpretentious spot with two dozen rooms, close to the sandy (volcanic grey) beach.

NISSIROS
Porfyris, DD; *Mandraki.*
Take a romantic room with a view out over the orange grove towards the blue, blue sea. It has its own pool, and a friendly, international clientele.

Hotel Three Brothers, D; *Mandraki.*
Basic, unpretentious spot, right by the harbour. One of the staff is multilingual and very helpful about ferry timetables and buses.

SIMI
Aliki Hotel, D-DD; *on the waterfront, Simi Town; tel.* 0241 71 665.
One of the elegant old houses on the waterfront, dating from the time when Simi was one of the richest islands in the Aegean. This is where the stars stayed when they were filming *Pascali's Island.* Close to the clock tower.

An exceptional place to stay in the upper town (Horio) is:

Panormitis, D; *Horio; tel.* 0241 71 354.
Plain, ascetic rooms in a 200-year-old monastery.

TILOS
Irini, D; *Livadia.*
Rural atmosphere, friendly service. Small hotel, many rooms with private shower.

If this is full, try:

Livadia, D; *tel.* 53 202.
Has a dozen or so fairly large rooms, most with private shower.

• *Kalimnos, famous for its sea sponges.*

that of the Cyclades. There is, nevertheless, one great difference – for years this island was only served by infrequent ferries, which means it has been largely ignored by visitors. Nowadays, sadly, this is changing, and the days of package tours do not seem far away. But out of season, and away from the beaten track, this island remains almost unspoilt.

In Classical times the island of Astipalea achieved notoriety as the home of the great boxer Kleomedes. Whilst fighting in the Olympic Games, Kleomedes unfortunately killed his opponent (one Ikkos of Epidavros). Kleomedes was disqualified, and the judges' decision outraged him so much that he stormed out of the games. He was still in such a fury when he arrived back at Astipalea that the locals were unable to restrain him. Going berserk, he set about the local school building and hurled its walls to the ground. Unfortunately, it was full at the time and all the children inside were killed. What happened to Kleomedes after this remains obscure.

The great medieval chronicler Stephanos of Byzantium once described Astipalea as 'The Table of the Gods', on account of the breathtaking beauty of its flowers and its abundance of fruit. Things have changed since Stephanos' day, although I am told that in spring the flowers are still very beautiful. Astipalea has the alleged distinction of being the only Greek island which has no snakes. For centuries it was also one of the greatest sponge fishing centres in the

Aegean. In the old days the swimmers would dive into the water clutching a rock to carry them down to sufficient depth, and then skilfully slice the sponges with their knife in the other hand, collecting them in a net bag. Sponges have been harvested here since earliest times. There are references to them in Homer and Aristotle, and they were used as padding, to stop chafing, inside suits of armour.

The island has just over a thousand permanent inhabitants, and over a dozen offshore islets and several shoals of rocks along the shoreline. On the map it has a curious butterfly shape. Its two 'wings' (14 and 11 km long respectively) are joined by a narrow isthmus. The main port, also known as Astipalea, is on the larger south-western wing.

Astipalea Town
On the E coast of the W half of the island, the port here was built by the Italians, who took the island in their Dodecanese campaign against the Turks in 1912. The town itself looks typically Cycladean – complete with a row of nine abandoned windmills. Beside them you will find extensive views out over the north of the island. There is also a Venetian castle, built in the 13thC by John Quirini – you can still see the Quirini family crest on the entrance.

Once, when the island was less barren, it must have produced an abundance of honey. Evidence for this comes from a story concerning an attack on the castle. The islanders, it is said, kept beehives on the ramparts. When the enemy advanced, the islanders goaded the bees into a fury and hurled them down into the face of their enemy.

Unfortunately the castle is now derelict, but you can still walk through the alleyways amongst the deserted dwellings.

Other places of interest: A 20-minute walk over the hill and down the coast from Astipalea Town brings you to **Livadia**, which has a good sandy beach and some tavernas.

Head north to the isthmus and you come to the fishing village of **Maltesana**. This place received its curious name because it was once the base for a gang of Maltese pirates, who plied their trade in the Aegean. Stories of hidden treasure in the nearby hinterland persist.

Further on, to the north of the eastern wing of the island, is the attractive natural harbour of **Vathi**.

KALIMNOS ⚓ ✕

60 km NE of Astipalea, 15 km N of Kos. Nearly two thousand years ago the Roman poet Ovid described Kalimnos as 'shaded with woods and fruitful in honey.' Now the island is grey, rocky and barren, with the exception of a few valleys between the high mountains, which rise to nearly 700 m.

The main industry here used to be sponge fishing, but now most of the sponges are affected by the disease which swept the Mediterranean several years ago.

Several of the houses and churches are painted blue and white. This custom is said to date from the Italian occupation during the Second World War, when the islanders took to painting their dwellings in the Greek national colours as an unspoken protest against the foreign invaders.

The ferry arrives at the port of Pothia, whose narrow streets make a perfect funnel to concentrate the sound of the speeding motorbikes and roaring car engines. The only thing worth seeing here is the **Museum**, which contains some interesting finds from the island's many caves. After this, it's best to leave town as soon as possible.

A pleasant spot to head for is the little beach resort of **Mirties** on the north-west coast. If you are looking for some night-time action, head out to Kandouni, 4 km south of Mirties, where there are a couple of lively nightspots. The best of these is Domus Bar.

Opposite Mirties is the volcanic island of **Telenedos**, which is reached by frequent local ferries across the 1.5 km strait. Here you can explore the beaches, visit a derelict monastery, and a ruined castle, before retiring to one of the tavernas in the island's single village.

A 40-minute bus ride west of Pothia takes you to **Vathi**. From here you can walk inland up a beautiful fertile valley filled with orange groves, fig trees and vines.

KOS
See Greece Overall: 11.

NAXOS
See Local Explorations: 10.

NISSIROS ⚓ ✕

60 km E of Astipalea, 20 km S of Kos. Once upon a time the sea god Poseidon was chasing the giant Polybotes across the Aegean. Unable to catch up with his enemy, Poseidon broke a lump off the island of Kos and hurled it after Polybotes, pinning him beneath it. And so the island of Nissiros was born.

In fact, Nissiros is a dormant volcano. The island is 8 km in diameter, and its cone is about 700 m high. It is renowned for its black sand beaches and its almond trees. The local speciality is *soumada*, a drink made from almonds that tastes like dissolved marzipan.

The ferry arrives at the port of **Mandraki**, a village of whitewashed and brightly coloured houses with balconies overlooking tiny twisting streets. Above the village is the usual ruined Venetian castle.

A nearby ruin well worth visiting is at **Paleokastro**. There may well have been a settlement here in Minoan times, although the present remains are largely Mycenaen and Classical. Some of the finds from this site are housed in the local museum at Mandraki.

If you are looking for pleasant beaches, head out east towards Pali, 5 km down the road. A further 2 km takes you to a brown volcanic sand beach at **Lies**. For something even more out of the ordinary, take a caique from Mandraki across to the island of **Yiali**, 6 km to the north. This isolated spot is renowned for its beaches.

The big sight at Nissiros – which attracts boat-loads of day-trippers from nearby Kos – is the volcano. This is still known as Polybotes, after the unfortunate giant. Catch a bus up from Mandraki, via the village of Nikia and take the short walk up to the crater itself. It is truly spectacular – a moonscape, but alive, with gushes of steam, a foul sulphurous stench and subterranean rumblings. This is no extinct volcano, as you quickly realize – its most recent eruptions were in 1522 and 1888.

PAROS
See Greece Overall: 12.

RHODES
See Greece Overall: 14.

SIMI 🛏 ✕
25 km N of Rhodes. The small (10 km long) island of Simi is almost encircled by two headlands from the Turkish mainland. However, its main contact with the outside world is Rhodes. During the high season the day trippers arrive here in hordes – but around three in the afternoon they start to leave, and all becomes quiet again.

The main port, where you arrive, is also known as Simi. It's in a beautiful natural harbour and was an important Aegean trading centre. For centuries the Simiots were famous throughout the Aegean as boat builders. Satisfied customers who tested the local product to destruction included Homer's heroes, the Crusaders and the Turkish

---

RECOMMENDED RESTAURANTS

AMORGOS - Katapola
Akrogiali, D; *in the main square.*
Cheap and cheerful island dining, with friendly informal atmosphere.

AMORGOS - Chora
O Kastanis, D; *on the main street.*
Country-style taverna serving slightly primitive fare at very low prices. Best for lunchtime snacks, although it is reputed to become lively in the evenings if there are enough people staying up here.

When I visited I was told by a German that the restaurant's name means 'The Chestnut', but a French student angrily disagreed and said that it meant something completely different, although he wouldn't say what. When the owner was asked to adjudicate, he awarded the table a further bottle of retzina and said that we could call his restaurant whatever we liked, so long as we didn't go on making too much noise during the siesta.

ASTIPALEA - Astipalea Town
Astropalea, DD; *lower town.*
Bar-restaurant where they serve high-quality, high-priced seafood. Lovely views, good for a romantic evening.

Viki's Taverna, D-DD; *lower town.*
Satisfying, rough-and-ready fare in a friendly informal atmosphere. Patronized by a lively, international student crowd.

A word of warning: not all Astipaleans are outgoing towards foreigners, and it is worthwhile checking your bill in all but the places I've recommended.

KALIMNOS - Arginontas
A welcome swimming spot 6 km up the road beyond Mirties.

Vanzanelis, D; *at the beach; tel.* 0243 47 389.
Pleasant, seaside taverna by lovely beach. They also have a few inexpensive rooms.

KALIMNOS - Mirties
Delfini, D-DD; *by the beach; tel.* 0243 47 514.
Ideal for a long, late lunch with a bottle of retzina, after a hard morning lounging on the beach.

NISSIROS
Mike's Taverna, D; *Mandraki.*
It is difficult to recommend this place too highly. An Australo-Greek-run establishment with the best qualities of both nationalities and some excellent inexpensive food, including

galley fleet. Unfortunately, the wood for the boats came from the forests on the mainland, and when access to these was cut off in 1912 as a result of the Italian invasion, the boat building trade collapsed. The effect was immediate and devastating – from being an island richer than Rhodes, Simi sank to penury. Even so, the old ship-builders' and merchants' houses remain, and many of them have been aesthetically restored.

Simi Town has no outstanding beaches, but there are a few remote little bays and coves around the coast. The main sight on the island is the large monastery of **Aghios Mihalis Panormitis** in the south, which attracts day trippers, but some of the more remote monasteries are worth a visit, too. Dedicated walkers should try making it to Aghios Emilianos by the sea on the extreme west of the island.

TILOS 🛏 ✕

35 km NW of Rhodes. Tilos is small (just 14 km long) and way off the beaten track. Despite this, it has started to attract day trippers from Rhodes. This is surprising, because it is a long way to come to a place without special attractions. The main thing here is the away-from-it-all atmosphere, which begins to seep in only gradually and takes possession of you after a few days.

You arrive at the small port of Livadia. This is not a bad place, but I suggest that you catch the bus across the island to **Megalo Horio**, and then on to the remoter beaches of Aghios Antonios and Eristo. Megala Horio, whose name in English, Big Town, may strike as a slight exaggeration, has a couple of things worth seeing. In the tiny local museum you can see the petrified bones of some woolly mammoths found in caves to the south of the island. Also, on the way up to the inevitable ruined Venetian castle, you will see the remains of some Pelasgian walls, said to have been built by the earliest inhabitants of Greece well over 10,000 years ago.

Take a one-hour walk west from Livadia and you arrive at the deserted village of **Mikro Horia** (Little Town). This is now deserted. According to the story I was told, its inhabitants all decided to move to Livadi one day, and simply took everything with them, right down to the tiles on the roofs. This story is supported by the absence of roofs on the derelict buildings, which are now frequented by the occasional goat. Only the little church is kept up.

Nearby are the caves where the woolly mammoths' bones were found. On your way you will also see caves which German soldiers are reputed to have lived in during the Second World War. This story is either untrue, or very intriguing. Why did these soldiers live in caves when they could have lived in houses with at least primitive plumbing and cooking facilities down in the village? Or were they a rogue unit that decided to go AWOL and sit out the war in a cave on a remote Greek island? Such things did happen, if you believe the film *Mediterraneo*.

---

a few unusual dishes.

Romantzo, D; *on the waterfront at Mandraki.*

Standard fare here, but it is an easy-going spot with a varied collection of friendly customers.

SIMI
Les Katerinettes, DD; *at the waterfront in Simi Town.*

Historic restaurant where the Italians signed their surrender on May 8th 1945, thus ceding the Dodecanese to the Allies. A plaque commemorates this event, which is remembered with annual celebrations. The navy puts in for a formal ceremony, followed by high jinks. The menu is well up to standard for celebrating a historic event of your own.

TILOS
Blue Sky Taverna, D-DD; *Livadia.*

Best of the harbour eating places, with a menu including many island favourites.

There are a number of pleasant seaside restaurants on the beach down at Eristos beyond Megalo Chorio, where they cook fresh seafood, caught locally or even harpooned by your own hands.

Aegean Islands

Rhodes
Around the Coast

75 km; map Michelin 980, 1:700000

Rhodes is the second most popular of all the Greek islands, after Crete. This is not simply due to its size. It has superb beaches, and all the resort facilities you would expect from a major tourist destination – but there is more to it than that. Despite the inroads of tourism, the essential character of the island remains, never far below the surface, even in the resorts.

The island offers photogenic beauty and historic sights to suit all tastes – from the medieval Crusaders' City in Rhodes Town to the white-washed houses and pebble-cobbled streets of Lindos, from the remote lighthouse island of Prassonissi to the lost Doric city of Kamiros. This route gives you access to it all.

In the gazetteer section which follows, the sights and places of interest marked on the map each receive an entry in the usual way, and there is an entry on Rhodes itself, worth reading first it gives further general and historical background.

Assuming you start from Rhodes Town, and drive in a clockwise direction, you drive south past the popular beaches and modern hotels of the resort strip, along the east coast – until you come to Tsambikas, with its monastery high on the hill. From here you drive 12 km south to Lindos, the second most popular spot on the island. Beyond here the coast becomes rather less developed. After passing south through Yenadi you drive along the dune-lined coast to Katavia. Here you can make a blue detour to the lighthouse at the southernmost tip of the island. Returning to Katavia, you head north along the west coast, taking in the Doric city of Kamiros, the famous 'Butterfly Valley' at Petaloudes, and Ialysos, before arriving back at Rhodes Town.

If you just make two or three stops at red sights, the circuit can be done in a day. But if you want to see some of the inland (blue) detours, allow at least a couple of days.

Rhodes makes an ideal base for island-hopping. You can take day trips to Simi, Tilos (see Greece Overall: 13) and the nearby unspoilt island of Halki. If you are feeling adventurous, you could try Karpathos, south of Rhodes halfway to Crete, or Kastellorizo, the faraway island to beat them all.

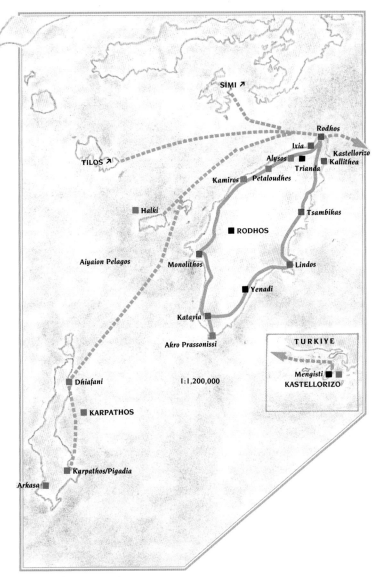

SIMI ↗

Rodhos

Ixia

Kastellorizo

Alysos
Kallithea

Trianda

Kamiros Petaloudhes

TILOS ↗

Tsambikas

Halki

■ RODHOS

Aiyaion Pelagos

Monolithos

Lindos

■ Yenadi

Katavia

Akro Prassonissi

TURKIYE

1:1,200,000

Mengisti ■
KASTELLORIZO

Dhiafani

■ KARPATHOS

Karpathos/Pigadia

Arkasa

TRANSPORT
Car hire firms are plentiful on
Rhodes, and the island has a
comprehensive bus system.
Coach excursions are also
available to all the main sights.
There are daily round-trip boat
excursions to Simi, Tilos and Halki,
and slightly less regular ferries to
Karpathos and Kastellorizo.

SIGHTS & PLACES OF INTEREST

ALYSOS

5 km SW of Rhodes, inland off road to the airport. This was once one of the three great cities of the island (Lindos and Kamiros were the other two). Now it is a ruin. The first settlement here probably dates from Phoenician times.

On the Acropolis you can see the remains of a 3rdC **Temple of Athena**, and to the south, a (reconstructed) 4thC BC fountain. From the top of the **Knights' Fortress** a wonderful view stretches before you over the upper end of the island. Also worth a visit here is the underground **Chapel of St George**, which has some 500-year-old murals.

IXIA 🛏️

West coast resort just outside Rhodes Town on the road to the airport. See Recommended Hotels, page 161.

KALLITHEA

On the east coast, 10 km S of Rhodes town. This is an ancient spa centre. The waters were even praised by Hippocrates, the 'father of medicine' more than two thousand years ago, and the

---

RHODES WINE

Rhodes has long been renowned for producing some of the finest wines in Greece. This is not much to boast about, admittedly, but things are changing. Recently applied American and EC knowhow is beginning to show in the vintages, and Greece is working hard to move into the quaffable plonk market at present cornered by the Bulgarians.

The light, dry white wines from Lindos make a pleasant accompaniment to seafood, but best of all are the reds. Some may find the Cair wines a little heavy, but the Chevalier du Rhodes is fine for most spicy Greek meat dishes. Those who like sweet wines should try the Malvesia (ancient Malmsey). There are *afficionados* of the local sparkling wine, although, in my experience, this still has a long way to go.

Italians attempted to relaunch the spa in the 1930s.

Nearby is a lovely little beach in the cove. The rocks here have become a favourite with the local scuba diving clubs; this is, in fact, one of the few places in Greece where this activity is officially permitted.

KAMIROS

28 km SW of Rhodes Town, off coast road. In Classical times this was one of the triumvirate of cities that ruled Rhodes. It was even mentioned by Homer. But when Rhodes Town became the island's new capital, Kamiros quickly faded, and was eventually abandoned and forgotten. It was only rediscovered just over a hundred years ago, when excavations began.

What we now see are the largely undisturbed ruins of a Doric city. If this doesn't interest you, the site is on an attractive hillside overlooking the sea, with a pleasant beach and a few tavernas at the foot of the slope.

KARPATHOS 🛏️ ✕

35 km SW of the S tip. This island is half a day's boat ride from Rhodes, but it's well worth making the trip if you have the time. Ferries run regularly from Rhodes Town. In marked contrast to Rhodes, this is off the main tourist track. The island is 35 km long, has some superb lonely cliffscapes and hidden coves, and inland there are a number of unspoilt villages. Alas a new international airport augurs ill.

We have some accommodation suggestions (page 161) at **Dhiafani**, the northern port where some of the ferries put in briefly before continuing to the main port of **Karpathos Town**; also at **Arkasa**, a pleasant village across the mountains from Karpathos Town, at the southern end of the west coast.

KASTELLORIZO 🛏️ ✕

Island 125 km to the E of Rhodes, with the Turkish mainland just 3 km away. Tiny Kastellorizo is the most remote of all the Greek islands and attracts few visitors – mostly adventurous souls who go simply 'because it's there'. Don't expect much. It's a barren spot, with just one small town, **Mengisti**, and no inviting beaches – but it does have a lovely **Blue Grotto**, one-and-a-half hours by small boat from town. See also Recommended Restaurants, page 165.

KATAVIA
S tip of Rhodes, 109 km from Rhodes Town. This is rather a lonely spot, as many of the houses are locked up, their owners away working in such far-flung places as Melbourne, St Louis and Rio de Janeiro.

Head south down the track and you come eventually to the southernmost tip of the island, where you find the lighthouse at **Akro Prassonissi**. In summer you can walk across the sand bar to the lighthouse, which is run by an old couple, but come the first storms of winter, the lighthouse is cut off from the mainland.

If you really want to get away from it all, try exploring the sand-dune-lined beaches along the east coast in the direction of Yenadhi. In July and

---

RECOMMENDED HOTELS

IXIA
Rodos Palace, DDD; *Leoforos Ialyssou; tel. 0241 25 222.*
Large establishment with a range of apartments overlooking the beach. Friendly international clientele; great for families. Large private pool.

KARPATHOS - Karpathos Town (Pigadia)
Seven Stars, DD; *Pigadia; tel. 0245 22 101.*
Over 30 rooms, many with private shower. Private pool.

Harry's, D; *Pigadia; tel. 0245 22 188.*
A pleasant spot. Island-style rooms with balconies, some with views.

KARPATHOS - Dhiafani
Mayflower Hotel, D; *on the waterfront; tel. 0245 51 228.*
Sound, standard rooms. Handy for ferry.

If this is full, people meeting the boat offer rooms.

KARPATHOS - Arkasa
Hotel Dimitrios, D-DD; *S end of village.*
A warm welcome; pleasant terrace for sunset watching.

KASTELLORIZO
Hotel Megisti, DD; *Megisti; tel. 0241 29 072.*
The only real hotel on the island, with a private swimming spot off the terrace – there are no good beaches on Kastellorizo. Only 17 rooms, so it is wise to ring ahead. The only alternatives are rooms in town.

TSAMBIKAS - Kolymbia
Hotel Kolymbia Beach, DD-DDD; *on the coast south of Tsambikas; tel. 0241 56 225.*
Tastefully designed modern hotel overlooking the beach. Also has own private pool, tennis courts, and golf nearby. Subject to block-booking, so be sure to ring ahead.

MONOLITHOS
Hotel Thomas, DD-DDD; *Monolithos; tel. 0246 61 291.*
Here you are away from the crowd, and you can cook for yourself if you like. There is a supermarket in town. Useful if you plan to stay for a few days to explore the south of the island.

RHODES TOWN
St Nikolis, DDD; *61 Ippodamou; tel. 0241 34 561.*
Superbly renovated old mansion in the street runing south from the Suleiman Mosque to the ramparts.

Cava d'Oro, DDD; *15 Kisthinou Street; tel. 0241 34 561.*
Right under the walls in the easternmost street of the old city, and very handy for the port. Authentic old-style atmosphere.

TRIANDA
Hotel Sun Beach, DD-DDD; *seafront; tel. 0241 25 284.*
Modern resort-style hotel complete with studio apartments. The wide range of sporting facilities includes private pool and tennis courts. Ideal for families. Out-of-season bargains sometimes available.

August, however, there tend to be rather more Robinson Crusoes per square mile than you may wish for.

LINDOS ✕

On E coast 45 km S of Rhodes Town. Lindos is a delight. It has rows of whitewashed houses and atmospheric streets paved with pebbles in true island style. Some of these houses were built in the 15thC by the Knights of St John, and several have quaint gates and courtyards. The **Acropolis** here contains the delightful **Temple of Athena**, which dates from the 6thC BC. Below the Acropolis is **St Paul's Harbour**, where the Apostle arrived in Rhodes nearly 2,000 years ago. If St Paul stepped ashore here today, the sight of so many shamelessly naked breasts on the beach would probably send him into a state of apoplexy. The trouble with Lindos is people – there are just too many of them and this has had a sad effect on the locals.

If you plan to buy a souvenir in Lindos, try their traditional lace but beware the hideous ceramics.

MONOLITHOS 🛏

Small town with a castle at the southern end of the west coast of Rhodes. See Recommended Hotels, page 161.

• *The Acropolis, Lindos, Rhodes.*

PETALOUDHES

15 km SW of Rhodes Town: turn inland just after the airport. This is the celebrated **'Valley of the Butterflies'**, which is filled in July and August with clouds of Jersey Tiger Moths that come to feed on the mulberry plants. It should really be called the Valley of the Moths, but this would hardly attract the tourists, who come in their droves, some fluttering, and often quite prettily coloured. You can see their red faces and brightly coloured plumage moving amongst the pools, waterfalls and bridges, watched in amazement by the visiting butterflies who have long found this delightful Valley of the Tourists a favourite spot.

RHODES - THE ISLAND

SE *Aegean, 150 km NE of Crete.* 'In Rhodes the days drop as softly as fruit from the trees,' wrote Lawrence Durrell in *Reflections on a Marine Venus* (still the most evocative book on Rhodes). But the island in which Durrell lived over 40 years ago has undergone a dramatic transformation. Like it or not, tourism has arrived. The beauties of such enchanting spots are no longer the preserve of a few fortunate travellers. What they described to the world in such glowing terms, the world now wants to see for itself. The process is inevitable.

Rhodes is named after the nymph Rhodos, who was a daughter of the sea god Poseidon, and loved by Helios the sun god. The island certainly lives up to its mythical pedigree. The sea caresses its beaches, and the sun shines lovingly from the sky.

In Classical times, Rhodes was famous for its sculptors, who produced three of the greatest masterpieces the world has ever known. The celebrated Laocoön wrestling with a snake is now in the Vatican, and the Winged Victory of Samothrace is now in the Louvre. The third, the Colossos of Rhodes, was a huge bronze statue of the sun god Helios which straddled the entrance to Rhodes harbour. This was one of the Seven Wonders of the World; ships sailed beneath it into the port, and the torch held aloft in its right hand was a beacon. To put this in perspective, just imagine a statue two thirds the height of the Statue of Liberty, cast in metal, well over two millenia before the first skyscraper.

The 30-m-high statue was brought down by an earthquake in 225 BC. Four hundred years later, its shattered pieces were dredged from the bottom of the sea and shipped to Syria. Here they were carried off on 980 camels to be sold and melted down. Indeed, far from being lost, pieces of the statue may well now be scattered throughout the museums of the world, in their ancient coin collections.

In 1306, the island of Rhodes was sold to the Knights of the Order of St John of Jerusalem, which had originally been a kind of Crusaders' Red Cross. However, well before they arrived in Rhodes their behaviour had begun to lapse. During their time here they often operated as little more than pirates

• *Rhodes Town.*

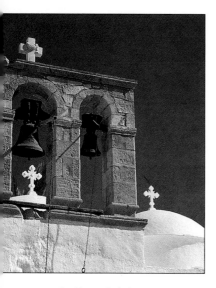

• *In the old part of Rhodes Town.*

fascinating history. Not surprisingly, it has become one of the great tourist destinations of the Mediterranean – attracting sun worshippers, hellenophiles and imbibers of exotic cocktails. Yet despite the ravages inflicted by this annual invasion, the island has not been completely spoilt. The islanders have done their best to maintain their island's essential qualities. They have maintained the prices too – you will find Rhodes one of the most expensive of the Greek islands.

RHODES TOWN ⌂ ✕
N *tip of the island*. The town itself consists of two distinct districts: the old and the new. The **old town** is the most interesting, and contains most of the sights. It still remains to a large extent the medieval crusaders' city that was occupied by the Knights of St John of Jerusalem five hundred years ago. Surrounded by protective walls and a moat, it is entered through its ancient gates.

Inside you can visit the **14thC Grand Master's Palace** and see the former site of St John's Chapel which contained the hand of John the Baptist. Be sure to take a walk down Knights' Street (modern Greek name: Odos Ippoton), which remains cobbled and passes the medieval Inns where the knights lived. The knights were divided into different 'Tongues' according to the different languages they spoke – and each 'Tongue' had its own Inn; the French Inn is the largest and most impressive. The street ends at Hospital Square where the English Inn is located.

Another essential is the **Knights' Hospital and Archaeological Museum** (Nossokomio Ippoton) which dates from the 15thC. The museum contains a number of excellent examples of Classical sculpture, reflecting the island's prestigious artistic history. The most outstanding is the little **Aphrodite of Rhodes**, dating from the 1stC BC. This is the statue that features in the title of Lawrence Durrell's superb book about Rhodes, *Reflections on a Marine Venus*.

Be sure to walk along the ramparts on the walls for some enchanting views over the town, especially the minarets in the Turkish quarter. The most impressive of the **gates** in the walls is

roaming the Mediterranean, answerable to no one except themselves. They accumulated large amounts of money and built up their organization efficiently, living well and cultivating the myth of their chivalry. Similarities found in the Mafia are no historical accident. Eventually, in 1522, the Knights were driven out by the Turks, and after a few years of wandering, finally settled in Malta. The Knights' original emblem is what we now call a Maltese Cross.

In 1912 the Italians took Rhodes from the Turks, along with the rest of the Dodecanese islands. They remained in control here until 1943, when the Nazis briefly took over. During this period, the long-standing Jewish community was deported to the camps of northern Europe. In 1945, the British took control of Rhodes and the Dodecanese for the Allies. Not until four years later did Rhodes at last become a part of Greece, which had already been independent for more than 120 years.

Rhodes has some of the most exciting beaches in Greece, and is said to have more hours of sunshine than any other Greek island. Fortunately, this is untrue: the winter rains keep the hinterland pleasantly green. The island has an enchanting beauty that is unmistakably its own and its many picturesque sights date from all periods of its long,

St Katherine's, which gives on to the harbour from the north-eastern sector of the city. **The Turkish Quarter**, which centres on Odos Sokratous, has a number of intriguing mosques, and some restored Turkish Baths dating from the reign of Suleiman the Magnificent.

Outside the old city is another fine mosque, **Murad Reis**, which has an interesting Muslim cemetery. The other main sight of the modern town is **Mandraki**, the north-western of the two harbours, whose ancient entrance was once straddled by the Colossus of Rhodes. The eastern breakwater contains the famous windmills, and ends at St Nikolaos' Tower, which dates from the 15thC.

Rhodes Town has a wide-ranging and frequently changing night-life. For a good night out, try **Garage,** 13 *Iroon Politechnou* – a popular disco-cum-nightspot which manages to transcend its ominous name. A couple of blocks west of the old harbour.

If you are planning a picnic, an excellent place for scrumptious Scandinavian-style sandwiches is **Kringlan's Swedish bakery,** 20 A*marandou,* in the modern town, just west of the old harbour. And if you need some fruit, just around the corner is **Nea Agora,** the New Market, opposite Mandraki.

SIMI
See Greece Overall: 13.

TILOS
See Greece Overall: 13.

TRIANDA ⌒
Part of the resort strip on the north-west coast outside Rhodes Town on the way to the airport. See Recommended Hotels, page 161.

TSAMBIKAS ⌒
28 km S of Rhodes Town on the E *coast.* The promontory here was once part of a volcano. Climb to the top and you will find a monastery with inspiring views out to sea and over the shoreline. Either side of the promontory there are excellent beaches – which, once upon a time, were a deserted, unspoilt paradise. At nearby **Kolimbia** you will find a pleasant little harbour with some tavernas.

RECOMMENDED RESTAURANTS

KARPATHOS - Karpathos Town (Pigadia)
El Greco, DD; *Pigadia.*
Highly recommended for its thoughtful service and well-cooked local dishes. Let the owner recommend you a good wine.

O Giorgios, D; *at the quayside.*
Lively, informal spot with friendly customers, who will tell you all you want to know about the island.

KASTELLORIZO
Savva's, D-DD; *main square.*
A real find, in such an out-of-the-way spot. Local dishes, well cooked, and exceptional seafood. An ideal place to linger and chat with adventurous travellers such as yourself, who are wondering what to do with themselves now that they have arrived. (If you have seen the Blue Grotto, try a day's swimming on nearby Aghios Giorgios island – the sunburn will give you something to talk about for weeks.)

For a change, try:

Little Paris, D-DD; *Megisti.*

LINDOS
The Rustic Taverna, DD; *Lindos.*
Not quite as inauthentic as its Anglophone name would suggest. Menu contains a few suprisingly original flourishes. Palatable, moderately priced wines, and a fabulous view.

RHODES TOWN
Oasis, DD; *Plateia Douleios.*
Easy-going spot by Omirou, the main street running east-west in the south of the old city. Respectable local wine.

Kon Tiki, DDD; *Limin Mandrakiou;* tel. 0241 22 477.
Delightful floating seafood restaurant in the old port with a range of Greek and international cuisine in a superb setting. But you pay for it.

Aegean Islands

Between Kastelli and Aghios Nikolaos
Crete - The North Coast

Up to 260 km; map Michelin 980, 1:700000

This route samples all the main ingredients of Crete. (To complete the picture, the three Local Explorations on Crete, numbers 13, 14 and 15, tell you how to explore the rest of the island in depth.) You will see an almost deserted peninsula, Venetian cities, one of the world's most famous archaeological sights, and a booming international resort. If you keep to the red sights, you can drive it in a day, but to give yourself time to enjoy everything, allow at least four days.

If you start at Kastelli, on the north-western tip of the island, you are within easy reach of several ancient sites, a spectacular beach, and some exhilarating mountain scenery.

Driving east, you soon get to the unspoilt Rhodopou Peninsula, with its religious sites and hiking paths along some of the island's most beautiful, unspoilt coastline.

A further 24 km along the north coast you come to Hania, whose ancient Venetian waterfront and harbour is one of the best preserved in the entire Mediterranean. Your route then continues east, with more coastal scenery and some spectacular views of the mountains inland, until you reach the 'oriental' city of Rethimnon, with its minarets and Venetian fortress.

The road now passes east along the rocky coastline, through a number of small resorts, until you come to the urban sprawl of Heraklion, the island's capital. Just 5 km south-east of Heraklion is the ancient Minoan site of Knossos, one of the archaeological wonders of the world. It is worth allowing a day to visit this site, before heading to the coast for a cooling swim.

From Heraklion you continue east along the coast, ending at the international resort of Aghios Nikolaos, and the popular beaches of the Gulf of Mirabello.

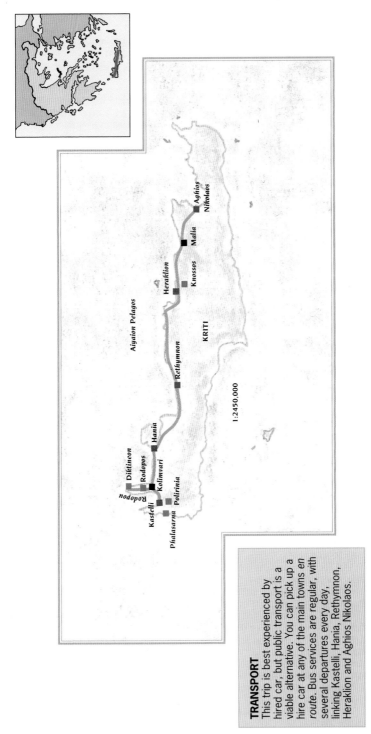

Aiyaion Pelagos

Diktineon
Rodopos
Rodopou
Kolimvari
Kastelli
Polirinia
Phalasarna

Hania

Rethymnon

Heraklion

Knossos

Malia

Aghios Nikolaos

KRITI

1:2.450.000

TRANSPORT
This trip is best experienced by hired car, but public transport is a viable alternative. You can pick up a hire car at any of the main towns en route. Bus services are regular, with several departures every day, linking Kastelli, Hania, Rethymnon, Heraklion and Aghios Nikolaos.

SIGHTS & PLACES OF INTEREST

AGHIOS NIKOLAOS ⟷ ✕

NE *coast, 66 km E of Heraklion*. People can be a bit snooty about 'Ag Nik', as the tourists affectionately refer to it. Yet, as with many popular tourist destinations, its initial and continuing appeal is the beautiful setting. There are superb views along the rocky coastline; the harbour with its quayside restaurants is charming, and in the heart of the town lies the celebrated 'Bottomless Lake'. In fact, the bottom of this lake was recently discovered to be 209 m down.

If you like international fun spots, this is the place for you. The British and the Germans are visible in the discos; Scandinavians and Dutch on the beaches; Americans, Czechs and French in the bars; Inca buskers play on the promenade; Italians and Belgians play volleyball with the Lebanese. There are even rumoured to be a few Greeks around.

HANIA ⟷ ✕

NW *coast 131 km W of Heraklion*. Hania was the capital of Crete until 1971. According to a local historian I once met, it shares with a city in China the distinction of being the oldest constantly inhabited city on Earth. There has certainly been a settlement here from well before Minoan times, although its present charm stems mainly from its Turkish and Venetian past. Indeed, it was once known as 'The Venice of the East' – an odd title for a city with no canals. The ancient harbour, with its well preserved quaysides, Venetian warehouses and famous lighthouse, is one of the most appealing ports you will see anywhere in the Mediterranean. (It featured in the film *Zorba the Greek*.) Near the harbour in the ancient quarter an old indoor market is the site of much histrionic selling and bargaining.

The car ferries from Piraeus berth at Souda Bay, some 6 km east of town. On the coast to the west some of the beaches are pleasant for swimming, and the city makes an ideal base for expeditions to the remote west of the island, as well as to the White Mountains which lie to the south.

An interesting **archaeological museum** contains relics from as far

EL GRECO

His real name was Domenicos Theotocopoulos, and he was born in 1541 at the pleasant little village of Fodele, 16 km west of Heraklion. He emigrated to Venice in the early 1560s, and was later to achieve his fame in Toledo. We can only imagine what the Spanish made of his tongue-twister of a name, and it was soon accepted by all concerned that he should be known as El Greco – 'The Greek'.

back as the Minoan era, discovered at excavation sites all over western Crete. The **Historical Museum** here is second only to the one in Athens, and contains many superb manuscripts from the Byzantine, Venetian and Turkish periods of the city's history – as well as relics from the Second World War. Be sure to visit the **Café Kriti** for the excellent Cretan dancing – to real Cretan music.

HERAKLION ⟷ ✕

Capital of the island, centre of N coast. Heraklion is, frankly, a mess. If a competition was run for the least attractive city on the Mediterranean, its only close competition would come from the rundown suburbs of Naples. That said, there is plenty to see and do in and around the city. Out of season it is worth strolling along the mole of the old fishing harbour with its Venetian fort. The small old quarter, too, has its charms at low season, although the decibel level remains high. Whatever the season, be sure to visit **Aghia Ekaterini**, which has a superb collection of icons, including some delightful works by Damaskinos, who, according to local legend, taught El Greco how to paint.

Heraklion has two excellent museums. The **Historical Museum** contains exhibits relating to the island's long and captivating history. During the 19thC, for instance, the island was placed under the joint protection of Britain, France, Italy and Russia. References to this period are to be found in Kazantzakis' great novel *Zorba the Greek*, where the widow is renowned for having shared her favours between the commanders of all four powers.

RECOMMENDED HOTELS

AGHIOS NIKOLAOS
Coral, DDD; 21 A*kti* I. K*oundourou; tel.* 0841 28363.

Large hotel on the sea front overlooking the harbour. Modern rooms, balconies with sea views. The big bonus here is the roof-top pool, ideal for a rapid suntan.

HANIA
Porto Veneziano, DD; V*enetian Harbour; tel.* 0821 29311.

Deservedly celebrated spot in the best part of town, down by the old port. The building used to be home to a Venetian nobleman in the old days, but has since been fully (and tastefully) modernized.

Contessa, DDD; 15 T*heophanous* St; *tel.* 0821 23966.

Superb old mansion with period furniture, yet modern plumbing. Excellently run by Manolis Androulikadis and his friendly staff. Ask for one of the top rooms with a harbour view.

HERAKLION
Xenia, DDD; 5 A*kti* S*ophocles* V*enizelou; tel.* 081 284000.

Top-class, modern hotel right on the front. Private pool, leafy gardens and terrace café. Be sure to take one of the rooms with a balcony overlooking the sea, as the other side of the hotel looks over a busy main road and a bus station.

Knossos, DD; 25*th* A*ugusto* St; *tel.* 081 283247.

Old-style Cretan (or Greek provincial) hotel, with a slightly faded charm, by the Morosini Fountain. Quiet rooms at the back have balconies overlooking the delightful domed church of Aghios Titos.

Next door to this hotel is the Venetian *Loggia*, a fine old palazzo which is now the Town Hall. Next to this is **Loggia**, a pleasant bar on three floors. The first floor has a 'romantic' Piano Bar. The second floor unexpectedly houses a brightly lit Women's Café, a concept which penetrated the machismo male Cretan

•T*ypical coastline, A*ghios N*ikolaos area.*

consciousness with some difficulty. Men are allowed in one at a time in the company of a female adult, if they promise to behave themselves. But best of all is the third-floor Roof Garden, which has music and a fine view over the city; it could almost convince you that Heraklion is a romantic spot.

KASTELLI
Castelli Hotel, DD; P*latia; tel.* 0822 22140.

Pleasant C-class hotel overlooking the main square, in the centre of town. Also has a decent taverna, with a range of local dishes.

Galini Beach, DD; *west of main Promenade; tel.*0822 23 288.

Bright rooms with balconies overlooking the sea, on the beach just five minutes drive west of town. Ring ahead and they'll reserve a room for you, even in August.

RETHYMNON
Seeblick, DD; 17 P*lastira; tel.* 0831 22478.

German-run establishment on the front between the Venetian harbour and the fort. The best rooms look out over the sea. Be sure to book in advance during the season, as this place is deservedly popular.

By far the most important museum in Heraklion, and indeed in all Crete, is the **Archaeology Museum**. This contains the greatest collection of Minoan relics in the world, most of which are from the nearby site of Knossos. I advise you to visit Knossos before coming to this museum, as your memory of the site itself will help to bring the exhibits alive. This is no idle recommendation – the pieces in the museum appear to have been laid out by a genius in the art of inducing boredom. Fortunately, at least where the frescos are concerned, he was defeated by his materials. More lifelike than Egyptian frescos, and more dynamic than the lapidary statues of the classical world, these frescos have a unique vividness. You can see and even get the feel of what it was actually like in Crete more than 3,000 years ago.

KASTELLI ⛴ ✕

The westernmost town in Crete, 47 km W of Hania. Despite the ferry terminal (5 km west of town) tourism has made little impact on Kastelli. In fact, its charm lies in its ordinariness: this is how the real Cretans live. Walk around the main square, and then head down to the sandy beach for a swim. Afterwards, try a plate of roast pork with garlic and a bottle of local red wine – one of the best 'local' meals you will find in Crete. Buses leave from the main square for Paleokastro (6 km), and from here you

• *Aghios Nikolaos.*

• *Knossos.*

can walk up to the site of **Polirinia**. The oldest ruins here date from the 8thC BC, but there are also Ancient Greek, Roman and Venetian remains, as well as spectacular views out over the north of the island. Although not much of a floralist, it was here that I was converted to botany. In spring, the mountainsides are covered with a breathtaking variety of wildflowers.

Buses from Kastelli also go to **Phalasarna** on the west coast. Be warned: this drive ends in a spectacular (or hair-raising, depending upon the driver) run of hairpin bends as the road plunges to the coast. At the journey's end, you will find an idyllic sandy beach washed by crystal clear water, and a couple of tavernas. Just north of the beach are the ruins of ancient Phalasarna, which was once the port of Polirinia. Owing to the shifts in Crete's geology, the ancient port is now almost 300 m inland.

KNOSSOS

5 km SE of Heraklion. This is one of the most extraordinary archaeological sites in the western world. At the entrance, the 20thC is here in all its tawdry glory. But inside, you enter the realms of a civilization whose mysteries are enthralling. Minoan civilization was thriving almost 4,000 years ago. This was the earliest great civilization in Europe, and provides a link between Ancient Egypt and the Classical era. At the time, its artefacts were the most

171

impressive in the ancient world, and its people appear to have lived a charmed life. It was essentially a peaceful civilization, and not until the Mycean Age do weapons start appearing amongst its relics. Many believe that it was Minoan civilization which gave rise to the legend of the lost paradise of Atlantis.

The main focus of the site is the **Palace of Knossos**, grouped around the central courtyard. Unfortunately this is a fake – reconstructed by the great archaeologist Sir Arthur Evans in the early years of this century: pedantic scholars often refer to it as an archaeological Disneyland. But the reconstruction was done with such imagination and flair that, in my view, it adds considerably to the site, bringing the whole place alive. It also provides welcome shelter from the fierce sun. For those who want to potter about amongst the more genuine bits and pieces, holes and mounds, authentic building site terrain extends for miles.

Even if you don't like guides, it is worth taking one for at least an exploratory tour, just to give you an idea of the scale and importance of what you are seeing.

RETHYMNON ✉ ✕

N *coast, 76 km W of Heraklion.* Rethymnon is the third city of Crete, after Heraklion and Hania. I've always found something oriental in its atmosphere. The skyline is pierced by tall minarets, some of the streets are lined with ancient Turkish balconies, and there are still a few Turkish fountains hiding in the back streets. The main sight is the ancient **Venetian fortress**, said to have been the largest fortress in the

old Venetian Empire. Yet when the Turks attacked Rethymnon in 17thC, it proved to be of little use. The Venetians barricaded themselves inside the fortress, and the Turks took the city within 24 hours.

Nowadays, foreign raiders come from the nearby beach resorts every night. Mayhem thrives in the discos and tavernas, and the locals barricade themselves in their houses to watch TV. According to a rather disgruntled older inhabitant I met: 'The Turks were at least a religious people – these modern invaders are just pagans!' He wasn't too concerned, however: he owned one of the local discos.

The city's main beach is very crowded and rather grubby. To the east of town are more inviting beaches, although in summer they tend to be overrun by the Visigoths of Dusseldorf and tanned pagans from Birmingham, whose alien habits are catered for with understanding and tolerance by the local descendants of the worshippers of Dionysios.

RODHOPOU PENINSULA

To *get there, turn north just west of Kolimvari, 24 km W of Hania.* The road leads to the village of **Rodopos**, and then it's mainly track. The peninsula is largely deserted, and excellent for hiking. The views can be spectacular, with vistas of steep rocky hillside leading down to clear, sparkling water. The improved road now runs to the church of **Aghios Ioannis** (St John). On 29th August people from all over western Crete come on a pilgrimage here, bringing babies whom they wish to christen John.

From here, a 16-km track takes you out to **Diktineon**, a spectacular site on the tip of the peninsula. Rumour has it that this track has now been 'improved' by a bulldozer. The last time this happened, the bulldozer itself had to be rescued, so be sure to check up on the state of the road before you set out. The Diktineon was a religious sanctuary in Ancient Greek times. Now there are some Roman ruins and a beach. According to legend, the site received its name from a *diktyon* (fishing net) which was used by a local fisherman to rescue a goddess who had dived into the sea to avoid the attentions of Minos.

RETHYMNON WINE FESTIVAL

If you are in Rethymnon during the third and fourth weeks of July, look out for this event. It takes place in the City park, off Dimitrakaki. Once you have paid your entry fee, you can drink as much as you like, sampling from the various barrels of local wine. Much hectic dancing and bacchanalian hilarity – good for a night out with a party. You can even get something to eat, from various little stalls.

RECOMMENDED RESTAURANTS

AGHIOS NIKOLAOS
O Vios Einai Oneirou, DD; K. *Sfakiani.*

Down the main street, leading south-east from the Bottomless Lake. Brilliant modern taverna, designed, built and run by Maro Dayiantis, (who cooks well, too). Pleasant leafy terrace and relaxed atmosphere to go with the name, which means 'Life is a Dream'.

Cretan Restaurant, DDD; *Koundourou.*

Superb waterfront restaurant serving top-class cuisine. A French couple I once dined with here claimed it served the only edible food on the island – 'or,' they added, 'perhaps even in all Greece.' Predominantly Continental cuisine, prepared by chefs. Respectable wines, and a mean lobster flambé.

HANIA
Akti, DD; *Venetian Harbour.*

My favourite taverna on the quayside of the old harbour. Try their excellent *kakavia* (Cretan fish soup) if it's available. Unfortunately it can become overcrowded during the evenings in summer.

Emerald Bistro, D; 17 *Kondilaki.*

If you have come all the way to Greece to have a good Irish stew, this is the place for you. Home-made Irish food (and even some Greek cuisine as well). Excellent Guinness. Conversation can be almost up to Dublin standards.

HERAKLION
Ta Psaria, DD-DDD; 25*th Augusto St.*

One of a number of good fish tavernas just off the Venetian Harbour. The waiters here are particularly helpful at recommending Cretan wines. Serves several unusual local fish dishes.

Gorgona, DD-DDD; *Sophokles; right on the waterfront west of the Venetian Harbour.*

Tasty seafood and local dishes. Be

• *Hania.*

sure to sit at a table right up against the glass partitions if the dreaded Meltemi wind is forecast.

KASTELLI
Papadaki, DD; *on seafront beside main road to Platia.*

Just the place for a long, easy-going lunch overlooking the sea. All the fish here is delicious, but their *barbouni* (red mullet) is superb, with a glass of local white wine.

RETHYMNON
Vangela, DD; *Platia Petihaki.*

On the central square by the Arimondi Fountain. Run by the redoubtable Vangela herself. There is usually a wide variety of excellent local dishes. Can be delightfully calm, can be absolutely riotous – chaos is an essential ingredient of many successful Greek restaurants.

Athens:
introduction

• *Opposite: Apollo.*

At first sight, Athens is the sort of place you wouldn't wish on your worst enemy. In August, with the temperature in the 40s, the streets packed with sweating, irritable tourists and persistent, irritating vendors, the sweltering sky dimmed by the notorious *nefos* (the eye-watering, throat tickling, gasp-inducing pollution cloud which gets trapped above the city in its bowl of hills), Athens is no one's favourite place.

However, if you do find yourself here in mid summer, just follow the sensible Athenian's example. Get up early to do what you have to do (such as seeing the many superb sights), then have a long, pleasant lunch, sleep through the heat of the day, and live it up at night.

This way, you'll find that Athens has much to offer. It is a city the way cities used to be – before the era of dehumanizing shopping malls and antiseptic *nouvelle cuisine* restaurants. Like all great cities, it has its own distinctive music (from traditional raffish *rembetika* to modern *bouzouki*). Its tavernas take you back to the original taverns of another age, and its streets have a zestful, racy life which has largely vanished from the cities of northern Europe.

Then there is Piraeus, one of the last old-style Mediterranean ports. Here the ships berth across the road, and the streets still retain a sailor-town atmosphere. Piraeus is just 20 minutes away from the centre of Athens on the Metro.

The main tourist sights of Athens need no gloss from me. The Acropolis, the Agora and the National Archaeological Museum are unsurpassed anywhere. Outside Athens you can visit the spectacular Temple of Poseidon at Sounion, drive to the woodlands of the nearby Parnitha Mountains, or go and live it up in the popular and lively resorts which line the Apollo Coast to the south-east.

So don't judge Athens by your first impression. Go easy – *seega, seega* as the Greeks say – and you'll soon learn to appreciate its charms.

USING THIS SECTION

Some of central Athens lends itself to exploration on foot, and I have devised two short walks (pages 178-183) for this purpose. As usual, you don't have to do the walks from beginning to end; indeed you don't have to follow them at all. The information in the walks can just as well be absorbed at a café table; and of course, the hotel and restaurant recommendations (pages 188-191), can also be consulted as and when needed.

Some important Athens sights and places of interest can't be taken in on the walking routes. These are featured in the alphabetical, gazetteer-style entries starting on page 184.

Following those, on pages 188-189, are important sights just outside Athens, again in the usual gazetteer style.

PUBLIC TRANSPORT

Athens has an extensive bus service. A single ticket costs 75 drachmae to any part of the city (though you can't change buses). You buy this before-hand at any street kiosk. You cancel your ticket in the machine as you board. Destinations are marked on the buses. The big snag is the overcrowding at peak hours, which can make it a very hot journey indeed in the summer. The best way around Athens is by the Metro. There is a single line which operates from Kifissia in the north down to Piraeus. The main city centre stations are at Omonia and Monastira-ki. Tickets cost 75 drachmae, plus 25 drachmae if you pass through Omonia either way.

Otherwise try a taxi. These are cheap and numerous. A short journey

ACCOMMODATION GUIDELINES

The best places for inexpensive accommodation in the centre of Athens are found around Omonia Square and in the Plaka district, the ancient quarter which lies just below the Acropolis. However, these neighbourhoods can become fairly frantic in summer – high temperatures, high decibels, high blood pressure all round. For a more relaxed atmosphere, try the Kolonaki district which lies north-east of central Syntagma. Here prices will tend to be somewhat higher.

If you're catching a ferry to the islands, your best plan is to stay in Piraeus because most boats leave early in the morning.

To find a hotel the easy way, go to the hotel reservations desk which is in the building of the National Bank on Syntagma Square. The only hotels they deal with are in our medium and expensive price bands (see page 12). They don't answer enquiries on the phone.

will cost you under 1,000 drachmae (for the taxi, not per person). The bad news: they're almost all full during the day. The good news: you can wave down taxis filled with people, and ask the driver if he's going in your direction. If he is, you pile in. (Prices are usually around the same as if you have the entire taxi to yourself. You have to bargain with the driver. But remember, everyone else in the taxi is not interest-

ARRIVING

To make economies, Olympic Airways have at time of going to press scrapped the bus services from both Athens airports to the city centre. Fortunately Greek taxis are so numerous and so cheap that this isn't a major blow. You'll see long rows of waiting taxis outside the arrivals gate of either airport. The trip into the city centre takes around 20 minutes and costs around 1,500 drachmae. (At night prices go up – around 50 per cent *in practice*, though officially

less.) These prices are for the taxi ride itself, and not per person.

The rail link through former Yugoslavia remains cut, so you're unlikely to arrive at a railway station.

If you arrive by boat at Piraeus, go to the Piraeus terminal of the Metro, which is right by the port. This has regular trains running directly into the city. (Monastiraki is the best station for the Plaka and the heart of the city.) Tickets cost 75 drachmae (25 drachmae extra if you go through Omonia).

ed in your economic situation and wants to get started.) There is a taxi rank on Syntagma, by the National Gardens. This is useful only in theory – there are never any taxis on it. There are also ranks at the main bus and train stations. These always have lines of taxis and queues of amazing length. (Where do all these people come from?) To be sure of a taxi, get your hotel to ring one for you. You'll be told that one will arrive in a quarter of an hour. Have a leisurely bath; and if you are lucky it will be there in three quarters of an hour.

NEIGHBOURHOODS TO AVOID

For years, Athens had a surprisingly good reputation, but things are begin-ning to deteriorate. This is partly because of the influx of refugees from the war-torn Balkans and deprived areas of Eastern Europe. If possible, avoid the Bazaar quarter, north of the Plaka, late at night. After midnight even Syntagma can become unpleasant at times.

Don't wander the backstreets of Piraeus at night. If you have to be out and about in this part of town, stick to the front by the harbour. This is bad enough, but there are always large groups of backpackers and tourists waiting in the cafés for the morning island ferries.

• *Time out, Athens.*

Old Central Athens

These two walks make a useful introduction to the city: they will help you get your bearings by leading you through the heart of the city, past many of the main sights, without having to worry about transport or finding the way.

The distances covered are fairly short – both around 2 km – which means that they are manageable even in the unbearable heat of the summer. However, some of the sights require some additional footwork if you're to see them properly: the best time to do the walks is as early as possible in the morning, before the heat becomes too fierce, or after the heat has started to die down in late afternoon.

FROM THE STADIUM
TO THE ROMAN FORUM
Start At the Stadium, off Platia Stadhiou, on Leoforos Vasileos Konstandinou, opposite the National Gardens.
The Stadium is situated between two hills, and follows the traditional horseshoe design of the ancient Greek stadiums. It was built in 330 BC for athletics contests. The straight part of the

• *The Acropolis, early morning light.*

track, along which the athletes raced, measures 600 ancient Greek feet. This was the equivalent of one *stade* – from which the word stadium is derived.

During Roman times, the Stadium's use degenerated, and on the occasion when Hadrian became Emperor it was the scene of an obscene bloodbath, when thousands of wild animals were baited and killed for the entertainment of the baying mob.

In the following centuries, the abandoned Stadium was used as a quarry, its marble pillaged for Athenian buildings. In the late 19thC, it was completely restored, at the expense of the wealthy Alexandrian-Greek philanthropist Georgios Averoff. It was then used to stage the first modern Olympic Games in 1896.

If it's not too hot, try the short climb up Ardhittos Hill, which rises just to the west of the Stadium. From the top you have one of the finest views out over the city of Athens with the Acropolis to the west, and the Hill of Lykabitos to the north.

From the Stadium, cross over Platia Stadhiou and into the National Gardens. Here continue west, parallel with Leoforas Olgas for 400 m until you come to the Byron Monument. Here cross south over Leoforos Olgas to the **Temple of Olympian Zeus.** Begun in 7thC BC, it was, on completion 700 years later in 131 AD, the largest temple in Greece (and the fifth largest in the Roman Empire). Originally it had over 100 columns, though only 16 of these remain standing today. For the opening ceremony Hadrian donated two colossal statues of the gods – one of Zeus and one of himself (as Emperor, he was also a god).

During the following centuries the temple fell into decay, but it was not entirely without use. For a time its abandoned ruins became the home of a medieval Stylite hermit, who, in common with others of his sect, renounced all physical comfort by taking up residence high on an architrave between two pillars.

The temple is surrounded by widespread contemporary remains, but just in front of the temple you come to Hadrian's Arch. Being gods, Roman emperors had little patience with mortal virtues such as modesty. Thus in 131 BC the Emperor Hadrian erected *Hadrian's Arch* to the glory of himself. This gate once marked the limit of the ancient Greek city, and stood at the entrance to the new Roman sector of Athens, known unsurprisingly as Hadrianopolis.

Cross back over Leoforos Olgas and into the National Gardens. Continue north for about 100 m, then turn west across Leoforos Amalias.

Here you come to **St Paul's Church**, the English church of Athens, which stands on the edge of the Plaka. From here you continue north along Filellinon, and after 30 m turn west along Kidathenaion. This pedestrian street leads you through the heart of the old **Plaka** district. This picturesque area, composed of steep little winding lanes, rises towards the slopes of the Acropolis, which towers above it, and can often be glimpsed between the roof tops. The Plaka is filled with little tavernas, and is one of the few parts of the city which manages to retain a distinct charm of its own.

As you continue along Kidathenaion

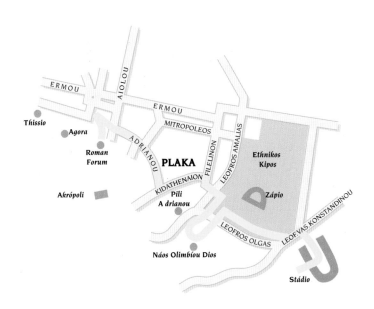

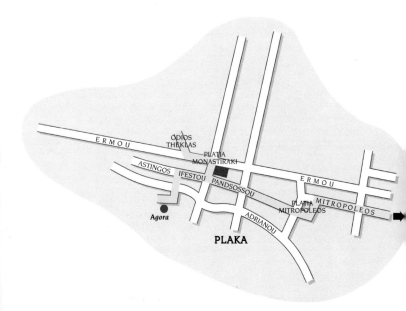

PLAKA

you will see on your left the **Greek Folk Art Museum.**

Folk art is often rather boring, unless you're specifically interested, but this small collection is an exception. The first floor has the predictable pottery, weaving and so on, well laid out. On the second floor is an imaginative reconstruction of an old village house, complete with a series of murals by the eccentric primitive painter Theophilos.

Kidathenaion leads you to a pleasant small square, where there's a café on the corner: an ideal spot to take the weight off your feet and refresh yourself with a cup of Greek coffee.

Just beyond here you turn right along Adrianou Street. This leads you across to the far side of the Plaka district, and in 400 m you arrive at the crossroads with Aiolou Street. Across the street you'll see the site of **Hadrian's Library**. All that now stands are parts of the remaining outer walls. Once this building contained a courtyard which was surrounded by 100 pillars. The building was intended to house one of the finest libraries of the classical world, in the tradition of the great library of Alexandria and its rival at Pergamum.

According to tradition the contents of the library were ravaged by a fire, during the course of which Thucydides' *History of the Peleponnese War* was destroyed. Fortunately the orator Demosthenes had just finished reading the *History*, and, so the legend goes, was able to dictate the entire tract, word for word, thus enabling it to be saved for posterity. The surviving version of this work runs to eight books, of which the last is incomplete. The experts say this is because Thucydides never finished it, but those of us who prefer to believe in the legend will realize that of course it only ended here because Demosthenes couldn't remember any more.

The building was finally laid waste in 267 AD, when the Heruli tribes invaded Greece.

Continue southwards down Aiolu and you come to the excavations of the **Roman Forum**. The site itself is railed off, and can be something of a disappointment at first sight. The feature that first strikes your eye is the ruin of a large Roman public lavatory – but on closer inspection you will find that there are some worthier objects of interest.

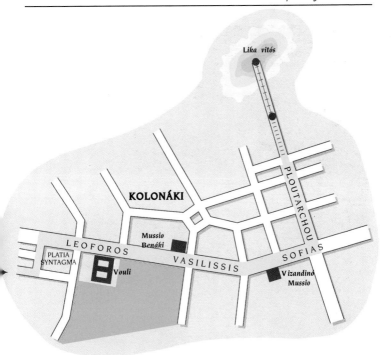

The market was built by Julius Caesar as an addition to the main Agora. There is a fine entry gate with columns and a Doric portico (the gate of Athena Archegetis). One corner of the site is occupied by a 15thC mosque, which has been 'converted' into an archaeological storehouse. It was once known as the Victory Mosque, because it was built to celebrate the Turkish capture of Athens.

Across the site from the mosque you can see the fascinating **Tower of the Winds**, which in ancient times served as a kind of clock and meteorological device. It was built in the 1st or 2nd century BC by Androkinos of Kyrrhos, who was probably a Syrian. The tower is octagonal, and each of its eight faces has a relief figure representing the appropriate wind, in a pose indicative of its properties. Zephyros the West Wind is shown scattering flowers, Apiliotis the East Wind bears fruit and corn, and Kaikias the north-east wind is shown spilling hailstones from his shield. By the south face of the tower you can see the remains of the water system which drove the chronometer. Also incorporated in the tower were early scientific instruments:

sundials, a wind vane and a compass.

FROM THE AGORA TO THE HILL OF LYKABETOS

Start The ancient Agora, whose main north entrance is on Adhrianou, the street named after the Emperor Hadrian which bisects the Plaka district.

As you leave the north exit of the Agora (details, page 185), you'll see a pleasant café over on Adhrianou: I recommend a pause here before continuing through busy central Athens.

Leave Adhrianou heading north. In 50 m you come to the crossroads with Astingos. This street is named after an Englishman, Frank Hastings, who died near Missolongi in 1823, fighting for Greek independence.

Turn right (i.e., east) along this street which becomes Ifestou, a crammed thoroughfare which was once the metal workers district, but now consists of shops selling all kinds of military junk (or memorabilia, depending upon your point of view), high-fashion jeans and modern clothes.

In just over 100 m, Ifestou disgorges into Platia Monastiraki, which is named after the 10thC monastery in its centre. This was the old Turkish bazaar

• *Monastiraki flea market.*

district, and still has a slightly oriental feel to it. The pavements are spilling over with lottery ticket vendors, nut sellers and stall holders, whose cries vie with the pandemonium of the traffic. It can be hellish on an oven-hot August day, so be prepared. The shops in **Monastiraki** are mainly geared to the tourist trade. For something that was once a little different, look out for the shop of Stavros Melissinos, the poet sandal-maker, at No 89. Stavros shot to fame when he made a pair of sandals for John Lennon, and at the same time passed on to him a few poetic gems. This historic feat was superceded when he made a pair of sandals for Jackie Onassis. After this, hacking out footwear and poetic gems for the likes of Bob Dylan and Kojak became commonplace.

Afficionados (and even readers) of poetry may want to take a short detour at this point. Just 50 m north-west of Platia Monastiraki, at the first right turn off busy Ermou as it heads west, you come to Odios Theklas. Byron lived here at No 11 during his first ten-week stay in Athens in 1809. The landlord's 13-year-old daughter reappeared as the Maid of Athens in his poetry.

Leave Platia Monastiraki by the main street from the south-east corner: Pandrossou. This takes you by Platia Avisinias, the site of the famous **Monastiraki flea market**, open on the grand scale Sunday mornings: the sweating, seething mass of humanity you see before you is but the weekday prelude. This market used to be good for picking up Ancient Greek and Roman coins at very reasonable prices – the prices still remain very reasonable, but the coins aren't always quite so ancient as they appear. However, some of of the tourist ware on display here is worth looking at, especially the leather bags, rugs, and *some* of the imitation Ancient Greek ware.

Continue east down Pandrossou, and in just over 200 m you emerge into Platia Mitropoleous. This square contains two churches. The larger, **Mitropolis**, is the Greek Orthodox cathedral, dating from the mid 19thC.

It's said to have been designed by four different architects simultaneously, and to have been built out of the remains of more than 70 churches which had been reduced to rubble by the Turks. More than a little of this shows in its pleasantly incongruous appearance.

To the south of Mitropolis stands the much smaller **old cathedral**, which has also suffered from the begriming action of the Athens atmosphere. The present building dates from the 12thC, though its foundations are said to be about four hundred years older. At the south side is the celebrated **Stone of Cana**, whose inscription identifies it as having been used as the table-top at the Marriage at Cana, where Christ performed his first miracle, turning the water into wine. This somewhat undistinguished looking block of grey marble was miraculously discovered at Elatea.

Take the north-eastern exit from Mitropoleos, which leads you along Mitropoleous Street. In 300 m you emerge into Platia Syntagma (often known as Constitution Square), the main square of Athens. Its centre is shaded by oleander and cypress trees, with statue-lined paths, and the outer part of the square has a number of large cafés.

On the east side of Syntagma is the former **Royal Palace**, which has acted as the Parliament (Vouli) building since 1935. (See also page 187.) Greece's constitution was proclaimed from the balcony here in 1843.

The north side of Syntagma is overlooked by the **Grand Bretagne**, Athens' most prestigious grand hotel. The building dates from 1843. During the Second World War the Germans and the British successively used it as their headquarters. When Winston Churchill visited in 1944, there was an attempt to assassinate him by blowing up the hotel from the sewers. (This failed, and the sewers of Athens remain as blocked as ever.)

From Syntagma continue east along Leoforos Vasilissis Sofias, which leads out of the square to the north. On your right you'll soon see the National Gardens, and after 300 m you come to the **Benaki Museum** on your left. For details, see page 185.

Leaving the museum, continue east along Leoforos Vasilissis Sofias, and in

• *Across Athens to the Hill of Lykabitos.*

a couple of hundred metres you'll see the **Museum of Cycladic and Ancient Art** on your left. For details, see page 185.

Continue two blocks east along Leoforos Vasilissis Sofias, then turn left down Ploutarchou. Here you'll see the British Embassy on your left. This street now leads you through the smart Kolonaki district. Eventually you begin to climb some steps. Some 500 m on, at the end of Ploutarchou, you catch the funicular which takes you to near the top of the **Hill of Lykabitos** for a superb view out over Athens. It is particularly fine at sunset, when the accumulated pollution in the air often produces a crimson glow as spectacular as any you'll see between here and the similarly polluted skies over Tokyo.

This unnatural aesthetic phenomenon can be observed in comfort from a café at the top of the hill, accompanied by a more natural product: a glass of ouzo.

SIGHTS & PLACES OF INTEREST

ACROPOLIS

If you see nothing else in Athens, see this. Despite its over-exposure to the ravages of history, pollution and fulsome admiration, it remains one of the world's finest sights.

The Acropolis, which literally means 'high city', is over 150 m above sea level, 400 m long by just under 200 m wide, and within easy reach of the sea – an ideal defensive spot for a settlement. The site was first inhabited around 5,000 years ago. Originally, its great walls made it unassailable. But in the 5thC BC the Athenians were advised by the Delphic Oracle (see page 92) to pull down their walls. The place was reduced to rubble and ashes by the invading Persians little more than a quarter of a century later.

But it was in the 5thC BC, during the Age of Pericles, that the Acropolis as we know it came into being. Its rebuilding coincided with Athens' rise to power and a golden age of civilization.

The Acropolis was not only a defensive citadel, but also a sacred site – and the perfection of the white marble temples built during this period continued to dazzle all who saw them during the following centuries. No building in Europe was to match the Acropolis in terms of architectural skill until the great Gothic cathedrals were built more than one thousand five hundred years later. (And these are only a technical improvement, remaining inferior in terms of architectural taste.)

The Franks in the 13thC were the first to use it again as a fortress. Later, the Turks turned it into a fortified mosque. In the mid 17thC the place was used as an arsenal, and some powder kegs blew up causing widespread damage. Forty years later it was besieged by the Venetians, who managed to score a direct hit with a mortar on the Parthenon.

Then in the early 19thC the Scottish grandee Lord Elgin arrived as British Ambassador. He took off home almost anything of value which could be lifted. By a rare freak of poetic justice, the cost of removing the objects eventually bankrupted him – thus completing financially what had already occurred morally. These ill-gotten treasures, which include the Parthenon frieze, remain to this day in the British Museum in London. Despite the determined campaign by the recent Greek Minister of Culture Melina Mercouri to have them returned, there appears no prospect of the so-called Elgin Marbles (the Greeks call them the Parthenon Marbles) being restored to where they belong.

During the 20th century, a considerable amount of restoration has been carried out on the Acropolis, and work continues apace. Yet it remains an uphill battle. The present successor to the Turks, Venetian mortars and Lord Elgin comes in the form of acidic air pollution from the factories and exhaust pipes of Athens. This has already begun eating deep into the ancient marble, and indeed into the brains of some of those concerned with its preservation. It has even been suggested that the whole thing be pulled down and replaced with an 'everlasting' white plastic replica.

Nevertheless, there is still much to see on the Acropolis. Here are a few of the features you should not miss:

The *Propylaia* were the ancient ceremonial gates to the Acropolis, designed and built by Mnesikles using two different types of marble (Eleusian and Pentelic). The original five gates had large wooden doors.

On the right of the Propylaia you can see the columned *Temple of Athena Nike*. This once contained a wooden statue of Athena Nike, the goddess of victory. Normally statues of Athena Nike were winged, but in this case the statue had no wings, so that the goddess of victory could never fly away from the city.

Once you have passed on to the main plateau of the Acropolis, you see ahead of you an area of marble rubble, with the graceful columns of the **Parthenon** to your left. This, the finest of all Greek temples, is a complex masterpiece which despite its size gives an impression of delicate simplicity. The building is full of subtle architectural sleights of hand that reinforce its visual eloquence. (For instance, the columns lean slightly inwards: so when viewed from floor level the tops don't appear further apart than their bases.) The temple was devoted to Athena and designed by Phaedeas, who was also responsible for the gold and ivory statue which it contained. Its pediments and friezes were decorated with painted sculptures, which stood against a blue background.

To the north of the Parthenon stands the second finest building on the Acropolis, the **Erechteion**. This was built between 421 and 407 BC and incorporates a number of earlier shrines. In the eastern portico are replicas of the famous Caryatids, the large female statues which supported the roof. The originals are at present in the Acropolis Museum, preserved behind glass from the corrosive gasps of their admirers and the hot air of the guides. The **Acropolis Museum** is beyond the Parthenon at the south-eastern end of the Acropolis. It contains a number of superb statues which somehow managed to elude the Venetian mortars and the attentions of Lord Elgin. Those who find the original Caryatids a little too gargantuan for their taste in female beauty should seek out the more delicate *Mourning Athena* (Room 6), a relief dating from the 5thC BC, or *Victory Undoing her Sandal*.

On those few days when the atmosphere is clear, there are fine views from the Acropolis south over the city towards the blue sea of the Saronic Gulf. And from the southern perimeter there is also a vertiginous view down over the Theatres of Dionysios and Herod Atticus.

AGORA

Just north of the Acropolis, south-west of Monastiraki, this is the next most important site in Athens, after the Acropolis. It was the bustling heart of ancient Athens, where business was conducted, gossip passed on, the latest news announced, and everyone from philosophers to nut sellers attempted to persuade the passing crowds what was best for them.

The Agora is now an amorphous muddle of ruins and relics, from a mixture of eras. But in the midst of all this there are some superb things to see.

The **Theseion**, dating from the 5thC BC, is one of the finest Doric temples still standing. Theseion means Temple of Theseus; however the name is a mistake: a medieval scholar misread Theseus for Hephaistus. Hephaistus was the god of metal workers and this used to be the district of the metal workers;

the modern street of Ifestou, just north of here, is also named after Hephaestus, and the tradition of metal working lingers in the area to this day.

Also worth seeing here is the **Stoa of Attalos**, which is a modern reconstruction of the original 2ndC BC arcade, with its covered walkway and row of pillars.

BENAKI MUSEUM

On Leoforos Vasilissis Sofias (east from Syntagma). If you find the large major collections, such as the one in the National Archaeological Museum, somewhat overwhelming, this is the museum for you. The exhibits here originally formed the private collection of the Greek philanthropist Andonis Benaki, who made his millions in the Egyptian cotton trade. The neo-classical mansion which houses the collection was once Benaki's Athens residence.

There may not be superb masterpieces as in the major museums, but what you can see here is amenable, making the different periods more comprehensible. The collection ranges from Bronze Age relics right the way through to 19thC pieces and relics from the War of Independence. There are also some fine paintings, including a couple of surprising early works by El Greco, as well as some wonderful icons.

MUSEUM OF CYCLADIC ART

4 Neophytou Douka St (off Leoforos Vasilisssis Sophias, east of Syntagma). Cycladic art flourished in the Aegean from 3000 – 2000 BC, and its primitive statues and earth mother figures have a grace which presages the classical beauty of later eras. In fact, some of these simplistic forms can be very stirring, and have had many recognizable influences on modern art. These are well illustrated by the comparisons you'll find on the third floor. Photographs of works by Picasso, Brancusi and Modigliani are displayed alongside photographs of Cycladic art. The British sculptor Henry Moore is also included in these comparisons.

NATIONAL ARCHAEOLOGICAL MUSEUM

At 28 Octobriou St, two blocks north-east of Omonia. This museum houses the finest collection of ancient Greek art

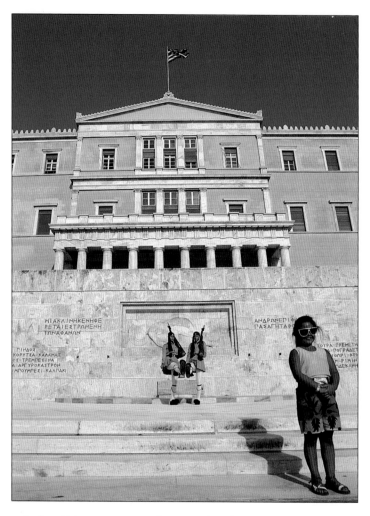

• *The Parliament Building, Athens.*

and relics which you can see anywhere in the world. It represents all of Greece with the exception of the finds made at Knossos, Delphi and Olympia. It also covers all periods from Archaic times through to the Hellenistic and Classical eras. All the exhibits are helpfully labelled in both English and Greek, a source of additional entertainment for those who find it amusing to spot where the translators have got it wrong.

If you intend spending any length of time here, it's worth buying a specialist guide to the museum. Also, by far the best time to visit is *after* visiting a number of the islands, digs and sites from where the exhibits originated. An

ancient amphora discovered in the sea off Mykonos suddenly comes alive if you've swum in that water.

One of the earliest and finest exhibits is the collection of frescos from Santorini on the first floor. These date from 16thC BC and were discovered less than 20 years ago. Yet they appear as fresh and vital today as they must have done to the ancient Minoan people who first saw them. My favourite is the picture of two boys boxing, and there's also a very good one of a fisherman with some fairly recognizable fish.

Also not to be missed are the museum's prize exhibits, including the Artemesian Poseidon in Room 15. This dark bronze statue originally had white ivory eyeballs, which must have looked fairly startling. Indeed, many of the statues in the museum would startle us if we could see them as their creators originally intended. All we see are the time-washed white marble relics of what were once brightly painted pieces. So preconceived are our notions of what classical statues should look like that it's difficult for us to imagine them coloured, without ruining what we perceive to be their timeless beauty.

In Room 4 you can see the famous **Mask of Agamemnon**, which was discovered by Schliemann at Mycenae (page 26). In fact the mask couldn't possibly be the mask of Agamemnon, as it was made for the funeral of a king who died 300 years before him.

Also not to be missed are: the Warrior of Marathon (Room 11), the 2ndC BC Horse and Jockey (Room 21), and the ceramics on the 1st floor. For insight into how sculpture developed from the Archaic to Classical times, visit Room 13 and the standing *kouroi* in the nearby rooms.

NATIONAL GALLERY
At the E end of Leoforos Vasilissis Sophias, at Leoforos Konstandinou. Worth a trip, if only for the few marvellous works by El Greco in the permanent collection. Often houses interesting travelling exhibitions.

ODEON OF HEROD ATTICUS
South of the Acropolis. This theatre is linked to the nearby Theatre of Dionysios (see below) by the ruined **Stoa of Eumenides**, a pillared arcade 170 m long with two stories of sheltered walkway. The Odeon dates originally from the 2ndC, and was completely restored in 1955. Nowadays, performances are staged here as part of the Athens festival. The accoustics from the stage area are legendary, and convey every inflexion of a speaking voice perfectly even to those in the very highest rows. As this isn't usually open to the public except for performances, it's best seen in conjunction with the Theatre of Dionysios, which is open to the public.

• *The Temple of Wingless Victory, the Acropolis.*

PARLIAMENT BUILDING (VOULI)
Syntagma. Outside it is the Monument to the Unknown Soldier guarded by two Evzoni. These crack soldiers are dressed for the heat of Athens in short kilts, long thick white woollen tights, and boots with red pom-poms. You have to be pretty tough to get away with wearing an outfit like this in public – and the Evzoni are renowned for their bravery. The changing of the guard takes place every hour on the hour. Girls wearing similarly short skirts may receive a wink.

THEATRE OF DIONYSIOS
South of the Acropolis. Besides being god of wine, Dionysios was the god of transformation, hence of masks – and thus of the early theatre.

This theatre, the oldest in Europe, is sculpted into the side of the Acropolis. Created in the 6thC BC, it was later expanded to take 17,000 people. It was where the Greek tragedies of Sophocles, Euripedes and Aeschylus were first performed, and where the citizens of Athens came to laugh at the savage satirical comedies of Aristophanes.

ZAPPEION (EXHIBITION HALL)
National Garden. The hall itself houses passing exhibitions of varying fatuity. But the cafés near here are a great open-air meeting place.

In the heart of Athens, you're surrounded by greenery – and to the west you can watch the sun set behind the Acropolis.

SIGHTS WITHIN EASY REACH OF ATHENS

For islands within easy reach of Athens, see Local Explorations: 6.

DAFNI

On the north-western outskirts of Athens on main Corinth road. In Byzantine times this former fortified spot guarded the access to Athens. The first temple on the site was a Sanctuary of Apollo (approximately 4thC BC), and the present monastery takes its name from the laurel (*dafni*, in Greek) which became sacred to Apollo after he fell in love with a nymph named Daphne. In ancient times the sanctuary was surrounded by laurel trees.

The original Christian monastery was founded here in 5thC, but this was sacked by barbarian invaders. What you see today was built in 11thC, and can claim to be one of the finest early Byzantine monasteries in the country. During the early 13thC, when French crusaders took over Attica, the monastery church became the burial place of the Burgun-dian Dukes of Athens.

The church has some fine mosaics, whose survival is something of a miracle. In the early 19thC this sacred spot was abandoned for a while, then served as a barracks, and afterwards as an asylum.

Just outside the walls there is the site of a marvellously profane wine festival which runs from July until early September. For a small admission fee you can drink as much as you like of the wines on offer. These range from the disgraceful, through the appalling, to the surprisingly acceptable – much the same as the imbibers. Be sure to eat before going in. The food on offer is poor and expensive.

FILI

Sometimes written Phyle. Head north about 12 km from Athens's outskirts on the road into the Parnitha Mountains to the village of Fili. From here you pass on into a barren stretch of the mountains, with gorges. At the entrance to one of these you will see the restored 14thC Moni Kliston (Our Lady of the Gorges.)

RECOMMENDED HOTELS

Athenian Inn, DD; *22 Haritos Street; tel. 72 34 097.*

A real find. In the heart of fashionable Kolonaki, just below Mount Lykabettos. A little over five minutes' walk from Syntagma and the National Gardens (which are south-west, and ideal for jogging). Apparently this hotel is still used by the Professor of Philosophy from Bologna who is convinced that Socrates was born in a house on this spot.

Electra Palace, DDD; *18 Nikodimou; tel. 32 41 401.*

Some people want the impossible: for instance, an air-conditioned hotel in the Plaka, with beautiful views out over the city (including the Acropolis), and perhaps a swimming pool to cool off in during the afternoons, and maybe even a roof garden for that romantic late-night conversation beneath the full moon. This is that impossible place, and surprisingly the prices aren't *that* impossible.

Grande Bretagne, DDD; *Syntagma Square; tel. 32 30 251.*

An Athens landmark. During the Second World War the Germans ruled Greece from here, and afterwards the British used it as their headquarters. Founded in 1874, the Grande Bretagne has been attracting the Sarah Bernhardts and Coco Chanels of this world ever since. Try an early evening aperitif in the bar if wish to alert the press, or the assorted minor celebrities, to your presence in town. The best rooms have magnificent balconies overlooking the Plaka towards the Acropolis, and air-conditioning as cool and efficient as the room service.

John's Place, D; *5 Patroou; tel. 32 29 719.*

The best inexpensive accommodation in the centre of Athens, just around the corner from Syntagma. Basic rooms and basic communal showers, but clean. The single room on the very top floor is a must for undeconstructed garret romantics: outside the tiny window, beyond the encircling back windows of the sweatshops, you can just see the Acropolis

Another 5 km beyond the village you come to an old Athenian fort, built in the 4thC to guard the direct route from Thebes to Athens. It has two towers and is picturesquely situated on a small plateau.

GLYFADA
Just over 30 minutes' drive from the city centre, south down the coast beyond the airport. You can swim at Piraeus, but you'll need a bath afterwards. Glyfada is the nearest resort to Athens where swimming can be pleasant. It's very much the kind of resort you'd expect to find at the end of the main airport runway outside one of the hottest and most polluted cities on the Mediterranean. Unless you're booked in on a package holiday, the only real reason for staying here is so that you can have a swim – or if you can't face the heat of Athens, and are prepared to drive in to see the sights each morning (which isn't such a bad idea as it may sound).

PARNITHA MOUNTAINS
See Greece Overall: 5.

SOUNION
About 67 km south-east of Athens, at the end of the main road along the coast. The Temple of Poseidon stands here, high above the Aegean in perhaps the most spectacular site in the land. The superb Doric temple was built in mid 5thC BC, and of its original 34 columns 16 remain standing.

This 'sacred headland' was mentioned by Homer, but it became famous largely because of its appeal to Romantic poets, in whom it would induce reverie. The hard-headed Romantic Byron visited in 1810, but instead of falling into a reverie the poet spent his time carving his name on one of the pillars. He later refered to it in Don Juan:

> *Place me on Sounion's marble steep*
> *Where nothing save the waves and I...*

Alas, you'll now find as many people here as there are waves crumpling the wide expanse of the sea all around. In the distance you can see the islands of Kea, Kithnos and Aegina and sometimes you can see as far as Serifos, which is

---

(floodlit at night) rising above the rooftops of the Plaka. Book in advance in season.

Phaedra, D-DD; 16 *Herefondos; tel. 32 27 795.*
On the corner of Adhrianou, the main street which runs through the Plaka. In a pedestrians-only district, so there's no noisy traffic at all hours. Nothing fancy in the way of decoration, but friendly, helpful staff and gregarious clientele (individualists all).

XEN, D-DD; 11 *Amerikis; tel. 36 26 970.*
North-west off Stadiou, just north of Syntagma. A haven for all women who have had enough of persistent local attentions – this is the Greek equivalent of the YWCA: a strictly women-only hostel. Fairly Spartan, but clean accommodation, with a good, but simple self-service restaurant. Friendly staff and clientele. Ideal for meeting people if you're feeling lonely.

IN PIRAEUS
If you plan to catch a boat to the islands, and have to spend the night in Athens, it's best to stay down in Piraeus. The boats leave so early that money is wasted on a full night in central Athens hotel.

For those who enjoy the low life, Piraeus still has one of the greatest concentrations of sleazy and flea-ridden hotels in Europe. But hurry, some of these historic spots are now modernizing, and becoming merely tawdry. Because I like to go to Piraeus without having to be accompanied by a lawyer or a minder, my recommendation does not fall into the above category.

Hotel Aenos, D; 14 *Ethnikis Andistaseos; tel. 41 74 879.*
A useful place to flop for the night. Contrary to the predictable and unfair witticisms, it does not live up to its unpleasantly punning name – even at the height of the high, high season. One of the men behind the desk is exceptionally helpful, the other is so much the opposite as to be an entertainment in his own right. They change shifts, so you just have to take pot luck as to who's on duty when you arrive.

• *Plaka restaurant.*

RECOMMENDED RESTAURANTS

American Coffee Shop and Restaurant, D-DD; 1 *Karageorgi Servias; tel.* 32 48 673.

For all who are beginning to suffer from the unremitting Greek cuisine, or who want to break themselves in gently, or who just can't be bothered – this is the spot for some reassuring and recognizable grub. The service is friendly, the English comprehensible, the menu ditto, and the service is conducted at a speed which would be considered treasonable in a more traditionally paced Greek restaurant. Good for a bite or a blow-out. But don't expect anything fancy.

Dionyssos, DD; *Lykabettos; tel.* 72 26 374.

This is the restaurant at the top of Mount Lykabettos, which rises above the Kolonaki district, north-east of Syntagma. To get here you take the funicular from Ploutarchou. Best views of the city, and the food is surprisingly good for such a spot. Romanticissimo.

Eden, DD; 3 *Flessa; tel.* 32 48 858.

A deservedly popular vegetarian place down a side street in the Plaka. Greek food lends itself to vegetarian cuisine: in poorer centuries local dishes had very little meat, and managed to disguise this in imaginative and substantial ways. So you needn't be disappointed with rabbit food and bowls of raw nutritionless nonsense. Out of season it can be very intimate and romantic; in season the waiters supply these ingredients.

Floca, D; *The Arcade, Panepistimou.*

An Athens institution: more of a café and meeting place than a restaurant, but you can get snacks. Situated in the arcade which runs south off one of the main streets connecting Syntagma and Omonia. Used to be a famous literary watering hole: Kazantzakis, Seferis, Elytis *et al* argued here. The standard of literary and political debate still remains high. Useful for discovering what the world looks like for those who consider Athens to be the centre of the Universe. Their cream cakes are disgustingly good.

Kouklis, DD; 14 *Tripodon Street.*

On a side street in the Plaka, west of main Adhrianou and running parallel to it. Strictly speaking this an *ouzeri* – where you come for an aperitif (usually an ouzo, hence the name) and dishes of little snacks (*meze*). These are among the gems of Greek cuisine, and now go a long way beyond the stuffed vine leaves and gnarled, fiery mini-sausages of yore. Kouklis is housed in an old Plaka mansion, whose walls are lined with some genuinely interesting old Greek photographs. (Contrary to normal practice, pretend you only want to look at the 'naughty ones,' and no one will mind you getting in the way.)

IN PIRAEUS

The best place to go for seafood is Piraeus, and the best place for seafood in Piraeus is down by the little harbour of Mikrolimano. (This is five minutes' walk east of the Zea Marina where the hydrofoils put in, or a 15-minute walk south over the hill from the main port.) Here the cuisine is as delightful as the waterfront setting. But be warned: it's very popular with Athenians. This means that if you book a table at a restaurant, you are likely to find that it has already been occupied by the time you arrive – and everyone will pretend that (a) they've never heard of your name or (b) that it is so impossible for a Greek to pronounce, let alone remember, that they were just being polite on the phone and didn't expect you to take them any more seriously than they took you. The trick is to get here early.

My favourite here is:

Canaris, DD-DDD; 50 *Akti Koumoudourou; tel.* 41 75 190.
Superb fresh fish and genuinely friendly, helpful service. Ask the waiter to recommend his favourite dish, and let him explain what it's made of, where it is best made (his island), and a good wine to go with it. Or just order lobster or red mullet and forget about your resolutions to start economizing. As a starter try baby octopus. I'm told that in the old days the owner would arrive at your table with your live lobster crawling up his arm – just to show you how fresh it was. Such hair-raising floor-shows are now, alas, a thing of the past.

more than 70 km away.

The most spellbinding times here are sunrise and sunset, when sometimes you can almost have the place to yourself.

In the afternoons, when the buses start arriving from Athens and the resorts, there is a daily free performance of a modernist minimalist symphony for camera shutters and international voices which lasts for hours – until the members of the orchestra are finally herded back into their coaches for their next performance at the Acropolis.

VOULIAGMENI

About 10 *km* S *of* Athens. This is the smart resort just beyond the outskirts of Athens on the Apollo Coast. You have to pay to get on to the beach. A popular spot with the Athens glitter set at the weekends, and in the evenings you can see them dining in the expensive restaurants amidst a galaxy of glittering bangles and bracelets.

The resort also has a small lake filled by a mineral water spring.

VRAVONA

About 25 *km* E *of* Athens, *on the coast*.
Just 1.5 km inland from the sea, in a wide marshy valley, stands the site of Brauron. At the bottom of the hill you can see the Sanctuary of Artemis, which was once the most sacred spot of the Artemis cult. The foundation of this cult is related in a long, complicated, often incomprehensible and largely boring legend. Much more interesting is the fact that the worshippers of Artemis the goddess of hunting often took part in divine orgies. Though how they squared this with the worship of Artemis is difficult to imagine. Artemis remained strictly a virgin, and was likely to take horrible vengeance on anyone who attempted to relieve her of her maidenhood. She was also known to punish sexual miscreants, even when their conduct was not at all threatening to her virginity. For instance, when one of her attendants had an affair with Zeus, she turned her into a bear.

The site itself is rather pleasant, and attracts less visitors than you'd expect, mainly because it's so difficult to reach. Only for those with a hired car – it's just not worth it by public transport.

<u>Northern Mainland</u>

Northern Macedonia

300 km (round trip); map Michelin 980, 1:700000

This is one of the least visited regions in the entire country. One of its historic highlights is the remains of the first capital of Ancient Greece, on a site which remained lost for over 1,500 years. The geographical high spots are the mountains which rise to over 2,500 m, forming the country's northern border. Close by, you'll discover Greece's own lake district where two of the lakes are among the finest wildlife preserves in Europe.

If you're starting from Thessaloniki, (where the exploration links with Greece Overall: 1), head west along the E86. This takes you to the old heartland of Macedonia and the remains of ancient Pella, birthplace of Alexander the Great. Further on, at Skidra, you can take a detour to see the so-called 'Royal Tombs' at Lefkadia. Just down the road is Naoussa, which produces the finest wine in Greece.

Continue along the main E86 and you enter the Greek Lake District. From Arnissa on the shores of Lake Vegoritas, drive on through Florina (near the border wildlife preserve of the Prespa Lakes) and south to the old fur-trading centre of Kastoria on Lake Kastoria. Continue south to the E90, where you turn east, passing the fascinating small mountain town of Siatista. From here head on through Kozani and then on to Veria, at which point you can take a detour down to Vergina, to visit the site of the tomb of Philip II, King of ancient Macedon and father of Alexander the Great. Then continue east along E90 until you reach Thessaloniki.

Even if you're just doing the drive, and not stopping off to see any of the sights, you will need a couple of days for this tour. To do the route justice you should allow at least four days. *Before setting out it is essential to read the warning on page 194.*

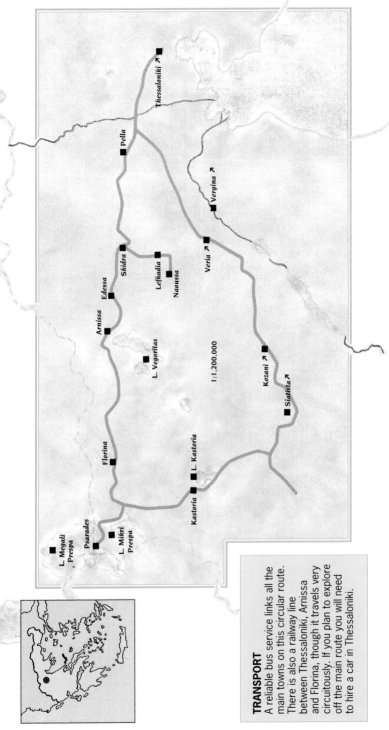

Thessaloniki ↗

Pella

Vergina ↗

Skidra
Edessa
Lefkadia
Naoussa
Veria ↗

Arnissa

L. Vegoritas

1:1,200,000

Kozani ↗

Siatista ↗

Florina

L. Kastoria

Kastoria

Psarades
L. Megali
Prespa
L. Mikri
Prespa

TRANSPORT

A reliable bus service links all the main towns on this circular route. There is also a railway line between Thessaloniki, Arnissa and Florina, though it travels very circuitously. If you plan to explore off the main route you will need to hire a car in Thessaloniki.

SIGHTS & PLACES OF INTEREST

ARNISSA

A picturesque village beside Lake Vegoritas, which denotes the start of the Greek Lake District – though in many ways the mountains here bear more resemblance to the Scottish Highlands. Lake Vegoritas is now filled with fish since trout from Switzerland were introduced just over 30 years ago. The island opposite Arnissa has the remains of an ancient mosque, all that is left of a village now beneath the surface of the water.

The highest mountain to the north is **Mount Kaimaktsalan**, which rises over 2,500 m and forms the border between Greece and the independent province of former Yugoslavia which

WARNING
Owing to the tense political situation which currently exists between Greece and the independent province of former Yugoslavia which calls itself Macedonia, travel is likely to be restricted in this region. You will almost certainly need permission if you wish to travel north or east (i.e., towards the border) off the E86 on the stretch from Edessa through Florina to Kastoria. There are even rumours that this stretch may soon be closed to foreigners altogether. Be sure to check at the main Tourist Office (GNTO) in Thessaloniki (8 Platia Aristotelous; tel. (031) 36 31 12) or with the Tourist Police (10, Egnatia; tel. (031) 52 28 21) *before you start your journey.*

• *Kastoria and lake.*

calls itself Macedonia. This mountain was the scene of continuous heavy fighting during the First World War and contains a memorial to the fallen.

EDESSA ⇌ ✕
A picturesque mountain town with a series of waterfalls.

FLORINA ⇌
This used to be a little Casablanca, with Yugoslavian entreprenuers crossing the border (13 km up the road) to load up with the flash and tacky capitalist goods so favoured by communist countries whose shops were stocked with less exotic tat.

For visitors not interested in making a killing in portable hi-fis or cornering the market in Madonna T-shirts, Florina nevertheless makes an ideal base for visiting the Prespa Lakes (Megali Prespa and Mikri Prespa), which straddle the border between Greece, Albania and modern-day Macedonia. Their remote reedy shores are home to an exceptional range of rare bird life, including some species of fowl which are now found practically nowhere else. Permission to spy in this region on our feathered friends is *absolutely* necessary (see warning above).

KASTORIA ⇌ ✕
This old town has an attractive position on a neck of land jutting out into a lake. Its name means beaver, and for years it was a fur trading centre. This contentious trade is now struggling, but continues.

The town itself is a rather nondescript mixture of drab modern flats and old houses raffishly decorated with storks' nests. The most interesting part of town is **Koriadi**, which is down by the south-eastern shore of the lake. Here, and to the north, there are a dozen or so fine old Byzantine churches. The most interesting of these is the 11thC **Panagia Koumbelidiki** which contains some delightfully garish 13thC murals.

For many centuries the town had a large Jewish population, but during the Second World War the entire community was shipped to the death camps. In 1949 the surrounding mountains witnessed the last bitter fighting of the Greek Civil War. At **Platia Makedonomakon**, north-west of the town centre,

---

RECOMMENDED HOTELS

EDESSA
Hotel Olympion, D-DD; *Odos Demokrias; tel.* (0381) 23 485.

A pleasant provincial hotel on the main street, close to the bus station. Not to be mistaken for the nearby Hotel Olympia on 18th Octobriou Sreet, which belongs to an altogether different order of cheapness.

FLORINA
Lyngos, D-DD; *tel.* (0385) 28 322.

Ideal as a base for visiting the nearby Prespa Lakes, or exploring the local mountains and unvisited villages. This hotel has a restaurant which is recommended for its pepper salad, the local speciality.

KASTORIA
Kastoria, DD; *Leoforos Nikis; tel.* (0467) 29 608.

North of the town centre by the promenade which looks over the lake towards the snow-capped mountains.

NAOUSSA
Megas Alexandros, D; *Platia Emborious; tel.* (0332) 27 511.

A suitably spartan spot in which to sleep off your vinous excesses.

---

there is a statue to the American general who 'assisted' the Greek army in this operation. The nearby quayside has fine views out across the lake towards the mountains (whose peaks are snow-capped for much of the year). The fishing boats which put out from here are of a traditional design, believed to be more than 2,000 years old, and unique to this lake.

KOZANI
See Greece Overall: 2.

LEFKADIA
This is the site of the greatest Macedonian tombs yet discovered. There are several tombs contained here, though only one (the best) is usually open to the public. Despite being called a Royal Tomb, it is almost cer-

tainly that of a Macedonian general.

Lefkadia is very much a place of the dead, and if you're susceptible to the ambience the murals inside can be spooky. One depicts Hermes and the dead general, and the others are portraits of the Judges of Hell. You may find this tomb locked. If so, ask for the keeper, who lives just down the road.

NAOUSSA   ✕
This hallowed spot produces the finest wine in Greece – usually under the name of the Boutari family. The red version gets better and better. For a sample of Naoussa at its best, try a bottle of the red 1986 vintage.

Behind the town rise the wooded slopes of **Mount Vermion**, whose peak is over 2,000 m high. It is a ski centre in winter. There are some fine walks through the woods.

PELLA
Pella was the capital of ancient Macedon, and the city where Alexander the Great was born in 356 BC. In those days it was connected to the sea by way of a shallow lake (the open sea is now some 30 km away). In 146 BC the Macedonians were defeated and Pella was sacked by the Roman legions. Everything of any value was carted off as booty to Rome. Over the centuries the waterway to the sea silted up, and the site of ancient Pella was lost.

Just over 30 years ago a local farmer began digging a new cellar for his house, and came across some marble pillars. Pella had been rediscovered. Excavations continue apace, but much of the city still remains to be uncovered.

As you approach this initially unprepossessing site beside the main E86, it is difficult to believe that this was the first real capital of Greece – more important even than Athens in its day – and the city from which Alexander set out to conquer to world.

The most interesting relics are certainly the mosaics, the best of which are displayed in the site **museum**. The site itself contains the foundations of several houses, a palace, shops and streets. Aristotle taught Alexander the Great here, and the celebrated trage-

dian Euripides wrote and died here, as did the poet Agathon (the Oscar Wilde of Ancient Greece).

PSARADES
In one direction you look out across the water towards Albania, in the other towards so-called independent Macedonia (part of former Yugoslavia). You can stay in a room in the local taverna. (It is possible to get to this village by bus.)

SIATISTA
See Greece Overall: 2.

THESSALONIKI
See Greece Overall: 1.

VERIA
See Greece Overall: 2.

RECOMMENDED RESTAURANTS

EDESSA
Xenia, DD; *tel.* (0381) 22 995.

In the centre of town, close to the park with the waterfalls, Xenia is government-run and surprisingly friendly for such an establishment.

KASTORIA
Ta Psaradika, D; *off Leoforos Nikis near Platia Makedonomakon.*

This *ouzeri* is actually in the lake on a platform. A popular early evening meeting spot for young locals, northwest of the city centre. Have an ouzo and *meze*: the food elsewhere in town is distinctly average.

If you're looking for a restaurant, the best place to try is the area around Mitropoleos/Platia Omonia, which is just over ten minutes' walk south of here.

NAOUSSA
Vermion, DD; W *of town; tel.* (0332) 23 013.

A restaurant with a pleasant mountain-side setting, renowned for its delicious locally caught fish. Try the fish with a bottle of the excellent local Boutari white – the waiters are very helpful on Naoussa wines (see Naoussa entry, left).

• *Naoussa.*

Northern Mainland

The Halkidiki

350 _km (round trip); map Michelin 980, 1:700000_

The distinctive three-pronged peninsula just east of Thessaloniki known as the Halkidiki is an area of dramatic contrasts. You see Greece at its holiest in the remote monasteries of Mount Athos, and at its most sybaritic in the huge resort hotels which line the Kassandra and Sithonia peninsulas. You can also visit the birthplace of the philosopher Aristotle, and the remains of one of Greece's first navigational canals, dug by the Persian Emperor Xerxes well over 2,000 years ago.

If you are following my route, and assuming you take Thessaloniki as your starting point, head south on the main road for the Halkidiki. About 5 km beyond the city limits turn off east towards Poligiros, the capital of the Halkidiki. Just beyond the turn-off there are some fine views as you penetrate the Holomondas Mountains, which rise to over 1,100 m. The trail continues through Stagira, then turns south along the coast to lerissos and Ouranopoli, the embarkation points for Mount Athos.

Retrace your route past Stagira, and then turn south at Paleohori. This leads you down to the Sithonia peninsula, with its picturesque circular coastal road. From here continue west to the Kassandra peninsula, which also makes a fine circular coastal drive. From Kassandra you can return north to Thessaloniki.

In a hired car, it would take you a couple of days to drive round this route. If you're planning to stop off at one of the resorts on Kassandra or Sithonia, or you have permission to make a four-day visit to Mount Athos, you should allow a week. As usual, you can just as easily use this section for random (or armchair) exploration of the region, without following the route.

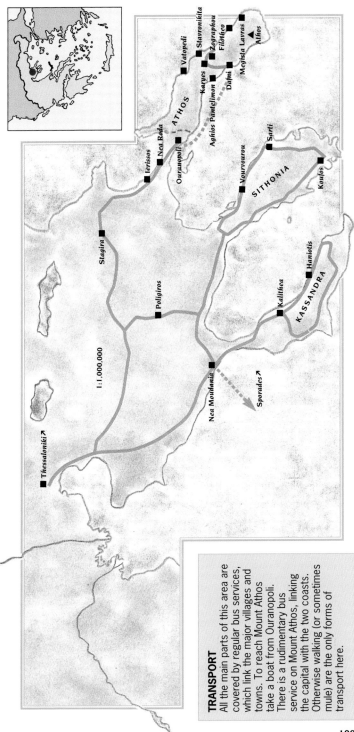

TRANSPORT

All the main parts of this area are covered by regular bus services, which link the major villages and towns. To reach Mount Athos take a boat from Ouranopoli. There is a rudimentary bus service on Mount Athos, linking the capital with the two coasts. Otherwise walking (or sometimes mule) are the only forms of transport here.

199

SIGHTS & PLACES OF INTEREST

IERISSOS
Nearby is **Nea Roda**, where you can see the remains of the canal which, according to one historian, 'was single-mindedly driven through the neck of the peninsula in 480 BC by the Persian Emperor Xerxes'. The canal was intended to save the Persian fleet from sailing around Mount Athos, where a decade previously they had lost 300 ships and 20,000 men.

KALITHEA
And Haniotis: see Kassandra, below.

KASSANDRA 🛏 ✕
This is the westernmost of the three peninsulas which jut out from Halkidiki into the northern Aegean. In the 19thC, during the Greek War of Independence, the inhabitants fought bravely against the Turks, but were eventually over-come and massacred. For years afterwards the peninsula was deserted, apart from a few isolated fishing settlements. Several decades ago it became popular with the city dwellers of Thessaloniki, who took to spending their weekends on its long sandy beaches. Then suddenly in the last ten years or so it was 'discovered' by the international tourist trade. Since then massive development has continued apace, with the building of large resort complexes, and groups of holidaymakers from all over Europe being ferried in from Thessaloniki International Airport. **Kalithea** on the east coast overlooking the Kassandra Gulf is the most popular of the resorts, and **Haniotis** has one of the finest long sandy beaches. From Nea Moudania you can catch a hydrofoil to the Sporadic islands of Skiathos, Skopelos and Alonissos (see Local Explorations: 8), which are now beginning to suffer from similar tourist overkill.

ENTRY TO MOUNT ATHOS
Only adult males are permitted to enter Mount Athos, and even if you qualify you will still require an entry permit, the acquisition of which is a suitably Byzantine undertaking. You must realize that the following procedure is what *ought* to happen, but you will be dealing with a dedicated bureacracy: there is no guarantee that it will.

First you must apply at your embassy or consulate (in Greece) for a letter of recommendation – impressing on the official your profound knowledge of and serious interest in Mount Athos, the Byzantine church or some similar Orthodox topic. (A frivolous interest such as philosophy or comparative religion may well cause you to fall at this early hurdle, and is likely to be anathema later.) Once your valuable letter has been extracted from an official, you are ready for stage two.

Take the letter together with your passport to the Greek Ministry of Foreign Affairs (2 Zalokosta Street, near Syntagma, Athens), or the Ministry of Northern Greece (Room 218 Platia Dikitirou, Thessaloniki), where the fun (at your expense) begins once more. Only ten visitors per day are permitted on to Mount Athos, and in summer the days are booked well in advance, so apply early. Your permit will allow you to stay on Mount Athos for only four days, and will undoubtedly be designated to begin on the day which is most inconvenient to you.

The best approach to Mount Athos is via the boat from **Ouranopoli** (7.45 am and noon in summer, 9.45 am only in winter). On board you surrender your permit and passport. The boat takes you to Dafni, where you travel by bus to the capital of Mount Athos, the hamlet of Karyes. Here you visit the police to get back your passport and permit, and then you must obtain another *essential* permit (*Diamonitirion*) from the Monastic Authorities in the yellow building. It costs 1,000 drachmae and allows you to stay at any of the monasteries on Mount Athos: you pay nothing further, as hospitality is free (though ascetic).

Having undergone your trials and tribulations at the hands of so many sacred and secular tormentors, you are now in a suitable spiritual state either to undertake your four days on Mount Athos or to lead a revolution.

MOUNT ATHOS 🚢 ✕

If you want to visit Mount Athos, see Entry to Mount Athos, opposite. If you can't obtain a permit, it is still possible to see Mount Athos from one of the boats which tour the coast, setting out from **Ierissos** and **Ouranopoli**, where there is a recommended hotel and several agreeable tavernas and cafés.

Mount Athos is the Holy Mountain (Agio Oros) of the Orthodox Church, and is considered as a separate theocratic republic within the Greek state. According to legend, the Virgin Mary was blown ashore here on her way to Cyprus, and declared the spot sacred ground. During the early centuries AD it was occupied by various hermits and misanthropes who lived in caves. The first recorded monastery here is **Megista Lavra** which was founded in 943 AD, but there had almost certainly been religious communities of some sort here since the 7thC.

In the following centuries nomadic Vlach shepherds and their families shared this remote peninsula with the monks, but stories soon began to circulate of scandalous behaviour more reminiscent of the ancient Greek gods than of a religious community committed to self-denial. As a result the Vlachs had to go, and the Byzantine Emperor issued a strict edict banning all women, 'smooth-faced boys' and female animals (even chickens) from Mount Athos – a ban which remains in force to this day.

The golden age of Mount Athos was in the 15thC, when 40 monasteries thrived here and there was a population of over 20,000 monks. The most recent monastery is said to have been founded during this period. Little of significance has changed in the past 500 years, apart from a drastic decline in the monastic population (now down to 20 monasteries with fewer than 2,000 monks).

Mount Athos has a capital, **Karyes**, which is little more than a hamlet. There is one old bus which runs a service along the only road connecting it

---

RECOMMENDED HOTELS

KASSANDRA - Haniotis
Ermis Hotel, D-DD; *tel.* Haniotis 51 245.
A pleasant small hotel in this lively resort.

KASSANDRA - Kalithea
Pallini Beach, D-DD; *tel.* (0374) 22 480.
A massive development with all the amenities you'd expect. If you want some privacy, try the chalets. This is very popular with families – the kids love it.

MOUNT ATHOS - Ouranopoli
Hotel Akrathos, DD-DDD; *tel.* (0377) 71 151.
Another resort development with a wide range of amenities including tennis courts and a private pool. Your last chance for some luxury before the monastic rigours of Mount Athos.

Xenia, DD-DDD; *down the coast on the edge of town; tel.* (0377) 71 202.
A government-run hotel pleasantly situated away from the rather tawdry strip.

RECOMMENDED RESTAURANTS

KASSANDRA - Haniotis
The best eating places are the tavernas which line the main square. Even at the tail end of the season there is still a fairly hectic nightlife here.

MOUNT ATHOS - Ouranopoli
The sea-front restaurants and cafés are great sunset-watching spots and are recommended, although they're mainly geared to the tourist trade and some are pricey. One which is slightly less on both counts is:

Manthos Taverna, D-DD; *left along the front.*
The seafood is delicious and some excellent local wines are available.

SITHONIA - Sarti
Ta Vrakkia, DD; *left along the front.*
A pleasant taverna right on the sea, with a lively clientele, where you can enjoy a jolly evening under the stars.

• *Fresco in the Church of Protaton, Karyes.*

to the landing stages on the two coasts (the peninsula is 10 km wide). You can catch caiques which run along the coast to the landing stages for other monasteries, or you can walk along the paths. You must reach the monastery where you are planning to spend the night before sunset, as their gates close irrevocably at this time. A friend of mine once arrived too late, in a state of extreme exhaustion and hunger after his long walk across the mountain. He spent the night huddled under a thorn bush, imagining that his boots had turned into chocolate and eventually chewing their laces.

This peninsula is one of the few stretches of coastline in the northern Mediterranean that has remained completely unspoilt. It is partly wooded, and crossed by isolated paths between the monasteries. The mountain itself, which is at the southern end of the peninsula, rises higher than 2,000 m.

The following are the main sights on Mount Athos:

At **Karyes** be sure to visit the restored **Church of Protaton**, which dates from the 10thC and many believe to be the oldest on Mount Athos. Its 14thC frescos are amongst the finest on the peninsula.

Stavronikita has a spectacular setting overlooking the sea on the east coast, and makes an ideal resting spot

for your first night on the mountain.

Megista Lavra is the showpiece of Mount Athos. It was founded over 1,000 years ago and now contains 15 separate chapels and churches. You can also see a superb mural of the *Last Supper* by Theophanes, the great 16thC Cretan icon painter. This monastery is at the end of the east coast and can be reached by caique, or a day-long walk from Stavronikita.

Filotheo is a friendly monastery where you sometimes get the chance to talk (in English) with one of the monks.

Vatopedi, on the northern stretch of the east coast, is also in a superb setting high above the sea. It is one of the larger monasteries and resembles a castle. It has a superb library containing more than 7,000 ancient books and manuscripts, which include such priceless gems as a copy of Ptolemy's *Geographia* and many rare old maps. A visit to Vatopedi, the most modern of the monasteries, will disabuse you of any notions you might have about the monks being naive primitives.

If you want to climb Mount Athos itself, there is a precipitous path up from Aghia Anna at the southern tip of the peninsula.

The west coast has a number of fine

monasteries which are closer together, including **Aghios Pantelimon** (a small community of Russian Orthodox monks) and **Zographou** (where the monks are Bulgarian).

NEA RODA
See Ierissos, page 200.

OURANOPOLI
And other places marked on the Mount Athos peninsula: see Mount Athos, and Entry to Mount Athos, page 200.

POLIGIROS
The small, uninteresting market town that is the capital of the Halkidiki.

SITHONIA ✕
An area that is more wooded and picturesque than Kassandra, and which has suffered slightly less from the effects of international tourism.

Vourvourou is set on a superb sweeping bay opposite the island of Nea Diaporos. But the most spectacular bay is at **Koufos**, near the tip of the peninsula, where there are impressive white cliffs. The coast north of here is hopelessly overdeveloped. **Sarti** is a popular resort on the east coast of the peninsula, with a pleasant taverna.

STAGIRA
The birthplace of Aristotle in 384 BC, with a statue of the great philosopher and logician to prove it. Unfortunately, the appliction of Aristotelian logic works against this statuesque proof: Aristotle was born in 384 BC in a small town.

• *Entrance to Vatopedi Monastery.*

There was no small town here in 384 BC.

Therefore Aristotle was not born here.

Regardless of statues and logic, Aristotle was born at *ancient* Stagira, whose remains are several kilometres down the road to Stratonion.

THESSALONIKI
See Greece Overall: 1.

VOUVOUROU
And other places on the Sithonia peninsula: see Sithonia, above.

HOSPITALITY ON MOUNT ATHOS

When you stay on Mount Athos you are subject to the Orthodox rule of hospitality. At night you are provided with a bed in a monastery, and you are also given a meal, which will be meatless, and often fairly basic. No payment is accepted for your bed and board. However, those who wish to make a contribution (or feel more at ease for having done so), can always leave money in the monastery church. This is not expected by the monks – there is no plate left conspicuously for your contribution. The usual place to leave your money is in the sand beneath the candleholders.

Be warned, you may find the beds harder than you're used to, and you may also find the food spartan, especially if you are walking long distances during the day. It is wise to bring along some kind of supplement to your diet, to give you the energy with which to continue your pilgrimage. Nuts and dried fruit are best. Don't bring chocolate, as it melts; or alcohol – your meals in the monasteries (even breakfast, in some of them) are usually accompanied by an everyday wine. As for the hardness of the beds: just look upon it as part of what you came here for.

South-Western Peleponnese

150 km; map Michelin 980, 1:700000

This is one of the least-visited regions of the Greek mainland, and I've included it to complement the mainstream Peleponnese areas covered elsewhere in this guide under Greece Overall: 7, 8 and 9. Indeed, the route links with Greece Overall: 7 and 8 at either end. Apart from Sparta (Greece Overall: 8) and Olympia (Greece Overall: 7), there are no major tourist attractions, just several interesting places to see, plus some superb beaches which often remain empty even at the height of summer.

Assuming you start at Sparta, you go west on the road for Kalamata. This takes you on a winding route through the Taigetos mountains, where you'll have a continous run of fine views up towards the peaks which rise to over 1,800 m. Just after Kalamata you can take a detour up to ancient Messine, the large mountainside site of a city that was destroyed by the Spartans.

Then you follow the attractive road which skirts the shores of the Messinian Gulf to Koroni and Methoni, the two former Venetian colonies in the south-western Peleponnese. From Methoni you head north to Pilos, on historic Navarino Bay. Above this you can visit the site of Nestor's Palace, which features in Homer's *Odyssey*. From here you continue north along the coast. This is one of the last undiscovered stretches of shore in the whole of Greece, with miles of long, isolated sandy beaches, without a soul to be seen.

At Tholo you can turn inland for a detour to the lovely Temple of Apollo at Bassae (Vasses), a beautiful expedition up into the mountains.

From Tholo the main route continues along the western Peleponnese coast to Pirgos. Here you turn inland for Olympia, site of the first Olympic games and one of *the* tourist spots of Greece.

You can easily cover all this ground in a day, but if you want to stop off and take a few side trips, allow two to three days.

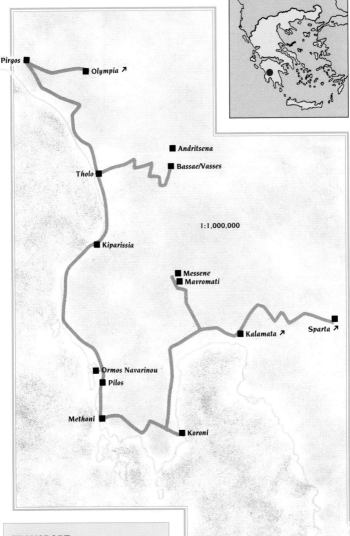

TRANSPORT
If you're planning to leave the main route, you'll need a car. Otherwise, you can cover the ground by public transport. Down in the remoter regions of Messinia, the south-western arm of the Peleponnese, the buses will tend to be very local, so make sure you allow time for connections. There is a railway which links Kalamata with Olympia, but if you take this you'll miss out on southern Messinia, which is the best part.

• Methoni Fort.

SIGHTS & PLACES OF INTEREST

BASSAE 🏛

Also known by its modern name of Vasses, this site is close to Andritsena, 51 km inland from Tholo. (Andritsena is an atmospheric small town, ideal for an overnight stop – see page 208.)

A superbly preserved Temple of Apollo is hidden deep in the mountains surrounded by gorges. Built in the mid 5thC BC out of local grey limestone by Iktinos, the architect of the Parthenon, it was surprisingly forgotten about for several centuries until the French architect Joachim Bocher re-discovered it in 1765. Whereupon the usual looting began: the inner frieze was carried off and auctioned in Zakinthos, bought by the British, and installed in the British Museum, where it remains to this day.

Unfortunately, the temple recently showed signs of falling down, and is at present housed beneath a tent-like structure, which has much the same effect as clothing the Venus de Milo in a space suit. The authorities keep promising that this unsightly garb is soon going to be removed – ring the Tourist Office at Olympia (tel. 0624 23 125) to discover if they have kept their word.

KALAMATA

See Local Explorations: 4.

KORONI 🏛

This beautiful little port of whitewashed houses and red tiled roofs was one of two Venetian strongholds in the Peleponnese. The other was Methoni, page 208, and together they were known as 'the eyes of Venice' because they kept watch on all ships that passed northwards into the Adriatic.

The Venetians first occupied this spot in 1206, and were here on and off until the early 18thC.

On the promontory above the village stands the ancient Venetian castle, whose citadel contains a Byzantine monastery.

Nearby there's good swimming at a lovely long sandy beach.

MESSENE

This is the site of the large fortified capital city of the ancient Messenians. Its 4thC BC surrounding walls stretched for more than 8 km, and were built in 85 days under the direction of the great Theban general Epaminondas, who intended to build a ring of forts through the Peleponnese to contain the Spartans. The plan was successful for a while, but in the end the Spartans destroyed the place.

• Windmill, Peleponnese.

In the midst of the scattered site is the pleasant little village of Mavromati. Above the village, providing a spectacular back-drop to the entire site, is Mount Ithomi, which rises to almost 800 m. The walk from the village to the peak takes an hour and a half. The path leads past a ruined 4thC BC Temple of Artemis, and at the top there's the Monastery of Voulkano, which was founded in the 8thC on the site of a Temple of Zeus. The present building dates from the 16thC and was in use until 1950.

METHONI ⇔ ✕
This was once the finest deep water port in the region, but the large bay has now silted up and is quite shallow. The place was mentioned by Homer, who speaks of the rich vineyards of the area. These remain to this day, along with olive groves and banana plantations. (According to a story I heard when I was last here, they also tried to grow avocados – but for some reason they all turned out the size of ping-pong balls.)

The Venetians took over Methoni in 1204, and it became a busy port on the trade route from Venice to Byzantium, Cyprus and the Levant. See also Koroni, page 206. Pilgrims would put in here on their way to the Holy Land, and during this period the cathedral was built.

The Turks attacked the place with vastly superior forces in 1500 and the Venetians held out valiantly on the islet of Bourdzi. Then news came through that Venetian troops from Corfu had arrived to assist them. Overjoyed, the Venetians began celebrating – but the Turks took advantage of this, slaughtered the lot and took over the city.

Later in the same century the great Spanish writer Cervantes was brought here after being captured by the Turks. (He refers to this in *Don Quixote*, in the tale told by the prisoner.)

There's a good beach on the bay, popular with windsurfers in the summer.

NAVARINO BAY
Now known as Ormos Navarinou, this large almost landlocked bay was the scene of the Battle of Navarino on October 20 1827. This was a decisive factor in the struggle for Greek inde-

RECOMMENDED HOTELS

ANDRITSENA
Theoxina Hotel, DD; *easy to locate in the town*; tel. (0626) 22 219.
Quaint provincial hotel – be sure to ask for one of the rooms with a view out over the mountains.

KORONI
Auberge de la Plage, DD-DDD; *by the harbour*; tel. (0725) 22 401.
Bright and friendly spot by the picturesque front.

KIPARISSIA
The railway line ends here on a stretch of coast with superb long sandy beaches.

Bassilicon, D-DD; 7 *Odos Alexopolou*; tel. (0761) 22 655.
Useful for an overnight stop, or as a base for the beaches.

METHONI
The bay area becomes very popular in the season, but there are always a few rooms on offer. For first choice try:

Iliodyssio, D-DD; *opposite the kastro*; tel. (723) 31 225.
Friendly staff and clean rooms at very reasonable prices.

PILOS
Be sure to ring ahead in the season as there are only a limited number of rooms on offer in Pilos, and these are sometimes all full.

Galaxy, D-DD; *near the beach*; tel. (0723) 22 780.
A small hotel, but comparatively large for Pilos and usually has a room free.

pendence, but came about by accident.

The Turkish fleet of Ibrahim Pasha was based at Navarino Bay, holding down the Greek insurrectionists in the Peleponnese. The combined British, French and Russian fleet sailed into the bay with the sole intention of intimidating the Turks, and forcing them to

RECOMMENDED RESTAURANTS

METHONI
Rex, D; *by the beach*.
   A pleasant, unpretentious spot whose menu has a few imaginative surprises amongst the usual *souvlaki* and moussaka.

PILOS
You'll find a row of pleasant tavernas, and a couple of slightly more pricey restaurants, on the quayside: all archetypal places for dining by the water beneath the stars.

leave the Greeks alone. During the night a jittery Turkish captain ordered his men to open fire, and in no time the entire bay was alive with blasts of gunfire and smothered in palls of smoke. When the furore eventually died down, it was discovered that the allied fleet had unintentionally inflicted an overwhelming defeat on the Turks. All 26 allied ships remained afloat, but 53 out of the 82-strong Turkish fleet were now at the bottom of the bay.
   Within three years Greece had become an independent state.

OLYMPIA
See Greece Overall: 7.

PILOS ⌂ ✕
Some 22 km N of Pilos is the site of **Nestor's Palace**, the scene of one of the more delightful episodes in Homer's *Odyssey*. Telemachus, son of Odysseus, visited Nestor to enquire about his father. After being feasted on the shore the visitor was invited to spend the night in the palace, where the King's nubile young daughter Polycaste and her handmaidens gave him a bath and anointed him with oil so that he emerged with his body 'looking like that of a god.' Which god is not mentioned, but my bet is on Priapus.
   The excavations of Nestor's Palace are superbly situated high above Navarino Bay, though the site itself is protected by a rather unsightly roof structure.
   To the joy of all concerned, a bath was discovered during excavations, as well as nearby pots which had contained olive oil. These can now be seen and steamily meditated upon.
   The wild flowers around the site in spring are particularly beautiful. Keep your eyes open for the bee orchids, whose blossom is a replica of a bee, intended to entice other bees to its nectar. These were first shown to me here by the renowned Mediterranean botonist Oleg Polunin.

SPARTA
See Greece Overall: 8.

THE DISCOVERY OF NESTOR'S PALACE

The American archaeologist Carl Blegen began excavating outside Pilos in 1939. Amazingly, within a couple of hours of starting to dig, he came across the palace archives, where he discovered more than 500 clay tablets inscribed with indecipherable writing. Ironically, these had survived the burning of Nestor's Palace precisely because it had been burned. The heat had fired the clay, baking it so hard that it survived three-and-a-half thousand years.
   On the very day Blegen discovered the tablets, Italy launched its invasion of Albania, and the Balkans were plunged into war. The tablets were hurriedly shipped to Athens and stored in a secret bank vault, where they remained undetected throughout the Second World War.
   The strange writing on the tablets was found to be Linear B, a script which had been discoverd at several other sites, including Knossos on Crete, but not on the mainland. Several experts had made attempts to decipher Linear B, all without success. An English architect and amateur cryptologist, Michael Ventris, began to suspect that the experts were mistaken in their belief that Linear B was a hitherto unknown language. He had a hunch that it was an early form of Greek, and in 1952 managed to decipher the script – thus proving the experts wrong, and at the same time showing that Greek was a much older language than anyone had previously realized.

Peleponnese

The Mani

170 km; map Michelin 980, 1:700000

This is one of the most remote and distinctive corners of Greece. It has not, so far, become part of the main tourist trail.

Much of the suggested route is on winding mountainous roads. If you are planning to tackle the expedition as a whole, it would be just possible to make it in a day. But this way you would only see the magnificent scenery, and have no time for exploring the hidden charms which make the Mani so special. Ideally, allow at least three days for the whole trip, or base yourself in the area and discover it in your own time.

If you start at Sparta, you can take a detour out to the Frankish castle at Geraki, which is at the end of a beautiful drive through the Lakonian mountains.

South of Sparta is the picturesque port of Githion, which has romantic associations with Helen of Troy. South-west across the mountains from here is Areopoli – one of the larger villages of the region. I suggest that after this you continue south, then turn off east for a clockwise circuit of the Deep Mani. Your next call would be Vathia, a typical Maniot village with some fine examples of the historic towers unique to the region. From Vathia you continue north, soon turning off for the coastal village of Mezapos, which is near the historic Castle of Maina.

The trail continues north back towards Areopolis, passing several remote Mani villages. This is a region of forgotten Byzantine chapels, and more of those strange defensive tower houses (used by Maniot families for self-defence in vendettas). From Areopolis you continue north into the Outer Mani, along a coastal road which has a continuous run of spectacular views over the sea and the mountains. This eventually brings you to the town of Kalamata, which is famed for its olives. From Kalamata a beautiful but precipitous road winds back across the mountains to Sparta.

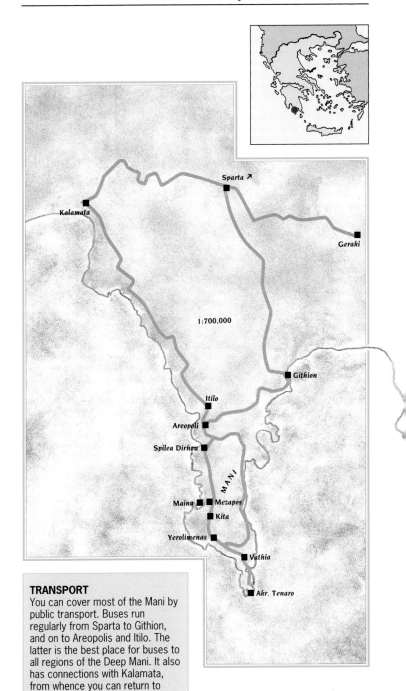

TRANSPORT
You can cover most of the Mani by public transport. Buses run regularly from Sparta to Githion, and on to Areopolis and Itilo. The latter is the best place for buses to all regions of the Deep Mani. It also has connections with Kalamata, from whence you can return to Sparta. However, you really will appreciate the freedom of a hired car or bike in this region.

211

SIGHTS & PLACES OF INTEREST

AREOPOLI 🛏 ✕

This is one of the larger and more amenable Maniot villages, permanent population 600. Maniots are old-fashioned and mistrustful of outsiders, but with a strong tradition of hospitality. They view with scorn such modern progress as education and female emancipation. The women still work in the fields in traditional costume: long black veiled mourning dress. Here you can sometimes hear them singing typical Maniot folksongs – a peculiar dirge-like lament. (A Maniot woman's lot was never happy: centuries of physical hardship, vendetta, repression and aggressively chauvinist menfolk seldom induce a colourful lifestyle.)

Areopoli has a number of delightful Byzantine chapels, some with frescos. Indeed, the remote mountain villages south of here are a treasure trove of such chapels and shrines. Unfortunately many are in a sad state of neglect, and some remain roofless despite their frescos. After a series of raids by Athenian 'art dealers', many of the chapels and shrines are now kept locked, forcing the crooks to bring ladders, so they can climb through the open roofs. Ask at the Dimarchio (Town Hall) in Areopoli about keys, and if you're lucky the guardian will take you on a tour. The best nearby villages with chapels are Pirgos Dirhou, Tsopakas, Erimos and Kounos – some of which are very remote.

CAPE MATAPAN

Marked Akr. Tenaro on the map, this is the southernmost tip of the Mani peninsula. It was off this cape on March 28 1941 that the British navy engaged the Italians, who lost three cruisers. Afterwards the Italian navy took no further part in the war.

GERAKI

This impressive spot, deep in the heart of the southern Peleponnese, is well off the tourist trail. The remains of a Frankish castle stand on a mountainside 5 km from the village. (Ask for the guardian of the castle in the village,

---

THE MANI AND GREEK INDEPENDENCE

The Maniots played a leading role in the fight for independence against the Turks, but once independence was achieved they quickly fell out with the first President of Greece, Capodistrias. In the time-honoured Maniot manner of dealing with such matters, they assassinated him. King Otho I, who was appointed in the President's place, sent in the army to subdue the region. The Maniots ambushed this invading force, stripped its members naked, and held them to ransom.

Having been forced to buy back his naked army, the King decided upon a more subtle approach. He invited the Maniots to form their own special militia, so that they could continue to fight for Greece. The Maniots leapt at this opportunity, and to this day the Maniot militia has a special place in the Greek army.

MANIOT VENDETTAS

These would start between two opposing families, for almost any reason at all. (The word 'honour' was usually invoked.) The one family would then attack the other, who would barricade themselves in their tower house. Prolonged gun battles would follow.

Such sieges sometimes lasted for *years* (on a few occasions for longer than a decade). Meanwhile the womenfolk – who weren't considered fit to take part in such honourable, manly pursuits, and were ignored by both sides – would continue about their business in the fields, bringing back food for their industrious men. Occasionally a brief amnesty would be declared, to help the women bring in the harvest.

The vendetta was considered finished when one family had wiped out the other – or the losing family came out and abased themselves before the winners. According to official accounts, the vendettas continued until the end of the 19thC. Others tell of smaller-scale unofficial conflicts persisting well into the 20thC.

and he'll take you on a tour.) The castle dates from the 13thC, and for less than a hundred years was a little outpost of Champagne in the midst of the Peleponnese. Also on the mountain are a number of chapels. Be sure to walk around the castle walls, which have superb views across the Lakonian mountains and down the valley in the direction of the distant sea.

The village of Geraki also has a number of delightful Byzantine churches, some of which are 800 years old. Aghios Athanassios has some fine frescos.

GITHION ⊨ ✕

This lovely little resort was once the port of Sparta. Behind the small tiled houses around the harbour you'll find narrow winding streets (one lined by Turkish houses with delightful balconies). Above, there's a ruined medieval castle.

The nearby small island of Marathonissi is joined to the mainland by a causeway. When Paris stole Helen from her husband Menelaus the King of Sparta, this was the spot where they first slept together. According to legend, Paris was said to have been so ecstatic after his first night with Helen that he built a small shrine dedicated to Eros, the god of erotic love and son of Aphrodite the goddess of love. When Menelaus arrived, hot on their trail, he didn't appreciate Paris's pious gesture. Incoherent with anger, in a fit of jealous rage he tore down Paris's shrine. In its place he put up two statues: one of Themis (the awesome Titaness who was responsible for justice) and the

---

RECOMMENDED HOTELS

AREOPOLI
Pyrgos Kapetanaki, DD; *Areopoli village*; *tel.* (0733) 51 233.

The name translates as 'little Captain's tower'. It is a real find: you can stay amidst traditional surroundings in a converted (but genuine) Maniot tower. Great for a night or two – but imagine what it must have been like to live here for a year-long vendetta siege.

Be sure to ring well in advance, as they only have half a dozen rooms.

Otherwise, try for an atmospheric room in the old part of the village along Odos Kapetan Matapan.

GITHION
Aktaion, D-DD; *on the quayside*; *tel.* (0733) 22 294.

Old-style pension on the front. Ask for a room with a balcony – great views.

KALAMATA
If you must stay in Kalamata, you're best off heading for the beach, which is 3 km from the town centre. Here you'll find:

Filoxenia, DD; *by the sea*; *tel.* (0721) 23 166.

A large hotel with a range of resort facilities, particularly friendly towards children.

Nautical buffs will be pleased to know that there is a nearby harbour where they can inspect rusted coasters and Greek freighters flying an exotic variety of flags of convenience.

MEZAPOS
Ask at the café about rooms, but be sure to ask early in the day during the season, to give yourself time to move on somewhere else in case they're all full.

VATHIA
A night here is something of an experience. It is as deep into the Deep Mani as you can get. The tiny village now has less than a dozen permanent inhabitants, but the Greek Tourist Board (GNTO) has refurbished a number of the ancient tower houses, and rents out rooms in them.

There's also a restaurant where you can meet up with adventurous souls like yourselves and hear how much the place resembles a lovely little spot just east of Kathmandu.

YEROLIMENAS
Akrogiali, D; *on the front*; *tel.* (0733) 54 204.

Right by the harbour of this old pirate port on the south-western coast, an ideal base for Deep Mani explorations.

other of Praxidica (the sadistic whip-yielding goddess of punishment).

With all this demolition and putting up of religious monuments, it's hardly surprising that Menelaus didn't catch up with Paris and Helen until they'd got safely to Troy – by which stage it was time to start the Trojan War.

The island now sports a Maniot tower, which houses a small museum.

KALAMATA 🛏 ✕
A very boring town, its sole redeeming feature is that it produces superb olives. Stop for your take-home can of olive oil, or a half kilo of the best olives in Greece, and then keep going.

It has a tragic recent history. On September 14 1986 there was a serious earthquake which wrecked the town and dozens of villages in the area. The main façade of the city has been restored, but you don't have to look far behind the scenes for evidence of what happened. The poorly constructed ugly blocks rushed up during the boom years of the 60s collapsed like poorly constructed ugly blocks. As

• *Defensive village, the Mani.*

a result, more than half the population moved elsewhere, and the place has never really recovered.

KITA
See Mani – The Peninsula, below.

MANI – THE PENINSULA
This is the middle peninsula of the southern Peleponnese. It is so isolated and its inhabitants so fierce, that for most of its history it has remained virtually autonomous. Neither the Franks, the Venetians, nor the Turks managed completely to subdue the wild Maniots. (According to a Greek friend of mine who isn't a Maniot, the name derives from the same Greek root as maniac.)

Left to their own devices, the Maniots continued with their usual way of life, which consists largely of vendettas and piracy. According to an early British traveller in the region, its inhabitants were 'famous pirates by sea and pestilent robbers by land.' In the late 18thC, several Maniot families emigrated to Corsica, where they apparently persist with their vendettas to this day.

To protect themselves from their neighbours, the families built distinctive defensive towers, which rise like astonishing mini-skyscrapers from the mountainous terrain. There are over 700 of these still standing, many as much as four hundred years old, and some of them as high as 25 m. The best places to see these towers are at the villages of **Kita**, Nomia, and at **Vathia** on the southern tip of the peninsula. Many of them are still occupied by the families which originally built them.

MEZAPOS 🛏

On the west coast of the Deep Mani, this village has a harbour, and many experts consider that it is the site of ancient Messe, mentioned in Homer's *Odyssey*. It makes a useful base for exploring the Deep Mani.

There is a fine walk south along the cliffs which takes you to a Byzantine church (Episkopi) with some interesting murals. Beyond here, 4 km on from Mezapos, you come to the **Castle of Maina**, on a rock which juts out into the sea. Built by Franks from the Champagne region in 1248 (what must they have thought of such a spot?), the castle is now deserted, but within its walls is the ruin of what is said to be one of the earliest Christian churches, dating from the 5thC.

SPARTA

See Greece Overall: 8.

SPILEA DIRHOU

The *spilea* or caves were discovered only in 1985 – by an intrepid dog who found a tasty cache of Neolithic bones, and made the mistake of showing one of them to his master. The caves are the most spectacular in Greece, and as atmospheric and exciting as you'll find anywhere. A boat ride takes you for over a kilometre across the lakes and up the subterranean river which runs through the caves. It's all very spooky, with spectacular coloured stalagmites and stalactites, and giant eels lurking beneath the surface of the deep, dark waters. Your guide will point out the usual 'spectacles' (features resembling dragons, the more mentionable bits of various Greek gods' anatomies, and so forth), but unfortunately this is at present all described in Greek – so be sure to buy one of the exotically worded guides in English at the entrance before you set off on your trip to hell and back. You are also taken ashore on a tour of some huge caverns, whose unexplored recesses reach at least as far inland as Sparta (a mere 50 km away) according to my guide.

VATHIA 🛏 ✕

See Mani – The Peninsula, page 214.

Exploring the Mani
By far the best way to get around the highways and byways of the Mani is by motorbike. Try Moto Mani, western end of the waterfront, tel. 0733 22 853.

RECOMMENDED RESTAURANTS

AREOPOLI
There is little choice here. The most unadventurous, but the most reliable if you're starving after a day's walking in the mountains, is in the Hotel Mani. If you have time, or a car, take the 3-km trip down to the sea at Limeni where there's a jolly beach-side taverna. The walk back up the slope at night will be sobering.

GITHION
The most picturesque eating area is on the front. There are half a dozen tavernas here, none of which is outstanding – and a couple are definitely over-priced. Choose carefully, and feast off the atmosphere which sealed Helen's fate.

KALAMATA
If you're looking for some of those fine Kalamata olives, head for the open-air New Market. This is over the river from the bus station, between the Museum and Ay Apostoloi church.

For something more substantial to eat in more pleasant surroundings, drive down to the sea, 3 km from the town centre. Here you'll find a number of beach-side tavernas (crowded at weekends).

<u>Ionian Islands</u>

The Island of Corfu

110 *km; map Michelin* 980, 1:700000

Corfu first became a tourist destination because of its astonishing beauty, and despite the inroads of mass tourism parts are still utterly spellbinding. It is like the *Mona Lisa* with a beard and moustache painted on her face: the original beauty remains, underneath; you just have to look harder for it, and ignore the rest.

The island is 60 km long: there is plenty of space. Away from the beaches, Corfu is green, with olive groves and cypress trees covering the hillsides. There is no circular route around the island, and the main roads all start from Corfu Town, otherwise known as Kerkyra.

If you want to tour the northern part, I suggest you head up the east coast towards Ipsos. For the first 15 km or so you will find an island vandalized by tourism – fish and chip shops are cheek-by-jowl with tacky pubs and discos. But after Barbati you come to small secluded coves, and just a few kilometres across the water looms the stark coastline of Albania. The main road turns west around the slopes of Mount Pantokrator, where you could make a detour to the unspoilt bays Kalami and Kouloura, and then follows the north coast, which has some lovely sandy beaches. Turn south at Sidari, then turn off west for Paleokastritsa, the island's 'beauty spot'. From here you can go back across the green interior to Corfu Town.

To see the southern part of the island, take the road out of Corfu town for Benitses. Persevere south through more tawdry scars of mass tourism until eventually you come to Missonghi. From here there are several spots worth exploring. Petreti is a surprisingly unspoilt fishing village further down the east coast. Alternatively you can head inland through the hill town of Aghios Matheos, and follow the tracks down to the remote beaches of the west coast. Nature lovers should try exploring the Korission Lagoon, which is renowned for its wildlife.

You can easily cover Corfu in a couple of days, but allow at least four if you want to see the island properly.

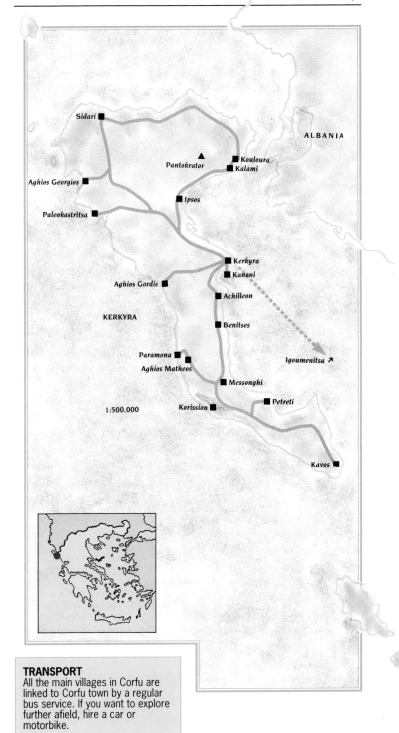

ALBANIA

Sidari

Pantokrator ▲

Kouloura
Kalami

Aghios Georgios

Ipsos

Paleokastritsa

Kerkyra
Kanoni

Aghios Gordis

Achilleon

KERKYRA

Benitses

Igoumenitsa ↗

Paramona
Aghios Matheos

Messonghi

1:500,000

Korission

Petreti

Kavos

TRANSPORT
All the main villages in Corfu are
linked to Corfu town by a regular
bus service. If you want to explore
further afield, hire a car or
motorbike.

• *Corfu.*

SIGHTS & PLACES OF INTEREST

ACHILLEON
This 19thC 'villa' was designed by the Italian architect Cardilo for Empress Elizabeth of Austria, and proves that bad taste is not a 20thC prerogative. After Elizabeth was assassinated, Kaiser Wilhelm II bought it.

Kaiser Bill was so enamoured by this fiasco that he spent every spring here until 1914, when he was forced to attend to a fiasco of a different nature. The villa itself is suitably grandiose – perfect for the casino which it was eventually to become. But it is in the gardens that a higher lunacy manifests itself. Here the rows of 'classic' statuary are of a surreal grandiloquence, which perhaps only the Victorians and the Wilhelmines were capable of achieving with a straight face. (Look upon it as 'The Marx Brothers meet *Last Year at Marienbad*' and this tragedy of taste is immediately transformed into superb slapstick comedy.) Some 15 km to the north-west you can visit the wonderful spot where the Kaiser used to set up a throne to watch the sun set over the sea far below. See this, and at a stroke Kaiser Bill is redeemed – anyone who set up his throne here couldn't be completely misguided.

AGHIOS GEORGIOS
See Paleokastritsa, below.

AGHIOS GORDIS ⋈
A spectacular bay on the west coast,

> **DETOUR – KALAMI AND KOULOURA**
> Approximately 30 km from Corfu town on the north-east coast, a steep road swoops down to two delightful bays in the shadow of Mount Pantokrator, Kalami and Kouloura. The taverna in Kalami, the White House, once belonged to Gerald Durrell's family, and serves delicious simple food. The second bay, Kouloura, is a tiny unspoilt fishing harbour, overlooked by a few houses and the single little taverna.

> **DETOUR – KAVOS ⋈**
> The resort at the very southern tip of the island, but popular despite its remoteness. There is an agreeable hotel here – see page 220.

where, above a long sandy beach, there are some fantastic rockscapes, which have an oriental look on the rare occasions when is a mist. There are also some massive hotel developments.

One miraculously surviving feature of pre-tourism Corfu is the informal, by-the-bottle vending of local wine. 'Miraculous' because this is the only wine in the world of which I could not bring myself to finish a single glass.

CORFU TOWN (Kerkyra) ⚓ ✕

For several centuries Corfu was ruled by the Venetians, and the graceful old buildings in the quiet back streets of Corfu town commemorate this. After the Venetians came the French, who characteristically built an arcade in imitation of the Rue de Rivoli. Then came

• Hilltop fortress, Corfu.

Greece at this time, Greek Independence was achieved in 1821, and the country's first president, Capodistrias, came from Corfu.

During 1858-9 Gladstone briefy served as High Commissioner of the Ionian Islands, and returned to Britain swearing that they would never be allowed to become part of Greece as long as he had anything to do with it. But in 1864, two years before Gladstone became Prime Minister, Corfu and the Ionian islands were ceded to Greece.

The former British High Commissioner's Residence, which overlooks Spianada, is now a museum. The exhibits include a suitably irrelevant collection of oriental carvings and Asiatic art. The former British Cemetery is just south of Theotoki Square. There is a statue to Lord Guilford amongst the twittering birds in the gardens in front of the Old Fort, and a street is named after him.

BRITISH CORFU

After the initial defeat of Napoleon in 1814 the Ionian islands became a British protectorate, known as the Septinsular Republic, which included the distant island of Kythera, off the southern Peleponnese. The administrative capital was Corfu Town.

Word soon spread of Corfu's beneficent climate and easy-going way of life, and it quickly attracted a rich harvest of well-heeled oddballs who had nothing better to do with their lives than be eccentric. Oddest of all was Lord Guilford who arrived here dressed in a white sheet with a gold ribbon around his head. (He was under the impression that in this garb he looked like Plato.)

In 1822 Lord Guilford founded the Ionian Academy, which a number of recent historians who should know better claim was the first university in Greece. (Plato founded the Academy in the 4thC BC.) Edward Lear, the nonsense poet who spent much time in Corfu during this period, was invited to become a professor at Guilford's new university, but turned down the offer in favour of writing poems about the owl and the pussycat and the dong with the luminous nose. One person who did lecture here was the poet Solomos who wrote the Greek national anthem.

Although Corfu was not a part of

the British, bequeathing a few cultural treasures of their own. You can still sit with a bottle of the locally made ginger beer (called *tsintsi birra* by the Corfiots), watching a game of cricket played in front of the former residence of the British High Commissioner, with the sound of a brass band practising in the background: a quintessentially British scene which no longer exists anywhere else in the world.

To get the feel of old Corfu, try walking in the backstreets inland from Arseniou (the northern *corniche*). Here the cats lie flopped out in the shade, and when you turn a corner you sometimes come across a delightful little square with a tree surrounded by railings.

According to the experts, the main sight in Corfu town is the famous Gorgon in the **Archaeological Museum**. But I'm afraid the Gorgon whose gaze was once said to turn men to stone also has this effect on me.

Much more interesting is the **Church of Aghios Spiridon**, the saint whose preserved body is kept in a large silver sarcophagus by the altar.

St Spiridon is the patron saint of Corfu, and half the local male population is named Spiro after him. St Spiridon himself was a Bishop of Cyprus in the early 4thC, and never had anything whatsoever to do with Corfu during his lifetime. But his remains ended up here over a thousand years later, after various wanderings around the eastern Mediterranean (including a long sojourn in Constantinople, followed by a 800-km journey on the back of a mule, accompanied by the equally ancient remains of St Theodora).

Since St Spiridon's arrival in Corfu he has led an active posthumous existence, saving the islanders from a famine, several plagues, and even on one occasion from the wrath of the Turks. Now he is brought out four times a year and paraded in a colourful procession around the streets. (The best is on August 11, St Spiridon's day, when he is accompanied by several enthusiastic brass bands, whose practising can be heard throughout town for weeks beforehand.)

For a pleasant walk which takes you

RECOMMENDED HOTELS

AGHIOS GORDIS
Chrysses Folies, D-DD; *set back from the beach*; *tel.* 0662 53 106.

The best-value smallish hotel in this picturesque (if popular) resort on the west coast.

CORFU TOWN (Kerkyra)
During the main holiday season, which now lasts from May to September, rooms can be almost impossible to find. If you're having difficulty, try one of the agencies on Arseniou, the road which runs up to the *corniche* from the old port. If you're planning on a staying for a week or so and would like a pleasant villa in some unspoilt part of the island, try the agency here run by the redoubtable George Varthis.

Hotel Constantinupolis, D; 11 *Zavitsanou*; *tel.* (0661) 39 922.

A friendly basic hotel down by the old port, with rooms looking out over the cafés and the quay, and above

the famous Mavros Katos (Black Cat) Café, which now, alas, is somewhat pizzarized.

Corfu Palace, DDD; 2 *Leoforos Dimokratias*; *tel.* (0661) 39 485.

If you're looking for a truly momentous place to stay, try the Corfu Palace, an extremely expensive hotel, but worth every penny. It has a rare and attractive blend of ancient and modern, with first-rate amenities including two pools, two tennis coaches, and so on. It retains the ambience of old-style Corfu.

Hotel Cypros, D-DD; 13 *Agion Pateron*; *tel.* (0661) 30 032.

Between the port and Spianada, the Cypros is a popular spot with discriminating international travellers.

KAVOS
Cavos Hotel, DD; *tel.* (0662) 22 107.

A pleasant holiday hotel, where most rooms have a private bath or shower, and with helpful English-speaking staff.

out of the town centre, head south of Spianada (The Esplanade), and follow the main seaside road all the way around Ormos Garitsas. At the very end of this you come to **Mon Repos**, the royal villa where the Duke of Edinburgh was born in 1921. As you might guess from its name, this villa is of Victorian British origin (and, as you would expect, you're not allowed in unless invited).

From here continue south in the direction of **Kanoni**, which is a couple of kilometres down the dusty road. This was the spot where the French set up a cannon to guard the entrance to the Halkiopoulos Lagoon (now crossed by the airport runway). From the café at Kanoni you can admire the view that launched a thousand travel posters: the little island monastery of **Vlaherna**, joined to the mainland by a narrow causeway, and the further tree-covered islet of **Pondikonissi**. You can walk down to the former, and take the small boat across to the latter.

You can end your walk with a rewarding drink, and if you're tired, catch the regular bus the 4 km back into town.

KANONI
See Corfu Town, above.

MOUNT PANTOKRATOR
Corfu's highest peak rises to just over 900 m and dominates the northern part of the island. It is possible to walk up to the peak, which has a small ancient chapel and a large modern telecommunications mast, from the village of Strinilas. Frauds can now drive to the top.

PALEOKASTRITSA ✕
This superb set of coves on the north-western coast, overlooked by an ancient monastery, is said to have been visited by Ulysses on his way home to Ithaka. Unfortunately this particular natural masterpiece has been heavily desecrated by modern development. Slightly less blighted is **Aghios Georgios** to the north.

PARAMONA
A small remote beach on the west coast beyond Aghios Matheos, where there is a pleasant taverna overlooking the bay.

RECOMMENDED RESTAURANTS

CORFU TOWN (Kerkyra)
Aegli, DD; *Spiniada.*

In the arcades which line the Esplanade, looking out over the famous cricket pitch, Aegli has an imaginative menu with some interesting seafood dishes. Try the superb fish in white wine sauce.

Bella Napoli, DD-DDD; *11 Skaramanga; tel. (0661) 33 338.*

Keeping Corfu's Italian tradition alive (even if the Neapolitans were among the few who never ruled Corfu).

To Nautikon, D; *150 N Theotoki Sreet.*

As you'd expect from the name, just the place to bring a sailor's appetite. All your old Greek favourites plus a lively young clientele.

PALEOKASTRITSA
This spot has a number of fairly expensive tourist restaurants right by the beach. The big speciality here is lobster, but don't expect it to be cheap, and don't expect it always to be lobster. It is sometimes crayfish, so be sure to go inside and point out your crustaceous victim.

For a more rough-and-ready meal, try:

Spiro's Taverna, DD.

Ideal for stoking up after an energetic morning lying on the beach.

If you want the best of both worlds – meaning the view without the crowds – head north up into the mountains towards the village of Lakones, and try:

Café Bella Vista, D-DD; *Lakones.*

A restaurant that for once lives up to this often misused name – with the idyllic ultramarine bays far below (and well out of earshot).

<u>Aegean Islands</u>

Islands Within Easy Reach of Athens
Salamis, Aegina, Poros, Hydra, Serifos and Sifnos

350 km (round trip); map Michelin 980, 1:700000

M ost of these islands can be visited on a day trip from Athens. Only Sifnos and Serifos, which are six hours from the main harbour of Piraeus by ferry, require a little more time.

The nearest island to Athens is Salamis, scene of the historic Battle of Salamis in 480 BC. To get there, make the short ferry crossing from Perama, just 5 km west of the city limits.

Aegina, 20 km across the Saronic Gulf, is more picturesque than Salamis, with some fine beaches and a well-preserved temple dating from the 5thC BC. After Aegina, the next island which the ferry calls at is Poros. The entry into Poros harbour is one of the most spectacular in the Aegean, with the town rising steeply above the channel just beyond the ship's rail. From here the ferry continues on to the artists' colony of Hydra. The main town has a lively nightlife. Inland, no cars or motorbikes are permitted, which makes the 20-km-long island great walking territory. There are chapels and monasteries to visit inland, and beaches along the coast.

Serifos and Sifnos are just over 100 km by sea from Piraeus. Sifnos is the more beautiful of the two, but also the more popular. I find Serifos more appealing. Although it is barren, it has a pleasant small port on a sandy bay, and inland its capital is one of the sleepy unspoilt wonders of the Cyclades (the rest of which are covered in Greece Overall: 12 and Local Explorations: 9 and 10).

If you want to visit all of these islands systematically, it will take you the best part of a week. It is far better to choose the ones you want to see and devote time to each. Be warned: owing to their proximity to Athens, all are very crowded during the summer season.

ATHINAI ↗
Perama
Piraeus ↗
SALAMIS
Saronikos Kolopos
Livadi
AEGINA
Aegina
Aghia Marina
POROS
Molos
HYDRA
SERIFOS
Hora
Livhadi
1:1,400,000
Kastro
Kamares
SIFNOS
Platis Yialos

TRANSPORT
The islands can only be reached by
ferry. For Salamis, you have to
take the car ferry from Perama.
There are regular services to all of
the others from Piraeus, with
several a day running to Aegina,
Poros and Hydra. These islands
are also connected to the mainland
by a fast hydrofoil service, which
runs from Zea harbour, just over
the hill from Piraeus port.

Temple of Aphaia, Aegina.

SIGHTS & PLACES OF INTEREST

AEGINA 🛏 ✕

Aegina would be a very pleasant island if it were anywhere else. Directly opposite Athens, it is perfect for an Athenian's day out with all the family. The main town **Aegina** has a lively working harbour, and the best beach is at **Aghia Marina**, 14 km away on the east coast. On the way here through the pine woods and the hills you pass the island's main site: the **Temple of Aphaia**, which contains extensive ruins dating from the 5thC BC. Aphaia herself was a nymph who fled from Crete to escape the lascivious clutches of old King Minos.

In the pre-tourist era, the great Cretan writer Nikos Kazantzakis lived on the island. In **Livadi**, just north of Aegina town there is a plaque outside the house where he wrote *Zorba the Greek*.

ATHENS

See pages 174-191.

HYDRA 🛏 ✕

This island was discovered by a small band of artists in the late 1950s, and over the years it gained something of a reputation as an artists' colony. Then the well-heeled Bohemian set moved in,

began doing up the fine old stone houses overlooking the harbour, and the place started to become a fashionable resort. Names began to arrive, trailing in their wake the inevitable flotsam of gossip columnists, *paparazzi* and gawpers. Prices began to shoot up.

The names are all but forgotten now, or have moved on to the latest fashionable watering holes. But many of the gawpers remain, and the prices can still raise the occasional eyebrow. This said, the island attracts an interesting, cosmopolitan crowd.

As Hydra has no cars or motorbikes, once you're outside the main town it becomes much more peaceful. Try walking 30 minutes west along the north coast to the little village of **Molos**, which has a beach and an offshore islet. There are several beaches in this part of the island, though they're mostly within caique range of Hydra Town. Walking inland you'll find a number of small chapels and monasteries. The best of these, the **Monastery of Zourvas,** is a couple of hours east along the donkey path and still has a couple of dozen inmates.

PIRAEUS

See pages 174.

POROS ⚓ ✕

The port of Poros is dramatically beautiful, with its whitewashed houses rising sheer from the sea beside the channel. Inland the island is covered with fir trees. There are some pleasant beaches and there is a picturesque 6thC BC **Temple of Poseidon** which still has a few columns standing. Unfortunately you probably won't be able to appreciate this because there are always people standing in the way. Visit the site on a sunny day in late October and you will appreciate how lovely it is.

SALAMIS

Was the scene of one of history's great disappointments. In 480 BC the Persian Emperor set up a marble throne on the nearby clifftop, so that he could dine and watch his fleet of a thousand triremes destroy the puny Greek navy. Unfortunately the result of this match turned out be an unexpected home win, which ruined his dinner. Many historians now believe that this Greek victory was even more decisive in the defeat of the Persians than the Battle of Marathon.

As for the island itself, there is noth-

AN ORIGIN OF RETZINA

When the Athenians abandoned Athens in the face of Xerxes' advancing Persian army, they were forced to leave behind all their wine. In order to render it undrinkable, they spiked all the barrels with the only fluid they had to hand – pine resin.

After their totally unexpected victory at Salamis, the Athenians returned home to celebrate. The only wine available was spiked with resin, but they no longer cared. In the heat of the moment it even tasted quite agreeable.

Since then the Greeks have continued to mix their wine with resin, hence the name retsina. If you have never been to Greece before, you will probably react to this wine just as the Persians were expected to. Others sigh with deep nostalgia as they knock it back in the dark cold winter of northern Europe. Give it a chance, and you may well develop a taste for it. It is, contrary to what you would expect, a refreshing drink.

RECOMMENDED HOTELS

AEGINA - Aegina Town
Hotel Marmarinos, D-DD; Odos Leon Lada; tel. (0297) 22 474.

You can't miss this hotel, which is just up from the harbour by the Tourist Office. Don't go for a front room with a balcony in the height of the season: the others are quieter.

AEGINA - Aghia Marina
Marina, D-DD; tel. (0297) 32 301.

A cheerful holiday hotel which has 25 rooms and is handy for the sea.

HYDRA
Orloff Guest House, DDD; Hydra Town; tel. (0298) 72 311.

This excellent establishment run by Irena Traghia is by far the best on the island. It is in a beautifully restored old house with a wonderful garden where you have breakfast, and has a very friendly clientele. Be sure to book a room *well* in advance, and not just for a single night.

Accommodation can be difficult to find in Hydra. If you have problems, contact the Tourist Police on Odos Votsi, close to the clock tower (tel. [0298] 52 205).

POROS
Pavlou, DD; Neorio Bay; tel. (0298) 22 734.

On the bay just north-west of the main town, right by the beach.

SERIFOS
Albatross Rooms, DD; Livadhi; tel. (0281) 51 145.

A cut above the usual rooms, these are handy for the harbour and the town beach.

SIFNOS
Benakis, D-DD; Platis Yialos; tel. (0284) 31 334.

In the island's best resort, this hotel is beside an attractive sandy beach.

ing much to see here nowadays. It is a popular weekend haunt of Athenians, and can get very sticky in summer.

SERIFOS 🛏 ✕
A bare little island, whose very name means barren. Nothing of any historical importance has ever happened here, its myths are incredible and boring, and the only thing it ever produced was iron ore, the supply of which has now been exhausted.

But if you want a peaceful time on an island that is easy to get to, and not yet overrun (except during the mad months of July and August), this is the spot for you. The main port, **Livhadi**, where the boats put in, has a row of tavernas and a semi-circular sandy bay. Over the hill to the west there are a couple of more secluded beaches.

Try the 2-km walk up to the capital **Hora**, which crowns the hill in the middle of the island: it is a true refuge. The houses are whitewashed, you can

• Hydra, *the town and harbour.*

detect remnant walls of the ancient castle, and there are a couple of sleepy little cafés in the sleepy little square.

There are some pleasant walks north of here, where the countryside is greener, and the beaches are more remote. Don't come to Serifos completely out of season, as the whole island closes down for the winter (October to April).

SIFNOS 🛏 ✕
Larger and greener than Serifos, and with much more to offer. In ancient times it was one of the richest islands in the Aegean. Unfortunately it is just too close to Athens, and is often completely overrun.

The boat puts in at the little port of **Kamares**, tucked beneath the rocks. On the other side of the island (just 8 km away) is the delightful village of **Kastro**, with its little cubist whitewashed houses and winding alleyways overlooking the sea. The best beach on the island is at **Platis Yialos**, on the coast just over 10 km south of Kastro.

RECOMMENDED RESTAURANTS

AEGINA
Aghia Marina has a lively nightlife and some congenial tavernas by the front. The food is of a high standard, but the prices reflect the Athenian clientele. Aegina Town has some pleasant cafés and tavernas by the harbour.

Espaterion, D-DD; *by the harbour.*
For delicious fish, try this restaurant, where the Greeks eat, so the food tends to be of a much higher standard than the usual tourist spots.

HYDRA
Restaurant Lulu, D-DD; *Odos Miaouli.*
On an island where the restaurants can be expensive, this one provides honest hearty fare at reliable prices.

Xeria Elia, DDD; *Platia.*
Dining with frills.

POROS
Zorba's, D-DD; *Kalavria; tel.* (0298) 22 739.

To reach Zorba's, cross the canal into Kalavria and head north-west along the front for five minutes. It is the place to come for a really wild night out with a memorable meal and some lively dancing, and a change from the cafés and restaurants along the front where everyone flocks.

SERIFOS
The tavernas and cafés are mainly on the front by the harbour. This is where everyone meets, and is the best place to eat out in the open. But if you want to get away from it all, and have simple fish for dinner, walk right around the bay along the beach to the very last houses, where there is a wonderful little informal anonymous café-restaurant. It is also recommended for an early evening drink and sunset-watching.

SIFNOS - Apollonia
Kypros, D; *Platia.*
A genuine old-style village taverna in the main inland village, which lives up to its name by serving a number of Cypriot specialities.

Aegean Islands

The Northern Aegean Islands
Thassos, Samothrace and Limnos

200 km (round trip); map Michelin 980, 1:700000

The northern Aegean islands have little in common save their geographical location. Thassos, the nearest to the mainland, is certainly the most picturesque in the traditional sense. It has miles of sandy beaches, and inland its mountainous slopes are green and wooded.

Samothrace is much more barren, its appearance as striking as that of any other Aegean island, except Santorini. Its dark cliffs tower above the sea, and inland its peak is the highest in the Aegean. In ancient times it was one of the holiest islands in Greece, with pilgrims from far and wide visiting the Sanctuary of the Greater Gods.

Limnos is a little dispointing after Samothrace, and its drab appearance is hardly improved by a large military base. Just south of here is Efstratios, one of the most remote and boring islands in the Aegean. There is little to see here but the rare monk seals who live in the caves. An exploration of these islands starts at Kavala on the mainland (see Greece Overall: 1). From Kavala it is an hour's journey by ferry to Thassos. This island has a circular coastal road which is particularly picturesque, with fine views over the shore and sea.

Return to Kavala, where you catch the ferry for Samothrace. From here you continue by ferry to Limnos, at which point you can make a detour to the lonely island of Efstratios. If you wish to extend your tour of the islands, take the ferry from Limnos to Lesbos (see Greece Overall: 11), from where you can continue island-hopping all the way down to Rhodes.

You can complete this journey in four days, but you should allow a little more time if you want to stop off and see a few of the sights.

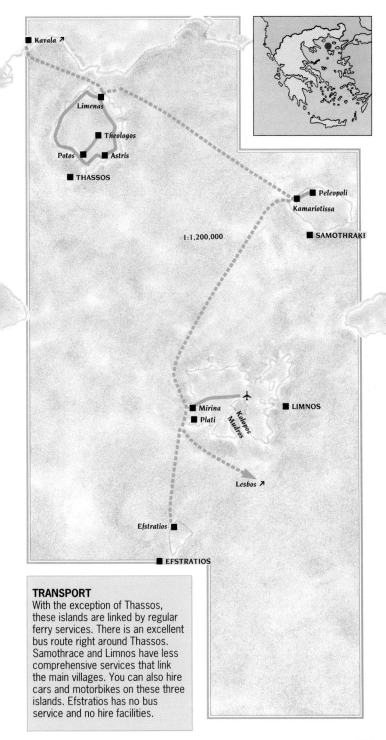

TRANSPORT

With the exception of Thassos, these islands are linked by regular ferry services. There is an excellent bus route right around Thassos. Samothrace and Limnos have less comprehensive services that link the main villages. You can also hire cars and motorbikes on these three islands. Efstratios has no bus service and no hire facilities.

• *Repairing fishing nets, Limnos.*

SIGHTS & PLACES OF INTEREST

EFSTRATIOS 🛏

Well off the beaten track and likely to remain that way. There is little to see here: no ancient sites, just one rather plain village of modern buildings (Efstratios), and the nearby beaches are unexciting. The beaches further along the island are a little more appealing, and the caves here are home to a number of rare monk seals.

LIMNOS 🛏 ✕

Limnos is a remote, barren island which has been heavily taken over by the military. Owing to its strategic position at the mouth of the Dardanelles, it could easily cut off all shipping to and from Istanbul and the Black Sea.

In ancient times the women of Limnos had a dispute with Aphrodite, and in retaliation the goddess made them

Local transport, Samos.

all repellent to their husbands by giving them hygiene problems which were beyond the power of mouthwash or deodorant. The husbands soon abandoned their conjugal privileges, and their womenfolk became so infuriated that in a fit of collective rage they murdered every man on the island. Not much later Jason and his sturdy band of Argonauts put into port to find an island full of frustrated women. Such was the sailors' reception that they ended up staying for two years.

The capital **Mirina** is on the west coast, and its streets have a number of attractive old Turkish houses. Until 1924 a large percentage of the island's inhabitants were Turkish, but they left in the exchange of populations which took place following the Smyrna Massacre. There are some attractive beaches north of Mirina, but if you want seclusion, head south to the more remote beaches along the rocky coast, such as **Plati**.

The **Gulf of Mudros**, the island's superb large natural harbour, was the base for the Allied Expeditionary Force which took part in the catastrophic offensive in the Dardanelles in 1915.

The Turks signed their Armistice here in the bay in 1918.

SAMOTHRACE

One of the most spectacular islands in the entire Aegean. Its dark forbidding cliffs rise sheer from the sea, and its inland peak Mount Tegari is over 1,600 m, the highest in the Aegean. According to legend, this peak was where the sea god Poseidon sat to watch the Siege of Troy – he must have had good eyesight, and the weather must have been very clear, because Troy was several hundred kilometres away.

In ancient times the island became famous for its **Sanctuary to the Greater Gods**, the extensive remains of which can be visited outside **Peleopoli** in the north of the island. This was where pilgrims were initiated into the mysteries of the Greater Gods, a cult of Thracian fertility gods. Around 700 BC these gods became absorbed into the pantheon of Ancient Greek gods – the Great Mother becoming Demeter, and so forth.

The initiation ceremonies which took

231

place here remain largely a mystery, as it was believed that anyone recording them would be struck down by the gods. At the risk of incurring this fate, I can reveal that there appear to have been two stages of initiation. The first involved a symbolic enactment of death and re-birth, with a joyous torch-light feast at the end of it. But those going a stage further were required to be of stronger stuff. The second stage involved a rigorous confession of all sins, and ended up with the initiate being baptized in bull's blood. These rites were almost certainly derived from earlier rituals, which may well have involved human sacrifice. Interestingly, the second stage was one of the earliest outside the Judaic tradition in which religion and morality were simultaneously combined.

On the present site you can see the remains of a Hall of Initiation (Anaktoron) dating from Roman times, as well as the foundations of the largest circular building in Ancient Greece, which dates from the 4thC BC. The Nike Fountain here was the site of the Winged Venus of Samothrace, possibly the most uncanny masterpiece of Western European sculpture. The statue was discovered in 1863 by French archaeologists, who shipped it to France, where it remains in the Louvre – though the French graciously sent back a (small) copy which can be seen in the site museum.

• *Thassos.*

A modern holiday hotel, with friendly efficient staff.

SAMOTHRACE - Kamariotissa
Aelos, DD; *on the front; tel.* (0551) 41 595.

Handy for the boat and as good a base as you will need on the island. It also has a private pool, which makes up for the disappointing beaches.

THASSOS - Limenas (Thassos Town)
Angelika, D-DD; *by the sea; tel.* (0593) 22 387.

A friendly hotel with clean rooms, many with fine views overlooking the beach. English and German speakers are on hand to help.

THASSOS - Skala Potamia
Miramare, DD; *inland from the harbour; tel.* (0593) 61 040.

A real find. This superb well-designed hotel has the best modern facilities in a superb setting – a little gorge above the village. Be sure to book well ahead – people who stay here have a habit of coming back. It is run by a friendly family.

RECOMMENDED HOTELS

EFSTRATIOS
If you want accommodation here, ask at one of the tavernas when you get off the boat. The rooms you'll be offered will be clean and cheap, but not much more.

LIMNOS - Mirina
Hotel Isfestos, D-DD; *tel.* (0254) 23 415.

The boats put in at the main port **Kamariotissa** in the north west, but the best beaches are on the south of the island.

THASSOS 🛏 ✕

The nearest Aegean island to northern Europe (only a little further from southern Germany than Paris is from London), which means that it has a hectic tourist season from mid June to mid September.

The beauty of Thassos is no fragile thing, and it is capable of absorbing a large number of people with only minimal damage. The coast is lined with long sandy beaches and coves, and inland the wooded mountainsides rise to over 1,100 m. Unfortunately the woods were extensively damaged by fire in 1985.

Thassos was always a rich island, and became famous in ancient times for its marble, oil, wine and gold (which was used for minting coins as far afield as Spain and Egypt). By the 5thC BC it had become a colony of the Cycladic island of Paros, and was ruled by Theogenes, a former boxing champion, who was said to have been fathered by the god Hercules. Thassos also produced one of the great athletes of classical times, Pausinias, who is recorded as having carried off nearly 1,500 sporting trophies at the Olympic Games.

The main archaeological site on the island is at **Limenas**, the capital (sometimes known as Thassos Town). This site contains the ruins of the classical and Roman city. You can walk along the ramparts and visit the ancient theatre, which is still used for weekly performances of Greek drama in the summer. Be sure to climb up to the acropolis, which has superb views over the island and sea.

The best beaches on Thassos are in the south. My favourite spot here is **Astris**, with its celebrated cliffs and limpid water – at its best in May or early October. Inland, the picturesque village of **Theologos**, just below Mount Ipsarion, is well worth a visit.

A word of warning: Thassos has a justified reputation for mosquitoes, but they can easily be kept at bay by a good repellent.

• (*Above, right*), *local produce*, *Thassos.*

RECOMMENDED RESTAURANTS

LIMNOS - Mirini
Best make for the cheap and cheerful tavernas along the front.

Club Avlonas, D; *just north of Mirina; tel.* (0254) 23 885.
The best disco on the island, in a superb rural setting.

LIMNOS - Plati
Gregory's, D; *tel.* (0254) 22 715.
A terrific restaurant with a friendly atmosphere – just the place for a lively night out. Wine, dine, and then out comes the *bouzouki* for some marvellous traditional dancing, with everyone joining in.

THASSOS - Limenas
Syrtaki, D-DD; *on the sea* W *of town.*
Go beyond the old harbour and you'll find Syrtaki right on the beach. Perfect for a romantic dinner and lingering over brandies – though at the height of the summer it can become hectic.

Aegean Islands

The Sporades: North-Western Aegean

Map Michelin 980, 1:700000

The Greek word Sporades means scattered. You can spend anything from three days to a fortnight exploring these scattered islands – either visiting one or two – or covering well over a hundred kilometres on an extensive island-hopping expedition.

Once upon a time the sporadic Sporades were the forgotten islands of the Aegean. Then they were 'discovered'. Skiathos has now become a colony of Essex and Skopelos is going that way.

Yet there's no denying that these islands are very beautiful, with their pine woods and rocky shores, and plentiful beaches. Those who want peace, and unspoilt beauty, can find it even on the main islands of the group if they persist along inaccessible paths. By the time you get to Skyros, or Alonissos and the tiny islands which spread out east into the Aegean, you're (mostly) in another world.

If you want to appreciate what a paradise these islands must have been, visit before or after the main season – which now extends from June until September.

You reach Skiathos from two ports on the mainland – Volos, and Aghios Konstantinos on the Euboean Gulf. From Skiathos you can island-hop on the regular ferries to Skopelos and then on to Alonissos. From the main port of Patitiri on Alonissos it's possible to travel on local caiques to the remote outer islands. Also from Patitiri you can catch a ferry across to Skyros. And from Skyros you can head back to Euboea (also known as Evia, see page 244) on the ferry for Kimi. (From Kimi you can get directly to Athens by bus in less than three hours.)

Once you're on these islands you'll find there's little in the way of formal roads. This means that there's usually not much more than a rudimentary bus service between the port and the main town. Often the only way to get about is by hired motorbike; even so, there are still regions which are only accessible on foot.

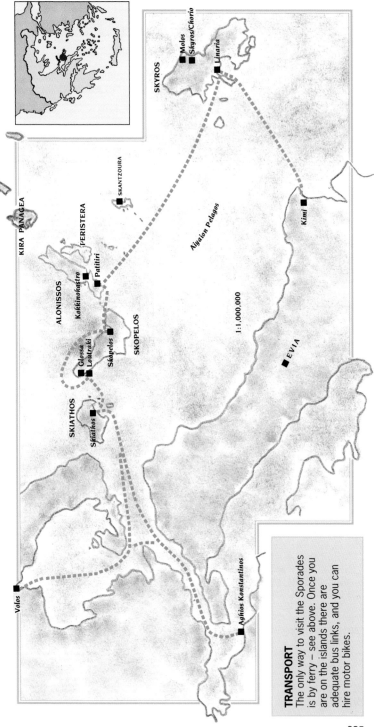

SKYROS

Molos
Skyros/Chorio
Linaria

SKANTZOURA

Aigaion Pelagos

KIRA PANAGEA

PERISTERA

Kokkinokastro
Patitiri

ALONISSOS

Kimi

Glossa
Loutraki
Skopelos

SKOPELOS

SKIATHOS

Skiathos

1:1,000,000

EVIA

Volos

Aghios Konstantinos

TRANSPORT

The only way to visit the Sporades is by ferry – see above. Once you are on the islands there are adequate bus links, and you can hire motor bikes.

SIGHTS & PLACES OF INTEREST

ALONISSOS ⇌ ✕
The furthest of the Sporades from the mainland, and the least developed for tourism.

Its capital used to be Hora, until the 1965 earthquake. Afterwards, during the dictatorship of the infamous colonels, and as a result of corruption and coercion, the villagers were forced to move out of their (easily repairable) homes down to the main port of Patitiri. Largely as a result of this, Patitiri has a tacky, makeshift air and is surprisingly ugly for a Greek island port.

As in the rest of the Sporades, you can still see many women wearing traditional dress. There are no important historical sights on the island, but there are some fine woodlands, nearly 30 km of coastline, and some good beaches – especially in the lee of the east coast, north of Patitiri. My favourite is the one at **Kokkinokastro** ('red castle'), which has a ruined castle; below the surface you can see the remains of ancient Ikos.

From Alonissos you can visit a number of nearby small islands which are uninhabited.

Peristera has some fine beaches and superb hidden coves. Night-time barbecues are often held here: alas, they are now becoming a little more popular and organized than they used to be – no longer characterized by the scenes of mayhem and abandon that one might wish for.

For more contemplative types, there's **Kira Panagia**, which has woodlands, two deserted monasteries, and a rather unprepossessing cave. According to local legend, this is where the Homeric Cyclops lived.

I'm told that the tiny island of **Skantzoura**, on the way to Skyros, has a small monastery still inhabited by a solitary, very shy monk. Apparently he can sometimes be spotted early in the morning, but otherwise sensibly pretends he's having a long siesta.

These islands are certainly remote, but don't expect them to be deserted in the yachting season.

KIRA PANAGIA, PERISTERA and SKANTZOURA, see Alonissos, above.

RECOMMENDED HOTELS

ALONISSOS – Patitiri
There are usually rooms available here, even at the height of the season. If you insist on a hotel, try:

Galaxy, DD-DDD; *Patitiri; tel.* (0424) 65 251.

Largish holiday hotel, which often still has a few rooms free even at the height of midsummer mayhem.

SKIATHOS – Skiathos Town
During the summer the hotels here are likely to be packed out, but there are usually a few rooms for rent. To find one, try any of the accommodation agencies which have sprung up along the front.

If you're planning a slightly longer stay, you might like to try **Skiathos Holiday Villas and Apartment Owners Association**, which operates from a kiosk.

Out of season, try:

Hotel Koukounaries, D-DD; *Skiathos Town; tel.* (0427) 22 215.

Pleasant small hotel with clean rooms and reliable amenities.

SKOPELOS – Panormos
Panormos Beach Hotel, DD; E *of Skopelos Town on the main (and only) road; tel.* (0424) 22 711.

There is a pleasant beach settlement on a bay here; the hotel is medium-sized and holiday-oriented. Most rooms have private bath or shower. Friendly informal international clientele.

SKYROS – Skyros Town
Xenia Hotel, DD-DDD; *by Magazia Beach; tel.* (0222) 91 209.

This government-run hotel offers the best of both worlds: it's handy for the beach, and close to picturesque Skyros Town. Also, it often has a room free when all others are booked out.

Otherwise, there are usually a few private rooms available in town.

SKIATHOS ⌨ ✕

This is a beautiful island, filled with beautiful pine woods, and surrounded by scores of beautiful beaches. But it has been blighted.

The boats put in and out at the main town, Skiathos, and the planes put up and down at the nearby airport. The remoter beaches are on the north-eastern coast (reached by walking or caique). The island also has a number of fine monasteries – though the monks have mostly abandoned them. The most atmospheric is **Evangelistria**, an hour's walk north of town, where you can sit and contemplate in relative isolation.

SKOPELOS ⌨ ✕

Skopelos means 'reef' in Greek, and the island's rocky coast lives up to this. Like its neighbour Skiathos, it has plenty of fine beaches, but it isn't yet quite so overrun by tourism.

The island's strategic position guarding the mainland port of Volos has meant that it has been conquered by almost every foreign power that has passed through Greece in the past three thousand years – from the Persians to the Romans, to the Franks and the Venetians, and so on...until eventually the pirate-admiral Barbarossa took the island for the Turks in 1538, and in customary fashion massacred the entire population.

Skopelos Town has small whitewashed houses, and is said to contain over a hundred churches and chapels. The island itself, like several others throughout Greece, boasts precisely 365 churches, chapels and monasteries. To reach the most spectacular of these, take the bus to the hillside village of **Glossa**, and then follow the path for one-and-a-half hours to the east coast. Here the monastery of **Aghios Ionannis** is spectacularly situated on a high rock overlooking the sea.

This island is famous for its plum orchards. Afficionados of the prune will be pleased to know that the local plum harvest is not all frittered away on frivolous products such as jam or fresh fruit. The pick of the crop is lovingly

---

RECOMMENDED RESTAURANTS

ALONISSOS – Patitiri

Along the front there's the usual line of tavernas and international mishmash of holiday bars ('Pub La Vie' and so on).

For a jolly evening meal, try:

To Dikty, D-DD; *on the front.*

Happy taverna with all your old favourites and friendly, flustered service.

SKIATHOS – Skiathos Town
La Piscine, DD-DDD; *Odos Evangelistrias.*

The top spot for a night out. You can have a drink, a meal, and dance by the eponymous swimming pool.

If you want something more traditional, at rather more traditional prices, try:

Stavros Taverna, D-DD; *Odos Evangelistrias.*

Just down the road from La Piscine, and much better than we deserve.

SKOPELOS – Skopelos Town
Ta Kymata ('The Waves'), DD; *on the front, close to the ferry berth.*

Eating out in Skopelos Town can be expensive, but by a miracle a few real tavernas have survived. This is the best of them.

If you fancy making a night of it, nearby is the best night spot on the island:

Platanos, DD; *on the front.*

A surprisingly interesting jazz bar, which doubles up in the mornings as one of those juice-and- yoghurt nutrition-free breakfast joints – presumably working on the canny principle that where you picked up your hangover the night before you are likely to return in order to get rid of it.

SKYROS – Molos
Marietas Taverna, D-DD; *at Molos beach resort just N of Skyros Town.*

Friendly spot close to the sea, with lively group of friendly international regulars.

baked in ovens to produce nature's wisest and most delicious fruit. (According to one of the pre-Socratic philosphers, the prune was the nearest thing to an embodiment of the human soul.)

The boat sometimes puts in at the ordinary little port of **Loutraki** before going on to the main port.

SKYROS ⋈ ✕
Largest of the Sporades, almost 30 km long, Skyros is remote from the main group.

This was the home of the legendary Atalanta, who achieved the notable twin accomplishments of being the fastest woman in the ancient world and also remaining a virgin. (The fact that she produced a son to Meleander apparently didn't alter this.) Atalanta swore that she would only marry someone who could run faster than her. Hippomenes took up the challenge, placing three golden apples in the path of Atalanta, who couldn't resist stopping to pick them up.

Skyros is just remote enough to have resisted the worst ravages of tourism. Its capital **Skyros Town** (often known as Chorio) is enchanting. With its Cubist whitewashed houses and labyrinth of steep streets climbing

• *Skiathos.*

towards its Venetian castle, it looks Cycladic (see Greece Overall: 12).

Here you can see a quaint bronze statue of 'imortal poetry' commemorating the minor British poet Rupert Brooke. This handsome lad caught the imagination of the British public with his sentimental poetry at the time of the First World War, and was for some years wildly overrated. He died at sea off Skyros in 1915, and immediately achieved immortality – becoming a symbol of the gilded youth which gave its life in the carnage of the First World War. His **grave**, in an olive grove overlooking the azure sea at the southern tip of the island, is one of the tourist sights of Skyros. It can be reached by a 10-km walk from Kalamitsa Bay, the pleasant beach just along the coast from Limani. It is hard to find, and if you want to make the pilgrimage the easiest way is by boat trip, details of which are advertised in Skyros Town.

Along the coast south-east of **Linaria**, the somewhat nondescript spot where the ferry puts in, is a pleasant beach at Kalamitsa Bay, from which it is a 10-km hike to Brooke's grave.

• *Opposite: Skopelos.*

Aegean Islands

Euboea, Andros and Tinos

Map Michelin 980, 1:700000

E ach of these three Aegean islands, close to the mainland, has a character of its own. It makes sense to explore them as a group (Tinos, though, is actually one of the outer Cyclades) but it will take a few days – see below. As with other island groups, such as the Sporades, there is little point in giving a guide to the distance covered.

The elongated island of Euboea, or Evia, hugs the shore so closely that it appears to be almost part of Attica: at one point, it is separated from the mainland by a channel only 40 m wide. There is a central mountain chain with several peaks higher than 1,000 m. The east coast is largely barren and inaccesible, but the western shoreline along the calm blue waters of the gulf has a string of popular resorts. Many of the inland mountain roads are extremely picturesque, especially the famous 'Eagle's Route' in the south.

In order to get to Andros, you have to return to the mainland. The ferry leaves from Rafina on the mainland to the port of Gavrio. From here you travel across the island to the attractive capital (also called Andros). Just south of here there's fine swimming at Korthiou Beach.

To complete the exploration, I suggest you continue on from Gavrio with the ferry to Tinos, one of the great pilgrimage centres of the Aegean, which has some lovely walks through mountain villages.

If at this stage you want to carry on island hopping, simply catch the ferry from Tinos to Mykonos, and then take in the central Cyclades – Greece Overall: 12.

To explore all three islands will take you about a week. Euboea is 150 km long; to do it justice allow at least three days. It will then take half a day to get to Andros, which deserves at least a couple of days. From here it's just a short hop to Tinos, whose main points of interest can easily be seen in a day – unless you plan walking through the villages around Mount Exobourgo (allow a day or two for this).

TRANSPORT

There are several ferry crossings from the mainland to Euboea, but in practice nearly all traffic goes via Halkida, the island's capital. You can catch a bus from Athens directly to Halkida. Regular buses connect all the main towns on the island; cars can be hired at Halkida, Kimi and Karistos.

A ferry service connects Rafina on the mainland with Karistos on Euboea. Another service connects Rafina with Andros and Tinos. To reach Andros and Tinos, you have to return to the mainland and connect with this boat.

MYKONOS

TINOS

▲ Exobourgo
■ Tinos

ANDROS
■ Andros
Ormos Korthiou

Gavrio

Messaria

▲ Oti

■ Karistos

EVIA

■ Stira

Kimi ■
Kimi ■
Lepoura

Dirfis ▲
Steni ■

Halkida ■

1:1,200,000

Rafina ■

Prokopi ■

Loutra Edipsou ■

241

• *Vatsi, Andros.*

SIGHTS & PLACES OF INTEREST

ANDROS ⇌ ✕
This is actually the northernmost of the Cyclades (Greece Overall: 12) and the second largest of that group after Naxos (Local Explorations: 10). It is within half a day's journey of Athens (via Rafina) which is why a number of well-heeled Athenians own smart villas here. But apart from the Gucci set, the island attracts a comparatively small number of tourists, and only a few foreigners, though this is very much a relative matter these days, especially during the high season.

The island is mountainous, green and prosperous; there is a surprisingly small permanent population. Its seagoing tradition ensures that even during the depths of a world recession the men of Andros are manning freighters throughout the seven seas.

The ferry puts in at the rather disappointing port of Gavrio. Here you can catch a bus across the island to the capital, named with the usual imaginative flair **Andros**. This is a lovely spot with marble paved streets overlooked by ancient balconies, and a ruined 13thC Venetian castle on a sea-girt rock reached by a small bridge.

Owing to the generosity of the local shipping magnate Goulandris, there are no less than three museums in Andros. The **Modern Art Museum** contains sculptures by the early 20thC Greek artist Tombros (an acquired taste) and often houses exciting travelling modern art shows. The three-star attraction of the **Archaeological Museum** is the Hermes of Andros statue, which dates from 4thC BC. The third museum, the **Maritime Museum**, to my intense irritation

• *Andros.*

always seems to be closed. (Last time I was told the curator was away at sea, an excuse which seemed appropriate enough – until I later learned that 'at sea' meant he'd gone on the ferry to Athens.)

Inland, be sure to look over the spookily almost deserted ancient village of **Messaria**, with a nearby abandoned 12thC church. The beautiful valley below has vineyards and lemon groves, and a few old Venetian pigeon towers (see Tinos, page 245). In an hour or so you can walk via Fallika village up to the lovely cliff-hanging **Panahandrou Monastery**, which was founded by Orthodox monks in the 10thC and still has some in residence.

The main resort on the island is the harbour village of Vatsi on the west coast (seething in summer), but the best swimming is south of Andros at **Korthiou Bay**.

EUBOEA (EVIA) ⇄ ✕

This is the second largest Greek island, after Crete, 150 km long and for the most part 20 km wide. It was created when the sea god Poseidon sliced it from the mainland with his trident; it's unclear whether this was an act of anger or mere caprice.

The resorts of the sheltered west coast are popular with Greeks and tend to fill up during the summer. (Generally, the further you are from the ferry crossings the less crowded the resorts.) The east coast of the island is a rocky wilderness and largely uninhabited, except at **Kimi**. The approach road to Kimi from Lepoura passes through some lovely unspoilt countryside, and there's a fine 12thC Romanesque church at Hani Avlonariou. From Kimi you can catch ferries to the islands of the northern Aegean – see Local Explorations: 7 and 8.

Inland, Euboea can be extremely beautiful. The drive from Stira to Karistos, along the so-called **'Eagles' Route'**, is one of the most spectacular in Greece. There's also a fine drive up Mount Dirfis (whose peak is over 1,700 m) to the village of **Steni**, which has a mountain stream running through the middle of it. The northern slopes of the mountain are covered with woodlands – good walking country.

The capital of Euboea is **Halkida**, a rather boring commercial town whose only point of industrial interest, its shipyard, is now largely defunct. Head for the old Turkish quarter of Kastro, and also see the front. Near the front is a **Byzantine Museum** in a former mosque.

If you stand on the bridge you can look down over the narrow channel of the Evripos. The water flows past here at around 6 knots. It continues in one direction for a few hours, suddenly abates without warning, and then flows equally fast in the opposite direction. This is likely to happen at least half a dozen times a day (and occasionally happens more than a dozen times). The phenomenon apparently defies all convincing scientific explanation. And for once there isn't even an unconvincing mythological one, despite this hav-

---

RECOMMENDED HOTELS

ANDROS - Andros Town
Xenia, DD; *on the front; tel.* (0282) 22 270.

Pleasantly situated, with many rooms looking out to sea. Efficiently run with reasonable plumbing, lighting; fairly clean. Rated two-star, which is not always as common as one would wish in the islands.

EUBOEA - Halkida
John's Hotel, DD; *Agelli Gobiou; tel.* (0221) 24 996.

More than 50 rooms; sporadically maintained roof garden; best value locally for price and hospitality.

EUBOEA - Karistos
Apollon Resort, DD-DDD; *at the beach; tel.* (0224) 22 045.

Largish resort hotel with good facilities; fine swimming.

This resort can get crowded in the high season, July and August. If you're having difficulty finding a room, contact the friendly local tourist office (tel. [0224] 24 130) which is north-east along the front from where the ferry docks.

EUBOEA - Paralia Kimi
Beis, DD; *on the front; tel.* (0222) 22 604.

Not to be mistaken for Kimi Town, which is a kilometre or so inland. Good swimmming, and an ideal base for exploring the region. Most rooms here have a private bath or shower; also handy for the northern Aegean island ferries.

TINOS - Tinos Town
Prices tend to be higher here than almost anywhere in the Cyclades, largely because of the pilgrimage trade.

Delfinia, D-DD; *on the front; tel.* (0283) 22 289.

Medium-sized hotel. Many of the rooms have pleasant sea views.

ing all the hallmarks of one of Poseidon's accomplishments.

According to a ridiculously unlikely, but curiously persistent, legend, Aristotle became so distraught at his inability to explain this phenomenon that he eventually threw himself into the channel and drowned. All we know for sure is that Aristotle did die here in 322 BC, after fleeing from Athens.

Other places worth seeing on Euboea include **Karistos**, at the southern end of the island, an attractive resort (far too popular in summer) with a good beach. From here you can set off up **Mount Oti**, whose peak is almost 1,400 m above the limpid waters of the Aegean. At the peak you can see the ruins of a pre-Hellenic building, which may well have been used for human sacrifice. It's known as the 'Dragon's House', and the locals are convinced that it is haunted.

The village of **Prokopi**, in the beautifully wooded valley of Klissoura, is also worth seeing. This region is part of the extensive estates on Euboea owned by an Englishman who was formerly a socialist Member of Parliament.

TINOS 🛏 ✕

This is the holy island of the Cyclades. In ancient times it was notorious for being infested with snakes, but the sea god Poseidon dispatched a flock of storks which got rid of them.

In 1822 a local nun called Sister Pelagia had a dream about where she could find a miraculous icon hidden underground. An icon was duly found, within a year the Church of Panagia Evangelista had been erected on the spot. And lo and behold the icon was soon working miracles.

The church still attracts pilgrims, whose numbers swell during the two festivals (25th March and 15th August) when the icon is brought out. It is then carried in procession over the bodies of sick and crippled pilgrims who lie in its path praying for a miracle. Below the church in the crypt is the cave where the icon was discovered. As you enter the church the bejewelled icon is on the left, with its poignant collection of votive offerings.

Tinos has a somewhat pervasive religous atmosphere and few beaches, but this does not deter the annual invasion of determined holidaymakers.

Inland there are several little villages clustered around Mount **Exobourgo** (1,700 m). As you walk amongst them, you will see a number of convents, ruined churches and scores of fascinating Venetian pigeon towers.

There are said to be over a thousand of these towers on the island, and some of them are masterpieces of naive art – notably lacking in Venetian sophistication. The Venetians used them as a source of eggs and meat.

RECOMMENDED RESTAURANTS

ANDROS

For a pleasant, unpretentious meal in a lovely setting head out to Stenies (a couple of kilometres north of Andros Town). This village is justly renowned for its flower-bedecked houses. After strolling through the village, continue on down to the sea at Yiala, where there's a friendly local taverna. Marvellous spot.

EUBOEA - Halkida

The best place to eat is along the front. The restaurants here are mainly used by Greeks, and consequently the cuisine tends to be of a reasonable standard. But watch out, some places can be a little pricey – especially the seafood dishes.

For less expensive dining, try inland, especially close to the Liosson bus station.

EUBOEA - Karistos
O Kavodoros, D; *Sachtouri Street; tel* (0224) 24 130.

A friendly, cheap and cheerful spot just two minutes into town from the harbour.

EUBOEA - Paralia Kimi
The best place to eat here is at one of the tavernas along the front.

TINOS
Steer clear of the large, overpriced restaurants on the harbour, unless you're feeling flush; the best area for reasonable food is in one of the tavernas in the market off Platia Venizelou.

Naxos, Central Cyclades

60 km; map Michelin 980, 1:700000

This is the largest, greenest and highest island of the Cyclades, with three peaks rising above 900 m. It lies about 170 km south-east of Piraeus. The rest of the Cyclades group is covered in Greece Overall: 12 – be sure to look at that section in conjunction with this.

Naxos beaches justly attract many tourists from northern Europe each summer, yet inland there are still several remote and unspoilt villages. You can also enjoy some fine walks along the paths through the groves of the fertile Tragea valley, which has a number of little chapels and ruined towers.

There are no famous historical sights here, but you'll find a number of castles and ruins, to say nothing of the *kouroi* (see page 249). Each one of these has its story to tell, and some of them are in strikingly beautiful settings.

The island is 25 km long and 20 km wide, but it seems much larger. This is because inland it is often mountainous, and there is no comprehensive road system with straight links between the main villages.

I suggest that the best way to tackle the island is to start from Naxos and head east along the road for Halki. This leads you through the picturesque Tragea Valley. From Halki the road continues up to the little mountain village of Filoti, with its 10thC Byzantine church. Shortly after, the road turns north skirting below Mount Zas, the island's highest peak. You then come to Apiranthos, a picturesque mountain village which has a small museum of Cycladic figurines. From here the road travels along the spinal ridge of the island, with superb views down to the Aegean on either side. Finally you come to the small northern port of Apolonas, which is a developing resort.

Distances on Naxos are short – despite the winding road it's just 49 km from Naxos Town to Apolonas. This means you can easily drive around the island's main roads in a day. Try taking your time, making an overnight stop at Apolonas, and returning along the north-eastern coast road, for a pleasant two-day trip.

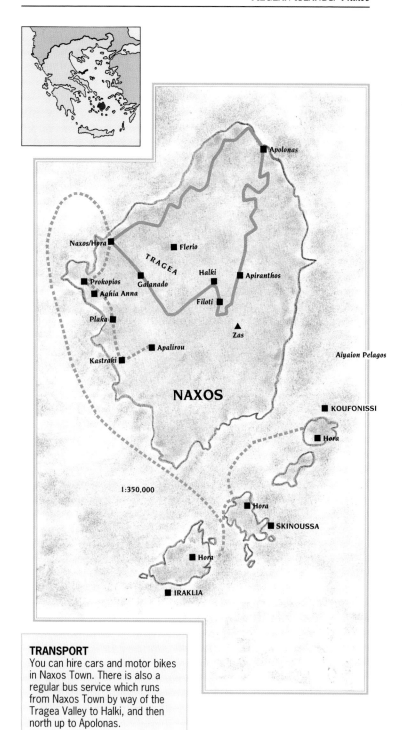

Apolonas

Naxos/Hora

Flerio

TRAGEA

Halki

Prokopios
Galanado
Apiranthos

Aghia Anna

Filoti

Plaka

▲
Zas

Aiyaion Pelagos

Apalirou

Kastraki

NAXOS

■ **KOUFONISSI**

■ **Hora**

1:350,000

■ **Hora**
■ **SKINOUSSA**

■ **Hora**

■ **IRAKLIA**

TRANSPORT
You can hire cars and motor bikes in Naxos Town. There is also a regular bus service which runs from Naxos Town by way of the Tragea Valley to Halki, and then north up to Apolonas.

SIGHTS & PLACES OF INTEREST

APOLONAS ⌖
Nearby there's one of the island's finest *kouros*, which was probably abandoned in the quarry here in 7thC BC. *Kouroi* are statues carved from stone (often marble), intended as monuments for the dead. They are usually larger than life-size male figures in formal, stylized poses. The earliest date from around the 7thC BC, resemble the statues of Ancient Egypt, and are almost certainly early Greek attempts to copy this art form. They are, in fact, forerunners of the great statues of the classical era. Several *kouro* are to be seen on the island, the most interesting being at **Flerio** in the centre of the island.

FILOTI ⌖
This village has a fine 10thC **Byzantine church** with 13thC wall paintings. From here you can walk in an hour to the top of Mount Zas, which is more than 1,000 m high and the tallest peak in the Cyclades. Breathtaking views greet the breathless conqueror.

Naxos is famous for its wines, which are usually named after the village where they are produced. My favourite is the one from Galanado. The island also produces a fiery spirit called Kitron. This is made from the local lemons, and comes in the usual three strengths (strong, very strong, etc). According to a local know-all I once met here, this liquor receives its distinctive flavour through the addition of lemon leaves at a certain secret stage of the distilling process.

The island's cheese is one of the best in Greece. On the menus nowadays it's usually called 'Naxos Cheese', and is hard, as distinct from the excellent and distinctive cream cheese which the island also produces. The latter goes particularly well with the fine island honey, on a slice of the rather ordinary island bread, if you like that sort of sweet-and-sour mixture.

NAXOS TOWN
Anixi, DD; *Kastro*; *tel.* (0285) 22 112.
A peaceful spot, in the upper part of town. Lovely views, and a gem of a garden.

If you want to be nearer the sea, try:

Iliovassilema, D-DD; *at Aghios Georgios beach*; *tel.* (0285)22 107.
A pleasant, smallish resort hotel just a short walk from town by the beach.

For hardened island-hoppers the best cheap place in town is:

Hotel Dionysios, D; *Kastro*; *tel.* (0285) 22 331.
In an old house in the upper town. Downstairs it is a youth hostel. Rough and ready, with cheerful (but not peaceful) clientele.

AGHIA ANNA
You can usually find an inexpensive room here, even in the height of the season.

APOLONAS
Hotel Adonis, DD; *tel.* (0285) 81 360.
Ideal base for exploring the northern part of the island. Be sure to book in advance, as Apolonas becomes a booming mini-resort in the summer season.

FILOTI
There are usually a few rooms available here, all inexpensive.

IRAKLIA
And the remote islands south-east of Naxos:
There are a few rooms available on Koufonissi, Skinoussa and Iraklia, though you may have to walk to the inland villages in season. If heading out here, it's best to take a sleeping bag. There are several pleasant beaches to camp on.

Half-way up the mountain is a huge **cave**, which according to a local legend is where Zeus was born (the mountain's name Zas is a form of Zeus). However, the Dikteon Cave in the mountains of eastern Crete (see Local Explorations: 14) are more usually accepted as Zeus's birthplace.

FLERIO
See Apolonas, *page* 248.

HALKI
A peaceful inland village above the rich green Potamia valley, usually known by the name of its river, **Tragea**. This valley contains vineyards and groves of olives and lemon trees, and paths lead through these groves, sometimes passing ruined Venetian towers or Byzantine chapels. A walk through this area is one of the best ways of experiencing inland Naxos.

IRAKLIA 🛏
And other islands south-east of Naxos, see Naxos Town, below.

MOUNT ZAS
See Filoti, *page* 248.

NAXOS – THE ISLAND
A curious history. In 1207 the island was captured by the Venetian Marco Sanudi, who virtually turned it into his own private kingdom. Under the protection of the Franks, he became the Duke of Naxos. Descendants of these early Venetians settlers still live in Naxos Town, where they form a small Roman Catholic community. In 1556 the Turks finally captured the island. Then for four brief years, from 1770 until 1774, it was ruled by the Russians.

The main legend attached to the island links the lovers Ariadne and Theseus with Dionysios, the god of wine, in an unlikely trio. Ariadne's famous thread enabled Theseus to escape from the Cretan labyrinth of her father King Minos; the pair then fled to Naxos. However, the faithless Theseus slipped off after spending the night with Ariadne, leaving her distraught. Then Dionysios, the boisterous god of dionysiac revels and orgies, appeared on the scene.

Dionysios was soon smitten with Ariadne – and having already lost her

• *Iraklia.*

heart to one rotter, she quickly fell for Dionysios. On their wedding night Dionysios gave Ariadne a crown of seven stars, and the two of them settled down to a life of bliss in her palace on Naxos. (During this period at least, Dionysios seems to have taken his customary wine, orgies and revels in moderation.) But Ariadne died, and the grief-stricken Dionysios tossed her bridal crown into the night heavens, where it can be seen to this day, shining as the constellation of Corona Borealis. To drown his sorrows, he resumed his dionysiac revels.

Parts of this touching legend are featured in a number of works of art, including most notably a delightful poem by Catullus, and the opera *Ariadne auf Naxos* by Richard Strauss. (Neither of these artists actually visited Naxos.)

NAXOS TOWN 🛏 ✕
Also known as Hora, this is the island's capital and the main harbour. It has the usual Cycladic whitewashed houses, and little alleyways with pots of flowers. (The geraniums are particularly striking.)

In the upper part of the village is the **Venetain Kastro**, built in the 13thC by Marco Sanudi, the first Duke of Naxos. Within the old castle perimeter you can still see the Venetian houses, many of which carry the carved stone crests of the ancient Venetian families. The present occupants of these houses are direct descendants of the original Venetian conquerors. Their small Roman Catholic community has its own bishop and **13thC cathedral** which contains some fascinating old family

• *Koufonissi.*

tombstones.

Nearby is the **town museum**, which has a few interesting Cycladic figurines and plenty of uninteresting Cycladic pots and paraphernalia. This museum used to be a school, and the young Nikos Kazantzakis (author of *Zorba the Greek*) was educated here for a couple of years. Uncharacteristically, he enjoyed it, according to his autobiography *Report to Greco* (which is his most interesting book, and less flawed by the heavy-handedness which mars his novels for many modern readers).

At the tower by the main gate into the Kastro enclave you can see a mark under the arch. This is the official Venetian metre to which all measurements on the island once had to conform.

Down by the port is the little island of **Palatia** (connected to the mainland by a causeway). The island contains the impressive 7-m-high **Portara** – reputed to be the gate of Ariadne's palace. Prosaic archaeologists are convinced that this arch is in fact the remains of an unfinished 6thC BC Temple of Apollo.

Just along the coast to the north of the harbour there's a wonderful place to swim called **Grotta**. There are caves, and beneath the surface you can make out the ruins of some ancient Cycladic buildings which are possibly 2,500 years old. Archaeologists have also discovered here what they believe to be the collapsed entrance to a tunnel which led to the Temple of Apollo on Palatia islet (though we know that this was really the secret tunnel which enabled Dionysios to slip out of Ariadne's Palace for the occasional revel with his satyric playmates).

If you want to get away from it all, take the ferry from Naxos Town to the group of little islands to the south-east of Naxos.

Koufonissi has begun to attract a few summer visitors, has a little village and a long sandy beach.

Skinoussa has just 50 permanent inhabitants, a tiny port and an inland settlement (Hora) a 20-minute walk up the hill.

Iraklia has a few more visitors than it used to. Its tiny port is in a superb setting, and you can walk to a beach and then on up to the capital (Hora) within an hour. This is the largest of the inhabited islands in the group and is just 7 km long.

PLAKA, PROKOPIOS AND OTHER PLACES ON THE SOUTH-WESTERN COAST 🏖

This region is famous for its beaches. The village of **Prokopios**, at the head of the coast, is just 7 km down the track south of Naxos Town. South of here is the pleasant little harbour of **Aghia Anna**, and beyond this you come to the marvellous beach of **Plaka**, whose white sand stretches for miles down the coast. (You can reach here by regular bus and caique from Naxos Town.) Beyond Plaka, reached by easily discernible tracks between beaches, there is the even more remote beach of **Kastraki**, whose southern end should be avoided because of sewage outflow.

Try the hour-long walk up from Kastraki beach to **Apalirou Castle**. This was besieged for several months during the 13thC by Marco Sanudi, and was the last place in the island to fall into Venetian hands. The castle is still surprisingly well preserved, and has some superb views out over the blue Aegean to Ios and more distant Cycladic islands. A track from here leads to Ano Sangri.

RECOMMENDED RESTAURANTS

NAXOS TOWN
By far the best eating area in town is up on the Kastro, where there are superb views. For a pleasant meal try:

Castro, DD; *Platia.*
Up on the square, with fine views and friendly service. They have some good Naxiot wines.

Vassilis, D; *Old Market.*
Your friendly, regular taverna: friendly prices, regular customers. Menu includes all the usual old favourites, including a few Naxiot surprises.

The best place to go for a drink is:

Diogenes; *Old Market.*
In the arcades. Serves vicious cocktails during its notorious three-hour happy hour. Serious prices and serious drinking begin at 9pm.

For dancing the night away, head for the discos at Aghios Georgos Beach. The first one you come to is heavily colonized by Vikings.

<u>Aegean Islands</u>

Chios, North-Eastern Aegean

Up to 250 km; map Michelin 980, 1:700000

Chios is one of the larger Aegean islands, 50 km long and 15 km wide. Its highest peak, Mount Pelineo in the north, rises to almost 1,300 m. Tourism has only recently arrived here, for a number of reasons. There are no spectacular beaches, and no really important historical sights. Also, history has been harsh on the island. During the 19thC it suffered an appalling massacre, which virtually wiped out the population. This was followed just over half a century later by a catastrophic earthquake which killed 3,500 people. More recently, a series of fires devastated the woodlands which used to cover the north of the island. Yet despite all this, Chios has its charms: remote, peaceful corners which grow on you the longer you stay.

There is no circular road around the island: the main roads all branch out from the capital. The main road south from Chios Town takes you through Vavili, with its unusually decorated church, and on to the village of Pirgi, whose houses are also decorated in a unique and striking way. From here you can continue down to the sea at Emborio, with a black sand beach nearby. Or you can take the road west through Mesta to Limenas on the far coast.

The main road north from Chios Town takes you to Volissos. From here you can go on to Aghia Markellas on the west coast, or up north through Aphrodisia to Ayiasmata. There are also roads from Chios Town to Nea Moni and Karfas.

Distances can be deceptive on Chios. For example, the distance from Chios Town to Volissos in the north is almost 50 km. By the time you've navigated all the twists and turns in the mountains, it will have taken much longer than you might judge from the map. Despite this, you should be able to see all the main sights of the island within three days – though you should allow a day or two more if you want to explore in depth or take the boat across to Psara.

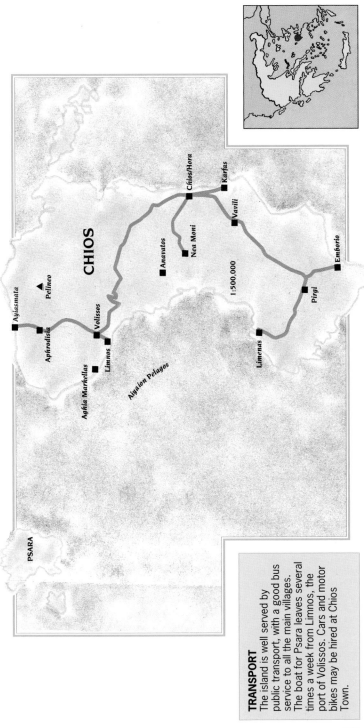

CHIOS

PSARA

Ayiasmata
Aphrodisia
Volissos
Aghia Markellas
Limnos
Pelineo
Anavatos
Nea Moni
Chios/Hora
Karfas
Vavili
Emborio
Pirgi
Limenas

Aiyaion Pelagos

1:500,000

TRANSPORT
The island is well served by
public transport, with a good bus
service to all the main villages.
The boat for Psara leaves several
times a week from Limnos, the
port of Volissos. Cars and motor
bikes may be hired at Chios
Town.

SIGHTS & PLACES OF INTEREST

ANAVATOS
See *Nea Moni, page 256.*

CHIOS – THE ISLAND
This island has a long history, marred by occasional horrific episodes. It was an independent state as early as the 8thC BC, and it is almost certain that Homer was born here during this period. Some five hundred years later, Chios took the unwise decision to declare war against the empire of Alexander the Great. In geographical and military terms, this was the equivalent of modern Liechtenstein declaring war on Europe. In the early Middle Ages Chios was ruled by the Genoese, before eventually becoming part of the Turkish Empire. Then in 1822 the island rose against the Turks. When Kara Ali Pasha sailed in with the Turkish fleet to put down the rebels, the Greek patriot Kanaris managed to set fire to his flagship and blow it up, killing Kara Ali Pasha. But the Turks were utterly ruthless with the islanders: 30,000 men were slaughtered; 45,000 were taken into slavery and the women were carried off to the harems. The island has never really recovered

• *Chios.*

from this catastrophe, and its depleted inland villages – many with deserted medieval dwellings – remain a silent memorial to the terror of that fateful year, which inspired the famous,

> ### MASTIC
> Is gathered from the lentisk bush (*Pistacia lentisca*): a nondescript, medium-sized dark green bush with reddish flowers and leaves in spring. The solidified resin is scraped from the bark. The gum was very popular amongst the inmates of Turkish harems – presumably because they had little else to do but sit around and chew it. The resin was also used in a variety of products from oil paint to lipstick, but the trade collapsed with the ending of the Turkish Empire early in this century.
>
> Nowadays the chewing gum is still sold on the island: most find its flavour unpleasant, sweet and perfumed; the original harem gum was unsweetened. Mastic is also used to flavour a fiery, sweet, faintly spicy spirit known as *mastica.*

• *Farmers, the Aegean.*

though rather romanticized painting by Delacroix, *The Massacre of Chios*.

Despite its troubled history, Chios has for the most part been a fairly prosperous island. Its men have always been great sailors, and a strong seafaring tradition persists to this day. But the island made its fortune as the world's greatest producer of mastic, a forerunner of chewing gum. This was widely exported to Europe and Asia. The five southern villages which produced mastic were known as the *mastichora* (the mastic towns), a title which they retain to this day.

CHIOS TOWN ⚓ ✕

The island's chief town, where the ferries put in, is larger than most Aegean island capitals, with a population of 25,000. Chios (or Hora, as it is sometimes still known) is very much a working town with a life of its own, and is not entirely dependent upon tourism, as is the case with many island capitals. It's not a particularly picturesque spot, but it gives you a chance to see how the real Greeks live, outside the enchanted goldfish bowl of tourism.

If you want to explore Chios Town, head inland to the **Genoese castle** and the old **Turkish quarter** which lies below it. Close to the castle is a square with the small **Turkish cemetery**. This contains several ornate Turkish gravestones, and the grave of Kara Ali Pasha (see page 254). Overlooking this square is the **Byzantine Museum**, housed in former mosque. This has a copy of *The Massacre of Chios* which the French romantic artist Delacroix painted in 1824. (The original is in the Louvre.)

Also of interest in Chios Town is the **Library**, with an interesting collection of stamps which once belonged to Dr Philip Argenti, the famous philatelist who lived for many years in London.

KARFAS 🛏 ✕
There is a fine, long sandy beach here, just 7 km south of Chios Town. Tourism came late to Chios, but here it's making up for lost time, with plenty of lost postcards, lost ice-creams and hotels with lost plumbing.

NEA MONI
This monastery is the island's main sight, a quarter of an hour's drive from Chios Town, at the end of a winding road which climbs up the slopes of Mount Epos. The name translates as 'New Monastery', but dates from 1049. It was founded by the Byzantine Emperor on a spot where a miraculous icon of the Virgin was discovered. The mosaics are amongst the finest of the early Byzantine period. The building and its interior decoration were the work of the best architects of the time, imported from Constantinople.

For centuries this was one of the richest monasteries in the Aegean, famous for its library. But in the 1822 massacre, the Turks murdered the entire community of monks, and plundered the building in search of booty. Then 59 years later the Chios earthquake took a further toll. The place has many ghosts, including that of the patriarch who rises from his grave in the garden to pray in the church at night, and the wailing spectres of three women who were drowned in the well.

Beyond Nea Moni you come to the village of Avgonima. A road leads from here about 2 km north to the deserted village of **Anavatos**, perched on its

---

RECOMMENDED HOTELS

AGHIA MARKELLAS
This spot on the largely unspoilt north-eastern coast is a real gem. If you plan staying in the north of the island, you can't do much better than rent a cell in the monastery here. The accommodation is suitably ascetic, but the place is spic-and-span and has a marvellous atmosphere.

CHIOS TOWN
Chandris Hotel, DD-DDD; *south of town; tel* (0271) 25 761.

Can claim to be something of a luxury hotel; own pool. More than 150 rooms, and despite block booking often has a room to spare at the height of the season. Excellent for children.

For the other end of the market, try:

Chios Rooms, D; *on the waterfront.*

Cheap and cheerful, handy for the ferry. Popular with the more discriminating backpackers.

KARFAS
This resort can be packed in the summer. If you enjoy the resort life and like it lively, try:

Hotel Yiamas, DD; *by the beach; tel.* (0271) 31 202.

A popular holiday hotel which attracts a friendly Scandinavian clientele. Right by the sea.

LIMNOS
It's possible to rent rooms in this tiny seaside spot. The best place to enquire is at the local taverna.

PIRGI
The Womens' Agricultural and Tourist Co-operative, DD; *office on way into village; tel.* (0271) 72 496.

This organization offers you a unique chance to live as the Greeks do. They have 44 rooms available in a wide range of homes throughout the village.

If they have no rooms available, or you want something a little more private, try the government-run GNTO bureau, which is on the main *platia*. This also rents out rooms, but in a number of rather more modernized village houses.

PSARA
Greek Government (EOT) Guest House, DD; *Psara village; tel.* (0272) 61 293.

This hotel, run by the Ministry for Telephones, is housed in what used to be the local jail. It has no bars of any sort, and you're allowed out on parole. The governor is very helpful about places where you can escape from it all.

cliff, with fine views. The village has a number of ruined churches, some with rather mediocre frescos. During the 1822 massacre, the villagers threw themselves off the cliffs rather than be captured by the Turks. A remote and atmospheric spot.

THE NORTH OF THE ISLAND ⌷ ✕
This part remains mostly sad and desolate. It has never really recovered from the 1822 massacre, and remains to a large extent deserted. Much of the woodland which covered the mountain slopes was devastated in a series of fires a few years back, leaving large areas of blackened wilderness.

If you do venture north, the bus will take you to **Volissos**, the main village of the region, legendary birthplace of Homer, with a ruined Genoese castle. About 5 km west there's a fine long sandy beach by the monastery of **Aghia Markellas**. Some 10 km north of Volissos there's a great little local spa on the coast at **Ayiasmata**, complete with its own mineral spring baths. To get here you pass through the unpromising village of **Aphrodisia** (unpromising in that it doesn't live up to its name).

PIRGI ⌷
One of the *mastichora* villages. Its houses are remarkably decorated with black-and- white geometric *xysta* patterns in the plaster. Their origins are obscure: some say they were imported from Italy, and that they are no older older than 19thC. The village now has a Womens' Agricultural and Tourist Co-operative which rents out rooms and runs a local scheme similar to that at Petra on the island of Lesbos – see page 139.

Below the village on the coast is the village's port of **Emborio**, which has a black pebble beach and the Bronze Age ruins of a city which once rivalled Troy. Now even this formerly remote patch of coast is beginning to feel the effects of tourism.

PSARA ⌷
This island (about 20 km north-west of Chios) once had 35,000 inhabitants, but since the 1822 massacre its population has fallen to a few hundred. During the summer there are several boats a week here from **Limnos**, the port of **Volissos**. You can stay overnight in what used to be the local prison (see page 256). It's a simple, out-of-the-way island, at present undergoing a 'reconstruction' programme by the French.

A schoolmaster I once met on Chios told me that in 1822, during the struggle for independence, the Greek parliament met here briefly – and thus, he insisted, Psara was really the first capital of modern Greece.

VAVILI
This village is 8km south of Chios Town. Twenty years ago the church here was decorated with frescos by an artist from Hawaii.

RECOMMENDED RESTAURANTS

AGHIA MARKELLAS
There's a wonderful taverna near the beach in the courtyard of the monastery.

CHIOS TOWN
Most of the best places to eat in town are along the front. These are not entirely geared to the tourist trade, which means that their cuisine is on the whole a step or two up from the normal. You'll also find a range of local and island dishes. However, my favourite is away from the harbour in the old quarter:

Hotzas, DD; T*zouri Street.*
This is the real thing, highly popular with the locals, always a recommendation.

KARFAS
There are a number of tavernas and restaurants along the beach. It's pure holidayland in the season, but none the worse for that when the moon is shining over the dark sea, you're halfway through your bottle of wine, and your food has at last arrived, even if it isn't quite what you ordered.

If your stomach is feeling in the need of something reassuringly ordinary which you can see and select for yourself, try the cafeteria at Hotel Yiamas – the kids love it.

Aegean Islands

Samos: Eastern Aegean

140 km; map Michelin 980, 1:700000

Samos is a wonderful island. It has some celebrated ruins, and plenty of beaches. Inland it's one of the greenest places in Greece, with vineyards and cypress trees, and charming, flower-filled villages amongst the mountains. Its wine is even celebrated in a poem by Byron ('fill high the cup with Samian wine'). The only problem is the international airport. During the season large parts of the north coast and the eastern corner of the island are overcrowded. This makes for lively resorts, but it hasn't done much for the island's superb hinterland – once so remote that some villages often didn't see a foreigner from one year to the next. It is a relatively large island, 35 km long by 15 km wide.

When I first came here in 1961, I went on foot to a village at the end of a track in the mountains. The villagers confidently informed me that I was a German. All evening, over my hosts' generously supplied wine, I argued for my true nationality – but to no avail. The village had received its last foreign visitor a few years previously. He had apparently been wearing jeans and was carrying a rucksack – just like me. When asked who he was, he had told them that he was a German. And that was it: nothing I could say would persuade them that I wasn't one too.

There's a circular tour you can make of the island, taking you to most of the main sights. Assuming you travel anticlockwise, head south from Karlovassi over the mountains to the small town of Marathokambos. Here continue down to the coast. At this point you can take a detour west along the coast to some fine beaches. Return the way you came, passing through Marathokambos and back to the T-junction with the main circuit road. Turning east you pass through a number of villages beneath the peak of Mount Ambelos. Continue down to the resort centre of Pythagorio, and then follow the road north to Vathy (Samos Town). From here you continue along the popular north coast back to Karlovassi.

The circuit can easily be done in a day. But if you want to spend time at some of the more interesting sights, and do some walking and swimming, you could make two or three days of it.

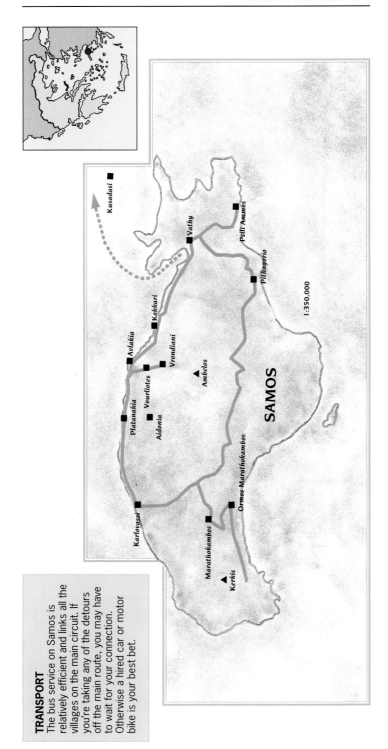

SAMOS

1:350.000

Kusadasi
Vathy
Psili Ammos
Pithagorio
Kokkari
Avlakia
Vrondiani
Vourliotes
Ambelos
Platanakia
Aidonia
Karlovassi
Ormos Marathokambos
Marathokambos
Kerkis

TRANSPORT

The bus service on Samos is relatively efficient and links all the villages on the main circuit. If you're taking any of the detours off the main route, you may have to wait for your connection. Otherwise a hired car or motor bike is your best bet.

SIGHTS & PLACES OF INTEREST

SAMOS - THE ISLAND

Samos has a long history, even for a Greek island. Its name derives from the old Phoenecian word for 'high'. The island's central peak, **Ambelos**, rises to more than 1,100 m; to the west of it, Mount Kerkis rises to 1,400 m.

The island was settled by the Ionians, and its fertile pastures eventually made it the richest island in the entire Aegean. It began trading as far afield as Spain and Egypt, and established colonies in the Black Sea and Sicily. Its golden era came in the mid 6thC BC, when it was ruled by the tyrant Polycrates. His court was famous for its intellectuals, and during this period the three greatest architectural and engineering feats in the Aegean were all constructed here: a great breakwater, a 1,000-m tunnel aqueduct, and a vast Temple to Hera, the island's favourite goddess. (According to legend, Hera was born in Samos. She was the goddess who watched over all living things, including vegetables, but she made the mistake of marrying the irascible philanderer Zeus. One day in a fit of jealous rage she had Zeus bound in chains, but he escaped and hung her from the sky by her wrists with an anvil attached to each ankle.) The Samian tyrant Polycrates ended up suffering an even worse fate, when he was tricked into trusting the Persians – who pounced upon him the moment he set foot on the mainland, and crucified him.

Despite this setback, civilization continued to flourish on Samos. Aesop, who wrote the famous fables, is said to have been born here (and in a few other places, as you'd expect of a fabulist). The philosopher Epicurus, whose disciples' cultivation of refined sensual pleasure gave us the word epicurean, lived here in the 4thC BC; and the astronomer Aristarchus, who realized 1,500 years before Galileo that the earth went around the sun, lived in Samos during the 3rdC BC.

But Samos' most famous son was Pythagoras, the greatest mathematician and philospher of his age – whose discovery of the intriguing peculiarities of the hypotenuse gave us all so many hours of pleasure at school.

Samos continued to flourish, though not so conspicuously, until the fall of

RECOMMENDED HOTELS

KARLOVASSI
Sandy Bay, DD; *by the port;* tel. (0273) 34 000.

Modern hotel, handy for the ferry. It also has the big bonus of its own private pool. Not too far from the local Limani Beach, either, though this can get very crowded.

ORMOS MARATHOKAMBOS
There are usually a number of rooms for rent here, even at the height of the season. There are also some attractive studio apartments in the area, especially at the beach settlements which are springing up along the coast to the west. Your best course is to enquire locally about these at the cafés.

PITHAGORIO
Expect the hotels to be booked solid during the summer. However, there is a helpful tourist information centre halfway down the main street, where you should enquire about rooms. My favourites are those run by the Lambis family, just back from the front. If all else fails, you can always try the top end of the market:

Doryssa Bay, DD-DDD; *just outside town by the beach;* tel. (0273) 61 360.

Large resort hotel, which also has a number of holiday chalets. This is mainly block-booked by package tour operators – but it's worth a tactful approach to the desk if you're having difficulty finding rooms in town.

All the amenities you'd expect of such a place, including tennis courts and private pool. Ideal for children.

VATHY
Hotel Eleana, D-DD; *on the front;* tel. (0273) 28 665.

Lovely old-style port house with views out over the bay. Handy for the jetty where the ferry puts in.

Byzantium in 1453 when it became a Turkish possession. In the 17thC the population became depleted and was replenished with settlers from Albania. To this day, descendants of these settlers are recognizable among the islanders for their fairer skin. In the years of easy-going Turkish occupation that followed, the island became virtually autonomous. When the Turkish authorities wrote to the Patriarch of the local Greek Orthodox Church saying they wished to build a mosque on the island, the Patriarch replied that he would only allow them to build one on the site of the former mosque. The Turks agreed to this, but then discovered that there had never previously been a mosque on Samos. So no mosque was ever built on the island – something of an oddity, when you consider that the island is only separated from the Turkish mainland by 2 km of water, making it the closest of all the Greek islands to Turkey.

NORTH COAST
The main resort is **Kokkari** – fishing harbour, stony beaches, lively tavernas. Best nearby beach: Tsamadou, interestingly named after Xanadu.

Places worth seeing: **Aidonia Gorge** – inland from Platanakia. The gorge takes its name from the river which flows through it, which takes its name from the Greek for nightingales,

---

VISITING MAINLAND TURKEY
Many people take the opportunity of a stay on Samos to visit Greece's enemy territory of Turkey. Here you can see the famous ruins of Ephesus, the greatest city in Asia Minor during the early centuries BC.

Catch the boat from Vathy for Kusadasi on the mainland. But be warned, it's a disencouragingly expensive trip, accompanied by a number of deliberately tiresome regulations.

---

which can occasionally be heard singing here.

Also: **Vourliotes**: a pleasant village 6 km inland from Avlakia. Another 2 km beyond here is the 16thC **Vrondiani Monastery**, which has superb views out over the coast towards the mainland.

PITHAGORIO ⇌ ×
This was the island's ancient capital, and was named after Pythagoras as long ago as 1955. The famous mole built by Polycrates is the foundation of the present jetty. A kilometre outside town is the entrance to the **Eupalinos Aqueduct** – a 1,000-m tunnel driven through the mountain in the 6thC BC to bring fresh water to the town. It is a

---

spooky and spectacular spot – get here just before opening time to beat the crowds. And 8 km west of the town, at the far end of Potaki Beach, are the extensive ruins of the famous Temple of Hera, which was twice the size of the Parthenon. Its sole standing half column comes as a disappointment after all the build-up, but those who enjoy pottering about among ruins will find a number of ancient lintels, carved stones, fragments and so on. Writing in 5thC BC, Herodotus described these three constructions (mole, hole and Hera) as the three greatest wonders of the Greek world during his era.

These superlatives need to be set in perspective by the fact that Pythagorio is now sheer holidayland, complete with a ghastly statue of Pythagoras and what I can only presume was his favourite hypotenuse. The hillside above is blighted by modern windmills.

SOUTHERN AND WESTERN SAMOS ⊨ ✕

These are the comparatively undeveloped regions of the island. The ferries arrive at Karlovassi, a somewhat nondescript spot, whose inland vineyards produce much of the famous wine.

From Karlovassi there's a good road south over the mountains to the delightful village of **Marathokambos**. Just below here is the beach at **Ormos Marathokambos**. Head west of here, and you come to a stretch of fine sandy beaches. The further you go, the remoter it gets – but much of this coast too is now becoming part of the coloured umbrella belt.

If you continue along the tracks north over **Mount Kerkis** and along the far western coast, you do at last get away from it all. According to a

• *Kokkari beach, Samos.*

local historian I met here many years ago, Pythagoras was imprisoned by the tyrant Polycrates in a cave somewhere on this mountain. I can find no mention of this anywhere else – though it is recorded that Pythagoras left Samos to live in Sicily after disagreeing with Polycrates.

VATHY ⊨ ✕

Also known as Samos Town, the island's capital is picturesquely situated on hills around a deep inlet. The Crusaders spread abroad the reputation of Samos wine, and thereafter ships from all over the Mediterranean would dock here. (In Medieval times Samos wine was used as communion wine in Rome.) Nowadays the port area is a tourist zone, and Samos wine serves more profane purposes. Yet despite the crowds and tourist tavernas, it's still a pleasant spot, with enough caiques and surviving old salts to remind you of the days not so long ago when this was just a sleepy backwater. The **upper town** (often known as Ano Vathy) retains a little of this sleepy charm in its dusty backstreets.

Amongst the palm trees of Vathy's main square, **Platia Pythagorio**, stands a large marble lion – a mark of the islanders' bravery. (Samians fought valiantly in the War of Independence against the Turks, only to be sold out afterwards by the politicians, who

• *Samos town viewed across the harbour.*

decided that the island should remain part of Turkey. Not until nearly 100 years later in 1912 did Samos become part of Greece.)

There's a beach just north of town (on the east shore), but the best nearby swimming is at **Psili Ammos**, 7 km to the south.

SAMOS WINE

The famous wine praised by Byron, and favoured during medieval times as communion wine in Rome, can prove a great disappointment. It is made from the muscatel grape, and outrageously sweet for many palates. The trick is to drink it with a cube of ice: this makes a pleasant light aperitif. If you take a bottle home, try it chilled with a dash of lime juice.

Samos also produces a white wine, often known as Samaina. This sometimes has a rather stalky taste, but is OK if well chilled. The same applies to the local rosé wine, Fokianos, which has a little more character than the white.

If you don't start off with high expectations, prejudging how you think these wines ought to taste, they can be pleasant.

Western Crete

160 km; map Michelin 980, 1:700000

I f you are having a Cretan resort hotel holiday, this expedition will provide a complete change. Designed around local bus and boat routes, it
takes you into the remote hinterland. You will see some grand mountain
scenery; and part of the route is covered by boat, visiting secluded villages along the south-western coast. There is an optional detour to one
of the most distant Greek islands of all, as well as an optional hike down
one of the finest gorges in Europe. The main part of the route can be
done in three days, but allow more if you want to see everything. As with
all the local tours in this guide, you don't have to do it at all. You simply
use the Sights & Places of Interest gazetteer to pick out places which
catch your fancy.

If you are undertaking the whole expedition, I suggest that you start
at Hania, and go west along the north coast – a somewhat nondescript
stretch of small resorts, with a growing number of modern hotels. This
is soon out of the way: beyond Maleme and the large military base you
turn inland. As the road begins to climb into the mountains you'll see
some spectacular views back over the north coast, as well as ahead
into the mountains, whose peaks rise to over 1,200 m.

The large coastal village of Paleochora comes as something of a sur-
prise after the remote mountain journey. Tourism has arrived here, but
not yet disastrously so. At this point you have several alternatives.

Those with time to spare should take a detour by catching the boat
for the round trip to the island of Gavdos, which lies 50 km south in the
Libyan Sea. It remains virtually unspoilt, and, for the record, remains the
southernmost point of Europe.

Alternatively, continue on the main trail by catching the ferry which
takes you east along the south coast to the beach settlement of Souyia.
If you fancy a tough five-hour walk with some breathtaking cliff-top
scenery, you can cover this stretch on foot, visiting the ancient ruins at
Lissos on the way. From Souyia the boats continue east along the coastline to Aghia Roumeli, at the entrance to the Samaria Gorge.

Another alternative from Paleochora is to catch an early morning
coach up to Ormalos village and plateau, in the heart of the White Mountains. From here you can make a four-hour walk down through the
Samaria Gorge to Aghia Roumeli on the coast.

From Aghia Roumeli the boats continue along the coast, calling in at idyllic Loutro on their way to Chora Sfakion.

From Chora Sfakion you catch the bus back to Hania, going through the White Mountains – Levka Ori – and more superb, rugged scenery.

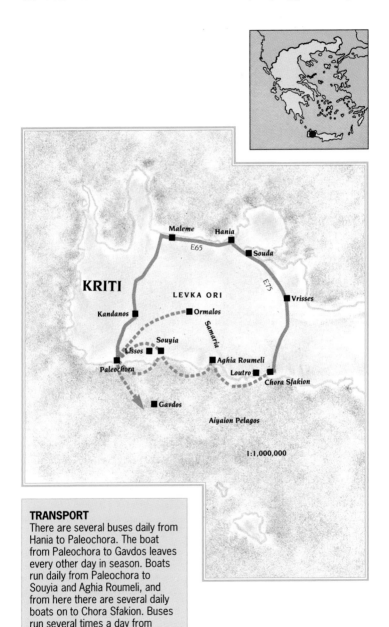

TRANSPORT
There are several buses daily from Hania to Paleochora. The boat from Paleochora to Gavdos leaves every other day in season. Boats run daily from Paleochora to Souyia and Aghia Roumeli, and from here there are several daily boats on to Chora Sfakion. Buses run several times a day from Chora Sfakion to Hania.

• Whitewashed church, Samaria Gorge, Crete.

SIGHTS & PLACES OF INTEREST

AGHIA ROUMELI ✕

This fishing village was once notorious for vendettas – as interminable and vindictive as any in Sicily. There is little to see here, beyond the cafés and tavernas overlooking the harbour. During the Second World War, this was the main disembarkation point for the Commonwealth troops after their disastrous defeat by German forces in the Battle of Crete; a small memorial commemorates this fact. An ideal base for long walks along the remote cliffs of the coast, or more ambitious expeditions into the White Mountains (Levka Ori).

GAVDOS ⛱

The boat leaves for this island from the quayside at Paleochora.

The southernmost land mass of Europe, Gavdos remains largely unspoilt. By Greek standards, it's not exceptionally beautiful – but there are several fine walks between the largely deserted hamlets inland, a few pleasant beaches, and some fine cliffs on the west coast. It's worth the four-hour walk to the 'last beach in Europe', if only just to say you've been there. But don't expect a welcome. The only sign of life here is usually a rather irascible lady with a herd of goats.

LEVKA ORI – THE WHITE MOUNTAINS

These mountains rise in places to around 2,280 m: their peaks are snow-

capped for much of the year.

The western region, around **Kandanos**, has many tiny hidden villages, as remote as they are beautiful. The best way to explore them is by motor bike, which can be hired in Paleochora. Here you can also buy a detailed map of the tiny roads and tracks which wind through the valleys.

The eastern region is even more remote, and mostly barren. This is the last remaining haunt of the famous Kri-Kri (Cretan Ibex), who appears with his striking horns on the coloured postcards. Many believe that this rare beast has not been spotted since the

• *Loutro.*

postcard photograph was taken. Even more rare and even less plausible is the near-extinct bearded vulture, which is so elusive that some say it's a figment of the ornithologists' imagination.

LISSOS

These ruins, of an ancient city which thrived in the 3rdC BC, are on the coastal cliff path betwen Paleochora and Souyia. The small Doric Temple of Asklepios, by what was once a sacred spring, has a fine black-and-white mosaic floor with depictions of birds. There are also two early Christian chapels, beside a barely discernible theatre.

LOUTRO 🖾

This tiny coastal village is completely cut off by mountains. The only way in is by boat or *very* determined hiking. It is (or was) one of the last truly undiscovered spots in the area. As with all such places, it only needs a few people for the place to fill up. However, it can still be idyllic in early spring and late autumn. There's good swimming from the rocks, no real beach.

MALEME

The airfield here was a major battlefield during the German airborne invasion of Crete in May 1941. In the course of this bitter chapter of the Second World War, more than eight and a half thou-

---

GUIDANCE FOR WALKERS
It's best to take a few elementary precautions if you're planning to walk along the cliff paths of the south coast, or setting off for longer hikes into the White Mountains (page 266). You may have to travel for hours without shade, and without meeting anyone. To avoid dehydration it's essential to carry water (at least one 2-litre plastic bottle per person). Be sure to cover up to avoid sunburn, and take a hat to avoid sunstroke. Also, make sure you wear shoes that can withstand the rocky terrain. On some routes it's best not to wear shorts, as the wiry scrub can be abrasive.

sand German and Commonwealth troops lost their lives. The nearby German cemetery contains four and a half thousand graves. As far as I know, Crete is the only place in Europe (outside Germany) where there are monuments to Germans who died in the Second World War. When I once asked a Cretan about this, he explained to me: 'Here we all fought like men. They deserve to be honoured.'

Just below the cemetery is the remains of a Minoan tomb.

PALEOCHORA ⚑ ✕
This pleasant, lively village at the southwestern tip of the island is overlooked by a ruined Venetian castle. (The 13thC walls are at present being restored – at the leisurely rate of around a yard a year.)

There's a long and beautiful sandy beach on the western side of the village, and a less populated stony beach on the

ANCIENT TIDEMARK
As you travel by boat along the south coast, you will notice a continuous black horizontal line running along the cliff face some 4 m above the water level. From the local fishermen I've heard several ingenious and astonishing explanations of this phenomenon (ancient gods, Turks, and so on). The true explanation is even more astonishing.

When the island of Thira (Santorini) blew up in the great eruption of 1500 BC, the geological plates beneath the earth's surface buckled, causing the entire coastline of this part of Crete to rise from the water. The line along the cliffs is the ancient tidemark.

It provides a telling indication of the colossal pressures beneath the earth's surface which caused the eruption. It also hints at the size of the tidal wave which must have been caused by this catastrophic event. Archaeologists believe that this tidal wave may have been responsible for the destruction of much of Crete's Minoan civilization. Such an event would have destroyed all coastal settlements throughout the Aegean region.

RECOMMENDED HOTELS

CHORA SFAKION
Panorama, D; *on the road to Hania*; *tel.* (0825) 91 296.

For once, somewhere that lives up to its name. On a hill just outside the village, with superb views out over the bay.

Xenia, D; *opposite ferry jetty*; *tel.* (0825) 91 202.

Ideal for tired travellers fresh off the boat. You'll get a warm welcome from the friendly proprietor. Be sure to ask for one of the rooms overlooking the sea – the others can be primitive.

GAVDOS
The little café by the landing stage has pleasant, simple rooms. Otherwise, take the motorboat to Korfos Beach, an isolated spot with rooms and a café-restaurant overlooking a fine bay. (The cook here makes the best Kakavia – traditional Cretan fish stew – I have ever tasted.)

LOUTRO AND SOUYIA
You'll find adequate, simple rooms on offer at both these places. You can't miss them at Loutro. At Souyia, walk the hundred metres from the jetty to the main beach settlement.

PALEOCHORA
Corali, D-DD; *on the eastern promenade*; *tel* (0823) 41 495

eastern side. (A 40-minute walk east along this coast brings you to the completely unspoilt paradise beach of Anidri.)

Paleochora's western sandy beach is famous for its lurid end-of-the-island sunsets, which may be observed whilst enjoying an equally lurid cocktail at one of the little cafés.

The sleepy main street comes alive at night, when the tables spill out from the cafés and restaurants. One or two of these still serve the nototrious mountain *raki* – which the locals like to drink fresh and warm from the still.

SAMARIA GORGE
It's difficult to exaggerate the beauties

Excellent rooms run by the friendly Kalogridis family. The two front rooms look over the balcony to the sea. The inexpensive restaurant downstairs is highly recommended.

By far the best hotel in town used to be the legendary Libykon, housed in a tumbledown Venetian Palace (Cretan version). Formerly the German army headquarters, it still contains the original candelabraed piano imported to entertain the troops, as well as the stage on which the local commanding officer (dressed in drag) is said to have regaled his men with renderings of *Lili Marlene*. (This stage can still be seen in the rather murky spare parts shop which now occupies much of the ground floor.) Long-term residents of the Libykon once included an Eskimo poet; a motorbike-riding 'freelance' anaesthetist from Berlin who was addicted to the writings of Thomas Bernhard; and an ex-merchant seaman writing a novel about a circus dwarf. Sadly, the place was closed down after a group of itinerant Syrian fruit-pickers turned the main corridor into a casbah – though rumours of its imminent re-opening persist. Opposite the Libykon, on the main road into town, is:

Pension Lissos, D; *on main road to Kandanos; tel.* (0823) 41 266.

Clean airy rooms, run by friendly proprietor who speaks English and German.

of this 14.5-km gorge, which descends over 600 m from the Omalos Plateau to the sea at Aghia Roumeli. (See page 266 for directions to the start of the walk.) The path begins with a rapid descent down the Xyloskalo – a wooden stepway through pine woods – and then follows the rocky bed of a stream. (There are a number of idyllic hidden pools amongst the rocks, where naked northern European nymphs and satyrs can occasionally be glimpsed having a forbidden dip.) Halfway down the trail you come to the deserted village of Samaria, and beyond this you pass through the 'Iron Gates'. At this point the rock face rises sheer for 300 m on

either side of the narrow path and the rushing waters of the stream.

After your hot four-hour walk, you can plunge into the cool clear sea at Aghia Roumeli, and have a well-earned *souvlakia* and glass of retzina at one of the beach-side tavernas.

The snag, as you will discover, is that you're not the only person to have heard of this wonderful spot – the Gorge attracts huge crowds. Even so, it's worth it.

SOUYIA 🛏

This remote settlement occupies one of the finest beaches on the south coast. Once it was a hippy paradise – but alas the days of excess and nightly high jinks are now a thing of the past (though there is the occasional spontaneous revival). The few cafés remain informal and convivial, with visits from the local mascot – a somewhat haughty pelican.

Inland there are unspoilt gorges and mountain tracks to some very remote villages.

RECOMMENDED RESTAURANTS

AGHIA ROUMELI
Zorba's, DD; *by the jetty*.

Pleasant spot with a terrace overlooking the quay where the boats come in. Good fish and salads.

CHORA SFAKION
Panorama Taverna, DD; *on road to Hania*.

Traditional local fare served on a high terrace overlooking the sea. Ideal for a romantic dinner.

PALEOCHORA
Christos, D-DD; *Eastern Esplanade*.

My favourite restaurant in Greece, run by the smiling Christos and his family (and dog). Sound, unpretentious local cuisine, excellent fish, and friendly clientele.

Michaelis, D; *main street by the kiosk*.

The best traditional Greek café in town, run by debonair moustachioed Michaelis and his son Giorgo. The place where everyone meets. A great range of gooey, sticky cakes.

Eastern Crete

320 _km; map Michelin_ 980, 1:700000

Here is an exploration of the the remote 'Far East' of Crete. You can visit a spectacular isolated monastery, and some excellent Minoan sites; there is fine mountain scenery, and some of the best beaches on the island. You could also take in the southernmost town in Europe, and visit the cave where Zeus was born. Nigel Mansell could probably do the circuit in a day, but if you want to see more than the chequered flag, you'd be best off allowing at least three days.

Assuming you start from from Aghios Nikolaos, head south along the picturesque coast road around the Gulf of Mirabello. At Sfaka a detour takes you north for the the little beach settlement of Mohlos. Returning to the main road, you continue east for Sitia, and then to the remote north-eastern tip of the island for the isolated monastery of Toplou and the beach of Vai, with its famous grove of date palms.

After Vai you can head south through the village of Palekastro to the Minoan ruins at Kato Zakros, going through some of the most remote and unspoilt countryside in the east of the island.

You have to retrace from Zakros to Sitia, where you take the road through the mountains for the south coast. Here you head west along the shore, passing through Ierapetra (the southernmost town in Europe), and then up into the mountains again. After passing through Aghios Vianos and Kastelli, you can detour east on the road up to the Lassithi Plateau, site of the famous Valley of the Windmills and the cave where Zeus was born.

Returning to the main road beyond Potamies, my route leads down to the coast, then east for the resort of Malia. From Malia it is a short stretch back to Aghios Nikolaos.

See also Greece Overall: 15, which links with this Local Exploration.

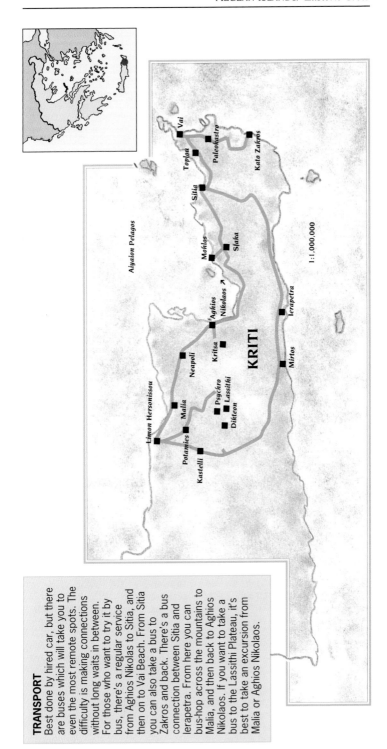

TRANSPORT

Best done by hired car, but there are buses which will take you to even the most remote spots. The difficulty is making connections without long waits in between. For those who want to try it by bus, there's a regular service from Aghios Nikolas to Sitia, and then on to Vai Beach. From Sitia you can also take a bus to Zakros and back. There's a bus connection between Sitia and Ierapetra. From here you can bus-hop across the mountains to Malia, and then back to Aghios Nikolaos. If you want to take a bus to the Lassithi Plateau, it's best to take an excursion from Malia or Aghios Nikolaos.

SIGHTS & PLACES OF INTEREST

AGHIOS NIKOLAOS
See Greece Overall: 15.

IERAPETRA ⛴ ✕
This is the only town on the south coast of the island – and as such claims to be the southernmost 'city' in Europe: in fact, you are further south than Tunis or Tehran. Apart from this geographical oddity, the place has little to recommend it. There are two rather ordinary town beaches, the usual Venetian fort, and 'Napoleon's House' (where the famous Corsican could possibly have spent the night of June 6 1798 en route for Egypt).

KATO ZAKROS ⛴ ✕
An idyllic little spot on the remote eastern coast of the island. There are just half a dozen tavernas by the beach, and a little harbour with fishing boats. Continue through the olive groves and banana plantations and you come to the Minoan ruins, which lie in a valley behind the village. The most important finds here were unearthed just 30 years ago. You can see the remains of a palace and a small town, dating from around 1500 BC. (Don't miss the cistern, which used to have terrapins living in it.) The caves in the nearby gorge known as the Valley of the Dead were once used as Minoan burial chambers.

KRITSA
This is sometimes known as 'the most beautiful village in Crete', and is famous as a handicraft centre. It's just 9 km inland from Aghios Nikolaos, and this has in many ways been its downfall. In the high season, the village is packed with day trippers. Even so, you only have to wander down the little side streets with their pots of plants, whitewashed walls and cats dozing on little stairways, to get the feel of what it must have once been like before people like us came along.

LASSITHI PLATEAU ⛴
One of the best reasons for visiting this spot is the great drive up to the plateau. It takes you through grand mountain scenery; then you emerge from the pass and see the plateau laid out below in its amphitheatre of mountains. Amidst the patchwork of fields are the famous windmills (most of which are disappointingly decrepit – though some still have sails which sometimes even revolve). From the village of Psychro it's a short drive to the **Dhiktaion Cave**, which has some fine stalactites and stalagmites, and according to legend is the birthplace of Zeus. (His father Kronos was in the habit of eating his offspring, so when Zeus was born his mother Kea gave Kronos a stone instead and hid the young god in the cave.)

MALIA ⛴ ✕
A popular north coast holiday resort with one of the best sandy beaches on the island (complete with tiny offshore islet and chapel). The entire town is given over to tourism. During the high

---

RECOMMENDED HOTELS

IERAPETRA
Petra Mare, DDD; *Sitia Road; tel.* (0842) 22 412.
Large luxury hotel, rooms tastefully furnished in 'Cretan style' (i.e., sophisticated ethnic, but unrecognizable to any Cretan). Claims to be the most southerly beach hotel in Europe.

Cretan Villa, D-DD; *16 Lakerda Street; tel.* (0842) 28 522.
A real find (if you can find it – north-east from Venizelou Square). A beautiful old Cretan house, complete with lovely leafy courtyard. Unlike the Petra Mare, this is authentic Cretan style.

KASTELLI
Veronika's, DD; *Xidas Road; tel.* (0844) 43 521.
Small, surprisingly modern hotel above a café-bar. Best in the region, though that's not saying much – there aren't many hotels in this region. Useful base for exploring the largely unspoilt country region of Pedhiadha.

KATO ZAKROS
Poseidon, D; *Kato Zakros; tel.* (0843) 93 388.

season the beach looks like a nuclear disaster area, the sand littered with badly scorched bodies struggling to recover from the effects of the radiation blast. At night the dead arise, and you can witness the transports of the damned in the infernal discos. Primitive civilization is alive and thriving in Malia – and if you wish to see the haunts of an earlier primitive civilization you can visit the nearby **Palace of Malia**. This Minoan site dates from 1650 BC, and was destroyed by a mysterious catastrophe in 1450 BC – long before the invention of the strobe lights and megadecibel sound systems which nightly threaten to destroy the brain cells of the present population.

MIRTOS

If you find Ierapetra and its nondescript surroundings rather depressing, it's worth heading on the 16 km or so for the pleasant seaside village of Mirtos. There's a long, rather stony beach, but the little whitewashed houses and tavernas have a charm of their own. Though you wouldn't guess, the place was completely flattened in 1943 by the German army as a reprisal against the local partisans.

MOHLOS ⇔ ✕

Once upon a time this was an idyllic spot. Just a couple of tavernas, a little harbour, a shingle beach and some rocky coves. It was bound to be discovered – but surprisingly it hasn't been entirely ruined (yet). There's even an island offshore, where recent excavations have discovered the remains of a Minoan settlement. (Swimmable, or take the local ferry.) Out of season, time stops still again.

Best of the limited options here: spartan rooms, shared shower. But a bonus is the terrace, which is highly romantic at night beneath the stars.

MALIA

Warning: finding overnight accommodation here can be a real problem during the season.

Hotel Poseidon, DD; *Beach Road, tel.* (0897) 31 312.

There's often a room going here, even at the height of the season. If you can, get one that overlooks the inner courtyard (far from the clamour of the busy street outside). Run by friendly Nikos, who is very proud of his easily comprehensible Inklish and Yerman. (When he's full, he'll do his best to find you a room in one of his friends' establishments down the road.)

MOHLOS

Sofia, DD; *on the front; tel.* (0843) 94 179.

Small, clean hotel. Be sure to ring and book several days in advance during the season.

PALEOKASTRO

Margot's, D; *Sitia Road; tel.* (0843) 61 277.

Really friendly guesthouse, run by German Margot. Good continental breakfasts with real German coffee. Deservedly popular – book well in advance during season.

PSYCHRO

Hotel Zeus, D; *road to the cave; tel.* (0844) 31 284.

Slightly austere accommodation, in a house on the village outskirts. Worth staying in the village overnight, just to see what it's like when the busloads have gone. Also has a pleasant taverna, where you can meet interesting, adventurous travellers like yourself.

SITIA

Victoria, D; *Konstantinou Karamanli; tel.* (0843) 28 080.

Friendly boarding house-type hotel. Shared showers on each landing. Pleasant garden. You can also make use of the kitchen to cook your own meals.

Ithanos, DD; *on the front; tel.* (0843) 22 900.

Large hotel by the sea with more than 100 rooms. Right in the centre of town, by the so-called park. Also has reasonable restaurant.

SITIA ⛵ ✕

A small town of block-built houses rises up the hillside overlooking the harbour towards the Venetian Castle. There's been a harbour settlement here since early Minoan times. Like so many other isolated ports, it was sacked in the 16thC by the famous pirate Barabarossa (who appears to have spent his time doing little else throughout this part of the Mediterranean). There's an interesting **Archaeology**

Museum which includes some pre-historic frying pans

TOPLOU MONASTERY

This isolated monastery is like a little medieval castle. Its isolation has meant that it has constantly been threatened through its centuries-long history. (Even the name Toplou is said to come from the Turkish word for a cannon.) Inside it's beautiful, with a small courtyard beneath the bell-tower, a domed chapel (with frescos), and a place where you can walk along the walls. Cretan partisans used to rendezvous here with British secret agents when the island was under German occupation during the Second World War.

• *Palace of Malia, Crete.*

If you're in Sitia in mid-August, there's a lively Sultana Festival. It's held just beyond the ferry terminal. Your entry fee guarantees you unlimited local wine – with the inevitable high jinks. Good Cretan music and dancing – which becomes more informal as the evening progresses.

VAI BEACH

The only wild date palm grove in Europe starts at the edge of this fine sandy beach. Twenty years ago this looked like the shore of a South Sea island. Nowadays you'd find it quieter having a picnic on Kurfurstendamm or Oxford Circus in the rush hour. Strictly an out of season spot – then it's well worth a visit.

RECOMMENDED RESTAURANTS

IERAPETRA
Manthos Palace, DD-DDD; *on the front.*
Don't be put off by the grandiose name – this is a genuine Cretan taverna. The seafood is excellent, and reasonably priced.

Taverna Karin, DD; *Sitia Road.*
Karin (who hails from Westphalia) serves a range of German and local dishes. Highly popular with her compatriots from the nearby Petra Mare hotel. Renowned for its healthy breakfasts.

KATO ZAKROS
Maestro, D-DD; *main square.*
The maestro himself is quite a character. He speaks good English and German, and like many self-appointed local experts has a highly imaginative grasp of local lore. Surprisingly, the food is equally imaginative and after a glass or two of wine you may even be bold enough to try the goat stew (which is excellent).

LIMON HERSONISSOU
Il Camino, D-DD *on the front.*
Great pizzas cooked in an authentic Cretan furnace, down by the

beach. For some reason very popular with Australians (who are convinced that pizzas were invented by an Italian Australian).

MALIA
Milos, DD-DDD; *Beach Road.*
Pleasant leafy patio restaurant serving a wide range of standard Greek fare. Can get hectic in high season, but good fun for all that.

Elektra Café, D; *Beach Road.*
Surrounded by all the tawdriness of inauthentic Greek tavernas and fake *bouzouki* music, this serves the real thing: genuine English-style fish and chips wrapped in newspaper (alas, Greek tabloids – you can't have everything).

MOHLOS
Sofia, DD; *on the front.*
Pleasant taverna with a range of local dishes. Friendly service and informal clientele.

SITIA
Zorbas, DD-DDD; *on the front.*
The 'in' place, right by the sea. It can get pretty hectic during August. Good seafood. Just the place for a romantic dinner under the stars on an out-of-season moonlit night.

Central Southern Crete

200 km; map Michelin 980, 1:700000

S outh-central Crete is perhaps most notable for its Minoan sites, and if you do all of this circuit you'll see not only these, but most of what the area has to offer: fine mountain scenery (with the opportunity to ramble through a spectacular unspoilt gorge); an idyllic near-tropical beach with a lagoon and palm trees; and some beautiful fishing villages. Allow at least three days if you want to take in all of the main attractions. Most of the sights make a great day's expedition in their own right.

Assuming you start from Heraklion, I suggest you head south across the mountains, detouring if possible to Zaros in the Messara Plain. Returning to the main road, you continue south to Aghii Deka and the Greco-Roman ruins at Gortys. About 16 km west of here, you come to the Minoan Site of Phaestos, second in importance only to Knossos. At Phaestos you are conveniently placed to make a detour to the famous beach-side caves at Matala. Returning to Phaestos, you continue west to the Minoan villa at Aghia Triada, and then on to the delightful fishing village and resort centre of Aghia Galini.

The trail now continues north-west through some fine mountain scenery, until you come to the turn-offs for the monastery and palm tree beach of Preveli, and the picturesque small resort of Plakias. The main road leads north to Rethymnon, Crete's 'oriental' city; going east along the coast road from here towards Heraklion takes you past several resorts and some fine coastal scenery.

This Local Exploration links with Greece Overall: 15 which, together with Local Explorations 13 and 14, completes the guide's coverage of Crete.

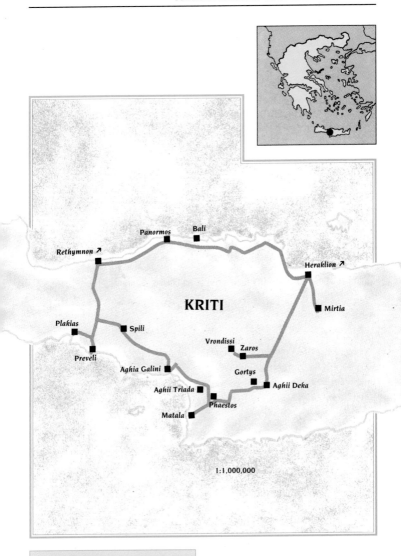

TRANSPORT
Best covered by hired car, but those who wish to travel by bus will find little difficulty. There are regular daily buses from Heraklion to Zaros, Matala, and Aghia Galini (passing Gortys, Phaestos and Aghia Triada). Buses run several times a day from Aghia Galini to Plakias, where you can catch the boat to Preveli beach. Plakias has connections to Rethymnon; between here and Heraklion there's a regular service.

SIGHTS & PLACES OF INTEREST

AGHI DEKA
See Gortys, this page.

AGHIA GALINI ✉ ✕
Aghia Galini remains as spectacular as it always was – a beautiful fishing village on a hillside with whitewashed houses and tiny streets leading down to a small harbour. Unfortunately, everyone has now heard about Aghia Galini, and there just isn't room for all the people who visit. Also, there isn't a good beach – just a narrow strip to the east of the village. This said, Aghia Galini is a lively spot, with a friendly atmosphere – and out of season you can still get a feel of what it used to be like. Some of the rooms above the harbour have breathtaking terraces overlooking the sea.

AGHI TRIADA
This small Minoan site dates from 1500 BC. In the old days the sea reached inland, to the foot of the nearby hills, and Aghi Triada probably

NIKOS KAZANTZAKIS, 1885-1957
Best known as the author of the novels *Zorba the Greek* and *Christ Recrucified*, he also wrote a poem *The Odyssey: A Modern Sequel*, whose 33,333 lines make it one of the longest ever written. His writing often has the intensity of Dostoevsky and expresses his uncompromising views on man's relationship with God, the world, and fate. He saw himself as a 'great' writer, and the tenor of his work is often at odds with the conventional world. Not a modest man, he let it be known that he was willing to share the Nobel Prize, as long as it was awarded to him quickly. He was tired of waiting. The Nobel Prize Committee was unimpressed by this generous offer, and Kazantzakis never received the prize. For all this, he was a profound and prolific writer, who remained proud of his Cretan origins – and was certainly the greatest Greek prose writer of his era.

served as the port for nearby Phaestos. In many ways it's a far more attractive site than Phaestos, with its shrine, smaller villa-type palace and market, complete with a line of shops running down the hill. The palace once contained a delightful fresco of a cat stalking a pheasant (the original fresco ended up in the Archaeological Museum in Heraklion).

BALI ✉ ✕
A small fishing village on the north coast, surrounded by rocky coves, with a backdrop of mountains rising behind. Alas, in the summer it seems as if all those who can't afford to go to the other Bali end up here, and the place can become badly overcrowded. Even so, you could try the so-called Paradise Beach if you like swimming and diving off the rocks.

GORTYS
This Greco-Roman site lies just outside the village of **Aghii Deka** (which means 'Ten Saints' and is named after ten early Christian martyrs whose remains were miraculously discovered at the bottom of the local pond after a child had a vision here in the 1920s).

Gortys was best known in Ancient Greek times for its legal code which was inscribed on tablets of stone. When the Romans took over Gortys, they incorporated these tablets into the Odeon, a 1stC AD theatre whose ruins are the most impressive part of the site. Also worth seeing is the church of Aghios Titos, named after St Titos who was consecrated as the first Bishop of Crete by St Paul in 57 AD. (Though judging from one of Paul's Epistles, he wasn't too impressed by the Cretans, whom he describes as 'liars, savage beasts and lazy curs'.)

HERAKLION
See Greece Overall: 15.

MATALA ✉ ✕
This small town with its sandy beach and fine caves has long been a focus of high fantasy (or legend, depending upon your point of view). The god Zeus swam ashore here disguised as a bull, bearing Europa on his back. (This legend may arise from an early visit by a Phoenician ship with the figurehead of a bull.) The famous caves, which over-

• *The beach, Preveli.*

look the beach, are carved out of sandstone, and were probably early Christian tombs created during the Roman era in the 1stC AD.

In the 1960s these caves became the most renowned hippy colony in the Mediterranean, giving rise to the inevitable legends: John and Oko slept here; Janis Joplin stayed awake here; and so on.

A pleasant seaside spot well worth visiting, even in our current, sober, post-legendary era.

MIRTIA
The village which was the birthplace of the great Cretan writer Nikos Kazantzakis, author of *Zorba the Greek*. It's less than half an hour's drive from Heraklion and well worth the trip, even if you've never heard of Kazantzakis.

Mirtia is a typically picturesque Cretan village, with whitewashed houses and little pots of flowers everywhere. The rather grand house where Kazantzakis was born in 1885 is now a museum, filled with all kinds of interesting memorabilia and Kazantzakis trivia

– just as the old egomaniac would have loved it to be.

Kazantzakis' tomb is on the Martinengo Bastion which overlooks Heraklion. He was refused an Orthodox burial owing to his controversial spiritual outlook, a curious blend of Buddhism, communism and Franciscan Christianity – anything but Greek Orthodoxy, in fact. Inscribed in Greek on his tomb are his immortal words: 'I hope for nothing, I fear nothing, I am free.'

PHAESTOS
This site contains the remains of the second largest Minoan Palace after Knossos. The palace was first built in 1900 BC, later destroyed by an earthquake, and partially rebuilt before the mysterious disaster of 1450 BC which destroyed so much of Minoan civilization in Crete. Apart from the fine views over the Messara Plain, this site can be something of a disappointment (especially after Knossos.) This is only partly because traditionally minded archaeol-

RECOMMENDED HOTELS

AGHIA GALINI
Hotel Acteon, D-DD; *Vassilios Ioannis Street; tel.* (0832) 91 208.

Rooms with sea views, on two delightful terraces. Plumbing, at last inspection, was antique, and may be temperamental. Friendly service.

Galini Mare, DD; *Main Road; tel.* (0832) 91 358. Away from the crowded centre, on the ridge, and often has rooms when others are full. Simple, tiled, spotless rooms, with excellent views out to sea.

BALI
Bali Beach Hotel, DD-DDD; *about two minutes from where the bus stops; tel.* (0834) 22 610.

Attractive modern hotel set on shelving coastline with its own private beach amongst rocks. Close to village; own restaurant.

MATALA
Bamboo Sands Hotel, DD; *Phaestos Road; tel.* (0892) 42 370.

Clean modern hotel with pseudo-classical touches. Take a room at the back, and you're right by the beach.

Pension Fantastik, D; *off Platia; tel.* (0892) 42 362.

Friendly spot with smallish rooms and balconies. Recommended for those who want peace and quiet.

PLAKIAS
Alianthos, DD; *Main Road; tel.* (0832) 31 227.

Clean, but rather ordinary rooms with private bath and balcony. Main plus here is that you're just across the road from the beach. (Not to be mistaken for the more expensive Alianthos Beach, which is on the way into town.)

Geronimo's, D; *ten-minute walk W of town.*

If high-season Plakias is too much for you, try heading out west of town along the track to Geronimo's taverna, a faraway spot which also has some rooms.

SPILI
A pleasant village: the shady cobbled backstreets, with balconies of flowers, are well worth exploring. See also Recommended Restaurants.

ZAROS
Idhi Hotel, DD; *on the edge; tel.* (0894) 31 302.

An unexpected find in such a spot. The main bonus is the garden and the private pool (which makes up for the lack of sea). Good restaurant.

---

ogists refused to contemplate any 'reconstruction' such as Sir Arthur Evans did at Knossos. Also, the imposition of the later palace on the earlier ruins makes it something of a muddle unless you're an expert.

The excavations of the ruins northeast of the palace uncovered the famous Phaestos Disc (now in the Archaeological Museum in Heraklion). The spiralling hieroglyphs on this disc are claimed as the earliest printing known to man, and are said to contain a mysterious 'secret'. The hieroglyphs remain undeciphered, although there have been the usual fantastic claims, including the suggestion that secret contained in the writing is in fact a description of visitors from outer space; the meaning of life; the earliest communist manifesto; and so on.

PLAKIAS 🛏 ✕
Once a back-packers' hideaway, Plakias is now a lively resort. Despite the onset of mass tourism, there are still some unspoilt sandy beaches nearby, and the backdrop of mountain scenery is superb. You can also catch boats from here to the idyllic Preveli Beach (below), with its lagoon and palm grove, just down the coast.

PREVELI
This isolated monastery was an outpost of Christian resistance to the Turks during the 18thC. More recently is was used as a hideout for fleeing British and Commonwealth soldiers during the German invasion of Crete. The soldiers were eventually evacuated by submarine from the nearby beach.

The beach is one of the most beautiful in Crete. The clear waters of the river flow down the gorge through a miniature jungle, complete with palm trees, to a small lagoon. The beach itself is sandy and idyllic – inhabited during waking hours by day trippers and at other times by a hardy band of modern-day Robinson Crusoes and Girl Fridays; though the latter are not the type you find assisting 20thC senior executives.

RETHYMNON
See Greece Overall: 15.

VRONDISSI
See Zaros, this page.

ZAROS 🛏
This low-key little town is the main market of the Messara Plain, Crete's most fertile region. The best day for the market is Saturday, when all the farmers come in from the surrounding area.

Worthwhile walk: ask in town for directions to the Zaros Gorge: it's about 3 km from the edge of town, with a path through it rather more than 3 km long. It attracts surprisingly few visitors, even at the height of the season, and has some superb mountain views. When you reach the end of the gorge, retrace your steps.

About 3 km west of Zaros at **Vrondissi** there is a church which contains some beautiful icons and 500-year-old frescos.

RECOMMENDED RESTAURANTS

AGHIA GALINI
Onar Restaurant, D-DD; *Taverna Alley.*
Right in the centre of things, yet with a fine view out over the harbour. Some tasty local specialities, also good fish.

Greenwich Village, DD; *Taverna Alley.*
Leafy terrace overlooking the town centre, where they serve great fish *souvlaki*, excellent with the local white wine. Good steaks, too.

BALI
Panorama, DD; *on the front.*
Lives up to its name with a great view of the harbour. There's a wide-ranging menu, but the best choice here is the fish. Ask what's fresh that day, or go for the swordfish steak, which is strong enough to live with their more-than-passable rosé.

MATALA
Zwei Bruder Taverna, DD; *Platia.*
Lively taverna, right on the main square. *The* spot during the season. Try the fresh fish, accompanied by the house white.

Olympia, DD; *on the front.*
First-floor restaurant with fine sea

SAKANAKI
This is the Aghia Galini speciality: a piquant, fiery meat and vegetable stew. Ingredients include aubergines, mushrooms, sausage, peppers and herbs. It's excellent with one of the heavier local red wines, and said to be a cure for an ouzo hangover.

---

view, serving a range of Cretan dishes; could be romantic out of season.

Fish Taverna, DD; *on the front.*
Excellent fish restaurant, up on the bluff, with a fine view across the bay towards the caves. Try their red mullet for a real treat.

PLAKIAS
Sofia, DD; *on the front.*
Run by the redoubtable Sofia Drimakis, who earned star-billing in the old hippy days. Now the place has been done up, but still serves great helpings of a great variety of dishes to a great variety of customers.

Julia's Place, D-DD; *W of the front.*
Worthy range of standard (not particularly Greek) vegetarian dishes, served by friendly English Julia. Relaxed place for meeting people.

SPILI
Loukakis, D; *off Platia.*
Renowned for the quality of its classic Greek dishes.